READING DISABILITIES
An International Perspective

READING DISABILITIES
An International Perspective

106706

edited by
Lester Tarnopol, Sc.D. and
Muriel Tarnopol, M.A.

University Park Press
Baltimore · London · Tokyo

Published 1976 by
UNIVERSITY PARK PRESS
International Publishers in Science and Medicine
Chamber of Commerce Building
Baltimore, Maryland 21202

Copyright © 1976 by Lester Tarnopol

Typeset by The Composing Room of Michigan, Inc.
Manufactured in the United States of America
by Universal Lithographers, Inc., and The Maple Press Co.

Library of Congress Cataloging in Publication Data
Main entry under title

Reading disabilities.

Includes index.
1. Reading—Remedial teaching. I. Tarnopol, Lester,
II. Tarnopol, Muriel.
LB1050.5.R38   428'.4'2   75-33977
ISBN 0-8391-0829-X

Contents

v

Contributors

Rita B. Balch, M.A.
Mental Health Associate, Gulf Coast Mental Health Center, Gulfport, Mississippi

Susan Ruth Butler, Ph.D.
Lecturer in Education, University of Sydney; Consultant Psychologist in Neurology, Royal Alexandria Hospital for Children, Sydney, Australia

June Cunningham, M.A.
Department of Psychology, Carleton University, Ottawa, Canada

Joep J. Dumont, Ph.D.
Professor of Education, Instituut Voor Orthopedagogiek, Katholieke Universiteit, Nijmegen, The Netherlands

Beth Gessert, B.A.
Researcher, Comparative Special Education; Teacher, Deaf and Physically Handicapped Children, London, England

Bjørn Glaesel, Cand. Paed. Psych.
School Psychologist, Lyngby; Editor, Skolepsykologi, Denmark

Carlos J. Robles Gorriti, M.D.
Child Psychiatrist and Psychoanalyst; Associate Professor and Visiting Lecturer, Hahnemann Medical College, Philadelphia, Pennsylvania; Head, Psychiatric Department, Children's Hospital, Buenos Aires, Argentina

T. Dudley Hagger, M.D.
Consultant Pediatrician, Healesville, Victoria, Australia

Harry H. Hall, A.B.P.S.
Consultant Psychologist, Salisbury, Rhodesia

Mogens Hansen, Cand. Paed. Psych.
Deputy Chief Psychologist, Lyngby; Coeditor, Skolepsykologi, Denmark

Sándor Illés, Ph.D.
Associate Professor of Psychology, Training College for Teachers of Handicapped Children, Budapest, Hungary

Mogens Jansen, Cand. Psych.
Research Director, The Danish Institute for Educational Research;
President, Danish National Association of Reading Teachers and Reading
Specialists, Copenhagen, Denmark

Thomas Kellaghan, Ph.D.
Director, Educational Research Center, St. Patrick's College, Dublin,
Ireland

Edith Klasen, Ph.D.
Clinical Psychologist, Scientific Director, Bavarian Association of
Kindergartens and Day Care Centers, Munich, West Germany

Marianne Klees, Lic. Psychologique
Assistant, Department Medico-Psychologique, Université Libre de
Bruxelles, Brussels, Belgium

Robert M. Knights, Ph.D.
Professor of Psychology, Carleton University, Ottawa, Canada

Betty J. Knych, M.A.
Professor, Communications, College of the Virgin Islands; Coordinator,
Educational Diagnostic Center, Department of Education, Virgin Islands
of the United States, Charlotte Amalie, St. Thomas

Othmar Kowarik
Professor of Education, Federal University of Vienna, Vienna, Austria

Doreen Kronick
Director, Integra Foundation; Past President, Ontario and Canadian
Associations for Children with Learning Disabilities, Toronto, Ontario,
Canada

Mei-Ho Lin Kuo, B.Ed.
Instructor in Education, National Taiwan Normal University, Taipei,
Taiwan, Republic of China

Wei-fan Kuo, Ed.D.
Professor of Special Education, National Taiwan Normal University,
Taipei, Taiwan, Republic of China; Member, Educational Commission
Rehabilitation International

George D. Logue, Ph.D.
Educational Psychologist and Vocational Counselor; Founder, Phoenix
School, Durban, South Africa

Zdeněk Matějček, Ph.D.
Clinical Psychologist, Child Psychiatric Center, Prague, Czechoslovakia

Mary L. McGinnis, M.S.
Learning Disabilities Specialist, Department of Education, Virgin Islands
of the United States, Charlotte Amalie, St. Thomas

Ildikói Meixner, Ph.D.
Training College for Teachers of Handicapped Children, Budapest,
Hungary

Ana Maria Rodriguez Muñiz, Psp.
Professor of Psicopedagoga, Salvador University; Head, Psicopedagoga
Section, Psychiatric Department, Children's Hospital, Buenos Aires,
Argentina

Arne Søegård, Cand. Psych.
Chief Psychologist, Lyngby; Coeditor, Skolepsykologi, Denmark

Yvonne Stewart
Honorary Secretary, Australian Federation of Specific Learning
Difficulties Associations, Sydney, Australia

Raija Syvälahti, M.A.
Teacher of Special Education and Reading Specialist, Helsinki, Finland

Lester Tarnopol, Sc.D.
Faculties of Psychology, Engineering and Mathematics, City College of
San Francisco, San Francisco, California

Muriel Tarnopol, M.A.
Lecturer in Counseling and Guidance, San Francisco State University;
Consultant, Pupil Personnel Services, South San Francisco Unified
School District; Consultant, Special Education Services Division, San
Francisco Unified School District, San Francisco, California

Grete Hagtvedt Vik, M.A.
Teacher, Learning Disabled and Educable Mentally Retarded, Tønsberg,
Norway

Acknowledgments

The editors gratefully acknowledge the assistance received from everyone who contributed to this volume. We are also most grateful for a generous Grant-in-Aid from CIBA Pharmaceutical Company, and especially for the continuing assistance received from Dr. Richard Roberts.

Also acknowledged with gratitude is the help received from Dr. Leonard Levine and Dr. Alan Simmons for documents and information concerning the master plan for special education in California; Ms. Becky Calkins for materials on the operation of the United States Bureau of Education for the Handicapped; Dr. Jeanne M. McCarthy for materials on the Leadership Training Institute in Learning Disabilities; and Mr. D. W. Brown and Dr. J. Tizard for a copy of the Bullock Report summary.

Grateful acknowledgment is also made for the assistance and encouragement received from Dr. Marguerite Dugger and Dr. Martin Dean in our work with the San Francisco Unified School District.

We are especially grateful to Dr. Edith Klasen both for her excellent paper on Germany and for her translation from the German of professor Kowarik's paper on Austria. We are also grateful to A. Alexidis for the very fine drawings and to Yung Wing-Sum for his calligraphy and guidance in the Chinese language in Dr. Butler's chapter on China.

Preface

In 1963, the legislature of the State of California adopted legislation permitting school districts to establish special education for educationally handicapped children. These children were defined as being neither retarded nor culturally deprived, and as having either a neurological handicap or emotional disorder, or both, such that their academic work was significantly below their intellectual capacity.

In 1966, we presented a resolution to the San Francisco Board of Education calling for the implementation of this program in the San Francisco Unified School District. At once, some board members declared that they appreciated our efforts, but they could not understand how a child of normal or higher intelligence could fail to learn to read! This anecdote epitomizes the problem of explaining the fact that a great many intelligent children can have specific learning disabilities that may prevent them from readily learning to read.

During the past 12 years, we visited a number of countries, discussed learning disabilities with professionals, lectured on the subject, visited schools and teacher training institutions, and observed and listened to many children, parents, teachers, and other professionals. The countries visited were Australia, Czechoslovakia, Denmark, England, Finland, Fiji, Greece, Israel, Italy, New Zealand, Norway, Sweden, Switzerland, and the Soviet Union.

During this time, we also edited the first two books of a series on reading and learning disabilities, *Learning Disabilities: Introduction to Educational and Medical Management,* C C Thomas, 1969 (Spanish edition, La Prensa Mexicana); and *Learning Disorders in Children: Diagnosis, Medication, and Education,* Little Brown, 1971 (Italian edition, Armando Armando Editore, Rome; Portuguese edition, Edart Livraria Editora, Sao Paulo).

After visiting the Scandinavian countries in 1973, we had an opportunity to travel to the Soviet Union where we met with Dr. A. R. Luria, and then visited the Institute of Defectology in Moscow. There we talked with Dr. T. A. Vlasova, the director, and Dr. V. I. Lubovski, head of the laboratory of higher nervous activity and psychology of abnormal children. We visited classes for deaf and hard-of-hearing children, which were just starting.

During our discussions with Dr. Lubovski, we talked about the need for a book summarizing the learning disabilities problem in many countries. It was thought that such a book would help developing countries by indicating the incidence of specific learning disabilities in intelligent children as well as the remedial steps taken in the more advanced nations. At the same time, the book would help the advanced countries by describing the work done in a great many different places. This information then could be used to improve the existing learning disabilities programs.

We agreed to edit the book in the United States, and it was also agreed that we would exchange manuscripts. However, we were cautioned that the new regulations in the Soviet Union did not permit either the publication of a foreign document or the sending of a Soviet paper without permission for its publication outside the country.

After returning to San Mateo, we wrote to about 30 well known authors who had published in the field of learning disabilities and requested manuscripts for this book. About 25 original manuscripts were received, and it was possible to include 19 of them in this volume. Each contributor was asked to attempt to use the following general outline:

1. Background of special education in your country
2. Statement of reading problem and percentage of children involved
3. Facilities for testing and diagnosis
4. Methods of testing and diagnosis
5. Facilities for remediation
6. Methods of remediation
7. Results of remedial methods used
8. Medications used, if any, and results
9. Case history of a child
10. Parent/professional organizations helping these children and their work

Originally, we asked for a statement about the learning disabilities problem in each country, but we soon found that most countries had only advanced to a consideration of reading and spelling problems, and so we changed the format to conform to reality.

Professor and Mrs. Kuo, of the National Taiwan Normal University, were to prepare the chapter on reading problems in Chinese, but they were unable to complete their research in time to prepare a manuscript. We were very fortunate to receive a manuscript on the reading problems of Chinese children by Dr. Susan Butler of the University of Sydney, who had just completed a book, *Impressions of China Today*. The chapter on China contains an addendum by Dr. and Mrs. Kuo based on preliminary results of their study of reading problems in Taiwan.

We hope that this volume provides the salutary effects intended for the benefit of children with learning and reading disabilities everywhere.

to the children worldwide who suffer from reading and learning disabilities; to their parents who perhaps suffer even more; and to the dedicated teachers, psychologists, speech, hearing, and language therapists, physicians, and other professionals who try to help these children and parents and especially to Matthew and Daniel, from whom we learned.

READING DISABILITIES
An International Perspective

CHAPTER 1

Reading and Learning Problems Worldwide

Lester Tarnopol and Muriel Tarnopol

It has often been asked how professionals in different countries view the problem of intelligent children who have great difficulty learning in a normal school situation, and what they are doing to help these children. Answers to these questions indicate that, in almost all industrialized nations, many professionals (educators, psychologists, speech therapists, physicians, etc.) are acutely aware of these issues and are actively engaged in their study and amelioration. In the emerging nations, on the other hand, more basic problems are so pressing that special education is often nonexistent.

This situation is documented by the 1971 study of special education by the United Nations Educational, Scientific, and Cultural Organization (UNESCO). The statements below were taken from the reported replies to questionnaires from the Secretariats of the National Commissions of member states. The respondent from Dahomey stated, "Handicapped children are in practice excluded from ordinary education." The Ethiopian reply stated, "Education is not compulsory for either handicapped or nonhandicapped children." From Syria came, "No special provisions are made for handicapped children." Tanzania's reply was, "There is no compulsory education either for normal or handicapped children." "No special education" is provided in Togo. And so it continues. Under the circumstances, these nations can hardly be expected to consider the plight of intelligent children with reading and learning disabilities.

In a survey by Waller (1974), an educator from Tanzania remarked, "As so many children never receive full time education, those with any type of problem would drop out unnoticed. It is a luxury for the better developed countries (that are) able to concern themselves with this prob-

1

lem." In reply to the question, "Is the problem of dyslexia (word-blindness or specific developmental language difficulties) recognized?" Malta responded, "In theory yes, in practice not yet." Saudi Arabia replied that there was no official recognition of the problem and no government funds were spent on any aspects of the problem. On the other hand, other responses indicated that official recognition is given to dyslexia, and government funds are spent on the problem in Austria, Canada, Denmark, Finland, France, Germany, Luxembourg, The Netherlands, Rumania, Sweden, Switzerland, and Tunisia.

Another fact that emerged from our study of learning problems in many lands was the disparity in the level of development of the programs for children with reading and learning disorders in the "advanced" countries. It became apparent that in many nations the study and treatment of specific learning disabilities had only reached the level of diagnosing and remediating reading or reading and spelling problems. Writing, arithmetic, and concept formation disorders were not generally being considered. Finally, in some countries, reading disorders in intelligent children were just beginning to be considered. Since the gamut of specific learning disabilities was less often being considered than purely reading and spelling problems, the thrust of this study will necessarily be in the area of reading disabilities.

It is most interesting to note that reading problems in nonretarded children are now acknowledged worldwide and that they have aroused great interest and activity among both parents and professionals in a determination to help these children. It has been established worldwide that for many intelligent children, reading and learning problems can be most persistent, even to the point where some American physicians have confined their practices exclusively to the treatment of this problem in children (Tarnopol, 1971). Since the problem is, of course, primarily educational, it has also become the most significant and extensive problem within special education. It is significant that the ability to read is now being seen as both a necessity and a right, especially in the industrialized nations.

This general attitude has probably been given its greatest impetus in recent California legislation which declares that all children, regardless of the nature of their handicaps, are legally entitled to an educational program that meets their needs. The legislation also states how this shall be done. Provision is even made for California's 95 free community colleges to receive state funding for special programs to help students (to 21 years of age) with learning disabilities. However, although this provision for older students has been available since 1964, the community colleges are just beginning to implement it.

READING DISABILITIES SURVEY

The Tarnopols received replies to a survey questionnaire from 16 countries: Argentina, Austria, Canada, China (Taiwan), Czechoslovakia, Denmark, Finland, Hungary, Malaysia, The Netherlands, Norway, Rhodesia, South Africa, Sweden, United States, and Venezuela. From this survey it was possible to make some generalizations about the incidence and handling of reading problems in these countries.

Because there are no internationally accepted standardized reading tests, it is very difficult to estimate the relative extent of reading problems in various countries. The replies to the question, "In your country, approximately what percentage of nonretarded school children have reading disabilities?" ranged from 1% in China to 33% in Venezuela, with a median of 8%. The problem of establishing the percentage of reading disabilities is, of course, compounded by the lack of an internationally accepted definition of this term. Most of the respondents defined "reading disability" as existing when a child read significantly below either his age or grade level.

Respondents from only seven countries replied that they have legislation to provide special education for nonretarded children with reading problems. These countries were Austria, Czechoslovakia, Denmark, The Netherlands, Norway, Sweden, and the United States. In the United States, such legislation exists in most, but not all of the states.

Half of the countries surveyed have special full-time classes for children with reading or learning disabilities; and all but three countries provide special part-time programs in regular schools for these children. The ratio of boys to girls who require remedial reading was most often stated to be three boys to one girl. Only seven respondents stated that their countries had a program of early case-finding and failure prevention.

Testing and Tests Used

In most countries, it was stated that children are usually tested for reading disorders by an individual. In a few countries, this testing is usually done by a team. The testing is generally performed by psychologists, educators (teachers), and speech therapists, in that order. The tests generally include, in the order of precedence, reading, standardized reading, intelligence, visual perception, visual-motor coordination, and auditory perception. Tests of equilibrium are seldom performed, which is interesting in view of the fact that at least two equilibrium tests have been invented which predict reading disabilities quite well. One static balance test was developed by Kohen-Raz (1970) of the Hebrew University of Jerusalem in conjunction with the Department of Pediatrics of Stanford University. On the average, pediatric and neurological examinations are sometimes done, while psychiatric examinations are less often performed.

The psychological tests most often used were the Wechsler Intelligence Scales, the Terman-Merrill-Binet Intelligence Tests, the Illinois Test of Psycholinguistic Abilities, and the Bender Visual Motor Gestalt Test, in the order given.

Almost all countries had special courses to train teachers how to teach children with reading problems. In seven countries, the psychologists had special training to test and work with children with reading problems. The number of school psychologists per 10,000 school children ranged from one-half to eight, with a median of two.

Causes of Reading Disabilities

The main causes of reading and learning disabilities were listed as neurological, followed by genetic, and in a few instances emotional causes were added. The respondent from Norway stated, "In our country the population is highly homogeneous and the language is relatively regular. Therefore, the main causes of reading disabilities are assumed to be of genetic or psychoneurological origin." From Czechoslovakia came, "heredity and minimal brain dysfunction." The Hungarian response included, "disturbances of the underlying neurophysiological and psychological functions; especially speech disturbances, very mild manifestations of aphasia, disturbed feed-back or motor processes in speech, and genetically based disturbances."

In most cases, the best methods of remedial teaching were listed as eclectic. Also mentioned were individual instruction, differential diagnosis followed by prescriptive teaching, and phonics.

Some respondents saw "teaching disabilities" as adding to the problems of children with learning problems. In Venezuela, the problem was seen to be related to inadequate organization of the school system. In Sweden the extent of reading problems arising from inadequate teaching was estimated as 10 to 15%. From Norway came the statement, "Even though the teaching profession is held in high regard in Norway, the traditionally trained teachers are too poorly qualified to provide remedial instruction. The college programs do not provide sufficient coverage of the special techniques used for detection and remediation of learning disabilities. Therefore, learning disabilities may arise, and be sustained, due to teacher incapability." This situation is certainly also the case in the United States and, we would imagine, in most countries.

The response from Hungary indicated some specific possible teaching flaws. "The faults that can occur in teaching reading are: wrong sequence in teaching letters; faulty associations between letters and pronunciation;

and not giving the longer words gradually enough, so that the children soon become overloaded." The German respondent stated that teaching disability is a problem "to a very limited extent. For example, Vienna schools never introduced the whole word method, yet there were just as many retarded readers there as elsewhere." In the United States, we have made a somewhat detailed study of the types of teaching errors which occur, and have introduced the subject in the chapter on the United States.

TERMINOLOGY

Disparity in terminology exists both among and within states. The lack of universally accepted designations for various types of reading and learning problems tends to handicap anyone attempting to study these problems. However, a more important consideration is the fact that differences in terminology are often associated with different opinions about the causes and remediation of these problems.

Although the existence of reading and learning disabilities in intelligent children is generally accepted, the etiology and treatment remain controversial. Considering these circumstances, the chapters from 18 countries and the Virgin Islands are remarkably similar with respect to these controversial issues./ The authors almost all agree that the etiology of reading disabilities in children of adequate intelligence is most likely neurological, with possible secondary emotional amplification, and it may often be genetic. Only the French literature is cited as generally giving precedence to emotional disorders as a primary cause of reading problems, with suspicion still being cast on the mother-child relationship. Cultural deprivation, lower socioeconomic status, and transient status are also cited in many nations as causes of reading problems, but not of reading disabilities.

Our authors generally appear to accept the concept that reading disabilities in nonretarded children are simply one manifestation of possible specific learning disabilities. However, the terminology for children with reading problems includes reading disabilities, dyslexia, specific language disorders, learning disabilities, perceptual disorders, instrumental disabilities, minimal brain dysfunction, brain damage, and so forth. In general, the reading problem is seen as difficulty in learning in the presence of adequate intelligence, instruction, and opportunity to learn.

Terminology in Different Countries

The terminology used to describe reading disorders in each country seems to be related to local developments. The term "dyslexie" was first suggested in Stuttgart by Rudolf Berlin in 1887 as a form of word blindness that had previously been described by Kussmaul (Wagner, 1973). This term is now in universal usage as dyslexia, following the English form of the word. Hungary, Austria, and Germany also use the term "legasthenia" (specific weaknesses in learning to read and spell) which was introduced by the Hungarian, Ranchburg, early in this century. The German-speaking nations also refer to reading-writing weakness (Lese-Rechtschreibe Schwäche).

British literature on the subject may begin with a Scotch ophthalmologist's (Hinshelwood) report in 1895 of some cases of word-blindness. This was shortly followed by reports from an English ophthalmologist (Morgan) and a school physician (Kerr) on cases of reading disabilities among intelligent children; one of the reports used the term "congenital word-blindness" (Strother, 1973). Today, in Great Britain, specific reading difficulty seems to be used globally to refer to reading, and perhaps writing, spelling, and number skills that are below a child's general abilities. Such children may also be called dyslexic or backward readers. The concept of learning disabilities often appears to be related to low intelligence (IQ as low as 50) in Great Britain.

The first Czechoslovakian publication dealing with reading problems appeared in 1904 and discusses a case of reading and writing retardation in the presence of adequate school achievement in other areas. The condition was referred to as "alexia" by a neurologist. Modern terminology in Czechoslovakia includes dyslexia and specific reading disability.

In Denmark, Edith Norrie established the Word-Blind Institute about 1931; however, her definition of word-blind has been the source of much controversy in their literature. At present in Danish literature, it appears that reading disorders may be called reading retardation, word blindness, learning difficulties, and learning disabilities.

In Canada, no common terminology has been adopted. Specific reading disabilities, educational disabilities, learning disorders, and learning disabilities are variously used. Belgian literature refers to instrumental impairments or handicaps to describe the condition of children whose peripheral organs function normally but who have academic problems associated with perceptual, psychomotor, and linguistic impairments. Finnish children with academic problems and who are not retarded are referred to as reading-writing disabled. Learning disabilities is also used. Rhodesian psychologists refer to the reading problem as dyslexia.

The term learning disabilities appears to be generally used in Ireland, The Netherlands, and the Republic of South Africa. Australians are talking about specific learning difficulties.

In Norway, disabled readers are grouped according to auditory, auditory-visual, emotional, and educational dyslexia. These terms were developed by Gjessing. They also speak of learning disabilities and specific reading disability.

In the United States, McCready reported on language disability in children in 1927. Orton invented the term "strephosymbolia" in the 1930's to represent a type of dyslexia which he saw as producing turned or reversed symbols due to ambiguous or lack of established hemispheric dominance in the brain. Presently, "specific learning disabilities" is used for the nonretarded condition, and "general learning disabilities" is used for the condition in the presence of mental retardation. "Specific learning disabilities" have been defined by the United States Office of Education to be "a disorder in one or more of the basic psychological processes involved in understanding or in using language." The disorder may involve speech, reading, writing, or mathematics. Excluded, however, are disorders arising from visual, hearing, or motor handicaps, mental retardation, emotional disturbance, or environmental disadvantage.

Physicians tend to use the term minimal brain dysfunction. However, about 40 different terms (Clements, 1966) are still to be found in the literature, with learning disabilities, specific learning disabilities, minimal brain dysfunction, and dyslexia occurring most often.

SOME FACTORS RELATED TO READING PROBLEMS

Although it is generally conceded that a major cause of reading disorders in intelligent children appears to be related to genetic and neurological dysfunctions with secondary emotional problems, there are still a great many children to be accounted for who may not be so classified. This is especially true in countries where the population is not homogeneous. For example, the population of the United States is quite inhomogeneous in comparison with Norway, and this may partly account for the great discrepancy in reported reading problems. Moreover, in the developing countries even the concept of specific learning disabilities tends to be a luxury too remote for immediate concern.

An overview of the sources of reading problems in school children suggests the following list based on Eisenberg (Tarnopol, 1969):
1. Excessive absences
2. Educationally deprived environment
3. Lack of environmental motivation
4. Lack of motivation due to emotional factors
5. Defects in teaching
6. Chronic illness or malnourishment
7. Severe vision or hearing losses
8. Mental retardation

9. Brain damage
10. Genetic or congenital brain dysfunction

Reading problems may be caused by any one or any group of these variables.

Environmental Factors

Reports from many countries indicate that lower socioeconomic status tends to be related to generally depressed reading and learning levels. Another factor related to low reading levels is minority status, especially when the minority comes from an ethnic or national group that does not have a history of educational development. The combination of minority status from an underdeveloped country and lower socioeconomic level places some children in double jeopardy. In many cases the problem is compounded by the fact that the child's first language is not that of the country whose school he is attending. Other environmental factors which tend to retard children's learning are transient status and any other things which prevent steady school attendance.

Minority status and speaking a foreign first language do not necessarily lead to learning problems. Those national or ethnic groups that have a history of educational achievement do not seem to have difficulty learning in a new environment. Some minorities even tend to have less than average difficulty learning in a new country. For example, Chinese and Japanese children, and Jewish children from Europe have tended to do very well, on the average, in the United States.

The National Reading Council in the United States wanted to determine the number of adult Americans who might be unable to "survive" in a technological society because they lacked practical reading skills. They, therefore, commissioned a study to measure the national "survival" literacy rate. The test included such items as the ability to fill out forms used for job applications, social security, a driver's license, and public assistance. By these measures, literacy was found to be approximately proportional to income; suburbanites tended to surpass both the inner-city and rural populations. Among those surveyed, the illiteracy rate of whites was about half that of blacks. On the average, women were found to surpass men in reading ability, and younger people were more literate than their elders. This latter finding seems to be related to the fact that the educational level has been steadily increasing in the United States, so that, on the average, young people have had more formal education than older people (Dempsey, 1972).

In a reading comprehension study done in 15 countries using a standardized reading test translated into each language, it was found that reading levels in the three developing countries fell far below those in the economically developed countries (Thorndike, 1973). In the economically poorer countries, major problems were found in the availability of educational facilities, teacher training, class size, special education, and remedial programs. This is an example of the debilitating influence that the total educational environment may have and seems to indicate that "schooling does make a difference."

Structure of Language

The structure of language in terms of the relationship between spoken and written language seems to influence the degree of difficulty encountered by children learning to read. Of the languages investigated in this study, it appears that the original Chinese pictographs may be the easiest to learn to read, followed by the newer ideographs (Figure 1, see also Chapter 8). The next in order of difficulty appear to be the most phonetic languages, probably followed by the less phonetic, and finally the least phonetic languages. In this respect, English appears to be one of the most difficult languages for beginners. However, there is some evidence that the order of difficulty may change for advanced reading comprehension.

A number of factors make it extremely difficult to adequately compare languages for difficulty in learning to read. The greatest problem is the lack of equivalent standardized reading tests in the different languages. Second, many countries do not have standardized reading tests that they can use to determine the relative reading levels of the children in their

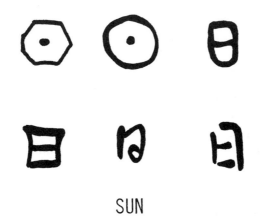

SUN

Figure 1. The evolution of written Chinese is demonstrated by the characters for sun. Evolution occurred from left to right and top to bottom for the characters shown. The early pictogram dating from the oracle bones of the Shang dynasty (1766 to 1122 B.C.) was a pictorial representation of the sun. Major changes occurred during the Chin dynasty (221 to 207 B.C.), the Han dynasty (207 B.C. to 220 A.D.) and in modern times. The final character is from the *Kai* calligraphy now used.

countries. For this reason, the percentages of nonretarded children with reading problems reported from different countries are often based on subjective estimates and are certainly not comparable. Since socioeconomic level, minority status, transiency, population homogeneity, adequacy of the educational system, and so forth, affect the reading level of a population, the problem of comparing languages for relative ease of learning to read is compounded.

Reading versus Spelling

Ordinarily, spelling is more difficult than reading for children with learning disabilities. In the German-speaking countries, spelling is a greater problem than reading for many children. In English, it has often been observed that after a dyslexic child learns to read well, he generally continues to demonstrate a severe spelling problem.

However, this is not always the case. In a study from Uruguay, Carbonell de Grampone (1974) cites cases of children who can spell better than they can read. A sample of 118 Spanish-speaking Uruguayan third-grade children were tested in both spelling and reading. Thirty-one (26%) spelled better than they read. Further testing confirmed the hypothesis that these children tended to have visual perceptual disabilities in the presence of good auditory perception. A review of the types of spelling errors made by these children confirmed that their auditory perception abilities were better than their visual perception abilities. They tended to make spelling errors such as omitting the *u* in *gui* or doubling *r* when it was not required. For example, writing *ginda* instead of the correct *guinda* (silent u), both pronounced the same; or writing *alrrededor* instead of *alrededor,* not realizing that this word is an exception to the rule of doubling the *r*. None of these errors has an auditory origin.

These children, who were poor readers, characteristically continued to read each word, letter by letter, when the other children were well along in the reading of whole words and phrases. This persistent decoding problem indicated the presence of a relatively severe visual perceptual disability which was confirmed by the tests. It was concluded that visual skills are important in reading Spanish. Good auditory perception may permit the child to learn his phonemes, to analyze the word into its component phonemes, and to master the grapheme-phoneme associations, but the ambiguities of adequate Spanish reading finally require visual learning.

IEA Study of Reading in 15 Countries

In an attempt to determine the reading levels of children in various countries, the International Association for the Evaluation of Educational

Achievement (IEA) developed a reading comprehension test, a reading speed test, and a test of word knowledge in 12 languages (Thorndike, 1973).

In this study, children in 15 countries were tested at ages 10 and 14 years, and in their last year of secondary school. These countries were Belgium (Flemish), Belgium (French), Chile, England, Finland, Hungary, India, Iran, Israel, Italy, The Netherlands, New Zealand, Scotland, Sweden, and the United States. Ordinarily, 10-year-olds who started school at age 6 would be in the fifth grade. In some countries, substantial proportions of each age group could not be tested because they were not at grade level. For example, in Chile, one-third of the 10-year-olds were either more than one year retarded or were not in school; in Hungary, 4 to 5% were more than one year retarded; in India, an unspecified percent were in grades 1 and 2; and Italy excluded 60% of their 10-year-olds because they were in the fourth grade. At the 14-year-old level, 43% of the children in Chile were no longer in school; in Hungary, 10 to 12% were either retarded or not in school; and in Israel, 16% were no longer in school.

Results were obtained from 15 countries, involving a total of 1,670 schools and 34,344 10-year-old students; 1,752 schools and 39,307 14-year-old students; and 1,209 schools and 29,474 students in their last year of secondary school.

The reliability of the comprehension tests was found to be high except in India and Iran where they appeared to be too difficult. The most dramatic finding was that the 12 developed countries with strong systems of universal education were very much ahead of the three developing countries in reading levels. Only 10 to 15% of the students in developing countries scored as well as an average student in the developed countries on a test of reading comprehension. It was suggested that the cause lay partly in the schools. The less developed countries had less well trained teachers and poorer resources, and consequently, a limited educational program. However, it was believed that the major differences lay in the home environments and society which gave the children meager verbal and intellectual stimulation.

In the 12 developed countries, the highest correlation was found between hours of instruction in the mother tongue and reading comprehension, $r = 0.47$. This was followed by the number of magazines in the home ($r = 0.36$), hours of reading for pleasure ($r = 0.29$), mother's education ($r = 0.23$), and father's education ($r = 0.14$). Since the most significant variable correlated with reading comprehension was hours of instruction in the mother tongue, it appears obvious that educational programs that substitute hours of any other instruction for reading and language seriously reduce the students' reading comprehension levels.

When reading comprehension was correlated with these variables for all 15 countries, the situation changed dramatically, indicating that other variables were more important determiners in the three developing countries. For example, the correlation between reading comprehension and the number of books in the home was $r = 0.85$, with the mother's education $r = 0.73$, and with the father's education $r = 0.60$. This indicates that the educational level of the family was the most important factor correlated with reading comprehension in the developing countries (India, Iran, and Chile).

REMEDIATION

Investigation of the approaches used in 30 countries to remediate reading problems in children indicates that no single method appears to have been adopted universally. Moreover, there seems to be no individual nation in which a single solution has been found for all reading problems.

Bullock Report

The British report, "A Language of Life," stresses the principle that there is no one method or philosophy that unlocks the process of learning to read (Bullock, 1975). The point is made that for four centuries the main arguments about how reading should be taught have been "advanced, contested, revamped, discredited, and rediscovered." The report continues, "Today's discovery was often yesterday's discard, unrecognized as such, or rehabilitated by some new presentation. There have certainly been advances, and some valuable innovations, but the major arguments are substantially the same as they have always been, and too much attention is given to polarized opinions about method." The committee further felt that improvement in the teaching of reading will come only from a detailed study of all of the factors involved and how they can be influenced. This understanding should influence teacher training, the organization of teaching, and other resources. Finally, the committee states, "The majority of children require precise, well organized instruction if they are to become successful readers."

Survey of Methods

Chall (1967) did a survey of methods of teaching reading from which she observed that people often tended to be emotionally tied (or "married") to a particular method of teaching, and so were constrained to defend it. Chall asked why some children fail to read. The replies from authors of basal readers, and from proponents of phonics, linguistics, alphabet reform, or language experience, all indicated that a return or new approach to their method would prevent reading failure. Chall stated that this emotional attachment was "more often characteristic of religion and politics than of science and learning."

Chall cites Fries' review of the literature from 1570 to 1900 on methods of teaching reading. He uncovered a "succession of discoveries and rediscoveries including alphabet reforms, word methods, sentence methods, phonic methods—each claiming to be the new, natural, true, logical way to begin reading."

Prescriptive Teaching

The thrust of this research appears to be that "there is nothing new under the sun." On the other hand, from our study of *remedial* reading methods in many countries, it may be concluded that something new has been added. A relatively modern innovation is prescriptive teaching. It appears that prescriptive or diagnostic remedial teaching is being done in all developed nations. The modern feature of such teaching is in the nature of the test battery used to diagnose specific learning disabilities (Tarnopol and Tarnopol, 1975). The tests explore the basic sensory learning modalities, including visual, auditory, and tactile perception; motor coordination and equilibrium; and the visual-auditory-motor cross modalities. In each sensory area, measurements may be made of reception; immediate, short-term, and long-term memory; integration; and expression. Finally, the results of these tests are coordinated with the results of tests of language, academic achievement, and intelligence. A further modern feature of testing is the development of standardized tests with population norms, which have been carefully checked for both reliability and validity.

Many psychologists, teachers, and language therapists are learning how to develop an individualized teaching program for children who have been tested. There is evidence that in severe cases of specific learning disabilities, this approach may succeed when other approaches to teaching the child have failed (Calancini and Trout, 1971).

Computer-assisted Instruction

Another method of teaching reading that appears to have some new features is computer-assisted instruction (CAI). Almost universally, it has been found that girls tend to learn to read better than boys in ordinary classrooms. In the United States, when the children are grouped for reading, the top group usually contains about 3 girls for each boy, and the bottom group generally has 3 boys for each girl. Atkinson (1974) reports that with CAI, boys appear to benefit more than girls, even though the girls as a group remain superior in reading. Boys improved in reading 42%

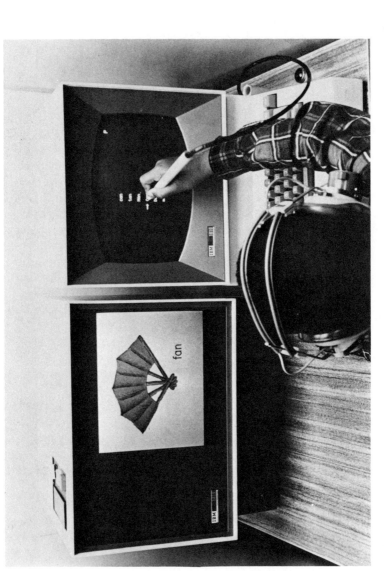

Figure 2. Student using computer to learn reading. This first-grade student is learning to decode whole words in a computer assisted instruction system. From *Introduction To Psychology*, Sixth Edition, by Ernest R. Hilgard, Richard C. Atkinson, Rita L. Atkinson, © 1975, Harcourt, Brace Jovanovich, Inc. Reproduced with permission.

over the control group while girls improved 17%. The results have been replicated in several studies.

Computer-assisted instruction was used to teach reading to first through third grade children (Figure 2). After about 5 years of research with CAI, the present orientation is toward developing low cost CAI that supplements classroom teaching, and concentrates on tasks that require individual instruction. The student terminal consists of a teletypewriter with audio headphones. This terminal is connected to a computer at Stanford University in Palo Alto, California. The teletypewriter provides the student with a printed copy of whatever he types and the computer's replies.

The CAI program focuses primarily on decoding but it also includes introductory reading for meaning and pleasure. The program has eight parts. A section of one part teaches the identification of the letters used in the beginning sight words. When the student has mastered these letters, he may enter the section containing the sight words. The computer keeps a continuous record of the student's achievement and programs him to the correct place at his learning level. The student automatically receives an amount of time in each section proportional to the number of items still to be learned before going on to the next part. Each student's progress is individualized according to mathematical formulas for the acquisition of reading that are used to specify the best scheme for sequencing his work with the computer.

After the pupil has learned a specified number of sight words, he begins exercises in phonics. This includes initial and final consonants and consonant-vowel-consonant combinations. Vowel sounds in isolation are not learned, in accordance with linguistically oriented curricula generally. Patterns of vowels and consonants usually found in phonemes are emphasized. After some phonemes are learned, the student is requested to construct words by adding appropriate consonants. Finally, decisions about what instruction to present to a student are made by the computer, based on a complete record of his learning history with the CAI program.

Kindergarten Screening

Another area in which decided advances have been made is in kindergarten screening for potential learning disabilities. Reading readiness tests have existed for a number of years. However, testing has been refined by the introduction of test batteries that are over 80% efficient in predicting reading failure. They may also give a differential evaluation of the child's strengths and weaknesses so that specific educational strategies for habilitation may be formulated.

Book (1974) reported on a test battery given to 725 kindergarten children to identify potentially high risk children for reading failure in the first and second grades. The battery included the Metropolitan Readiness Test, the Bender Visual Motor Gestalt Test, and the Slossen Intelligence Test. On the basis of test scores, the children were divided into six diagnostic categories. At the end of first and second grades, the children were given tests to measure their reading levels, which were divided into six reading-level categories. Four hundred thirty-five children were tested in the first grade for reading level. The correlation between diagnostic category and reading-level category at the end of the first grade was very significant ($r = 0.99$, $p < 0.001$). Similarly, at the end of second grade, for reading tests given to 219 children, the correlation between diagnostic category and reading-level category was very significant ($r = 0.99$, $p < 0.001$). By the end of the second grade only 1 child failed to make as much progress as the tests predicted, and 27 children did better than expected.

Jansky and de Hirsch (1972) developed a kindergarten screening test battery to predict reading failure. The tests in this battery include: Letter Naming (the child is asked to name 6 printed letters); Picture Naming (name 22 pictures); Gates Word Matching Test (find the words that are alike); Bender Visual Motor Gestalt Test (6 designs are copied); Binet Sentence Memory (repeat a list of sentences).

Those children who fail this predictive screening battery may be given a diagnostic test battery composed of 19 tests as follows: Oral Language A (six tests), Pattern Matching (four tests), Pattern Memory (five tests), and Visuo Motor Organization (four tests). From these test scores a diagnostic profile is derived that is used to formulate a remedial program for the child.

The screening index was given in kindergarten to 268 children. It correctly identified 79% of the failing readers at the end of second grade. The index also singled out as risks 22% who achieved average or above average reading levels. These tests were done on a high risk population in New York City. Of 347 children, the percentages of those who failed to learn to read by the end of second grade were 16% white girls, 23% white boys, 41% black girls, and 63% black boys. The screening index correctly identified 86% of the white boys, 79% of the white girls, 77% of the black girls, and 76% of the black boys who later failed reading.

Probably the most extensive kindergarten-level project to screen for potential learning disabilities is the one in Buenos Aires in 1972 reported by Gorriti and Muñiz (Chapter 2). The project was prompted by the fact that about 58% of the children in Argentina dropped out before completing elementary school. Although this drop-out rate may not be unusual among South American countries, this action of the National Board of

Education indicates a sincere desire to modernize the educational system in Argentina.

Twenty-five thousand children were screened with a battery of tests similar to those used by Book, or Jansky and de Hirsch, with the notable addition of Piaget's operational tests. It is also interesting to note that the Bender Visual Motor Gestalt Test appears in all three batteries and the Metropolitan Reading Test is in two batteries. Another important generalization is that, based on many studies, over 90% of the children with learning disabilities show evidence of visual-motor and motor coordination deficits as established by such tests as the Bender, Marble Board test, and neurological examinations for "soft signs."

Finally, all three kindergarten screening studies (Book, Jansky and de Hirsch, and Gorriti and Muñiz) were linked to projects for attempted habilitation or remediation. The Argentina study has the possible advantage that its findings, both in terms of screening for learning disabilities and follow-up special education for the children who need it, may be applied in the many Spanish-speaking countries of South America.

Remedial Methods Often Used

All of our authors seem to be in agreement on one aspect of remedial teaching. Children with reading and learning disabilities fare best in a well structured, organized environment. Permissiveness is never recommended. All are also in agreement that counseling or psychotherapy given to the child does not remediate his learning problems. Sometimes counseling is recommended to help the parents understand and deal with the problem, and, at times, psychotherapy is recommended as an adjunct to remedial teaching to assist the child in overcoming severe anxiety.

Within a structured teacher-pupil relationship and environment, the most often used technique of teaching appears to be a multisensory approach. The child is taught through several sensory learning modalities simultaneously or consecutively or both. Most often used are the visual, auditory, kinesthetic, and tactile senses for learning. It is also almost universally agreed that these children must overlearn everything much more than an average pupil. Finally, there seems to be consensus on the desirability of preventing beginning learners from making errors. Incorrect first impressions tend to be most difficult to eradicate and often form a base upon which further errors may multiply. It is not believed that beginning pupils learn well by trial and error.

The concept of diagnostic remedial teaching seems to be widespread. In conjunction with this approach, nearly all nations have adapted or developed diagnostic test batteries. There also appears to be general agreement with the concept that early diagnosis and prevention of reading and learning disabilities present the most hopeful approach to remediation.

Among the remedial teaching methods most often cited by educators in different nations are those of Gillingham and Fernald. These methods have in common a multisensory approach. However, the Gillingham method is based on alphabetic phonics and the Fernald technique uses the whole word approach.

The Gillingham method (developed by Orton, Gillingham and Stillman) uses visual, auditory, and kinesthetic reinforcement of associations made between sounds and symbols. First the sounds of letters are learned, followed by small phonetic groups of letters. Phonics drill cards are used, beginning with those words for which the sound-symbol relationship is the same. Spelling and reading are taught simultaneously. New sound-symbol combinations are then learned, continuing the use of multisensory reinforcement. Teachers who use this method have reported generally good results with their handicapped children.

In the Fernald method, the child selects a word he wishes to learn, regardless of length. The word is written or printed by the teacher and the child traces the letters saying each part of the word as he traces it. This process is repeated until he can write the word from memory. The initial learning stages are: tracing a word with the finger, writing the traced word from memory, writing the word as a whole rather than by sounding it out, and using the words in meaningful groups. Many teachers also have used this method with satisfactory success when teaching children with learning disabilities.

Montessori and Frostig have also been influential in the development of remedial programs in a number of countries. In several countries linguistic studies of the language have been made and programs have been developed utilizing these results. Letters and sounds are sometimes presented for children to learn based on their frequency of use. Color-coding of vowels, consonants, and combinations of letters such as diphthongs may be used to help the child learn. Signs, such as arrows, may be used to help children start to read in the right direction, since many of these children have directionality problems. Sometimes the letters or diphthongs being presented are framed so that they stand out. The configurations of words may be outlined to aid in the whole word method of presentation.

In the teaching of handwriting, which tends to be a problem for most learning disabilities children, a simplified cursive alphabet may be used. For these children, cursive writing is often easier than printing and they are much less prone to reversals with cursive writing. Austrians and others stress handwriting skills, not only because these handicapped children can learn to write quite legibly, but also because it may be used as an aid in the development of both word perception and memory. A great deal of attention is paid to spacing on the page and proper proportions between upper and lower case letters. For learning purposes, practice proceeds from large muscle movements to the small muscles. Finnish primary workbooks stress proper sequence using arrows. Tracing perfect models provides visual and kinesthetic reinforcement (Figure 3).

The teaching of reading and writing (calligraphy) in Chinese appears to be a very structured, rote, repetitive process. It also seems that the children spend more time learning to read and write Chinese than is the case with Western languages. This combination of factors should partially account for the fact that China claims the lowest reading problem rate of all of the nations surveyed. Another factor which should reduce both the

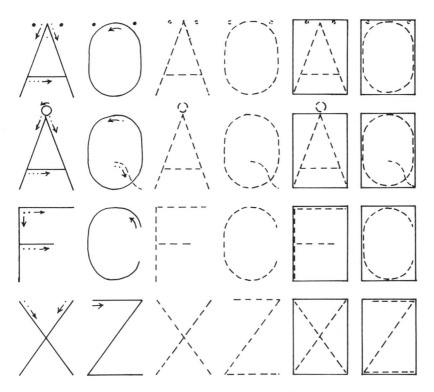

Figure 3. Shown is a page from a Finnish first-grade writing workbook. It illustrates the authors' appreciation of the fact that beginning students benefit from tracing perfect models. Arrows start the children writing in the desired sequence of strokes. The letters are large and present a strong visual stimulus. The child at this level of development is not required to draw the letters from memory. Source: Harjula, S., Syvälahti, R., and Virtanen, T. (1970) *Kirjoituksen Alkeet 1* Helsinki: Werner Söderström Osakeyhtiö. Reproduced with permission.

reading and writing problems of beginning learners in Chinese is the teaching method. The children spend a great deal of time tracing over perfect models on plastic sheets. They also use paper that has lined squares printed on it to aid them in practicing calligraphy.

Moreover, Chinese pictographs have a logical structure based on pictured objects. These original pictographs tended to convey a clear meaning which even children or uneducated people had no difficulty grasping, as indicated in Figure 1. Subtleties in written forms, such as the transition from pictograph to ideograph to phonogram, came later. The process was probably similar to the changes in form which have shaped the Western languages. Since Chinese is so completely different from the written languages of the West, it would be most interesting to acquire some comparable research results that might help determine the incidence of neurogenic learning disabilities among Chinese children.

TEACHER TRAINING

Research and experience, worldwide, on the reading and learning problems of children, indicate that the learning process is extremely complex. The intricacies of the learning process have been subjected to a great deal of scrutiny in the past several decades by multidisciplinary teams of professionals. This work may be said to be generally the product of special education since the most profitable studies have been those performed with handicapped learners. The results of these studies have led to the remedial teaching methods used in many countries. These approaches to serving handicapped children comprise the main thrust of this volume, and they indicate the direction that teacher training could most profitably take.

We have often heard educators state that the child who has no learning disabilities and who has adequate intelligence and motivation will learn in spite of poor teaching. It appears that this may be only a half-truth. In the IEA survey of reading in 15 countries, Thorndike (1973) found that in Iran, India, and Chile, the 14-year-old children were so far behind their counterparts in the countries with a higher economic level of development that they "seemed almost illiterate." Part of the problem was indicated to be related to the low level of teacher training and the lack of special education in these countries.

On the reading comprehension test at the 14-year-old level, only the top 2% (approxmate) of the Indian and Iranian students scored above the lowest 2% of the students in New Zealand, Scotland, England, and The Netherlands. One can hardly postulate that intelligence and socioeconomic differences favored the poor and average achievers in the developed countries over the better readers in Iran and India. Therefore, it seems logical that the educational systems must be very different, giving an advantage to children in the developed nations. These data seem to favor the hypothesis that children with good ability tend to learn more in the better school systems with better teaching than do similar children with less adequate teaching.

It has also been said that the child with learning disabilities seems to be unable to learn in the presence of poor teaching. This generalization tends to be substantiated by both research and experience. Jansky and de Hirsch (1972) reported that they asked the principals to rate the teachers in 5 public schools where the children were "at risk." In the primary classes taught by the teachers rated as adequate, 23% of the children failed to learn to read by second grade. However, 49% of the pupils failed who were taught by the teachers whom the principals had characterized as poor teachers. It was pointed out that inexperienced teachers were frequently assigned this most difficult task of starting high risk children on reading in the crucial first two grades. It was also stated that the problem tends to be compounded by the high rate of turnover among young teachers. Finally, they stated, "It is well known, moreover, that the reading curriculum in teacher-training institutions is poor." Jansky and de Hirsch see the reading problem as arising in part from a combination of inadequate teacher training and the inexperience of beginning teachers.

Similarly, throughout South America, a comparable situation may exist. We have been unable to find any evidence of special education for children with reading and learning disabilities in the public schools of Argentina, Brazil, Chile, Colombia, Mexico, Peru, or Venezuela. Reports from all of these countries indicated that there were, however, private facilities available to assist these children.

The problems of education in Mexico may be typical of those in many South American countries. Primary education is compulsory in Mexico. However, there are not enough schools or teachers to educate all of the children. In rural areas, there may be no schools available. In Mexico City, many of the schools have three shifts; three different groups of children and teachers attend the schools at varied hours during the day. Teacher training is unable to include such esoteric curricula as the treatment of reading and learning disabilities.

Special Education in the U.S.S.R.

Since the activities in the U.S.S.R. on behalf of handicapped children are of great interest, we shall summarize some of our observations in this respect. The Russian Federated Soviet Socialist Republic maintains a center in Moscow called the Institute of Defectology. This institute does research on the diagnosis and correction of children's disorders, and maintains pilot educational programs with small numbers of children to develop methods of teaching handicapped children. The results of these studies are then made available to educators throughout the Soviet Union. The Institute concentrates its work in the areas of blindness, deafness, hard-of-hearing, mental retardation, motor defects, speech and language deficits, reading deficiencies, and learning disabilities. This last area was added about 1969.

The research and correctional work are performed by teams of specialists including physicians, psychologists, speech and language therapists, and educators. The approach to an individual child's problems includes establishing a definite diagnosis and finding means of compensating for the defect, while attempting to correct the defect if at all possible.

An attempt is made to provide children in special schools with about the same education that they would receive in a regular school. The concept is that a handicapped child graduating from a special school should have an education equivalent to children from regular schools. The difficulties inherent in accomplishing this with handicapped children are readily admitted. Handicapped children may also receive vocational higher education so that they may become productive citizens.

The government has issued instructions to the effect that handicapped children are to be assisted by early special training and home upbringing methods, based on the theory that prevention of difficulties and compensation for handicaps are easiest at the preschool ages. At school age, there is a mandatory 8-year program to correct or compensate for the handicap. This also includes a general educational curriculum similar to regular school.

The Soviet psychologists do a great deal of testing, but do not rely on psychometric test scores. Rather, they depend on qualitative, clinical judgments to assess a child's problems and to develop a retraining or compensatory educational program. Dr. A. R. Luria stated that he saw this as a major difference between American and Soviet psychologists.

Implications for Teacher Training

With heterogeneous grouping of children in classrooms, it appears that primary teachers need a great deal of training in how to teach if they are to be adequate teachers. There seems to be general agreement that primary education is crucial because it tends to set the pattern for the children's future academic development. At the very least, a good start eases the way, and a poor start acts as an impediment to further learning.

Cronin (1969) states, "Teachers are often at a loss to define the difficulty of children who exhibit developmental lags or lags in learning and/or behavior. The child, easily discouraged, unpredictable in behavior and in school achievement, with short attention span, easily set off, or who cannot accept criticism, poses a challenge to the classroom teacher, puzzling and difficult to solve."

Research on teaching reading seems to indicate that it is desirable to have criteria by which different types of reading retardation may be identified to permit appropriate remedial training. Moreover, it is generally conceded that adequate reading achievers should not be taught in the same way as problem readers; nor do all problem readers respond to the same treatment.

Bond and Tinker (1967) and Kaluger and Kolson (1969) have suggested methods of classifying groups of readers according to degree of retardation. Three general classifications are suggested; namely, the developmental reader, the corrective reader, and the remedial reader.

The developmental reader is defined as the child who achieves at approximately his ability level as derived from his mental age. The mental age is found by intelligence testing.

The corrective reader may be defined as a child who has a relatively minor reading problem that would ordinarily be remediated by his regular classroom teacher or by some tutoring. The teacher need only determine the nature of the child's problem and apply appropriate corrective assistance. To be able to help such children, teachers need some diagnostic skills and remedial techniques.

The remedial reader is considered to be a "seriously disabled reader" (Kaluger and Kolson, 1969). He is reading well below his capacity as determined by his mental age. In general, such children can understand material well above the level at which they are able to read. Characteristically, these children tend to get very low scores on tests of reading speed, very low to low scores on "word naming" tests, and much higher scores on tests of reading comprehension; but all scores tend to be well below their reading expectancy levels as derived from their mental ages. To educate these children, teachers need both diagnostic and remedial skills in depth.

A dramatic example of prescriptive teaching based on differential diagnosis comes to mind. At the learning disabilities center of the University of the Pacific in San Francisco, it was found that the usual remedial methods could not help Frank learn to read above the preschool level. Differential diagnosis based on a battery of tests indicated that he had a very severe problem of visual perception which interfered with his ability to acquire sound-symbol relationships. At the staff conference, it was decided that he would have to be blindfolded to learn to read. When this was done, Frank quickly learned to read using the kinesthetic-auditory modalities. Thereafter, reading could be tied to the visual modality and Frank learned to read.

Recent research has indicated further implications for diagnostic training for remedial teachers. For example, it has been found that both visual and auditory figure-ground deficits have profound diagnostic significance. In Belgium, Klees (Chapter 6) has found that "children presenting (visual) figure-ground impairment, which is always associated with an overall picture of instrumental (perceptual, etc.) difficulties, remained severely maladapted to the ordinary school environment, despite individual psychological and pedagogic help, if their IQ's were (below 110)." Children with higher IQ's usually managed to compensate with remedial help. The implication for teacher training is that special skills are required to remediate children with visual figure-ground deficits.

Auditory figure-ground deficits pose a different problem. In Australia, Keir (in press) found that 38% of 197 children presenting with learning problems had auditory figure-ground deficits (ability to repeat words heard with different levels of background noise), including 19 children (10%) with very severe deficits. Keir stated, "The nature of the auditory problems which children with poor figure-ground differentiation skills have in a noisy classroom is reflected in some typical comments one hears from their teachers: 'He hears me only when he wants to'; 'He can't pay attention'; 'He can hear well enough but he won't listen.' " It is readily seen that these children ought not be considered for open classrooms.

Since case-finding of children with learning disabilities is best done by regular classroom teachers, these teachers need diagnostic skills. These same skills, more adequately developed, may be used to find methods of teaching corrective readers in the regular classroom.

There appears to be a trend toward having children with reading and learning disabilities remain in regular classrooms. Also, in most of the countries surveyed, referrals of children for special help are increasing faster than services can be arranged. Since all of these children cannot be accommodated in special programs, regular classroom teachers will continue to be faced with these children. Therefore, teachers require special educational techniques in addition to their general education if they are to cope successfully with this problem.

The first implication of the worldwide nature of the reading problem is that many teachers need more training in how to teach reading. A general introductory course, or even two courses in reading methods, would not appear to serve the purpose.

The second implication appears to be that teacher training is best when practical. It has often been observed that teachers who have had courses in reading or learning theory may be completely lost when they enter a classroom with real children. Kirk (1972) cites an interesting example. When organizing a special program for brain-injured children, three teachers were hired. Two teachers held Ph.D. degrees with learning specialties. The third teacher held an M.S. in special education. In the classroom, the

Ph.D.'s were completely unable to apply their learning theory in any practical manner while the teacher with the Master's degree demonstrated the ability to invent, design, and create varied approaches to teaching. She proved to be a successful teacher because she could be practical. In this respect, it has been our experience that a great many inexperienced teachers are unable to translate theory into practice; they need substantial help in this area.

The third implication for teacher training seems to be that teachers need to learn diagnostic teaching. That is, they should be able to diagnose a child's learning problems either from observation while teaching him, or with the use of appropriate tests. On the basis of this diagnosis, the teacher should be able to develop a program for each child who has a different basic learning style from the rest of the class.

A fourth implication for teacher training is the need for ongoing in-service education. It has been observed that education students may be given a great deal of theoretical and practical information, but that these data may remain completely meaningless because the student does not have contact with a class of children. This same training, given after the teacher has received some practical experience on-the-job, tends to become internalized and useful. Moreover, it has been observed that there is so much to learn about teaching that almost all teachers seem to be able to benefit from appropriate in-service education. One caution should be observed, however. The educational program must be both appropriate and practical; otherwise the results will not be worthwhile.

CONCLUSION

We have been impressed by the fact that in every country that we visited, there was an awareness of both the existence and the needs of intelligent children with specific reading and learning disabilities. In those nations where no special educational provisions are as yet made to assist these children, many people are attempting to bring this matter to the attention of the appropriate educational or governmental authorities. Most of the industrialized nations now have special programs for these children and it appears that there is a rapidly growing movement to develop similar programs in other countries. There is reason to feel optimistic about future developments in helping children with reading and learning disabilities worldwide.

REFERENCES

Atkinson, R. C. 1974. Teaching children to read using a computer. Amer. Psychol. 29:3.

Bond, G. L., and M. A. Tinker. 1967. Reading Difficulties, Their Diagnosis and Correction. Appleton-Century-Crofts, New York.

Book, R. M. 1974. Predicting reading failure: a screening battery for kindergarten children. J. Learning Disabil. 7:1.

Bullock, A. 1975. A Language for Life. Summary of the report of the Committee of Inquiry. Department of Education and Science, London.

Calancini, P. R. and S. S. Trout. 1971. The neurology of learning disabilities. In L. Tarnopol (ed.), Learning Disorders in Children. Little, Brown, Boston.

Carbonell de Grampone, M. A. 1974. Children who spell better than they can read. Acad. Ther. 9:5.

Chall, J. 1967. Learning to Read: The Great Debate. McGraw-Hill, New York.

Clements, S. D. 1966. Minimal Brain Dysfunction in Children. NINDB Monograph No. 3. U. S. Department of Health, Education, and Welfare, Washington, D.C.

Cronin, E. M. 1969. Case finding and treatment: the teacher. In L. Tarnopol (ed.), Learning Disabilities: Introduction to Educational and Medical Management. Charles C Thomas, Springfield, Ill.

Dempsey, D. 1972. The right to read. In Duggins, J. (ed.), Teaching Reading for Human Values in High School. Merrill, Columbus.

Jansky, J., and K. de Hirsch. 1972. Preventing Reading Failure: Prediction, Diagnosis, Intervention. Harper and Row, New York.

Kaluger, G., and C. L. Kolson. 1969. Reading and Learning Disabilities. Merrill, Columbus.

Keir, E. H. Auditory information processing and learning disability. In L. Tarnopol (ed.), Brain Function and Learning Disabilities, University of Rotterdam Press, Rotterdam. (In press).

Kirk, S. A. 1972. Input lecture. Final Report, Volume II, Leadership Training Institute in Learning Disabilities. Department of Special Education, University of Arizona, Tucson.

Kohen-Raz, R. 1970. Developmental patterns of static balance ability and their relation to cognitive school readiness. Pediatrics.

Strother, C. R. 1973. Minimal cerebral dysfunction: a historical overview. In F. F. de la Cruz, et al. (eds.), Minimal Brain Dysfunction. New York Academy of Sciences, New York.

Tarnopol, L. (Ed.) 1969. Learning Disabilities: Introduction to Educational and Medical Management. Charles C Thomas, Springfield, Ill.

Tarnopol, L. (Ed.) 1971. Learning Disorders in Children: Diagnosis, Medication, Education. Little, Brown, Boston.

Tarnopol, L., and M. Tarnopol. 1975. Program for educationally handicapped children in California. Danish J. School Psychol.

Thorndike, R. L. 1973. Reading Comprehension Education in Fifteen Countries. Halsted Press, New York.

Wagner, R. F. 1973. Rudolf Berlin: originator of the term dyslexia. Bull. Orton Soc. Vol. 23.

Waller, E. 1974. Provision for dyslexia overseas. The Dyslexia Rev. North Surrey Dyslexia Society, England.

CHAPTER 2

Learning Problems
in Argentina

Carlos J. Robles Gorriti and Ana M. Rodriquez Muñiz

In Argentina there are no statistics available for determining the extent of the learning problems of children. Based on our experience, a rough estimate of children with normal intelligence presenting learning problems appears to range between 10 and 25% of the total school population.

There are no schools available for this category of child even though there are special classes and schools for the retarded, the cerebral palsied, and more recently, for the psychotic. In approximately 1966, educators became aware of the problems of children without physical handicaps or severe emotional disorders and set up in each school "gabinetes psicopedagógicos" or psycho-educational consultation rooms staffed by specialists in education and educational psychology. In the past, the psychiatric department of general hospitals handled the consultations requested by school authorities, and also in some situations gave remedial education.

It was the work of these psychiatric departments, particularly in the area of diagnosis of learning problems, that led to the community awakening to the need to develop appropriate facilities for children with learning problems. A first and urgently needed step in this direction was the design of a research project to evaluate the extent of the problem and the need for preventive as well as remedial programs. This was the first government attempt to investigate learning problems in education.

Probably, the action of the government was precipitated by the realization that a staggering number of children, 58.3%, dropped out of elementary school before graduation. This occurred in spite of the fact that elementary school attendance was compulsory. Apparently, this was a very difficult law to enforce.

In 1972, the National Board of Education in collaboration with the

United Nations developed a plan, "Program for the Promotion of Health and Education," aimed at improving the educational yield and avoiding the large number of grade repeaters that leads to elementary school drop-outs. This project studied 25,000 children who were ready to begin school in 491 elementary schools in the city of Buenos Aires in 1972. It was a comprehensive study focused on the medical aspects of learning immaturity and case-finding to discover children with difficulties in reading, writing, and mathematics. Also included in the project was the training of 975 teachers to help them learn the tests they were to administer. The tests selected included the Metropolitan Readiness Test, the Perspective Organization Test by Santucci (1963), the Bender Visual Motor Gestalt Test and Piaget's (1961, 1966, 1967) operational tests.

The data from this project are still being broken down, but it can be stated that approximately 35% of the children demonstrated significant delay in maturational readiness for first grade. Included in the program planning is the creation of special classes for the children exhibiting lags in maturation to be given the readiness they need for successful first-grade experiences. It is our feeling that this study is beginning to modernize the concept of "school readiness" and will influence the future of education in Argentina.

METHODS OF TESTING AND DIAGNOSIS

We believe that a carefully taken history of each child's psychological, educational, and medical background is of utmost importance for arriving at a working diagnosis. We pay particular attention to the child's motor development, its sequence, and any interference with its normal development, such as casts due to fractures or bedrest for prolonged periods.

In the school history, the child's first contact with school is considered most important. A teacher's report is generally requested with observations of the child's classroom behavior and attitude towards learning. We may also visit the school to observe the child in his classroom and on the playground.

Very important information is obtained from observing the child's workbooks and written materials. This gives us many clues about both the child and the teacher, including the teacher's method of teaching, his ingenuity, and attitude toward the child. We also note the child's handwriting, spelling errors, reversals, neatness, and ability to write on the lines and keep margins, among other things.

If the child's history or other tests indicate the need, we also perform a neurological evaluation for "soft signs" and a psychiatric evaluation, including projective tests. We assess the level of each learning function using a number of tests, collecting detailed information about each function. A test which is widely used in Argentina is the "Maturational Test for Reading and Writing" which was constructed by local educators (Morales et al., 1958). This test evaluates a number of different learning functions including stereognosis, visual and tactile figure-ground discrimination, visual-motor coordination, fine muscle coordination, spatial orientation, number concepts and so forth. In general, it tests the most important functions required for school readiness. Other learning functions tested are the following.

Intelligence

The Wechsler Intelligence Scale for Children (WISC) is used between the ages of 5 and 15 years. The Stanford-Binet Test is used from 2 to 5 years. We also use Piaget's methods to assess the child's intellectual developmental level. We test for conservation at various ages. Conservation of sets is at the 6- to 7-year-old level, conservation of weight appears at ages 8 and 9, and volume conservation occurs at ages 11 and 12. We also check mathematical development using Piaget's methods.

Visual-Motor Coordination

The Koppitz evaluation of the Bender Visual Motor Gestalt Test is used.

Laterality and Dominance

We use Zazzo's techniques to assess dominance of eye, hand, and foot (Zazzo, 1963). Normally, dominance of one side should be achieved by 5 or 6 years. We observe a number of activities such as drawing, threading a needle, kicking a ball, and the direction in which the child writes his letters. For example, does he write an "O" clockwise or counterclockwise?

Spatial Orientation

This function is explored in three different ways. (1) According to Piaget the knowledge of right and left develops in three stages. An average child recognizes his own right and left hand by about 5 years of age. By 8 years he is able to tell right from left on another person. Finally, by age 11, he can distinguish right and left among three objects which he is facing. (2) Head's Test (1926) is used as follows: the child follows instructions such as, "Touch your right ear with your left hand"; the child imitates the hand movement of the examiner (9 to 10 years); the child imitates a figure drawn on a card (about 12 years). (3) The child demonstrates his understanding of words having spatial meanings such as above-below, outside-inside, near-far, in-on, around, etc. Children usually know these concepts by about 4 years of age.

Time Orientation

The child is asked the meanings of words such as yesterday, today, tomorrow, and to name the days of the week, the months, and the seasons.

Rhythm

The Stambak Test (1951) is used to test memory for rhythmic sequences. The child listens to a sequence of taps and reproduces the pattern heard.

Body Image

The Goodenough Draw-A-Man is used. Also the child may be asked to name parts of his body, and the Object Assembly subtest of the WISC may be used, as well as finger recognition.

Muscle Coordination

Large muscle coordination is checked by observing jumping, and climbing up and down steps. Small muscle function is assessed by observing cutting, tying knots, and threading beads or needles.

METHODS OF REMEDIAL EDUCATION

Remedial education is begun after a detailed analysis of the child's deficits has been made. Re-education is done in small groups or individually. Grouping is done homogeneously in relation to age, personality traits, and learning problems. At first, we work on developing the deficit functions, rather than the symptoms of defective reading, writing, or arithmetic. Later, we tackle the symptoms proper using different teaching methods based on two principles: (1) A multisensory approach (visual, auditory, proprioceptive, tactile) is used. (2) The child's strongest sensory function is used as an anchor pathway.

The different materials used in remedial teaching must be easy to handle; the texture, size, and color should be varied, and generally attractive enough to keep the child's interest alive. Everything in the teaching environment, blackboard, desk surface, walls, should be devoid of disturbing stimuli that might interfere with the child's ability to pay attention. In general, the level of the child's motor skills and spatial relations will determine what tools to use and the space needed. For example, the poorer the motor coordination, the larger the movements and the more space the child will require. It is important to graduate incoming stimuli according to the child's ability to handle them and to ensure that a given stage of development is well established before moving on to the next one.

Recess and cathartic discharge activities should be planned according to the child's needs. A stable routine and sequence of activities are of utmost importance. These children need an environment that is stable and predictable to help them develop internalized order and inner controls.

MEDICATION

Many drugs are used, even though the results are rather disappointing. Medication appears to have the greatest positive effect on hyperactive children and those with marked free-floating anxiety. Combined learning disabilities and hyperactivity are treated with amphetamines, methylphenidate hydrochloride (Ritalin), or deanol (Deaner), in the order of effectiveness. In our experience, only 15% of the children seem to derive benefit from these medications. However, it is worthwhile to try drugs for a few weeks to determine if one will work.

Children whose learning is jeopardized by intense anxiety frequently find relief with the use of major tranquilizers. The immediate result is an increase in attention span and power of concentration. The most frequently used drugs are thioridazine (Mellaril), chlorpromazine (Thorazine), trifluoperazine (Stelazine), and the minor tranquilizer, diazepam (Valium). Any of these drugs is effective in at least 50% of the children treated, reducing their anxiety to manageable levels.

CASE HISTORY: PETER

Reason for Referral

Peter was a boy 6 years and 3 months old. He was referred by his kindergarten teacher because he had a short attention span, did not complete assigned tasks, and was always in a hurry to finish. He also had difficulty in counting and in copying drawings, and he did not participate in playing ball or rough-housing. An evaluation was requested to determine the possible existence of a learning disability and to decide if he should be promoted to the first grade.

Behavior during Examination

Peter was an average-size, good-looking child, with a mild lisp; he was cooperative throughout the examination. He frequently showed marked signs of free floating anxiety. He was unable to wait and constantly asked for new stimuli, "What's next? What shall I do?" He was in such a hurry to start new tasks that he did not wait to understand the instructions fully.

He did not ask for explanations or help and frequently adopted an omnipotent attitude followed by an error. However, he was able to accept limits, usually followed by better organized behavior. As time went on his mistakes became more frequent due to decreased attention and increased anxiety. When the task demanded more attention, he made a game out of it and ignored the examiner's requests. He was loquacious and had a good vocabulary with well constructed sentences. He appeared unable to tolerate silence.

Family History

The family history revealed a paternal grandmother who had compensated for severe dyslexia. She had poor spatial orientation and could not understand a simple road map in spite of being a well-educated, sophisticated, world traveler. She also made gross spelling errors. His maternal aunt also probably had mild dyslexia. Peter's three cousins, two of them identical twins, were also dyslexic.

Both parents were free of learning disorders. His mother was a registered nurse and his father was a lawyer and a businessman. Peter's father was a young man who was an outstanding sportsman and could not tolerate Peter's clumsiness and poor coordination in outdoor activities.

The mother appeared anxious, loud, and unable to set limits or to keep a well organized home. There were no set schedules for meals or sleeping, and the children were free to roam their suburban streets. The mother frequently yelled at Peter who would freeze in terror. There were two other children in the family, a brother 4 and a sister 2 years old.

Developmental History

Peter's psychosexual development and neurological maturation were within normal limits, except for a crying spell at age 6 months that ended with a seizure. An electroencephalogram (EEG) taken at that time showed marked dysrhythmia. He was medicated with diphenylhydantoin (Dilantin) until this evaluation, when his EEG was normal.

Peter's social maturity level was within normal limits. He had many friends and was able to stay overnight at a friend's home. He was an independent, strong-minded boy who adjusted well in preschool. However, even though he was a conscientious worker, he could not do the assigned tasks.

Psychological Findings

Peter's WISC Full Scale IQ was 80 and his Verbal IQ was 85 with a Performance IQ of 79. The subscale scores showed marked scatter giving the impression of higher intellectual potential (Table 1). The very low Information score of 4 was related to his anxiety which reduced his concentration. The high score of 11 in Comprehension reflected good

Table 1. Peter's WISC scores (Full Scale IQ 80)

Verbal IQ 85	Scaled scores	Performance IQ 79	Scaled scores
Information	4	Block design	7
Comprehension	11	Object assembly	6
Similarities	7		
Arithmetic	8		

reality testing and emotional makeup. The low performance scores suggested poor visual-motor coordination and spatial orientation.

On the Bender Visual Motor Gestalt Test, Peter scored below 5 years (Figure 1). In this test the geometrical designs are copied by the child, one at a time, on a plain sheet of paper, from individual designs presented on cards (Figure 2). Using the Koppitz scoring method, some of the Bender designs indicated organicity in spite of his age. These included rotations, lines instead of dots, and skipping a whole line of dots. The designs were disseminated in chaotic fashion throughout the page. In drawing the designs, he constantly changed the direction of his pencil movements. However, these were more frequently from right to left, as with left-handed individuals. Laterality tests revealed that Peter was ambidextrous with a tendency toward right-handedness. His right eye was dominant but he showed no foot dominance.

Peter's human figure drawing scored below 5 years of age on the Goodenough scale (Figure 3). In this drawing, as well as on the WISC face assembly, he had problems with the eyes and mouth. The body images were not well integrated.

Fine muscle coordination was adequate except for the ability to draw lines within limits. Tactile figure-ground perception was found to be missing so that the possibility of learning through tactile experience was nil and the level of his exploratory activities was at the 3- to 4-year-old level. A number of sensory learning functions were below his age level. These included tactile form identification, visual-motor coordination, visual figure-background discrimination, immediate recall of simple drawings, object seriation, and the ability to copy a simple design or letter. This evidence indicated that Peter was not ready for first grade.

Discussion

This was a preschool child with a three-generation family history of dyslexia. His neurological examination was essentially negative except for a history of crying and a borderline EEG at 6 months of age.

Figure 1. Peter, age 6 years, 3 months. Bender Visual Motor Gestalt Test, scored below 5 years.

The home environment was chaotic and this did not help the child internalize sequencing of events or to experience a predictable future. These experiences are important for learning to delay gratification and to tolerate frustration. Also, a number of sensory learning functions were maturationally delayed. We speculate that with this history, if the child is not helped at this time, he will evidence a full-blown dyslexia when he is faced with academic learning tasks in school.

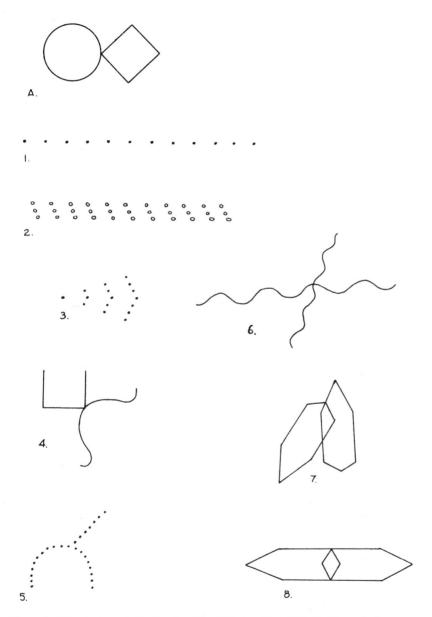

Figure 2. The designs of the Bender Visual Motor Gestalt Test. These designs are presented individually on cards and the child copies each design as best he can.

El papa   un chico "tiene 3 ojos"   la mamá

Figure 3. Peter drew his father, his mother, and a child. The child has three eyes, *tiene 3 ojos*. Using the Goodenough scale, the drawings were assessed at less than the 5-year-old level.

Recommendations

It is recommended that the lagging sensory learning functions be developed before any corrective academic teaching is attempted. Otherwise the child will be exposed to further failure. Once these functions are brought to the required level of maturity, the learning process will unfold swiftly. The recommendations include the following:

1. Develop a structured, integrated body image through special exercises. Proceed from the large muscles to the small ones. Use proprioceptive and tactile stimulation both externally and internally (thorax, abdominal cavity).

2. Help the child achieve dominance (hand, foot, and eye) through special exercises. Once this is achieved, spatial orientation will follow.

3. Develop other skills through the appropriate use of tools like scissors,

hammer, and so forth. This training may be done in small groups and should include activities like throwing, boxing, climbing, and jumping, aimed at discharging pent-up aggression. About 3 to 6 months of intensive work, 3 times weekly, in sessions of 2 to 3 hours, with appropriate recesses, should prepare the child for teaching proper.

4. Parent counseling, to diminish their anxiety and help in the child's management, is advised in the form of group counseling.

This type of program is done on a private basis at the Children's Hospital Psychiatric Department since neither the public nor the private schools have such programs. Therefore, the child is not able to attend school during this period.

REFERENCES

Benton, A., O. Hutcheon, and Seymour. 1951. Arithmetic ability, finger localization capacity and right-left discrimination in normal and defective children. J. Orthopsychiatr. 4:756.

Head, H. 1926. Aphasia and Other Disorders of Speech, Cambridge.

Koppitz, E. 1968. El Test Gestáltico Visomotor para Niños. Guadalupe, Buenos Aires.

Morales et al. 1958. Cuándo empezar a enseñar? Lopez, Buenos Aires.

Piaget, J., and A. Szeminska. 1967. Génesis del Número en el Niño. Guadalupe, Buenos Aires.

Piaget, J. 1961. La Formación del Símbolo en el Niño. Fondo de Cultura Económice, Mexico.

Piaget, J. 1966. Psicología de la Inteligencia. Psique, Buenos Aires.

Santucci, H. 1963. Perspective Organization Test. In R. Zazzó (ed.), Manual para Examen Psicológico del Niño. Kapeluz, Buenos Aires.

Stambak, M. 1951. Le probléme du rhythme de developpement de l'enfant, et dans les dyslexics d'evolution. Enfance Vol. 480.

Zazzó, R. 1963. Manual para el Examen Psicologico del Niño. Kapeluz, Buenos Aires.

CHAPTER 3

Learning Disabilities in Australia

T. Dudley Hagger
With an Addendum by Yvonne Stewart

Australia was colonized as a number of isolated, independent states, and when the Australian Commonwealth government was formed in 1901, the responsibility for education remained with the six state governments. Local municipal government has never played any significant part in Australian education.

The Commonwealth Department of Education is responsible for the education of the comparatively small populations of the two territories— Australian Capital Territory and Northern Territory—and also has an important financial function. During World War II the most important sources of taxation were given by the states to the Commonwealth, which undertook to reimburse the states on an agreed formula. The states are, therefore, in a position to complain about their poverty and to blame educational deficiencies on the Commonwealth. The Commonwealth, on the other hand, is able to say about any particular educational project, that it is up to the states to decide how they allot the money the Commonwealth grants them for education.

In addition, education is by far the largest item in any state budget. In 1970, for example, it was responsible for 27% of total expenditure by the state governments. Education thus becomes the best target for pruning when the states feel an urgent need for money elsewhere. With this system it is perhaps not surprising that Australia spent only 4.3% of gross national product on education in 1970—a lower proportion than in most industrialized nations.

Another way in which education in Australia differs from that in some other countries is in the importance of nongovernment schools, which are attended by 22% of Australian children. Over 80% of these private schools are Catholic parish schools which are plagued by inadequate financing and staffing difficulties. With the best will in the world, it would be almost impossible for them to deal adequately with a problem in special education as large as the learning disability problem. State education departments have therefore tended to accept responsibility for providing special services to the Catholic schools. Although the situation varies from state to state, it is largely true that these services have been unequal to the task of providing adequate help even to the learning-disabled children in departmental schools, so that children in Catholic schools tend, at present, to have very little chance of receiving such assistance.

Besides the Catholic parish schools there is a sprinkling of more exclusive private schools which have tended to regard themselves as catering mainly to the intellectually as well as socially elite, and therefore as not needing to be unduly concerned about handicapped children. In the past few years, however, a number of them have recognized and accepted their responsibilities concerning learning disabilities and have appointed counselors and full-time remedial teachers to their staffs.

THE SPELD MOVEMENT

Origins

Awareness of learning disabilities as a special problem was, at first, slow to develop in Australia. Dame Jean Macnamara, a Melbourne pediatrician, was greatly interested in the education of physically handicapped children. At the time of the poliomyelitis epidemic in 1938, she had been impressed by the teaching ability of Mona Tobias, a state education department teacher who, on her own initiative, had obtained permission to visit, and help with their studies, some of the victims of this disease who were unable to attend school.

Later, Dr. Macnamara, who worked with victims of cerebral palsy, came to realize that there was a group of apparently intelligent children, some, but not all, of whom were spastic, whom she referred to as having the "can't read, can't spell" syndrome. She probably either picked up that term from or suggested it to J. R. Gallagher who published an article "Can't spell, can't read" in the *Atlantic Monthly* in 1948. She met and discussed these problems with Dr. Gallagher in Boston in the 1940's.

Dr. Macnamara transmitted all the information she could gather on the education of handicapped children to Miss Tobias. This lady was endowed with that first requisite for remedial teachers, the almost instinctive ability to understand a child's attitudes and feelings about his problems. She also possessed the confidence and experience to make certain that such a child left the first interview with the feeling that he could now succeed. In the late 1950's, Miss Tobias was influenced and encouraged by a copy of "The First Seven Years of the Gillingham Reading Program at the Francis W. Parker School," which Dr. Macnamara had obtained from the United States. However, Miss Tobias' important work received no publicity and was not widely known until the development of the Specific Learning Difficulties Associations (SPELD) in 1968. In 1970, Miss Tobias became the first SPELD Overseas Scholarship holder.

At the University of Queensland, Professor Fred Schonell established a remedial education center in 1951. After Schonell's death this was re-named the Fred and Eleanor Schonell Educational Research Centre. The particular interest of the center was reading problems, and a course was conducted for a Certificate in Diagnostic Testing and Remedial Teaching. This course was the only one in Australia aimed specifically at training "remedial" teachers. That term is used in this chapter to describe teachers specializing in helping intelligent, underachieving children. Most Australian states sent a few teachers each year for this training until, in 1971, the course became absorbed into a 3-year Bachelor of Education degree. (In Australia, until very recently, degrees were granted only by universities, and almost all primary teachers received their training and certification from teachers' colleges, which are not affiliated with universities.)

There is no doubt that the presence of the Schonell Centre in Queensland was an important factor determining that Queensland should be the first state to form one of those parent-professional associations which have been so largely responsible in this country for awakening interest in learning disabilities, both among the community at large and also among educational administrators.

Development

In 1968, administrators and educational psychologists did not generally regard neurologically based learning disabilities as a problem. Their attitude was that if such conditions existed they were rare and not amenable to help. The large numbers of intelligent, but academically failing children were thought to be in that plight either because of bad teaching or more often because of emotional and social handicaps which were more the responsibility of the parents and community than of the educational system.

If such a child happened to be referred by a school for psychological assessment and help, he would be likely already to have experienced failure for several years, and then would have to wait a further year for his turn for assessment. In the unlikely event that special teaching help was thought to be warranted, there might well have been another year before a place was available in a special group. Naturally, only exceptionally gifted teachers and exceptionally lucky children made good progress in these conditions.

The Australian College of Speech Therapists played an important role in initiating the rapid developments that followed. In 1966, the annual conference of that college had been addressed by Dr. W. A. Dibden (Director of Mental Health Services, South Australia) on the possible relationship between cerebral dysfunction, failure to learn, and disorders of behavior. In 1968, the college organized a Symposium on Dyslexia in Melbourne. On the final day, a move was made for some continuing action aimed at relieving the plight of dyslexic children (Harrison and Hooper, 1968).

A parent-professional association, the Queensland Association for Children with Learning Problems, had already been formed in Brisbane a year or two earlier. It performed some valuable pioneering work and was instrumental in arranging important visits by overseas experts.

Following the Melbourne Dyslexia Symposium, committees were set up in each state and the first Specific Learning Difficulties Association was formed in New South Wales in October 1968. Within the next 18 months, a SPELD group had been formed in each of the six states and two territories. In 1970, a loose national body was created under the title "Australian Council of SPELD Associations" (AUSPELD).

In most states these associations were at first met with resistance and even active opposition from established educational authorities, but by and large they have now developed a satisfactory modus operandi by seeking to understand the problems of the administrators, being moderate and constructive in their criticisms, yet asserting vigorously the case for recognition and help for learning-disabled children.

While the SPELD associations themselves would probably be surprised at this judgment, it does seem that their efforts have met with major success in comparatively quick time. From the position of widespread denial on the part of education authorities in most states, and almost complete unawareness on the part of the general community, the point has been reached where at least those members of the general public who are interested in education know roughly what a specific learning difficulty is, and have some idea what should be done about it. In addition to this, educational administrators have already found it necessary to plan some reorganization of their facilities for dealing with these children. Of course, this does not mean that the battle is over. Administrators appear to be playing down the size of the problem they had so long claimed did not exist and to be making their plans on far too small a scale.

Their first task was clearly to awaken awareness in the educationally

minded members of the community, and among teachers. On the necessary basis of that awareness they then had to convince politicians and
educational authorities that there really was an important and solvable
national problem on which money and effort would be well spent.

SPELD went to work through public meetings, articles in newspapers
and professional journals, SPELD publications, news items on radio and
television, and quite importantly, visits by overseas experts. Except in
Western Australia, it was not until a good deal of ground work of this kind
had been done that official approaches to departments of education and
various political bodies met with much success.

Developments in Western Australia were different in several respects.
Due in large measure to the fine planning and persuasive personality of its
first president, Elaine Michael, The Dyslexia Association of Western Australia (now known as SPELD) very early achieved a position of respect-
ability and of some influence in that state. It has been the only member of
AUSPELD to receive substantial financial aid from its state government.

Australians have always been more impressed by statements from a
foreign visitor than from an indigene. Added to that is the undoubted
quality of the visitors; there can be no doubt of the value to the SPELD
movement of the visitors Australia has had in the past few years, particularly the Tarnopols, Marianne Frostig, Sam Clements, John McLeod,
Macdonald Critchley, and Barbara Bateman.

TODAY'S PROBLEMS

Policy-making Problems

No one would question that the better the classroom teaching and the
greater the classroom teacher's understanding of the subject, the fewer the
number of intelligent children who get into serious learning difficulties
which then demand remedial help. Prevention is better than cure. Nor
would many question the general principle that (other things being equal)
handicapped children should be educated either in the normal classroom
or in a setting as near to, and as fully integrated with the normal classroom
as possible.

On the other hand, we have to accept that in present day conditions,
however good the teacher and however liberal the facilities at her disposal,
there will always remain a proportion of handicapped children, including
some with learning disabilities, who do not and cannot cope if taught full
time in the ordinary classroom.

The first problem of policy making then is, "Where should the main
emphasis be placed in dealing with learning disabilities? Should it be on

training and facilities for ordinary classroom teachers, or should it be on specialist teachers?"

Professor Bateman's visit to Victoria in 1972 has brought this previously latent problem out into the open. Her message to Australia was that the most important thing to do for a child with a learning disability was, after preliminary analysis of the individual task, to provide him with very expert, precise teaching. Victorian administrators were quick to grasp this message and the inferred answer to their policy-making problem: "It is best to keep these children in their own classrooms. Most of them do not need psychological assistance; they only need better teaching. Very few of them, indeed, will ever need a special teacher if the ordinary teacher is trained to cope." In the writer's opinion this answer is inadequate in the Australian scene without important qualifications.

The first qualification arises from the fact that, so far in Australia, most of those who propose the classroom teacher as the answer have done very little to prepare classroom teachers for the job, and even less to provide them with the facilities they would need.

Preparation for the task would require an understanding of variations in childhood development and of the different ways in which children with learning problems function, as well as a practical familiarity with a wide variety of teaching methods—familiarity in the sense of having actually used these methods with underachieving children, under supervision. In reality, preservice primary teacher training in Australia appears recently to be moving toward academic upgrading with greater content of theory, rather than toward providing knowledge and experience of a variety of practical teaching methods. In-service training of the required kind for classroom teachers, as judged by the Victoria Education Department's efforts today, can hardly be taken seriously.

Failing to provide facilities for the required classroom organization is an even more crucial inadequacy. Ask almost any grade one teacher if more training would enable her to cope with the nonachieving children in her class. She will reply, "I might then at least know what to do, but while I look after the 4 or 5 needing individual help, who will look after the 30?" Both Bateman (1971) and Englemann (1969), while advocating that the main attack on the problem be through the classroom teacher, make it clear that they think the classroom teacher needs organizational help for this purpose.

An innovation which is very popular today is the "open" classroom or school. Dividing the children into groups or clusters with different learning tasks can provide a better opportunity for individualized help than does a formal classroom. Such help can come from older children, classroom teachers, or specialist remedial teachers. But it must not be overlooked that this arrangement can also add to the difficulties of some children, especially if the school building has not been designed for the purpose. What about children with an auditory figure-background problem? They are common, and their confusion in an ordinarily noisy classroom is bad enough. In an open school it can be even worse. And what of the hyperactive, distractible child? With an open plan he may well need more segregation than with a formal classroom. Until such time as we have more consistently effective drugs, or more simply applied behavioral techniques than Patterson's (1965), the writer believes that a special withdrawal room should always be available for young hyperactive children.

A second important policy-making problem is posed by the existence in Australia of a feeling of uncertainty, expressed among a proportion of both professional workers and parents, concerning the fundamental value of educational remediation. Increasing awareness of the problem tends to produce increasing desperation about inadequate facilities to cope with it. Makeshift solutions and short cuts then become the order of the day. No one can blame, for instance, a secondary school, lacking any outside help, if it sets up a makeshift "remedial group." Such a group will often consist of children who have experienced persistent failure for 7 or 8 years, and a teacher with little or no special training for the task. Disappointing results from this sort of "remedial" teaching inevitably sow doubts in the minds of some people about the value of educational remediation in general.

Then there is the "short cut." "Wouldn't it be wonderful if a course of eye-muscle exercises, or training in gross muscle coordination as used in crawling, or even a ready made set of perceptual training exercises, would solve many of these learning problems!" Some people are sure to want to try these short cuts. Many forget that such a trial is an experiment. When initial enthusiasm fades and results do not live up to expectations, further doubt is added to previous uncertainty about the value of all "educational remediation."

When there are so many peripheral activities claiming to make easy the difficult but central task of remedial teaching, and so many makeshift programs for carrying out such teaching, there is serious danger that the evidence of good results from adequate, early, remedial teaching will be forgotten. All who experience such doubts should keep by them reports like those of Schiffman (1962) and Rawson (1968), and should be reminded frequently of the very good results being obtained in their own communities by trained and experienced remedial teachers working in proper circumstances.

The immediate problem for the policy makers is the urgent need to provide more properly trained resource teachers, specialists in teaching intelligent under-achievers, and to see that they are provided with facilities to carry out their work.

Problems in Cooperation

Few areas of human endeavor have attracted such multidisciplined attention as have learning disabilities. Nevertheless, multidisciplined groups have been rare in Australia, outside hospitals and research centers. There have, therefore, been problems of cooperation between different professional groups who have not been accustomed to working together. To this problem is added another, arising from the provision of services by multiple agencies.

In Melbourne, for instance, services for children with learning disabilities are being provided by at least a dozen different agencies, each tending to emphasize the approach of one particular profession. Communication between these diverse agencies is, in practice, rare and often ineffective. These agencies tend to develop diverse frames of reference for their thoughts and statements on learning disabilities. Sometimes they speak a language which is barely intelligible to workers in the other agencies. It is only to be expected that there will be clashes of opinion, often based less on real conflict than on misunderstanding.

These clashes can be illustrated in the field of nomenclature. Physicians will use terms like developmental dyslexia or minimal brain dysfunction, thinking they will communicate the need for adequate remedial therapy. Psychologists will be alarmed because these terms somehow have come to mean to them that the problem of the children concerned is hopeless, and it is not worth spending remedial effort on them.

Or again, in considering etiology, a worker from one agency will claim that he has evidence for a genetic basis for learning disabilities, or another will say that minor brain damage is the trouble. Someone else will hotly deny such organic bases and say that he is quite convinced that the problem is nothing more than a lag in maturation; yet another will say that he has good evidence for the implication of socioeconomic causes, or of poor teaching in large classes; another will be quite adamant that the child's motivation is the real problem. If only these people from different agencies met and talked often enough, they would almost inevitably integrate their points of view.

One of the first important contributions toward the development of understanding and cooperation between the great variety of interested agencies and professions in Australia was provided by AUSPELD when it initiated, and organized jointly with the Australian National University, an

Australia-wide Workshop on Specific Learning Disabilities held in Canberra in 1972. This workshop brought together representatives of half a dozen different professions from all the states and territories. It was also the occasion of the first direct Commonwealth government financial contribution to the solution of the problems associated with learning disabilities. Much more such activity is needed.

TESTING AND DIAGNOSIS

Facilities for Testing and Diagnosis

In general, not only are current Australian facilities for diagnostic services for failing children grossly inadequate in quantity, but they are also sometimes unsatisfactory in form, because they were not designed for multidisciplinary study of problems. Although the last year or two has seen a rapid increase in recognition of these deficiencies, there has not yet been any great improvement in the facilities themselves.

The ratio of psychologists employed as guidance officers by the state education department to the number of children in the schools, varies considerably from state to state. Western Australia has the best provision with approximately 1 psychologist to 2,500 children in government schools. Yet, those working in the Western Australian service feel their numbers are insufficient. In the more populous states to the east, the ratio is more like 1 to 12,000. However keen the worker may be, the resulting case load makes adequate attention to the various needs of individual children impossible.

In private schools, the diagnostic services provided are usually by arrangement with private practitioners, and they therefore impose additional financial burdens on the parents.

In most parts of Australia, diagnostic collaboration with a member of another profession such as a medical practitioner, is a slow and cumbersome process. New South Wales has the unique advantage of about a dozen multidisciplinary health centers in or near schools around the metropolitan area of Sydney. These are administered by the health department, and they employ psychologists, speech therapists, social workers, and psychiatrists as well as school medical officers and school nurses. There is also a large and very well equipped suburban health center specifically set aside for investigating problems, including learning disabilities, of country children who are brought to Sydney for that purpose.

In each state there are a number of rather small and specialized services associated with universities, teachers' colleges, and hospitals. Diagnostic services for learning-disabled children are provided at these centers by part-time and sometimes voluntary work on the part of members of the academic staffs concerned.

A rapid development in the past year or two has been in the number of psychologists entering private practice in educational counseling. This seems an inevitable development in view of the over-all failure of departmental services to rise to the need.

Victoria has seen, in 1972, the opening of a private nonprofitmaking center for the assessment and remedial teaching of children with specific learning difficulties. Known as "Gould House," this is supported by private donations, charges fees subject to income, and employs, in addition to remedial teachers, a part-time staff of psychologist, psychiatrist, pediatrician, speech therapist, and physical education teacher.

Most of the nondepartmental centers for learning-disabled children have been set up since 1970. They are an indication of the rapidly growing interest in learning disorders, and they have an important function in relation to research and to the training of psychologists and teachers. However, none of them can hope to make a contribution in any major way to meeting the need for services, as distinct from their value as research and training centers. In Australian conditions, the service need can only be met by government departments of education. There can be no doubt that until the departmental services are enlarged and updated the majority of Australian children with learning disabilities will continue to remain undiagnosed and unsatisfactorily managed.

Methods of Testing and Diagnosis

In Australia, the use by teachers, even specialist remedial teachers, of diagnostic tests is discouraged. In Victoria their use by other than registered psychologists is illegal. This applies to such tests as the Illinois Test of Psycholinguistic Abilities, the Frostig Developmental Test of Visual Perception, and the Wepman Auditory Discrimination Test. The same even applies to some tests specifically designed for use by teachers (for example the Slosson Intelligence Test) and some which were devised by workers other than psychologists.

Screening Tests It is noteworthy that many Australian workers in the field of learning difficulties express great concern that emphasis in planning should be put on prediction or recognition of affected children during their first weeks at school, with a view to prevention of the worst effects of school failure.

The Health Service of the Melbourne City Council, which is responsible for preschool centers in its area, is developing, in close cooperation with the School Medical Service, a schedule which promises to provide the first-grade teachers at related primary schools with a very useful guide to the handicaps which individual school beginners may experience. The search for pointers to specific learning difficulties is in the forefront of this investigation.

In New South Wales, a number of schools are using the Teachers' School Entry Screening Test prepared by Marlene Sheppard. With this test goes a developmental program designed to improve "pre-reading" skills among children who score poorly on the test items. As yet, no controlled study has been published of the predictive validity of the test or its developmental effects. It can be said, however, that its use by teachers will at least help them to study and understand the children in their care.

Professor McLeod, while working in Queensland, developed a simple "School Entrance Check List" intended to be completed by parents at the time of a child's admission to school, and also a more comprehensive "Dyslexia Schedule" for use by professional diagnosticians. The check list is being used in some schools in Queensland as an aid to early identification of children likely to be plagued by reading problems.

Attainment Tests   Because of the dearth of trained educational psychologists, and the restrictions on use of diagnostic tests, the teacher will usually have to be satisfied with tests of educational attainment, backed by her own experience. At the same time, the principle of full and accurate diagnosis before treatment is accepted by the great majority of Australian workers as the eventual aim.

There is, of course, a considerable choice of tests of attainment in word recognition, reading comprehension, and spelling. North American tests are seldom used because of the differences in both vocabulary and spelling between America and Australia. Three tests normed in Britain are, however, commonly used here. They are the Schonell Word Recognition Test, the Daniels and Diack Standard Reading Tests, and the Neale Analysis of Reading Ability.

Australian tests in common use include the St. Lucia Graded Word Reading Test (based on Schonell), the Gap and Gapadol Group Tests of Reading Comprehension, and the ACER Primary Reading Survey Tests. An interesting recent publication is the Domain Phonic Test Kit, which also contains a series of exercise sheets suggesting methods of handling the various weaknesses revealed by the test.

Diagnostic Tests Used by Psychologists   What of those children who do have the benefit of a full diagnosis? Which individual tests are used to help in prescribing the best ways of handling their teaching? In general, the Wechsler Intelligence Scale for Children (WISC) remains the mainstay, both because it is often helpful in backing up a subjective judgment of how much progress the remedial teacher might reasonably aim for, and also because the individual subtests may provide a helpful profile of contrasting abilities in different areas.

The next most common group of tests might well be projective tests such as the Rorschach, the Children's Apperception Test, and the Goodenough Draw-A-Man Test. An understanding of motivation and family dynamics tends to be regarded by Australian workers as being of major importance in handling intelligent underachieving children.

Depending on the individual diagnostician, the Illinois Test of Psycholinguistic Abilities (ITPA) might be the preferred supplement to the WISC. This would often be backed up by tests of visual perception or visuo-motor abilities such as those devised by Frostig or Bender. The Wepman Auditory Discrimination Test is also occasionally used to supplement the auditory channel subtests of the WISC and ITPA. The Wepman test may tend to be replaced in this country by the recently published Domain Phonic Test Kit which includes a test very similar to the Wepman.

Diagnostic Tests Used by Other Professions   Speech therapists in Australia are well trained in the use of tests as well as in therapy for children with disability in language development. Following are some of the tests most commonly used by Australian speech therapists in the investigation of anomalies in the development of spoken language in addition to a variety of articulation tests.

1. The Houston Test for Language Development
2. The Mecham Verbal Language Development Scale
3. The Developmental Sentence Score (Laura Lee)
4. The Northwestern Syntax Screening Test (Laura Lee)

In the few multidisciplinary centers, or in exceptional cases, an individual diagnostician might seek help from a member of a medical discipline such as psychiatry, neurology, pediatrics, or ophthalmology. The EEG is rarely used for the investigation of learning disabilities, except for research purposes or occasionally to exclude petit mal or other epileptic variants. In addition to a routine general medical and neurological examination, the medical practitioner might employ a variety of tests for "soft" neurological signs, such as the Oseretzky Test of Motor Abilities and the Harris Tests for Lateral Dominance, etc.

Training of Diagnosticians

Training for clinical and educational psychologists has been very difficult to obtain in Australia. The common requirement for psychologists employed by education departments has been a university degree with a 3-year major sequence in psychology, preceded in some states by training and experience as a teacher. Such a graduate will have had little or no experience in the use of relevent tests, and so will then require further in-service training provided largely by his more senior colleagues.

Recently, the Australian Psychological Society has decided that admission to full membership should require a prerequisite 4th university year or its equivalent. In 1972, for the first time, a 2-year part-time post-graduate course in educational counseling has been offered in the Applied Psychology Department of the Royal Melbourne Institute of Technology, and no doubt other similar courses will be developed in response to the requirements of the Psychological Society. An additional legal requirement for registration in Victoria is a 3-year period of postgraduate work supervised by a registered psychologist.

Students of speech therapy in Australia, especially at the Victorian School of Speech Science, receive a good deal of instruction in relevant areas, and their training includes familiarity with and supervised use of such tests as the ITPA and numerous language development tests. In addition, many of them have been teachers before they became speech therapists, so they are well qualified to have an understanding of the diagnosis (and for that matter, therapy) of learning disabilities in the language area.

For professions other than psychology and speech therapy, no special training in diagnosis of learning disability is at present available. Pediatricians, neurologists, and psychiatrists are not provided with training in learning disabilities. It seems very desirable to provide some introduction to this problem in the formal training of all medical practitioners. General practitioners, for example, are often called upon for advice concerning the disturbed behavior induced by school failure, and need a considerable understanding of learning disabilities and their interaction with personality if such advice is to be soundly based. They should also have a thorough knowledge of the value and limitations of medication in assisting children with learning disabilities. Until now they would be fortunate indeed if this occurred during their undergraduate training.

To sum up the Australian position with regard to special testing and diagnosis, it could be said that most workers consider it to be an important prerequisite to treatment. However, few members of the professions have had any opportunity for training in the use of tests other than on-the-job training, and fewer again (except those in private practice) have the time to use those tests with which they are familiar.

PERCENTAGE OF CHILDREN INVOLVED

There will always be arguments about the incidence of any disability which occurs with all grades of severity. Three Australian reports are available which point to an incidence of 10% of otherwise fully capable children who have a disability severe enough to require special help. None of these three investigations looked for disability in areas other than reading and spelling.

A reading attainment survey of 31,000 children entering Victorian secondary schools in 1968 (Education Department of Victoria, 1971) showed that 14.7% of these children were 3 years or more retarded in reading skill. This survey made no attempt to identify the cause of the reading retardation, but neither did the 14.7% include children of above-average intelligence who may have been retarded less than 3 years in reading. In fact, the reading attainment of a further 16% was retarded between 1.5 and 3 years.

A most interesting and carefully conducted survey was carried out in Western Australia in 1970 and has been reported by White and White (1972). It surveyed 107 children constituting the third grade population of three schools in the country district of Busselton. Nineteen of those surveyed, though above the 25th percentile on a group intelligence test, had reading and/or spelling ages at least a year below their chronological ages. These children were subjected to detailed individual testing and in 8 of them, factors other than perceptual or psycholinguistic immaturities were judged to be responsible for the reading retardation. This left 9 boys and 2 girls (10.3% of the total population) whose reading retardation was related mainly to such immaturities.

This study proceeded to two further interesting investigations. One was a study of children in the same population who were below the 75th percentile on the general ability scale but had reading and/or spelling ages at least a year higher than their chronological ages. There were 10 of these children. The other investigation was the analysis of the number of "significant immaturities" (a score more than one standard deviation below mean for age on the Bender-Gestalt or a single subtest on the WISC or ITPA). Three or more such immaturities appeared to impose a critical handicap, and two seemed to be borderline in the sense that, of four such children, three were retarded in reading but one was advanced.

Another Australian survey which sought to separate the different causes of reading retardation is the one recently undertaken by R. J. Walsh, Professor of Human Genetics at the University of New South Wales, as a preliminary to his study of the genetic factor in dyslexia. His results have not yet been published, but in a personal communication, Professor Walsh states that in a suburban school population of 462 8-year-old children, 5.0% (7.6% of the boys and 1.9% of the girls) were regarded as having primary reading retardation or specific dyslexia, with an average reading age retardation of about 1.5 years. Children whose disability was accompanied by a history of possible brain damage were excluded.

Professor Walsh has also recently made a study of the genetic aspects of specific dyslexia as defined by Critchley—reading retardation associated with possible brain damage was excluded. He indicates that a preliminary analysis of the figures shows a very high percentage of positive pedigrees. He also states that the inheritance may be explicable on the basis of an autosomal dominant gene with incomplete penetrance, provided one accepts a different degree of penetrance in males and females. However, he states that another possible explanation would be multifactorial inheritance.

This writer, in a consecutive series of 200 children diagnosed as having specific learning disabilities, found 31% to have brain damage as a possible etiological factor. Since most workers do not exclude children with minor brain damage from the category "learning disability" so long as over-all intelligence is not reduced below the average range, Professor Walsh's figures considered with my own would suggest an over-all figure of 7 to 8% of intelligent children with serious reading disability.

Concerning the relation of minor brain damage to learning disabilities it is important to note that in most cases we are dealing with a history suggesting possible brain damage, rather than with unequivocal evidence that the brain has in fact been damaged. So disabilities classified as possibly due to brain damage may sometimes in fact be of genetic origin. We should also remember Matějček's work suggesting that when the brain is subjected to a widespread noxious influence, its main effects in any particular child may be on those brain functions which are vulnerable by reason of genetic factors.

It is therefore of interest to record that in the writer's 200 cases there was a family history of learning problems almost as often among the possibly brain-damaged 31% as among the remaining 69%. One of the cases also provides interesting support for Matějček's views. She was one of a pair of intelligent identical twins, both of whom showed evidence of perceptual disability and whose mother had a reading disability. The sister was coping at average attainment levels and was therefore educationally inconspicuous. In the case of the failing twin, there was strong evidence of perinatal brain damage. In other words, her learning disability had presumably become conspicuous because of the effect of brain damage on a genetically predisposed function.

For these reasons, and because educational management appears to be identical, the writer prefers to include possible brain-damaged children, who otherwise qualify, in the category of specific learning disability.

MEDICATION

In Australia there has been little or no systematic use of medication as a means of combating disabilities in learning. Insofar as this writer is aware, there have been no Australian reports published specifically on such treatment. This section will therefore largely be based on personal experience.

At the Australian Workshop on Specific Learning Difficulties at Canberra in 1972 (proceedings published by AUSPELD) the present writer contributed a paper which advocated greater use of medication, especially that with amphetamine or methylphenidate, as a means of controlling hyperkinetic behavior. This suggestion was not well received by a majority of the medical practitioners in the audience, even though they were more experienced than most Australian practitioners in the management of learning-disabled children. Among the Australian general practitioners, pediatricians, and psychiatrists who deal with the medical problems of these children, medication is seldom employed, and when it is, the most commonly used drugs are probably the tranquilizers. There is active opposition by many to the use of the stimulants, probably based on the present cultural reaction against drugs and a lack of experience of their effect on exceptional children. To quote Dr. Dibden in the Canberra discussion: "If it acts on the rest of the body, it's called a medicine; if it acts on the brain, it's called a drug."

The author is quite sure that medication is of crucial value in a proportion of selected cases. These cases fall into two categories, those children depressed by their school frustrations and those with short attention spans. The depressed children usually seem to be helped to a quite worthwhile degree by antidepressant medication, especially in the first few weeks after diagnosis when the medication seems to make them more willing to accept and adapt to a new educational program.

With hyperactive, distractible children of short attention spans, the big problem is the unpredictability of the effects of medication—which is another way of saying, "lack of precision in diagnosis."

When using any of these medications, the practitioner should give as much care to the choice of drug or drugs and the adjustment of dosage as he does in treating epilepsy. He should carefully collate weekly reports from parents and teachers (both desirable and undesirable effects) during the first few weeks of treatment, and review at increasing intervals thereafter. The author usually advises that medication be stopped for a fortnight at intervals of 6 or 12 months, as a guide to continuance or cessation of treatment.

It is the impression of this writer that, used in this way, medication is a quite worthwhile adjunct to management in at least half the cases in which its trial has been personally advised.

EDUCATIONAL REMEDIATION

Facilities

Much the same can be said of facilities for remedial teaching as of those for diagnosis. They are grossly inadequate.

The writer is most familiar with the situation as it exists in the State of Victoria. Here the educational department, until recently, has relied mainly on what are variously known as Opportunity Remedial Centres or Remedial Centres. These vary somewhat in function but each is staffed by one "special" teacher and they enroll children with a variety of handicaps. The commonest would perhaps be children with borderline mental retardation, specific learning disability, emotional disturbance, social disadvantage, and those coming from families who have recently migrated to Australia and still speak a foreign language in the home. Although these centers are usually situated in a school, most of the children with learning disabilities who attend travel from surrounding schools for perhaps one half-day a week; transportation is provided by the parents. It is not possible to know how many specific learning-disabled (SLD) children would be treated in these centers, of which there are approximately 70. A very rough estimate is between 500 and 1000 children. The state has an annual new intake into its schools of about 70,000, so that if one assumed that 10% of school children needed help for learning disabilities, and such help was needed for an average of 1 year, it is evident that these centers would be coping with no more than about 1 in 10 of the SLD children in need of help.

The department has been concentrating for 2 or 3 years on an attempt to have learning disabilities dealt with in the ordinary classroom. Unfortunately, there has not been due recognition of the need to relieve classroom teachers from some of their routine duties so that they can give the individual and small-group instruction needed. Additionally, the preparation of classroom teachers for the task leaves much to be desired.

The official means of providing this preparation has been by setting up a demonstration unit which the department hopes to repeat elsewhere. With only about ten staff members and an additional load of advisory duties in schools, this unit has been required to "train" 10,000 teachers, in its 4.5 years of existence, for the task of helping failing children in their classrooms. The duration of such a course of training is no more than 2 or 3 days. It says much for the dedication and ability of the demonstration unit staff that in spite of these remarkable conditions, they have, in fact, made a quite worthwhile contribution toward the adequate education of these children. In addition to the demonstration unit, the department has set up a number of special education centers, usually staffed by one or two trained special teachers. These centers are providing a worthwhile service in the areas where they are situated in the form of attainment testing and advice to classroom teachers.

Outside the state school system there are trained remedial teachers who work either at private schools or as independent private practitioners. The majority of these teachers were trained at the Schonell Centre in Queensland in the days when it provided a certificate course. Because there is no traveling problem, remedial teachers in private schools are often able to take children for brief periods daily, rather than the half-day weekly which tends to be the rule in departmental remedial centers.

Finally, there are the remedial teaching services situated in hospitals, universities, teachers' colleges, and at Gould House.

In the other Australian states, services for educational remediation run on somewhat similar lines to those in Victoria. A heartening aspect of the situation in Queensland is that a 10-week, full-time in-service course has now commenced at one of the departmental teachers' colleges, thus replacing (for Queensland teachers) the course previously conducted by the Schonell Centre. It is anticipated that the supply of trained remedial teachers will thereby be expanded rapidly over the next few years. It is also planned to give all new teachers, in their preservice training, some insight into the problems of learning disabilities.

For the moment, however, Western Australia probably has the distinction of providing Australia's highest ratio of remedial teachers to children, as well as being the best supplied with educational psychologists. The training of these remedial teachers leaves something to be desired, but they are selected, experienced teachers and they receive very good support from the departmental psychologists. In 1971, there were 32 remedial teachers operating within the department. Nine teachers dealt with 168 children in full-time classes, 14 provided help on an itinerant basis to three schools each, and nine operated in secondary schools. In other states, classroom teachers in secondary schools usually have to cope with the large numbers of children coming to their schools with confirmed learning disabilities. Secondary teachers have had no official training in methods of teaching either reading or elementary arithmetic.

It is impossible to obtain accurate figures for the over-all ratio of trained remedial teachers to children because there are no relevant statistics from the private schools, and also because, at least in Victoria, special teachers at opportunity remedial centers divide their time between children with a variety of handicaps. Nevertheless, an estimate of one trained remedial teacher to 10,000 children enrolled in schools throughout the nation would be reasonably accurate. In contrast to these figures, it is interesting to note that the Catholic schools in the Diocese of Wagga in New South Wales have recently adopted the policy of providing one trained remedial teacher to every 300 children enrolled. This can be regarded as an adequate and realistic aim, particularly because the city of Wagga houses the Riverina Institute of Technology, at which a course in remedial teaching is available.

The statistics given above take no account of the amount of remedial teaching arranged privately by desperate parents who are prepared to pay the extra costs involved. The amount of teaching done in these circumstances is even harder to estimate than the official provision. Counting only those teachers who have some claim to special training in this area, it is the author's guess that the amount of this unofficial service would about equal that provided by the Department of Education.

One of the annoying frustrations of people seeking better provisions for educational remediation (annoying because it is so obvious and preventable) is that in most states there is no structure for promotion of remedial teachers employed by education departments. In order to obtain adequate promotion, such a teacher has to leave the field in which he or she has specialized. Administrators have had this glaring anomaly pointed out to them on numerous occasions for years, but most states seem no nearer to appropriate action.

One other source of remedial help should be mentioned. The Education Department of Queensland, at the instigation of the SPELD Association and the Country Women's Association, has organized two successive summer camp schools for SLD children from remote country areas. At these schools the 15 children who attend are tested by a psychologist and the mothers are given instructions in suitable methods to employ at home to help their children. A similar, but nondepartmental, summer camp was held in Melbourne in December, 1972. Much of the work was on a voluntary basis and the parents paid a small sum to defray other expenses. Several psychologists shared the testing of some 30 children and supervised a large number of helpers, including students of teaching and of medicine who provided one-to-one teaching in half-hour sessions interspersed with swimming and other play activities.

Methods of Educational Remediation

There are no prescribed teaching methods in Australia. Schools, and even individual teachers, have almost complete autonomy in deciding what their methods shall be. The same is true of remedial teachers, no two of whom employ the same procedures. Add to this the traditionally emphasized principle that a child with a learning disability should have a tailor-made program for his particular weaknesses and strengths, and it can be seen that it becomes a very difficult task to summarize the methods used for educational remediation in Australia.

There are, of course, some individual teachers who base their approach on a recognized formal program. In Perth there is a full-time remedial center whose work is based on Delacto procedures. Another full-time Perth group is using DISTAR. A third has adopted the Duffy program. This is essentially an etymologically based attempt at analysis of English spelling, together with exercises in language development. In Victoria, Queensland, and possibly some other states, a number of physical educa-tion teachers have taken an enthusiastic interest in devising programs for children with problems of motor coordination. At Gould House, physical education is combined with music as a means of developing sequencing and associated skills. There is no doubt that these also help with self-realization and motivation.

Centers with a strong bias toward one particular method are the exception. The great majority of Australian remedial teachers are found to be using parts of a great variety of programs, and to be modifying their repertoires frequently as a result of reading and attendance at lectures, seminars, and workshops. This may help to account for the phenomenal success of the journal *Remedial Education,* published quarterly by the Australian Remedial Education Association (editor, R. C. Davidson, 40 Canterbury Road, Toorak, Victoria 3142) and frequently containing de-tails of remedial techniques from a variety of sources. Another popular Australian journal is *The Slow Learning Child* which has been published for many years by the Schonell Centre, University of Queensland, and which interprets its title as including intelligent children who are educa-tionally retarded as well as the intellectually retarded.

If any over-all statements can be made about remedial methods in this country, it might be that they tend to adopt an alphabetic phonic approach (in a period when look-say has been popular) and to include multisensory procedures. Hence it might be claimed that they owe a good deal to Gillingham and Fernald, though tactile as well as kinesthetic methods seem to receive a good deal of emphasis, and in this respect they might be said to derive from Montessori. One occasionally sees a machine such as the Language-master, but aids and apparatus tend to be impro-vised.

For all this seeming lack of sophistication there are some very good results being achieved. When adequate reports are available it would be surprising if Australian results from centers with trained remedial teachers are far behind those of most other countries.

Training for Educational Remediation

It should be noted that there is as yet only one university chair in special education in Australia (at Monash University), though it is anticipated that Queensland will follow suit in the near future because of the donation of $20,000 by the Queensland SPELD Association for this purpose. But universities are only a partial answer to this problem in Australia.

A SPELD statement (1971), which summarized the problem of specific learning disabilities in Australia, categorized as "the most urgent need of all" the setting up of training centers for specialist teachers. It also emphasized the need, in Australian conditions, for these to be at undergraduate rather than at graduate level. The reason is that the centers should be able to admit practicing primary school teachers who, in Australia, rarely hold university degrees.

There is good evidence that the scarcity of training centers is not beginning to be overcome. In 1969 there was only one undergraduate training center available in Australia specifically for remedial teachers. In 1973 there are at least eight, and it is expected that this number will increase rapidly for the next few years.

The way in which these training activities have increased can be credited in large measure to the work of the SPELD associations. This was recognized by the Director-General of Education in New South Wales (D. J. A. Verco) when he said, in opening a seminar at the University of New South Wales in 1971, "For a good many years we arranged for the training of remedial teachers in Queensland and we in New South Wales are much indebted to the work of the University of Queensland for this provision. A few years ago we had only 31 such people but that number, in the last two or three years, has almost doubled. The fact that we have been able to do this has been in no small measure due to the fact that the work of SPELD has created that atmosphere of understanding on the part of administrators, on the part of those who hold the purse strings of the community, on the part of even the community itself and its readiness to provide funds in educational endeavor."

An important point about these courses is that they often make it an essential prerequisite that teachers undertaking the course should have already completed several years' experience as classroom teachers. The type of person seeking to work in special education in this country has hitherto been of particularly high quality, well motivated, and sensitive. This may partly be due to the lack of financial incentive, but the policy of selection of suitable applicants from the ranks of experienced, practicing teachers will be one safeguard toward maintaining this high standard.

ADDENDUM: RECENT DEVELOPMENTS IN AUSTRALIA
Yvonne Stewart

Government Committee Inquiry and Report

In December 1972, E. G. Whitlam, Prime Minister of Australia, appointed an Interim Committee for the Australian Schools Commission to examine the position of both government and nongovernment primary and secondary schools throughout Australia. Its purpose was to make recommendations for the immediate financial needs of those schools, the priorities within those needs, and the measures appropriate to assist in meeting them.

The committee submitted its report to the Minister for Education of the Australian government in May 1973. In the preceding 5 months it had surveyed Australia's 9,500 schools, sifted through the many submissions made to it, and consulted with educators in making its inquiries. The Committee's recommendations were accepted by the Australian Parliament, and subsequently the Schools Commission was formed. The report of the Interim Committee has been published under the title "Schools in Australia." This paper draws heavily on the findings and recommendations of this report.

AUSPELD Submissions

The Australian Federation of Specific Learning Difficulties Associations (AUSPELD) made detailed and comprehensive submissions to the Interim Committee. AUSPELD stressed the needs and priorities of children and adults with specific learning difficulties, and was pleased that the Committee's report stated that attention should be given to "the particular needs of schools for the handicapped, whether mental, physical, or social, and the needs of isolated children."

The Committee devoted one chapter of its report to "Equality of Opportunity," an important social goal which Australian schools have been given a major responsibility for achieving. Observing that the Australian concept of equal opportunity has been confined to public schooling, the Committee expressed the view that, regarding the spread of population in Australia, the degree of equality of provision which has been achieved is, by world standards, impressive. However, as AUSPELD would contend, this equality of opportunity has not previously been provided for children who are handicapped by their learning disabilities. It is therefore of interest that, in considering handicapped children, the committee suggested "special education" for children with physical and mental handicaps and included this area in the range of programs for which grants have been recommended.

The committee recommended to the Australian government that grants should be provided which would cover programs in the following areas: general recurrent resources, buildings, school libraries, disadvantaged schools, special education, teacher development, and innovation. The programs for schools for the disadvantaged and for handicapped children provide grants in relation to the pattern of disadvantage and the incidence of handicap in the community. Programs for teacher development and for innovation are available to all schools and school systems.

The committee was impressed with the need to provide primary school teachers with sufficient knowledge of remedial education techniques to enable them not only to identify children with learning difficulties, but also to offer treatment in the less serious cases. It also considered that specialists in remedial work should be available to all primary schools to cope with children with severe learning problems. AUSPELD believes that these particular recommendations are partly the result of its submissions and of the climate of understanding and concern for children with learning disabilities which it helped create.

AUSPELD also submitted evidence of the difficulty of retaining remedial teachers in their particular specialty because of reduced promotional opportunities. The committee agreed and reported: "It is argued that loss of qualified people from special education represents a serious impediment to the over-all standards of teaching in this area. The committee accepts that there is a problem and draws the situation to the attention of state education departments in the hope that something can be done to improve the promotion prospects of teachers engaged in special education, particularly in view of the substantial expansion in the number of such teachers which should flow from the committee's recommendations."

Grants for Teacher Training

The Committee reported that "there is an acknowledged need for increased specialist assistance to children in normal classes experiencing specific learning difficulties." Accordingly, recurrent grants were recommended for the employment of additional remedial teachers. Emphasis was laid on the need for preschool education, and in particular, its value for children who may have intellectual handicaps, language disorders, and deafness.

Grants exceeding $1,000,000 are being made available in 1974–1975 for training courses for teachers of handicapped children and, in addition, grants for the replacement of teachers-in-training in 1974–1975 will exceed $8,000,000. Great stress was also laid on the need for the in-service training of teachers; the committee recommended that more than $7,500,000 be set aside for this.

An important recommendation of the committee was that "the Minister should request the Australian Universities Commission and the Australian Commission on Advanced Education to investigate the provision for the training of teachers of handicapped children at universities and colleges, and to make financial recommendations to ensure the adequacy of such provision." A radical and sweeping change of attitude in Australia could be brought about by the recommendations of the Interim Committee, and it is interesting now to report on some of the developments since the acceptance of the report in the Australian Parliament in November 1973.

Some Recent Developments

It would be impossible to cover adequately the host of exciting developments that have been and are taking place in the community, but it will serve to give some examples.

The Department of Education in New South Wales has greatly extended its Division of Guidance and Special Education. Within the Division of Special Education, particular emphasis has been placed on the concept of resource teachers to implement the finding of the Schools Commission. "There is a general agreement that as many handicapped children as can adequately be cared for should be educated in the normal groups where they may share in social life. . . ." The trend is that, instead of itinerant remedial teachers who had previously been employed by the Department of Education, the emphasis should be on the development of resource teachers. Such teachers would be specially trained and would work in close liaison with classroom teachers and counselors. They would help children with all types of learning problems by giving them part-time help within their regular schools. As a result of this, there has been a tendency to cut down on special full-time classes. The department is hopeful that there will be a development of multipurpose special schools which will serve as a back-up to these resource teachers and be available for the children who need more prolonged and specific help.

Presently throughout New South Wales, there are 140 remedial teachers and 30 resource teachers. In 1968, when SPELD began, there were only 19 remedial teachers, all of whom had received their training outside New South Wales, mostly in Queensland. It is envisioned by the department that up to 200 teachers a year will be admitted to 1-year courses within the various colleges of advanced education.

Innovation

The report of the Interim Committee placed emphasis on the importance of encouraging research. "Although research may stimulate innovation, it often tends to be 'discipline-oriented' rather than 'mission-oriented'; and it is not necessarily directed towards achieving practical ends. In any event, its nature usually precludes it from bringing about improvements overnight. The creation of change in schools requires action at the work face, the actual implementation of new processes, as well as the conduct of research in the traditional sense. The committee holds the view that interaction among colleagues is vital if the will of the profession to innovate and to bring about beneficial change is to be strengthened. It hopes for change by fostering opportunities, providing stimulation, and rewarding initiatives on the part of those in and of the schools themselves—teachers, parents, pupils and local community." Accordingly, the committee has proposed that funds should be available to support, at the school level, special projects of an innovative kind or with implications for change.

The Schools Commission has been engaged in the direct administration of a $6,000,000 program designed to stimulate or innovate projects which may affect individual schools, or be mounted at a school system or even at national level. It is intended that funds will be allocated in such a way that a considerable number of small-scale projects within schools will be supported, in keeping with the commission's aim of encouraging initiative at a grass-roots level.

Progress Report

In a report issued by the Schools Commission in 1974, a brief outline was given of the progress which has been made in various aspects of the Schools Commission's recommendations. All the programs are at an early stage and are being constantly reviewed to ensure that they achieve their stated purposes. Of particular interest to AUSPELD, with its concern for learning-disabled children, are the programs for schools for the disadvantaged, for special schools (handicapped children), for teacher development, and for special projects (innovations).

In relation to programs for handicapped children, the Schools Commission has allotted general recurrent grants totaling $4,000,000. This sum will be distributed through state governments, and will be available to reduce class size and improve facilities for handicapped students.

In programs for teacher development, more than $7,500,000 has been provided for 1974-1975 under Schools Commission programs to assist state governments with the costs of in-service education for teachers in both government and nongovernment schools. Government school teachers will fill approximately 80% of the places available.

The Schools Commission will provide nearly $2,000,000 in 1974–1975 for the establishment of education centers to be operated by committees formed from the teachers from government and nongovernment schools, and other members of the community who have an interest in education. Already the Schools Commission has received 70 applications for funds for such centers throughout Australia. Funds have been allocated, and four centers have been established in New South Wales, three in Victoria, two each in Queensland, South Australia and Western Australia, and one in Tasmania. Other applications are under consideration.

The main features of teacher-development programs at this stage within the several states are as follows.

New South Wales   Over $900,000 from Schools Commission funds will be spent on in-service education in 1974. Twenty-nine applications for the funding of education centers in New South Wales have been received.

Victoria   In-service programs for teachers in Victorian schools will be expanded 10-fold as a result of the Schools Commission funding. Over $250,000 had been used in the first 3 months of 1974 to initiate a series of courses, to establish administrative arrangements, to acquire a printing plant for course materials, and to provide for evaluation of the effectiveness of programs. Twenty-three applications for funding in Victoria have been received.

Queensland   In Queensland, an In-Service Training Committee has made recommendations for the various needs of teachers for refresher and extension courses. It was expected that more than $240,000 would be spent in the first half of 1974. Fourteen applications for the funding of education centers in Queensland have been received.

South Australia   In South Australia, the Education Department and independent schools are sharing Schools Commission funds for teacher development. A working party has prepared schedules, and there has been a substantial increase in the number of release-time scholarships available to teachers. Five applications have been received for the funding of education centers in South Australia.

Western Australia   In Western Australia, consideration has been directed to the provision of week-long courses to primary teachers in remedial reading techniques and extension work in basic subjects. Four applications have been received for the funding of centers in Western Australia.

Tasmania In Tasmania, eight additional administrative and coordinating staff members and four additional support staff members have been appointed. Each of the three existing teacher centers will receive allocations with the objective of enabling all teachers to participate in in-service courses in 1974–1975. Three applications have been received for the funding of education centers in Tasmania.

Conclusion

In rationalizing its recommendations, the Interim Committee for the Schools Commission laid emphasis on the right of every child, within practicable limits, to be prepared through schooling for full participation in society, both for his own and for society's benefit. To this end it accepted the obligation to make special efforts to assist those whose pace of learning is slow.

It commented that in the past, educational expenditure has been weighted in favor of those who learn most easily and who therefore persist at school longer. The committee judged that some alteration in the balance of expenditure in favor of earlier stages of education, to consolidate a more equal basic achievement between children, is desirable.

In stating that the principle of recurrent or lifelong education had considerable attraction, the committee expressed its belief that every member of society is entitled to a period of education at public expense, and that those who leave school early have a claim which they should be able to make at a later date.

The adoption of this report was a milestone in the history of education in Australia, and in particular, it was of great significance in its emphasis on children with special needs. It must be a challenge to educators in Australia to fulfill its high ideals and humane concepts.

APPENDIX

Addresses of AUSPELD and Its Constituent Associations:

AUSPELD, c/o SPELD, New South Wales, P. O. Box 94, Mosman, 2088, NSW.
SPELD Australian Capital Territory, P. O. Box 129, Kingston, 2604, ACT.
SPELD New South Wales, P. O. Box 94, Mosman, 2088, NSW.
SPELD Northern Territory, P. O. Box 4739, Darwin, 5791, NT.
SPELD Queensland, P. O. Box 22, Kenmore, 4069, Qld.
SPELD South Australia, P. O. Box 83, Glenside, 5067, SA.
SPELD Tasmania, Acton Road, Rokeby, 7019, Tas.
SPELD Victoria, P. O. Box 146, Camberwell, 3124, Vic.
SPELD Western Australia, Community Development Centre, Selby St. and Stubbs Terrace, Shenton Park 6008, WA.

REFERENCES

Bateman, B. 1971. The Essentials of Teaching. Dimensions Publishing Co. San Rafael, Ca.

Engelmann, S. 1969. Preventing Failure in the Primary Grades. S.R.A., Chicago.

Harrison, R. N., and F. Hooper. (Eds.) 1968. Proceedings of the Dyslexia Symposium. Australian College of Speech Therapists, Melbourne.

Patterson, G. R. et al. 1965. A behaviour modification technique for the hyperactive child. Behav. Res. Ther. 2:217.

Rawson, M. 1968. Developmental Language Disability: Adult Accomplishments of Dyslexic Boys. The Johns Hopkins Press, Baltimore.

Remedial English Teaching in the Secondary School. 1971. Education Department of Victoria, Melbourne.

Schiffman, G. 1962. Dyslexia as an educational phenomenon. In J. Money (ed.), Reading Disability: Progress and Research Needs in Dyslexia. The Johns Hopkins Press, Baltimore.

SPELD Victoria. 1971. A SPELD Statement. Melbourne.

Walsh, R. J. 1974. Personal communication.

White, J., and M. White. 1972. Perceptual and psycholinguistic factors in retarded and advanced levels of reading and spelling skills. Slow Learn. Child 19(2):117. University of Queensland, Brisbane.

CHAPTER 4

Reading-Writing Problems in Austria

Othmar Kowarik

By the end of the last century, physicians in Europe described reading and spelling deficits within the framework of aphasia. They studied adults who had lost their previously established reading skills. The causation was thought to be brain lesions, and the syndrome was called alexia. Besides such acquired deficits, physicians also described children with congenital reading weaknesses. These weaknesses were called congenital word blindness, partial illiteracy, and in the English literature, developmental alexia, strephosymbolia, and dyslexia.

Ranschburg spoke of legasthenia. This term has been adopted in the German-speaking countries. Linder's definition of legasthenia has been generally accepted: "By legasthenia, we understand a specific weakness in learning to read (and consequently to spell) despite otherwise normal or (as compared to reading capacity) relatively high general intelligence."

Recently, the term reading-writing weakness (in Germany, the widely used abbreviation is LRS for Lese-Rechtschreibe Schwäche) has become most generally adopted.

Pyschologists and educators who were familiar with the condition tried to increase teachers' understanding of the reading-writing disabled child. Suggestions for treatment were offered in order to penetrate as intensively as possible the practices of everyday school routines. In doing so, many relied on foreign literature. But specifically Austrian research was needed since results gained in countries with differing languages could not be expected to be valid for Austria. At first, interest in reading disabilities was most apparent. German-speaking children, however, have even greater diffi-

---

This paper was translated from the German by Edith Klasen.

culties in spelling. Thus, writing disability is attracting more and more interest now.

The classroom teachers noticed primarily two facts: the bizarre reading and spelling mistakes, and the disparity with the student's general intelligence as well as his scholastic achievement in other subjects. Dyslexia seemed accompanied by specific errors, such as letter reversals, omissions, substitutions, repetitions, and difficulties in the perception of whole word, visually or conceptually. The frequency of errors also seemed a characteristic of dyslexia. Not less apparent were difficulties best termed as secondary symptoms. They consisted of behavior problems of varying flavor and degree. Usually, however, it was almost impossible to determine which symptom was primary and which was secondary. Researchers were in general agreement, however, as to the polyetiological origin of dyslexia.

Since the syndrome varies so much from case to case, efforts were made during the early stages of research to classify particular types and degrees of the condition. Results of statistical and empirical studies were not without influence on therapeutic practice. The training first applied soon developed into specific methods of reading therapy and special educational programs. These often went far beyond regular teaching, in method as well as in theoretical conceptualization.

The therapy of dyslexia in Austria thus is never restricted to symptomatological treatment. In our thinking, legasthenia is not merely a technical learning disturbance, but a problem in education, a pedagogical challenge. Simple exercise, mere tricks, or certain techniques are not the answer. The treatment of the whole person is a special educational task. In this curative area of education, there is still a chance for "healing." Therapeutic education can never mean assistance in an isolated section; it must always have in mind the treatment of the total person.

AUSTRIAN PROGRAMS FOR DYSLEXICS

A few years after World War II, the Vienna Psychological Consulting Service to Public Schools, directed by Schenk-Danziger, started to develop special aid to dyslexic pupils. As time went on, more and more officials in the public school system were won over to the idea. Eventually enough was known about the problem so that a few special classes for dyslexics could be established in various Vienna schools.

In these classes it became possible, for the first time, to gather experience on a broad scale. After a while it became apparent that the newly established classes had considerable negative side effects. As a result, during the academic year of 1962–1963, Vienna schools began to hold special groups for dyslexic students, instead of full-time classes. These groups were available at the primary as well as the secondary public school levels.

At the time of this writing, Vienna has 27 full-time teachers involved solely with special teaching on a small group or individual basis. Remediation is offered to the dyslexic children during regular classroom hours, and within the school the children regularly attend. Severely dyslexic students meet their teachers 3 times a week, 30 minutes at a time. About 1,000 pupils are presently enrolled in this type of program, representing about 0.6% of the total school population. The special teachers usually remain for 2 of 3 years at the same school in order to teach the children for several consecutive years, if necessary. The reading teachers stay in close touch with their students' classroom teachers. Together they work out a schedule so that every teacher knows at what time a student is to be released in order to attend his special group. The regular classroom teacher tries to help the dyslexic student catch up on important classroom work missed during his special instruction. Dyslexics of secondary school age (10 to 14 years old), to whom no special programs were available at the elementary level, or whose reading-writing difficulties became apparent at a later stage, now may enroll in special programs of the type described above.

In contrast with the full-time classes for legasthenic pupils, these part-time group arrangements have worked successfully and without major difficulties. This is not too surprising if one keeps in mind that, especially in the beginning, therapeutic remediation should be done on a one-to-one basis. Only in individual treatment can the unique aspects of each case really be taken into consideration.

Speech therapists on the staff of the public school system do not work exclusively with pupils having speech problems. They also take care of dyslexics who, besides their other problems, have a deficit of the dysphasic type.

Selection and enrollment of students in need of special programs take place on the basis of teachers' recommendations. The teachers also work closely with school psychologists and remedial reading teachers.

In almost all recreation centers run by the city of Vienna, there are now courses offered every afternoon, taught by licensed teachers, and attended by 6 to 8 dyslexic children. Each child can have 1 or 2 extra hours a week of special instruction. Yet another program consists of introductory courses offered at teachers' colleges to teachers in all fields who are interested and want to learn more about dyslexia and its treatment. These courses inform teachers of the manifestations of legasthenia and familiarize them with the working material developed by the city's school officials for the dyslexic group programs.

Austrian schools finish formal classroom hours between noon and 2 p.m.; thus, teachers are free to teach or attend special courses in the afternoon. At this time, teachers can also work with their dyslexic students if no other special program happens to be available at their school. The Austrian government distributes textbooks and other work materials, according to a special law, free of charge to students or their families. Within the framework of this special arrangement, any teacher may request books and materials for his dyslexic students and they are provided free.

In addition to the special programs already described, there are arrangements within the Austrian provinces for close cooperation between child guidance clinics and groups of dyslexic students. Courses are offered at the clinics on a regular basis and outside regular classroom hours. In this case, parents are required to pay a fee (which is legally controlled and within acceptable limits). In some provinces, welfare or church charity organizations reimburse these fees to needy parents.

In the larger cities, private individual help is available. In these cases, however, parents are on their own as far as the financing is concerned.

There are also courses offered by the teachers' colleges of all Austrian provinces. These are continuing education courses for teachers. They last a whole academic year and aim, in time, to familiarize all Austrian teachers with the theoretical as well as the practical aspects of dyslexia, including diagnostic and therapeutic procedures.

School psychological services in Austria were able to show by statistical data that next to mental retardation, dyslexia is the most frequent cause of learning disabilities. As a direct consequence of this finding, dyslexia now has been built into the curriculum of all Austrian teachers' colleges; no more new teachers will be trained without being informed about this widespread learning problem. Those who would like to major in legasthenia therapy must take a class or seminar on the subject over a period of 1.5 academic years. These classes are designed to present theories on the causation of dyslexia, its various manifestations, its frequency at different age levels, school types, sex, and such accompanying factors as left-dominance, dysphasia, brain lesions, etc. The student teachers also are expected to learn about the influence which social milieu, educational practices, or teaching techniques may exert in either increasing or decreasing dyslexic symptoms. They are required to know about secondary emotional overlays, and about various remedial programs on an international level. Diagnostic methods of various kinds are shown to them. Last, but not least, student teachers are made familiar with all materials available in German-speaking countries. As students learn to develop treatment programs, four types are to be differentiated and specified: (1) individual aid by a special reading teacher, (2) small-group remedial teaching by the classroom teacher, (3) individual treatment by the regular classroom teacher, and (4) special classes for students in secondary schools.

This kind of training is designed to prepare the future teacher in such a way that he will be able to detect dyslexia early among his students, and will also enable him to provide adequate remedial as well as psychological help for these students within the regular classroom.

In the future, teachers should be able to prevent minor dyslexic symptoms from growing into real learning problems—for instance, simply by his choice of teaching method, which he would apply according to the student's particular needs. Children with more severe reading-writing difficulties, he will refer during their third or fourth grades, at the latest, to special reading teachers. These measures will also prevent the development of serious secondary symptoms (emotional overlay).

DIAGNOSTIC PROCEDURES

In almost every regular classroom we find students of average-or-better intelligence who encounter great difficulties in learning to read and write. Their spelling often remains poor over a considerable period of time. Their reading and writing skills are always far behind their achievement in other areas. The degree of these reading difficulties differs from student to student and their spelling errors—whether more visual or more auditory in character—show no common characteristics.

In order to help a severely dyslexic child through a wisely chosen program of exercises, we must first arrive at a detailed diagnosis. Degree and manifestation of the learning problem must be determined as precisely as possible. It is never sufficient to administer a reading test alone. Reading and writing skills are to be compared to general potential, emotional development, social adjustment, etc. Only the discrepancy between reading-writing ability on the one hand and achievement level in other subject areas makes the dyslexic deficits apparent. Since the child's whole academic life is affected by the learning disturbance, early recognition and effective treatment are of decisive importance.

According to our experience in Vienna a diagnostic evaluation must include:
1. History taking (illness, speech development, familial trends)
2. Development in school (grades, including those of previous years), teachers' reports, behavior, present achievement level
3. Laterality tests (hand, eye, leg)

4. An intelligence test
5. Diagnostic achievement tests, consisting of:
   a) Single-word recognition
   b) Oral reading
   c) Digit reading
   d) Dictation
   If necessary this battery can be extended by these tests:
   e) Single letter reading (all letters of the alphabet, but not in the usual sequence, also combinations of vowels and consonants)
   f) Single-letter writing
   g) Single-digit writing
   h) A spelling and syllabication test without visual material
   i) A sound-association test (the child is orally presented with sounds which he is expected to tie together into words)

During first grade, diagnostic achievement tests can be given only to children who have been taught by the synthetic reading method. They must be asked to read letters already known to them, in new combinations. We watch for the following signs:
1. Difficulties in sound-symbol association
2. Difficulties in tying sounds together
3. Directional confusion (such as always beginning to read a word at its second letter)
4. Inversions or reversals of letters, sequencing mistakes
5. Inability to perceive a word as a whole
6. Reading resistance

When children write to dictation, we watch for these signs:
1. Printed letters or digits horizontally or vertically reversed
2. Tendency to move from right to left during writing process
3. Completely irrational sequencing of letters
4. Inability to isolate sounds and consequent omission of letters
5. Reversed letter sequences
6. Inability to isolate a word from a sentence

At the beginning of the first grade the test for legasthenia includes the School Readiness Test by Edtfeldt. Since the symptoms will be fully manifested only at a later stage, diagnostic assessment will be more adequate when carried out at age 7.5 years or later. Our standardized tests therefore are designed on second- and third-grade levels. The reading tests measure, aside from time used and quantity of mistakes, the number of reversals or inversions of letters and sequences.

Austrian experience has shown that no dyslexic evaluation can be complete unless it includes a spelling test. The spelling deficit is as much part of legasthenia as is the reading disability. The reading problems usually are more quickly removed than the spelling difficulties. Removal of the reading problems alone cannot be considered a complete "cure." When we evaluate the spelling disability we must distinguish between the degree, which expresses itself in the frequency of mistakes, and the symptomatology—the kind of mistakes the student makes. Dyslexic students will, for instance, consistently omit certain letters, they will have problems with capitalization, and they confuse certain vowels or cannot differentiate certain consonants.

Dyslexia of minor or medium degree tends to be amenable to treatment rather quickly. Therefore, from third grade on, diagnostic procedures must begin to emphasize spelling more than reading. In fact, we select potential special-class students during the first weeks after summer vacation, in cooperation with classroom teachers and school psychologists. The psychologist tests each potential dyslexic. Generally only students with an IQ of 90 or more are accepted into special programs (according to the Wechsler Scales).

It is generally known that achievement in school is not automatically linked with intelligence as measured by intelligence tests. It depends largely on such supporting functions as memory, perception, perseverance, concentration, responsibility, eagerness to learn, competitiveness, goal orientation, etc. In the case of legasthenia, these supportive functions show constitutional shortcomings. In the area of perception, for instance, we may see an inability to isolate parts from the whole, in visual or in auditory contexts, and the visual memory may be weak in storing visual symbols, singly or in groups. The Wechsler subtests, Object Assembly and Picture Completion, often are solved much better by dyslexics than by nondyslexics. On the Similarities and Picture Arrangement subtests, they usually do equally well. On the Arithmetic, Block Design, and Comprehension tests, however, dyslexics usually earn lower scores than nondyslexics.

Patterns different from the one described above are found especially in cases with cerebral implications. Here the performance scale may yield much lower results on all subtests than the verbal scale. Dysphasics also show subtest profiles of various kinds; they usually score especially poorly on the Vocabulary subtest.

FREQUENCY OF DYSLEXIA IN AUSTRIA

Schenk-Danziger conducted a testing program in 1956 which included 2,000 Viennese students. The folders of 1,402 children from 46 different classrooms, all second graders, were evaluated. The sample contained 718 boys and 684 girls. Repeaters were excluded from the sample. The average age of the group was 8 years and 1 month. We found 4% severe dyslexics and 18% mild dyslexics in this sample.

Among the severely dyslexic students, the boy to girl ratio was 2:1. Although these percentages of 4 and 18 may appear high, they are in reality even higher, since the sample excluded all repeaters and all those who already had been placed in special classes.

The research conducted by Schenk-Danziger included only city children. During more recent years, research in rural areas has shown that dyslexia rates are even higher, especially among second graders, in these areas. Part of the explanation could lie in the fact that rural school districts have fewer special class facilities; thus the sample contained less selected subjects, including repeaters.

THERAPEUTIC TREATMENT OF DYSLEXICS

Not every child with reading-writing difficulties is severely affected by the learning problem. Type and degree of affliction differ from child to child. Thus there is no material or method which would be 100% effective for remediation. Only on the basis of the child's individual pattern of problems can the therapist design a treatment plan for him. An exact diagnosis is paramount. Specific training will, at first, concentrate on areas in which the learning problem is lightest in degree and thus can be most easily overcome. This educational principle of from easier to more difficult steps must be applied in special education as much as in general education. For the dyslexic child who has already experienced failure, it is of utmost importance that he achieve success as soon as possible, even if only minor. Learning resistance will diminish in proportion to the progress the student himself can see in his work. Praising words are needed and are of educational significance. It is also important to strengthen newly gained skills by planned repetition and practice, by the arousal of the student's curiosity, and by the activation of his motivation by presenting him with attractive, attention-holding work material. Children need frequent and varied practice as well as repetition. This is especially true for dyslexic children. If a new subject had been introduced at the past class meeting, then today's class would begin with a summary of what had been covered. Repetition at larger intervals is also needed to reinforce and maintain skills previously learned.

Independent of the method a teacher may apply in the primary grades, he should pay special attention to the sounds and letters which are generally known to be difficult for dyslexic children. He should work on establishing firm associations between sounds and abstract symbols. In doing so he seeks to activate as many senses as possible: sight, speech, hearing, and motor functions. Weak sensory functions will thus be supported by those that are better developed.

Visual help would consist of, for instance, coloring or framing certain sound or letter combinations presented in written or printed form. A great number of dyslexic children have articulation problems. The speech-motor functions need to be strengthened through exercises like whispering, reading aloud, repeating words after the teacher, and pronouncing a sentence together with the teacher. Should a child, for instance, always confuse two letters (such as d and t), it is necessary to first strengthen each letter separately. After each is well learned independently, the teacher can teach the child to distinguish between the two letters. Children also enjoy rhyming as a way of learning sounds. It is also an easy way for some children to learn.

Correct auditory functions are essential to effective reading and writing. One must be able to distinguish single sounds, especially similar ones, and this often requires extensive practice in dyslexic cases. Auditory training should emphasize voiceless and voiced consonants, diphthongs, blending sounds, and the like.

Visual signs, such as arrows below the words, can be used to point out word beginnings or word endings. Many reading-writing disabled students fail to acoustically differentiate between the first and last letters of a word. These should only be practiced after the child has learned to distinguish between voiced and voiceless letters.

Analyzing words by syllables or letters and synthesizing parts into a whole word are especially important functions which must be practiced to teach the child the "architecture" of words, the sequence of letters and sounds. Visual as well as auditory differentiation will increase by adequate auditory practice.

Good handwriting helps in the perception and memorization of words. It is therefore important to stress good proportions between lower and upper case letters, and also regular spacing. Writing practice should always start with large muscle movements and proceed gradually to fine motor practice. We encourage children to "write" letters in the air; later they write on large chalk boards, then on large sheets of paper spread on tables, and eventually they write on regular sheets or tablets.

When letters are taught, their directional or spatial positions have to be indicated from the start to help differentiate such letters as b, p, g, M, and W.

In Austrian classrooms, two to three children sit at tables in rows. We place a lefthanded child at the left side of a classroom table and teach him a position which will prevent him from covering or erasing with his own hand that which he has written.

Every educator knows that we can practice only those functions that have developed sufficiently. Thus it is important to work, on the primary level, on a small but precise vocabulary. It should contain the most frequently needed words and these should be practiced extensively, with frequent repetitions. The teacher must avoid presenting too many words to the child. It is better to learn fewer words correctly than many that he does not know how to write or read. Insecurity grows with each mistake a student makes, and failure hampers his progress.

An experienced teacher will be able to develop, by a multisensory approach, the learning functions of all his students, whether they are primarily visual, auditory, or motoric learners. What cannot be done in the classroom (where children sit in rows, facing the teacher) probably can be practiced in the gymnasium; this includes orientation in space, balance, directional exercise, etc. ("stand on your left foot; point to your right knee; put up your right hand; pass me running, on the right from left").

A regular teacher can also help the dyslexic child by sometimes practicing with him alone, or in a small group. He may give his dyslexic students small special assignments (reading a paragraph at home, preparing a special sentence before class, memorizing special words, writing down something from memory). Regular teachers may work with the dyslexics of their class in small groups during extra hours; only in severe cases are they referred to special classes.

The Austrian publishing company, Jugend und Volk, together with the Austrian Federal Publishers, put extensive practice materials on the market, designed especially for students with reading-writing disabilities. The authors of this material, consisting of about 20 text and workbooks, are Kowarik and Kraft. These materials were developed on the basis of concrete educational experience with dyslexics of preschool to secondary school levels and much effort was expended to make the workbooks as interesting and entertaining as possible. There are enough variety and quantity now to permit parents or teachers to choose what seems to be right for a particular child, group, or stage.

Parents and teachers know that learning and practice remain ineffective as long as we cannot engage the child actively and pleasurably in the process. Increased reading exercise, pages of copying work, daily dictation of just any text, will do nothing to alleviate the child's learning problem. No one likes to work on subjects in which he has failed. Failure produces discouragement, anxiety, and the fear of failing again. To entice dyslexics to try and practice once more, they must first be helped to develop new motivation. A good way to do this is to permit them to play games at first.

Skills already gained by the child may be used to increase visual and auditory differentiation, concentration, memory, general knowledge, etc. Games for dyslexics should be carefully selected to train as many skills simultaneously as possible (attention, orientation, memory, judgment, etc.) but they should also be neither too difficult nor too simple for the child's present level of maturity and skill. Even in the case of games we maintain the rule: rather two steps too simple than even half a step too difficult. The child must have a real chance to engage fully in the game, to enjoy it, and to win.

Games, of course, introduce the danger that therapy is reduced to mere play. It is basically a question of judgment how to best integrate play learning into special classes. In many cases it suffices to use games in the beginning stage, just long enough to revive the student's interest in learning and participating. All group games have two advantages in comparison to games a child plays by himself. These are competition and checking by others. Competition arouses interest; the participation of other players prevents cheating. If adults participate, such as a father, mother, or teacher; this serves to increase his interest. Nonverbal games such as puzzles and peg boards should be used infrequently; reading and vocabu-lary-building games are of greater importance and should outweigh mere time-filling games.

Word games should be carefully matched to the children's current academic level. Enumerations of animals, objects, city names, etc. can serve to practice alphabetical sequencing—difficult letters, such as X, Y, and Z can be excluded if necessary. Here are a few examples of word games which provide concentration and fun at the same time:

"I travel to Arizona. I travel to Arizona and Baltimore. I travel to Arizona, Baltimore, and California. I travel to . . ."

"My mother buys: apples, butter, coconut . . ."

Games played by the student himself must be matched carefully to his educational needs to indirectly meet his weakness in attention, spatial orientation, laterality, visual or auditory discrimination, perseverance, motor skills, directionality, etc.

Viennese students showing difficulties in visual perception (b-d, p-q, ei-ie) first work from Workbook 7. Empirical studies have shown that these exercises serve to reduce errors of spatial orientation in small print. The dyslexic child must learn to recognize easily and with certainty the forms as well as the positions of the figures (Figure 1). The student also needs to practice selecting certain figures from similar-looking ones, even as their positions in space keep changing. Aside from visual form percep-tion and constancy we thus also develop his spatial orientation (left, right,

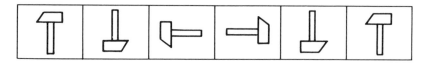

Figure 1. Fill in with blue the hammers pointing to the right. Fill in with red the hammers pointing to the left.

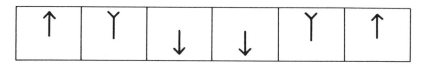

Figure 2. Trace all real arrows pointing up with brown, pointing down with green.

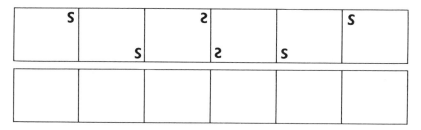

Figure 3. Copy all hooks in the boxes below. Make sure all are copied exactly like models. Trace all S's with red.

Figure 4. Copy the letters in the squares on the right. Make sure they are the same, and are in the same part of the box. Name the letters aloud as you work. Trace all b's in blue.

top, bottom, Figure 2). To the visual and spatial experience we add psychomotor exercises. They must not be too difficult for the dyslexics with retarded motor skills, many of whom have laterality problems in addition, or have been changed in their handedness (Figure 3). In all training, visual, auditory, or motor, left-to-right directionality must be observed and stressed, i.e., the direction in which we read and write. Whenever we work with language symbols we make sure that the visual and motor components of the exercise are joined by auditory practice (Figure 4).

Figures, symbols, letters, and digits are arranged in such a way that they will form, if colored correctly, a symmetrically colored picture. Thus a quick check of the completed exercise is possible. Speed practice can easily be added to the use of the work sheets which serve to reduce difficulties in spatial relationships. "The hook is in the top right-hand corner of the first square, it is shaped like an S. The second hook is in the . . ." (see Figure 3).

Drawing from dictation—which can be done as group exercise—provides excellent practice in concentration. The dictation may go like this, for example: "In the first square of the top row put a slanted line from the left bottom corner to the right top corner. In the second square to the right in the top row, draw a line from the left top corner to the right bottom corner. Leave the third square empty . . ." The faster the dictation, the higher the degree of difficulty. As homework, the student may copy designs and add them together in long chains.

MEASURES TO PREVENT SECONDARY SYMPTOMS

Quite frequently we observe certain behavior problems which are associated with reading-writing weakness. Many dyslexic children appear immature for their age. In the beginning, the young pupil seems to feel comfortable in his role of a small child. He rarely compares his own achievement with that of his peers and tends to overestimate his abilities. He is self-confident. Dyslexic students often maintain this attitude and it constitutes an apparent disparity with their mental potential, physical development, and chronological age. They may dislike academic challenge and try to ignore or escape scholastic expectations.

Eventually, the dyslexic gradually becomes aware of his lags in performance. To try to catch up does not enter his head, however. His naive attitude toward life prevents him from the necessary introspection. Instead he tries to compensate in other areas (to make better grades in arithmetic, physical education, geography).

In the first through third grades, reading seems to be a particularly sensitive point. The dyslexic suffers long-range blows to his self-image. Since spelling is a critically important subject in many schools, his failure in this area adds to the problem. Each day his realization increases that reading and spelling are decisive skills in academic endeavor. He usually does not attempt to meet the problem by more effort, but he tries to escape. Failure causes depression, and underachievement in other subjects as well. Thus students with dyslexic problems of long standing that have remained unrecognized and untreated, often have poor grades in all academic areas. Dyslexic students who have never read a book voluntarily have little chance of obtaining good grades; they are too far behind in knowledge and information. Discouragement prevents them from paying attention in class. Teachers often describe them as daydreamers; they may call such students playful, insecure, withdrawn, shy, and limited in attention span. Dislike for all academic work can lead to passive as well as active behavior problems. Frustration often causes escape or defense mechanisms. Pressure exerted by parents or teachers may cause aggression, withdrawal or resistance. Some tend to overcompensate and become show-offs, clowns, bullies, and the like.

Especially among younger children, a strong association exists between good grades and degree of peer acceptance. Classmates usually see the poor student exactly in the same way the teacher does. This adds a heavy burden to his academic difficulties. The stress increases and disables the student even further; thus a vicious circle is established.

No educator denies the value of praise. Countless experiments have shown that adults as well as children react favorably to acts which have pleasant consequences; they tend to repeat them. Negative criticism, on the other hand, has negative consequences, especially with slow learners. Dyslexics, more than others, need praise and acknowledgment. Usually, however, the good students are reinforced rather than those who might need it. Leniency alone is not enough; the dyslexic student needs success, progress and support by the group. The teacher must acknowledge all gains. If he fails to do so, the anxiety of the disabled learner may increase to the point where he cannot cope with the challenge. He may fail in tasks which are easy for his classmates and begin to consider himself a total failure.

Students react differently to continuous failure. Some react passively; they are discouraged, they give up. Indifference, concentration problems, inattentiveness, and lack of interest are effects rather than causes of the reading-spelling problems. Others react actively; they become rebellious, destructive, aggressive, and disruptive. In both cases secondary symptoms may become more important than the primary learning problems. In older children, cause and effect can no longer be clearly distinguished. The well known psychologist Hunger-Kaindlstorfer has a large private practice in Vienna for dyslexics. In 1965 she reported, at a convention in Berlin, that among 113 of her cases there were 87 with light to severe secondary behavior problems.

Every dyslexic must exert more effort in class than his peers. More concentration is needed on his part. Naturally, he tires more easily. The

Table 1. IQ vs. numbers of boys and girls

Wechsler IQ	No. of boys	No. of girls
91–100	80	41
100–110	89	48
111–120	43	26
121–130	24	2
Above 130	3	0

teacher notices how often he sits and dreams, how disinterested he appears, how little he seems to participate. Instead of criticism, he needs more frequent breaks, more gentle stimulation, more support.

Reading-writing difficulties can be reduced by patient, remedial treatment. Often they disappear completely. When grades go up, behavior improves also. Only if the secondary symptomatology has grown into fully developed neuroses must we expect further emotional problems and thwarted development. This indicates how important it is to treat second-

Table 2. Spelling errors from dictation: special classes

Level of education	Range of errors	Mean errors
Second graders		
At beginning of special class	16–47	23.9
At midterm	3–15	8.7
At end of year	0–8	3.8
Third graders		
At beginning of special class	11–37	26.6
At midterm	5–22	13.1
At end of year	3–14	8.9
Fourth graders		
At beginning of special class	9–32	13.7
At midterm	2–12	5.7
At end of year	1–10	5.3
Above fourth grade		
At beginning of special class	14–36	29.8
At midterm	9–27	19.7
At end of year	6–22	16.1

ary as well as primary symptoms; better yet, to never allow the secondary overlay to develop.

FOLLOW-UP STUDIES

Between the academic years 1962 and 1963, and 1970 and 1971, I have had 356 reading-writing disabled children in my special classes (239 boys, 117 girls). All of them were carefully tested, psychometrically and academically. Their Wechsler IQ's ranged from 91 to 138 (see Table 1).

These students were 7 to 14 years old. The majority were second and third graders. Table 2 shows the test findings using normed dictation tests. In all grades we see declining numbers of spelling errors. The decrease occurs at different rates in the various grade levels. The mean values show that the most rapid success occurred at second-grade level. The older the students, the slower the success rate in general.

A comparison of grades in language and reading subjects shows that

Table 3. Grades of students in special classes

Level of education	Grades (%)[a]				
	1 (A)	2 (B)	3 (C)	4 (D)	5 (F)
German: up to grade 4					
Before special class	0.0	3.4	46.5	44.1	6.0
After 1 year of attendance	1.5	16.3	45.7	33.9	2.6
After 2 years of attendance	3.9	27.3	39.2	29.1	0.5
Reading: up to grade 4					
Before special class	3.2	37.7	39.5	18.1	1.5
After 1 year of attendance	9.7	47.8	34.9	7.1	0.5
After 2 years of attendance	19.6	54.4	21.6	4.2	0.0
German: above 4th grade[b]					
Before special class	0.0	0.0	21.7	78.3	0.0
After 1 year of attendance	0.0	0.0	35.4	64.5	0.0
After 2 years of attendance	0.0	29.6	42.5	27.9	0.0

[a]The grade range is from 1 to 5; the highest is A.
[b]At these grade levels, grades for German and reading are combined.

Table 4. Follow-up study of 323 pupils from special class

Observations	Boys (N = 215)	Girls (N = 108)
Getting along normally in school	170	96
One or two repetitions before special class	19	6
One repetition during remediation	5	2
One repetition after remediation	21	4

the grades go up distinctly after 1 and 2 years of special remediation. The grade in the regular class is given completely independently of how the student does in his special reading course. Table 3 shows the distribution of grades.

In Austria grades range from 1 to 5; the highest (A) is 1, and the lowest (F) is 5. These tables indicate that the majority of dyslexics make their most rapid advances during the first year of remediation class. However, older students show marked success only after their second year of special help.

In only 323 of the cases was it possible to obtain further data for the follow-up study (215 boys, 108 girls). Of the total group, 22 (16 boys, six girls) had already repeated a grade once. Three had repeated twice.

After the first year of remediation, seven students (five boys, two girls) still had failing grades in either German or reading. Of the remaining students none needed to repeat during the treatment period. After successful dismissal from the special class, none of the students encountered significant learning difficulties any more. Within the course of their entire further school attendance, 25 of the 323 (21 boys, four girls) had to repeat once more. Eighteen boys and two girls failed in German or reading. The remaining five students had failing grades in mathematics, English, or other subjects. Table 4 gives an overview of the findings discussed above.

All districts of Vienna introduced special classes patterned after those which I had designed and from which the sample studied here had been taken. The dyslexia classes in all of the other Austrian regions are conducted according to the principles developed in Vienna. Thus it may be assumed that studies in other Austrian school districts would yield findings much in accord with those reported here.

CHAPTER 5

Learning Disabilities in Belgium

Marianne Klees

A disturbing feature of school performance in Belgium is that 48% of the children find it difficult to reach the final year of primary school without repeating either one, two, or even three years. This percentage does not include children attending special classes. This situation causes dismay and problems in many families and distinctly limits the social potential of the children concerned. Discounting the mentally retarded, motor-handicapped, sensory-handicapped, and severely emotionally disturbed children in this group, there still remains a large proportion of intelligent children who fall behind in the primary grades. Their failure is perplexing.

Dopchie et al. (1971) analyzed the various causes of school maladjustment in a group of 146 children attending a guidance clinic at Saint-Pierre Hospital, University of Brussels. The frequencies of appearance of the main causes of school maladjustment were:

1. Emotional factors only   34%
2. Mainly emotional   28%
3. Mainly instrumental   24%
4. Mainly intellectual   9%
5. Instrumental factors only   2%
6. Mainly organic   2%

The authors add that in almost two out of three cases there were several factors operating (usually instrumental and emotional disorders).

Abstracted by the editors from a monograph-length manuscript submitted by M. Klees.

EDUCATION IN BELGIUM

Elementary education (6 years) is free in all schools subsidized by the state. All schools which satisfy the standards imposed by the state are subsidized. School attendance is compulsory for eight years of completed schooling.

Forty-five percent of all children attend official schools organized by the state, provinces, or communes. Fifty-five percent attend independent schools, primarily Catholic.

Adaptation classes are available to provide temporary help to children who have adjustment problems. These children benefit from scholastic guidance organized by psycho-medico-social centers subsidized by the state. It is estimated that 7 to 8% of the school population attend the special classes which are organized by the state, provinces, communes, or independent schools.

Eight types of special education are available as follows:
1. Slightly mentally retarded
2. Moderately and severely mentally retarded
3. Behavioral problems
4. Physical handicaps
5. Children who are ill
6. Visually impaired
7. Hearing impaired
8. Instrumentally impaired

INSTRUMENTAL HANDICAPS

For several years we have been studying intelligent, instrumentally handicapped children who experience difficulty at school. Instrumental handicaps include perceptual, psychomotor, and linguistic impairments. Instrumental impairments occur in the presence of normal visual and auditory acuity and include auditory, visual, kinesthetic, and tactile perceptual dysfunction as well as visual-motor, psychomotor, and speech and language disabilities. In French, they are called "troubles spécifiques du développement." Examination of children with instrumental handicaps often reveals concomitant organic, neurotic, or psychotic disorders, or mental retardation.

Attempts to detect specific relations between instrumental disorders and specific learning difficulties in reading, writing, spelling, or arithmetic yielded no positive results. This indicates that these academic functions are too complex to be related to either the simple or multiple sensory etiological processes that can be isolated by our present methods. This tends to indicate that there can be no certain prediction of school learning difficulties based on an evaluation of instrumental abilities in a preschool child, especially when there are intellectual and/or affective compensations.

Emotional disturbances may make instruments which were initially only slightly impaired, completely unusable, or may even create further impairments. Thus, although instrumental impairments may be considered as "quasineurological" disorders, they must be viewed in the context of the child's whole personality, in relation to his past experience, and the investment which the child and those around him place in this experience and present activities.

In our clinical practice we had observed similarities between certain instrumental characteristics displayed by motor-handicapped subjects and those of children with simple instrumental impairments but without proven cerebral lesions. For instance, both showed impaired figure-ground discrimination. In view of the frequency of association of these impairments with school difficulties, we studied the possible role played by instrumental impairments in general, and by impaired figure-ground discrimination in particular, in the development of school learning difficulties.

INSTRUMENTAL IMPAIRMENT AND LEARNING

Children presenting a high risk of failure in kindergarten and those intelligent children who fall behind in school were considered for study. We were concerned with children of normal intelligence, without sensory or neurological impairment, or serious emotional problems. Our general objective was to gain a better understanding of the relationship between instrumental and educational symptoms often associated with behavioral problems.

The children studied came to a guidance clinic where it was established that instrumental impairments were the basic cause of their school difficulties. It was observed that visual figure-ground impairment (Frostig Figure-Ground subtest) coincided with significant frequencies of school difficulties in children of normal intelligence. These observations derived from the inclusion, since 1965, of the Marianne Frostig Developmental Test of Visual Perception (1963) in our battery of instrumental tests. The Frostig subtest, Figure-Ground, consists of a series of increasingly complex embedded figures which the subject is asked to find and outline.

Preliminary Studies

Preliminary data to check our hypothesis were gathered from several groups of children including: 68 children in first grade, 117 kindergarteners, 28 pairs of twins 5.5 to 9 years of age, and 32 dyslexic children aged 8 to 12 years. These children were tested intellectually and instrumentally, but were not kept under observation or helped afterwards.

A preliminary survey was devoted to determining the frequency of Frostig Figure-Ground (FFG) perceptual deficits as related to school difficulties in unselected children of normal intelligence, aged 5 to 8 years. An FFG deficit was said to exist if the child's standard score on this test was 8 or less, or at least one standard deviation below the mean. In a sample of 93 unselected children in kindergarten and first grade, eight (8.5%) had FFG deficits with average or higher intelligence levels, without gross neurological, sensory, or emotional disorders. All of these children had school difficulties. Further, among the 32 dyslexic children, 19 (59%) had FFG deficits in the presence of normal intelligence. In most cases FFG deficits were found in a constellation of visual-perceptual problems. Very frequently there were also associated motor problems, especially dysrhythmia.

Among the 28 pairs of twins, 4 pairs were premature (birth weight under 2,000 grams). All of these premature children were found to be below the average range (90 to 110 IQ) in intelligence. Eleven (29%) of the 40 intelligent twins were found to have FFG deficits in the absence of gross visual deficiencies. Six of the 11 had learning disabilities, and two whose IQ's were above 120 had no school problems. Thus, six (15%) of 40 intelligent twins had both FFG and learning disabilities.

Bertrand (1969) reported on the relationships between reading and spelling problems and scores on a number of psychometric tests for the 32 dyslexic children (previously mentioned) aged 8 to 12 years, with Wechsler IQ's above 90. These children did especially poorly on the Frostig tests, the Wechsler Intelligence Scale for Children (WISC) performance tests, and in copying Rey's complex figures. Tetrachoric correlations were calculated between each psychometric test and subtest score and the number of visual-perceptual errors each child made on a reading test. Perceptual errors of four types were considered; namely, visual confusions, omissions, additions, and inversions. The single highest correlation found was between Frostig Figure-Ground scores and total perceptual reading errors (r = 0.74). Similarly, the Frostig Figure-Ground subtest gave the highest correlations with visual-perceptual errors made on a spelling test taken by the children. These correlations were: FFG versus omissions, $r = 0.65$; FFG versus static inversion, $r = 0.64$; and FFG versus total perceptual spelling errors, $r = 0.62$.

All of these data indicate a strong relationship between visual figure-ground deficits and learning disabilities. This prompted a more detailed study of the relationships between instrumental handicaps and learning disorders in intelligent children.

Instrumental Impairments and Learning Disabilities

Twelve preschool children and 22 school-aged children were studied, all of whom had been followed by us for at least 2 years. The group included 27 boys and seven girls, 5 to 10 years of age, all of whom presented simple instrumental impairments not complicated by other anomalies. They ranged in IQ from 90 to 135, with a median IQ of 109, on either the Terman-Merrill Intelligence scale or the WISC.

None of the children appear to have suffered from emotional isolation from the mother as infants, and they appear to have received adequate psychomotor stimulation. Sitting and walking were achieved at the normal age by all children except for four premature ones. However, frequent falls were indicated by parents, and motor coordination difficulties became apparent in kindergarten.

Perception Difficulties of perception and spatial orientation were quite evident in the children's drawings. The most serious cases sometimes made two-dimensional models when working in Plasticine, e.g., the tree was flattened. Several children with figure-ground deficits exhibited this characteristic. Spatial confusion was sometimes apparent in language, e.g., high-low, left-right, inside-outside, and so on.

Visual spatial deficits sometimes resulted in difficulty with discriminating letters, directions, and orientation. These children had great difficulty with organizing space around them and needed fixed landmarks for constant reference. The older children could not read or draw maps of familiar places (younger children were not tested). An impaired sense of sequence often produced major rhythm disorders as well as difficulty in learning the days of the week, the month, the year, as well as time.

At the first interview, the parents of four children (and later numerous others) reported instrumental impairment in a parent which was identical to that of the child, raising the question of heredity and indicating the possible amplifying effect of distorted stimulation from these parents.

Intelligence tests are often contaminated by factors of perception. Separating perception and judgment items sometimes gives a clearer picture of a child's abilities. This proved important when testing this group of children. For example, on the Columbia test, logical reasoning is measured by both visual-perceptual and categorical judgment items. When retested, children with instrumental impairments often improved on the categorical judgment items (due to learning) but remained handicapped on the perceptual items, giving a more adequate assessment of their intelligence.

Thirty-two of the children were assessed for visual memory of geometrical designs. No child obtained a score in the normal range and 12 children were below the first percentile.

Results on Frostig Tests In the group of preschool children, half obtained a Perceptual Quotient (PQ) equal to or less than 100 and all of the school-age children obtained PQ's below 106 on the Frostig Developmental Test of Visual Perception. Twelve children were found to have very poor eye-hand coordination. Seven children performed poorly on the perceptual form constancy subtest which measures the ability to recognize circles and squares regardless of their size and position. Nine children had difficulty with the subtest, Position in Space (finding the object in a group which is the same as the stimulus figure, and finding the object which is different from the others in a group). Seven children had difficulty copying designs composed of straight lines connecting dots (copies are made on sheets containing only the dots).

The Frostig Figure-Ground subtest was the most difficult for these children. Twenty-five of 34 children (74%) scored 8 or less on this test compared with 16% in the total population. Most of the children received their lowest scores in this subtest. In all cases except one, FFG impairment was associated with other instrumental deficits.

Educational Disabilities Twenty children had difficulties in all aspects of mathematics; of these children, 18 had reading disabilities and 17 had writing disorders.

The difficulties with number concepts, number language, and the space and time orientation involved in sequencing numbers tended to persist in spite of remedial teaching. Their calculating difficulties could not be compared with those of mentally deficient children; their reasoning faculties were absolutely unimpaired and often provided compensatory mechanisms of surprising complexity.

REMEDIAL TEACHING

In French publications, the rehabilitation of school children experiencing learning difficulties is always considered in special categories: either reading-spelling, mathematics, or writing disorders. The correction of multiple aspects of learning disabilities in which instrumental deficits play a part is rarely studied as a global problem.

There is also some uncertainty in French schools of psychology as to the etiology and even the reality of learning disabilities. These difficulties tend to be seen in the light of emotional interference by child-family and child-school relations.

Very few schools in Belgium provide special education in conjunction with ordinary teaching to help children with instrumental difficulties. At the time of our study, those which existed did not accept children before second grade. We therefore found it necessary to create an experimental class for a small number of these seriously handicapped children. They were to be given special education based on their tested needs for as long as necessary to prepare them for re-entry to regular schools. It developed that the first year was prolonged into a second, third, and fourth year, which we termed "transition" years.

Remedial Methods

Educators must respect certain principles. We shall discuss the way they were applied to teaching the children in this study. Working in homogeneous groups diminished the anxiety stemming from the unequal competition in regular classrooms which is very traumatizing for these children. Group work permits the stimulation of competition at a level which the children can handle. Every child contributes towards structuring the others. In this sense it is a very active kind of teaching which does not lead to overdependence on the remedial teacher. Group work therefore has an advantage over individual remediation, which is valuable only if limited to one or two sessions per week.

The attention of these children tends to fluctuate from one moment to another. They react immediately to everything. They are hyperemotional and lack a sense of proportion and control. Since it is assumed that one of the main disturbance factors is emotional, we try to reduce their distractibility by improving the environment (reducing noises and background disturbances), by manipulating social contacts (showing that one understands the child's confusion), and by facilitating the selection of useful information from the variety of stimuli always present. It is sometimes erroneously thought that if an instrumentally impaired child is stimulated a great deal, he is bound to learn something. We found that this situation only confused the child and prevented any learning.

We found a discordance between knowledge apparently acquired, and its automatic use. This difficulty tends to persist and characterizes the fragility of these children. Simple acts, such as rereading a short word, continue to require energy equal to or even greater than that originally expended when it was first read. Experience indicated that repeated exercises, for which normal children show great endurance, are not to be recommended as a training method for these children. We believe that systematic and repetitive techniques for acquiring automatic reading, writing, and calculating must be abandoned and replaced by free spontaneous activities, geared to the child's interest.

In 1970, we decided to provide the specific instrumental remediation needed for each child. We planned an intense individual schedule with several specialists in each case. Very soon the artificial character of these methods became clear. We found that such organization (or disorganization?) confused the child by creating relations with too many people. It hindered his attempt to structure the various therapies received. Moreover, no account was taken of the position occupied by instrumental impairments within the framework of the child's education as a whole. Thus we came to the conclusion (which agrees with most American research findings) that, contrary to what is recommended for preschool children, school-age children require instrumental remediation within the activities in which the problems appear. That is, while learning reading, writing, spelling, and arithmetic.

We believe that great importance must be attached to the need for communication and linguistic curiosity, i.e., to the real driving forces invested in spoken and written language. The use and development of spoken language were therefore considered as the basis of all teaching and as indispensable for emotional growth. It is most important that the remedial teacher gain the child's cooperation, and that she not be afraid of talking undramatically about the child's problems when he wishes to do so.

The aim is to help the child by creating a favorable situation, enabling him to fight efficiently against the sources of his anxiety and inhibitions. This is quite the reverse of a totally permissive attitude.

It is desirable to diminish the interferences of the child's handicaps while offering him opportunities for creative activity or play based on educational material. For instance, a magnetic board and magnetic letters and numerals are indispensable. They give children the chance to correct their mistakes without the impression of failure. They also allow the children to manipulate and actually feel all the possible symbolic arrangements of the written language or figures, helping them to understand temporal and spatial flow.

We believe that the development of spoken communication is crucially important for these children who are so ill at ease with self-expression. The teachers were most struck by the children's difficulties in verbal expression, their reluctance to participate in oral class activities, and the repercussions in writing. Closer observation revealed poor vocabulary, imprecision in the use of terms, and poor use of phrases. These tended to be compensated for by mimicry, gesturing, and onomatopoeia. Linguistic "economy" often reflects the child's lack of erotization or his inhibition at using the instrument of language whose effects are unsatisfying to himself and others. The causes of these problems appear to be auditory-verbal perception deficits, with confusion of similar sounds and an inability to distinguish a specific sound within a series of sounds. This leads to serious difficulties in memorizing what was badly perceived originally, and to confusion about the meanings of words and complex verbal statements.

Remedial Reading

The methods used for learning to read were phonetic and gesticulatory. Coding and decoding took place at the same time for obvious reasons. The child wishes first to draw, then to express himself, and then to write his name. Writing his name is a real sign of the expression of his personality. The graphical expressions, which he cannot grasp until he learns to read, provide the deep motivation for learning to read and write.

This does not mean that writing and spelling were learned simultaneously. Children who were obviously not ready to learn to write, because of their severe motor difficulties, were urged to transcribe their expressions with the aid of magnetic letters on a magnetic board. They were trained to write, by appropriate exercises, at different stages.

When a child asked a question about spelling an unknown word, the spelling was always given to him. This was done to avoid a wrong first impression, since the critical effects of early errors are difficult to correct later. As often as possible, the teacher chose simple words of current usage or words spelled phonetically. This vocabulary is not confined to poor or limited expressions such as "the cat and the rat." On the contrary, the children's writings revealed a richness which stemmed from good motivations.

In this system, the teacher must present the letters and sounds in the order of their frequency of use in the language. Color coding was also used; consonants in blue and diphthongs in red.

Other exercises consisted of dictation and reading of meaningless syllables, after informing the children of this fact. Dictation of complex syllables was frequent in the beginning of the year, in order to emphasize the various phonemes and their temporal sequences in words. As soon as the children reached a certain reading level, the texts read and dictated to them related to their activities, games, and conversations. Long after the sequences of sounds in words were no longer a problem, categorical notions continued to represent an obstacle, in spite of numerous spoken language and vocabulary exercises.

At the beginning of the year, children with severe handwriting problems did their dictation using mobile magnetic letters. They performed numerous pre-writing exercises on the board with chalk, on paper with a brush, and eventually with a pencil. After a while, they showed the desire to write their dictation on the blackboard, then on large pages, and later in a copybook.

Teaching Arithemtic

The children's principal weakness lay in grasping the number concept and its invariant character. The concepts of number and invariance are absolute prerequisites of any general mathematical reasoning ability. As a result, the most elementary operations remained insurmountable for a long time.

With regard to the origin of such deficiencies, in the older children, who should long since have acquired these abilities, it is difficult to determine whether it is the acquisition of the elementary logical processes that is delayed, or if it is that the understanding of the symbolism involved in any statement of relation is hindered by emotional inhibition at the oedipal level. This is not just an epistemological question. The answer indicates the need for either remedial teaching oriented towards the logical activity, or a psychological approach designed to overcome the inhibition. It is necessary to bear this distinction in mind, especially if it does not emerge clearly on first contact with the child, as is the case with less intelligent children.

In children with instrumental impairments, delay in the logical processes of thought is the main etiological factor. In subnormal or phobic children, the oedipal regression takes precedence over reasoning. The distinction between logical delay and emotional inhibition is even more difficult to estimate in practice than in theory since the two interfere with each other continuously.

For a long time manipulation was used as an essential concrete activity through which to develop symbolic and operative thought (grouping, matching, correspondence, and exercises in serial order). Nevertheless, we felt that such exercises were of little help in the understanding of number concepts. It was only through the child's own body that he could arrive at the fundamentals, i.e., through psychomotor remediation to enable the child to act and feel the numbers, the rhythms, and the sequences. Handling small numbers and counting in small groups of numbers seemed to be a fundamental step which had to be mastered before progressing, to avoid creating inhibitions due to anxiety at being lost in a strange dimensionless world. This demanded a great deal of energy, ingenuity, and time. Gradually, the numerical concepts were constructed and the child's vocabulary of quantities became larger and more accurate.

RESULTS OF REMEDIATION

The five children in the preschool group who presented no figure-ground perception difficulties, but who were nevertheless given help because of the unfavorable prognosis suggested by language problems, managed to progress satisfactorily. In contrast, in the early months of first grade, the other children in this group who had presented figure-ground perception difficulties were already showing signs of poor adaptation in reading and arithmetic, whatever their intelligence and in spite of appropriate preventive help. However, after a full year, all the children who received appropriate help managed to overcome their school retardation, except one, who made slow progress. Also, continuous individual help was necessary for two of them whose functioning remained fragile for a further year.

Our findings concerning the predictive value of figure-ground perception problems were not known to us when we initiated the special classes. Thus, FFG deficits were not criteria for selecting the children admitted to these classes. It was the severity of their school problems or the affective reactions of the children which led us to remove them from ordinary classes and transfer them to special classes. None of these children had been able to keep up in a regular class.

Appropriate remedial help was given to all 22 school-age children, either as individual help, 1 or 2 hours a week while they remained in a regular class, or in the special full-time classes created by us.

We found that the six slightly handicapped children rapidly regained normal development. The three dysphasic children, afflicted only with handicaps of expression and not of perception, were also making good progress with no further problems. These children were very intelligent but were not regarded as "normal" from the psychoaffective point of view. Two of the three dysphasic children showed good progress, in contrast to the third who had been brought for psychological examination at a later stage. All three were of good intelligence with "normal" affect.

The development of nine out of the 15 very severely instrumentally handicapped children was very slow and remained so in some cases after 2 or more years. On the other hand, the remaining 6 children in this group eventually improved to a satisfactory degree. This lack of consistency between the intensity of the instrumental impairments and the progress of the children induced us to undertake further analysis.

As soon as we considered figure-ground impairment as a prognostic criterion, things became much clearer. Children presenting figure-ground impairment, which is always associated with an over-all picture of instrumental difficulties, remained severely maladapted to the ordinary school environment, despite individual psychological and pedagogic help, if their IQ's were between 90 and 110. Children with the same problem but higher intelligence, managed (provided their emotional balance was satisfactory) to gain enough benefit from the curative measures to compensate for their school difficulties.

On the other hand, children presenting instrumental difficulties without figure-ground perceptual impairment recuperated more easily, even with an IQ as low as 90. Consequently, in this group of 34 subjects, the diagnostic and prognostic value of figure-ground perception was confirmed.

SUMMARY

In summary, during the 2 years of observation, out of nine children without figure-ground perception problems, seven (78%) were able to attend ordinary school with auxiliary help. Two (22%) required full-time special teaching for 1 year, after which they went back to the ordinary school.

Whereas, out of 25 children with figure-ground perception problems, only four (16%) were able to remain in the ordinary school system (three of them had received preschool preventive treatment); 21 (84%) had to be transferred (despite auxiliary help) to special classes where they remained for at least 2 years, and some were still not ready to go back to ordinary school.

Our experience also demonstrates the importance of early treatment. Children helped before the age of six progressed well, whereas the likelihood of children over six making poor progress increased in proportion to the length of time that the failure situation had been allowed to persist. This underscores the amplifying role of the emotional reaction to the failure—the feeling of inadequacy—whose influence is extremely difficult to distinguish from that of the instrumental factors, especially in children over 9 years of age.

Finally, we feel that the remediation of school difficulties associated with instrumental handicaps for children 5 to 8 years of age depends on numerous factors of which the main ones, in order of importance, are:
1. An early start on appropriate remedial teaching
2. The emotional and relational adjustment of the child to his family and school environment
3. Intelligence

Although our findings do not permit us to assume a cause and effect relationship between visual figure-ground deficits and learning disabilities, they nonetheless help improve the accuracy of early detection of school maladjustment in certain cases, and to suggest preventive measures.

REFERENCES

Bertrand, H. 1969. Etude Qualitative chez 32 dyslexiques des fautes de lecture et d'orthographe comparées aux performances à des tests de perception visuelle. Licence thesis, School of Psychology, Brussels University.

Dopchie, N. et al. 1971. Recherche sur les facteurs d'inadaptation scolaire. Ed. Inst. de Sociologie (Université Libre de Bruxelles) 1:160.

Frostig, M., P. Maslow, D. W. Lefever, and J. R. B. Whittlesey. 1963. The Marianne Frostig Developmental Test of Visual Perception. Consulting Psychologists Press, Palo Alto, Ca.

CHAPTER 6

Learning Disabilities in Canada: A Survey of Educational and Research Programs

Robert M. Knights,[1] Doreen Kronick, and June Cunningham

For centuries the proper education of children has been of utmost concern to all peoples of the world. During the last few decades the teaching of special groups of handicapped children has been emphasized. This chapter presents an overview of Canadian policy and activity concerning children with learning disabilities. As a survey of the nation's practice in the area, this review must necessarily be selective in emphasis and therefore will not discuss many programs. The first section of this report presents the policies of government and private organizations, at both federal and provincial levels, which have influenced the nature of educational programs available for the learning disabled child. The second section is a brief description of the standard educational approaches to the problem of learning disabilities in most school boards across Canada. The third section discusses some of the rather unique methods of training and education and is particularly selective in that it makes no mention of many Canadian programs and facilities. In the fourth section, the major centers involved in conducting and publishing research studies in the area of learning disorders are discussed, along with their major focus of interest and experimental findings.

[1] R.M.K. was on Leave Fellowship Grant No. W73-0572 from the Canada Council during the preparation of this manuscript.

97

EDUCATIONAL FACILITIES

Government Policy

In Canada there is no federal office of education and all legislation concerning special education is the responsibility of the province. Consequently, there is a wide range in extensiveness and sophistication of the services available to the learning disabled child. There are also considerable differences in the way special education is funded, ranging from almost global provincial subsidization to expenses being carried exclusively by the municipality. Two of the provinces of Canada have legislation requiring school districts to educate children with special needs, whereas the other provinces have loosely worded exclusion clauses whereby it is even possible that a student can be prohibited from receiving a public education.

Volunteer Organizations

Volunteer organizations have played an important role in the development of facilities in Canada. The first volunteer organization specifically concerned with the learning disabled was formed in Toronto in 1964. Up to that time, effective services were scarce and served a minimal proportion of the population—the majority of the learning disabled children in Canada enjoyed neither diagnostic nor treatment facilities. The original volunteer organization assisted so many communities in initiating their own organizations that the Canadian Association for Children with Learning Disabilities was formed in 1969. The emergence of volunteer organizations across the nation, whose thrust was social action as well as professional and public education, spearheaded remarkable changes in the field. These changes have been evident in all facets of professional education and in-service training, with altered models of service and the provision of a spectrum of programs from early detection and stimulation to special education, counseling, recreation, job placement, and employer sensitization. There is still room for improvement in both the quality and quantity of services offered. Nevertheless, the growth from virtually no known services to an extensive accommodation of the learning disability population in merely a few years is an impressive step.

GOVERNMENT STUDIES

CELDIC Report

A 3-year, multiprofessional study of troubled children in Canada was organized by the Commission on Emotional and Learning Disorders in Children (CELDIC, 1970). The Association for Children with Learning

Disabilities played a critical role in its inception and the official sponsoring organizations also included The Canadian Association for the Mentally Retarded, The Canadian Council on Children and Youth, The Canadian Rehabilitation Council for the Disabled, The Canadian Welfare Council, and Dr. Barnardo's School, the latter being a British service and funding organization. After an extensive survey of the patterns of service delivery, the commission produced an incisive report which concluded that 1,000,000 children in Canada required special educational assistance and that this number constituted a national emergency. The report dealt extensively with the inefficient and fragmented means whereby the nation served its troubled youth, and also recommended a number of alternative approaches to the problem. Standardization in education was stressed with attendant changes to occur in teacher training, class size, and support services. Consequently there has been a national movement away from sheltered classroom placement, with increasing consideration given to creating an environment in which the learning disabled child can remain in the educational mainstream.

The sponsoring organizations of the Commission on Emotional and Learning Disorders have been involved in some joint efforts towards the implementation of their report on a national level. Provincial branches have been working collaboratively on the development of programs and in some of the provinces, notably Manitoba, committees have been established at the local level. In fact, it is at the local level that the most effective effort can be expended to ensure an optimum use of resources and coordinated delivery of services. The Manitoba government has organized a committee for implementation composed of representation from the Ministries of Health and Social Service and the Commission on Emotional and Learning Disorders Task Force, the latter being a group representing every organization serving children in Manitoba. In Alberta, the Association for Children with Learning Disabilities and the Edmonton Public and Catholic School Boards organized a CELDIC implementation conference involving all agencies serving youth and interested lay persons. Participants at this conference developed a set of recommendations which resulted in provincial funding to the school systems and to the Edmonton preschool screening project, as well as the establishment of two pilot project areas in rural Alberta to study service delivery systems to the learning disabled. In British Columbia, the Medical Services Foundation funded coordinator and secretarial services for purposes of implementation of programs. The result has been several interagency-sponsored conferences in the areas of concern such as teacher education and rehabilitation of juveniles, with the charge being directed at adjustments in professional training and service delivery.

Some of these adjustments have occurred, for example, in Victoria, where all children's services provided by the Human Resources, Education, and Health Departments are coordinated and delivered from one office. In Ontario, a Super Ministry was established over Health and Education to provide for joint funding and supervision of programs that were previously under separate departments. In the Atlantic provinces a committee was appointed to study the special education needs. Essentially, the committee's recommendations closely paralleled the recommendations in the CELDIC report. In addition, it urged parent involvement in all levels of service planning and also proposed that some facets of teacher and paraprofessional training, planning, coordination, and operation of special education services take place on an interprovincial basis.

SEECC Report

A national study was conducted by the Canadian Committee of the Council for Exceptional Children, in collaboration with the National Institute on Mental Retardation, concerning the training of teachers for special education programs. This study culminated in the SEECC report, "Standards for Educators of Exceptional Children in Canada" (Hardy et al., 1971), dealing with current provision of services and teacher training and some of the issues that should be considered in designing future training programs. The report has proven timely with the increasing thrust towards development of undergraduate and graduate courses in special education.

Collaborative Efforts

It is evident that one of the ways in which Canada has shown leadership in developing services for children with learning disabilities has been through collaborative, interagency efforts, locally, provincially, and nationally. Many of the services which previously served narrow diagnostic categories of children have combined their resources and now serve many children with different developmental deviations. The crossing of the lines of discipline and orientation is increasingly evident. For example, parents representing local associations in Edmonton and Toronto have been involved in designing professional training at the University of Alberta and York University. In several cities in Canada the local groups of the Council for Exceptional Children and the Association for Children with Learning Disabilities function as a combined group and a successful working relationship has been established. In such instances, the usual parent-professional dichotomy does not exist, but instead both groups share a combined commitment to a common goal. Recently the Canadian Paediatric Society published "A Practical Office Manual" (Crichton et al., 1972) in which two pediatricians, a psychologist, and an educator collaborated in an attempt to provide practical information to family doctors and pediatricians concerning means of assessment and treatment for the learning disabled child. Similarly, Kronick has written and edited several books for parents, reviewing the roles of medicine, education, psychology, and parent-group organizations. In addition, these books present suggestions for dealing with the problems of children with learning disabilities (Kronick, 1969a, 1969b, 1973). She has also compiled a directory for learning disabilities help across Canada (Kronick, 1970).

Cooperative and multidisciplinary methods are also demonstrable in some of the recent educational programs set up across Canada for the treatment of children with learning disabilities.

STANDARD EDUCATIONAL APPROACHES

As a result of pressure from private and government organizations the importance of developing special educational facilities for the learning disabled child has recently become evident to school boards across the country. Consequently, most Boards of Education in the larger centers of Canada have incorporated professional consultants and special classroom programs into their systems to serve the learning disabled child as well as children with mental retardation, emotional disturbances, and behavioral problems. Some smaller school systems do not provide the more extensive services available in the cities, but they do often have at least a consulting psychologist or special education teacher, whose function is to assess children with special problems and to suggest appropriate teaching procedures to the regular classroom teacher.

The Carleton Board of Education in Ottawa, Ontario typifies the extent of facilities available for children with special learning disabilities and other problems in a large urban center. The Board serves 37,000 children and has a variety of specialists including six psychologists, four social workers, five special education consultants, four speech correctionists, one speech therapist, and one counselor for the hearing impaired. In addition there are two attendance officers. These consultants are involved in assessments of individual children, the development of special training programs, and work in conjunction with regular and special classroom teachers. Although many children with learning disorders are able to function within a regular classroom, there are 19 special classes for learning disabilities, as well as four social adjustment classes, three rehabilitation classes for learning disabilities that become evident at the intermediate level, and 19 opportunity classes which include some children with learning disabilities and higher functioning, educable retarded children. There are six resource units in the various elementary schools and 11 resource units for children with learning problems at the secondary school level. Each unit has a part- or full-time specially trained teacher.

The concept of a resource unit or a resource room is a very popular and recent development in helping learning disabled children to cope within the standard educational system. A highly effective resource room program for high school students has been organized and implemented in Toronto, Ontario. The resource teachers describe their program as directed toward meeting the needs of students who are capable of following a regular high school schedule as long as they have additional assistance. The resource rooms are set up in collegiate schools which prepare students for university entrance, in composite schools which cater to the general level student, and also in academic and vocational training schools. Students are first recommended for the program by their classroom teachers or guidance personnel and assessed by the Board of Education psychologists to determine the area of their disabilities. They are then considered for entrance to the program by an admission board consisting of psychologists, special educators, guidance staff, and administrators from the elementary feeder schools and from the secondary schools concerned.

The service is not like a special class placement since the students follow a regular high school program, except that one of the periods in each school day is set aside for individual remedial and tutorial help in the resource room. The student's program is adjusted to stress strong abilities and interests. Ontario has recently adopted a secondary school credit system which allows for maximum flexibility in subject choice.

Each student is repeatedly counseled concerning the kind and extent of help available to him. Remedial programs are chosen by the student together with resource room staff. Much emphasis is placed on the multisensory approach in both the remedial and tutorial programs, and the interaction between one teacher and one student is stressed as a method of facilitating both oral and written expressive language.

Regular meetings to discuss the progress of resource room students involve participation by the psychologist, guidance counselor, principal, and all the subject teachers of a particular student. The student's strengths and weaknesses are outlined, while the regular teachers inform each other about the student's classroom behavior. Strategies for improving the student's function in all necessary areas are then discussed. Added intercommunication with regular staff is facilitated with memos, evaluation check sheets, and phone calls concerning individual students.

Parents are acquainted with resource room programs and expectations of the school, and information is obtained from parents which may help in understanding the student. When a parent, teacher, or student expresses concern over courses, assignments, or progress, a meeting is called which may also be attended by the other concerned staff. The student is always included. He takes an active part in all decision-making since he is the one who must take ultimate responsibility for himself.

Generally, it has been observed that resource room students are able to cope adequately on their own in high school after 2 years of resource room help. Spare period study time in the resource room is continued as well as extended time for examinations when necessary. At the end of about 2 years, students have developed a fairly clear idea of their own strengths and weaknesses, realistic goals, and strategies to compensate for learning difficulties.

SOME UNIQUE EDUCATIONAL PROGRAMS

Edmonton Preschool Screening Project

In September 1972, the Edmonton Preschool Screening Project was initiated following a 3-year pilot project. The Edmonton Board of Health, the Glenrose Provincial Hospital Departments of Speech Pathology and Audiology and Psychology, and the University of Alberta Hospital Orthoptic Clinic are participating in the project under the directorship of Dr. Jean Nelson, with funding provided by the Medical Research Foundation of Alberta. Children from ages 4.5 to 5.5 years are assessed by public health aides on psychological tests as well as tests of hearing, vision, speech, and language.

All test results are stored on computer tape, and modern data retrieval techniques are used to select each child with a disability and also a matched control child. All findings are available to the local board of health physician who examines the suspect children and interprets the findings to the parents and family doctor. Children are then referred to developmental programs. In 1973 the government of Alberta introduced legislation which provides special grants for handicapped students in preschool programs. This should serve as impetus for additional program development.

Acadia University Project Trailer

In 1970, Dr. T. Tillemans of the School of Education at Acadia University in Wolfville, Nova Scotia, began a program, Project Trailer, designed to deliver services to children in the surrounding school districts, as well as to provide preservice training to future teachers and in-service education to practicing teachers. After an invitation by a school principal, the trailer is parked on the school grounds for up to 6 months. Under faculty supervision, a graduate student is placed in charge of administration and organization of services available from the trailer.

Undergraduate and graduate students from the university screen the school children with an assessment battery including the Acadia Test of Developmental Abilities (a group test designed for this purpose), teacher's referrals, or student rating scales to determine the children who require additional help from project trailer. The diagnostic-remedial techniques utilized are oriented to the child's past and present. There is an attempt to locate the primary disability, as well as an effort to probe the secondary emotional repercussions in the history of the interaction between the child and his environment.

The project views education as a process of interaction among teachers, future teachers, graduates, undergraduates, parents, and children, in which everyone has something to offer and much to learn regardless of his age. The trailer brings new concepts to the schools and provides support for those who wish to try them. The university consults with school personnel as to the best method of delivering services to all children in a school district who, since January 1973, have lawfully been entitled to appropriate instruction. It assists school boards in identifying children with learning disabilities, offers in-service education by videotape via extension department, assists in volunteer training, and helps school personnel in formulating problems and seeking answers.

The original trailer project has been expanded into a double trailer program, a farm program for children with mental and physical handicaps, a diagnostic center, an adult training program, and a high-risk identification and intervention program. These programs operate on an interdisciplinary-interagency basis involving local resources and employing universities for backup support. They are intended to serve as models of integrated, complementary services for the province.

The McGill University, Montreal Children's Hospital Learning Centre

The Learning Centre was formally established at the Montreal Children's Hospital in 1960 under the direction of Dr. M. Sam Rabinovitch. It was launched as a result of the common concern of psychiatrists, psychologists, and pediatricians for children who have great difficulty learning in a manner and at a rate expected of them, particularly in a school setting. The Centre's staff and facilities are now jointly sponsored by Montreal Children's Hospital and McGill University, with a considerable portion of its funding from a private donor. The staff includes two full-time English-speaking psychologists, one full-time French-speaking psychologist, four part-time psychologists, a consultant psychiatrist, an expert on behavior modification, a social worker, a student social worker, an optometric consultant, a physician, one English- and one French-speaking teacher, three part-time teachers, three teachers seconded to the Centre from the Protestant (English) school board, and art and music specialists.

There is an extensive assessment battery administered, after which the staff decides whether the child requires tutoring at the Centre or whether he can receive sufficient assistance from his own school. The teachers who have been assigned to the Centre from the school board provide an outreach service for children on the Centre's waiting list for tutoring or assessment, for children who have been in some of the Centre's programs in the past, and for children who are referred by the school board. As a result, these teachers spend part of their day working directly with children at the Centre, and the remainder of their time with these and other students in the regular school system. The Centre provides materials for classroom teachers and the Centre's staff visits the teachers sufficiently often to ensure that suggested changes are implemented.

Since the Learning Centre's inception its staff has had a particularly positive orientation toward parent inclusion. Parents frequently are encouraged to be present during the entire diagnostic procedure so that they can begin to comprehend the difficulties their child is having. Following diagnosis, each parent is enlisted as an active participant in the therapeutic program. Parents are not encouraged to continue the same lessons and programs used by the Centre's staff, but are advised to apply similar techniques to everyday living in the home. Parents are kept fully informed of all the methods used to assist their child in making progress. The child's teacher at the Centre provides the link between the Centre and the home by listening to parents, making suggestions to them, and dealing with their questions and anxieties. Individual counseling with the social worker is provided when required, and also fathers' and mothers' groups have been organized to provide education and counseling.

Currently three additional programs are in operation: a summer program for elementary school children; a summer program for adolescents which provides educational instruction as well as sports, crafts and special projects; and a big brother/sister program supervised by the Centre's social worker, with emphasis on the development of social and independence skills for the learning disabled.

Centre for Educational Disabilities, University of Guelph

In 1965, Dr. Denis H. Stott opened a clinic in Guelph, Ontario, for "troublesome" children (Stott, 1966). He has proposed a behavioral (but not behavioristic) theory of learning disabilities and mental retardation in which he emphasized that most of these children have developed false learning styles or cognitive processes. He defines appropriate learning behavior as that which involves: (1) attention, (2) the ability to withhold impulsive responses, (3) motivation towards competence, and (4) social motivation to be involved in appropriate learning tasks. Correction of the inadequate learning styles utilizes standard learning principles to develop the appropriate learning behavior. His training programs are set within a game context in which appropriate problem solving and learning style are rewarded as they bring success. All the games demand attention, reflectivity, and confidence. They are self-correcting, and knowledge of the outcome of the response is immediate so that the child can relate it to the learning style he has used. To this end Dr. Stott has developed a number of detailed training kits for parents and teachers.

The Integra Foundation

The Integra Foundation was formed in 1966 by a group of parents, professionals, and businessmen. Their intent was to determine methods of teaching the learning disabled child other than within a formal academic model. Other objectives involved the provision of important supplementary experience for students of relevant professions, and the operation of seed services which would serve to encourage the establishment of other programs throughout Ontario.

The first program developed in 1967 was Camp Towhee, a 6-week residential camp for learning disabled children. The Foundation determines the children suitable for the camp from psychiatric and psychological data supplied by school boards, clinics, and other sources, as well as by staff interviews. Before the camp session, the child, his parents, and the Integra staff establish social, behavioral, and remedial objectives for the summer. A comprehensive picture is obtained of his current academic standing, current remedial approaches employed, and his teacher's goals and concerns—all this material is taken into account in planning the formal and informal aspects of the youngster's summer.

Staff at the camp includes a psychologist, consulting psychologist, pediatrician, psychiatrist, two language therapists, and four special education teachers. All the camp counselors are students or practitioners in the field. There are three adult counselors for each group of six children, and this staff is augmented by remedial and activity personnel, thus allowing for individualized remedial programs as well as regular camping activities. The remedial staff functions as aides to the counselors, teaching the counselors the methods of remediation and behavioral management techniques through the camping and self-care aspects of the program. Some of the most exciting and creative facets of the program occur in "remediation through camping."

Parents visit the camp at midseason and the last weekend. They meet with a senior staff person to review the precamp goals and the child's accomplishments, to obtain suggestions for home and school management, and to decide on the necessity for additional professional services. The parents, school, and referring agency then receive a detailed copy of this material. When a Towhee camper acquires the social and behavioral skills to function in a regular camping situation he is referred to such a setting.

The Foundation also has a full-time community liaison staff consisting of a psychologist, social worker, special education teacher, and child care worker. This team provides a global follow-up program to children who are enrolled for services, with the emphasis being to orient and utilize local agencies and professionals in providing family therapy, speech therapy, remediation, or recreation.

The Integra Foundation provides workshops throughout the province for parents, teachers, recreation personnel, students, and other professionals concerned with the diagnosing and educating of the learning disabled child. In addition to assuming primary sponsorship for a number of services, the Foundation becomes involved in shared programming throughout the province. Examples are the Wellesley Remedial Program, which serves as an individualized supplementary program to school remediation for about 50 elementary school children in the Toronto area, and the operation of a day camp in collaboration with the Clarke Institute of Psychiatry, York University, and the Hospital for Sick Children.

RESEARCH PROGRAMS

Victoria, British Columbia

Dr. William Gaddes established the first neuropsychology laboratory in Canada in 1963 at the University of Victoria. The general emphasis of the research included comprehensive assessment of children with learning disorders and/or brain lesions, and the utilization of the test results for planning educational programs. His initial work involved the development of the Dynamic Visual Retention Test in which serial order was added to a visual retention task. In this task the child is required to identify changes in a simple pattern of lights presented sequentially. The test was found to discriminate reliably between brain damaged and normal children.

A major contribution from the Victoria laboratory was the collection of normative data on a wide variety of neuropsychological tests for children, including some of the Reitan (1964) modifications of the Halstead (1947) tests (Spreen and Gaddes, 1969). Dr. Gaddes has also been concerned with providing educators with information about brain-behavior relationships, especially in the areas of handedness and cerebral dominance. This type of knowledge assists teachers to comprehend a child's capabilities and limitations (Gaddes, 1969).

Vancouver, British Columbia

In the Psychiatry Department of the University of British Columbia, Dr. Harry Klonoff has completed several factor analytic studies of a large neuropsychological test battery, as well as investigations of the psychometric characteristics of acute and chronic brain syndromes. The results of the factor analyses are complex; to briefly summarize, it was found that the number of factors identified increased with age from 9 in the younger group (5 to 8 years) to 19 in the older (9 to 15 years) age group. It was also noted that whereas some factors corresponded to the verbal-performance division of the WISC, a large number of the factors were independent of the psychometric measures of intelligence. For the younger children, there were 5 factors that were independent of intelligence measures, including tasks such as finger oscillation speed and the visual matching of shapes. In contrast there were 14 factors that appeared for the older groups, suggesting that there is an increasing degree of independence between neuropsychological and intelligence variables (Klonoff, 1971a). Studies comparing acute and chronic brain damage were performed. Analysis of the neuropsychological test battery provided differences in test pattern between the two groups. Both groups showed signs of psychological deficits when compared to normal children on 25 out of 32 variables. A study of the sequelae of head injuries in children found that the short-term effects were predicted from the neuropsychological test results, but the correlation with long-term effects was much less reliable (Klonoff, 1971b).

Windsor, Ontario

Dr. Bryon Rourke and his students at the University of Windsor Psychology Department and the Imperial Order of Daughters of the Empire Regional Children's Centre have completed several studies investigating the correlates of Verbal and Performance IQ levels on the Wechsler Intelligence Scale for Children (Rourke, Dietrich, and Young, 1973). They found that in older children with learning disabilities, a verbal-performance IQ discrepancy was reflected in other auditory-perceptual and visual-perceptual neuropsychological tests; however, this relationship did not occur when similar comparisons were made in children under 8 years of age. Another area of investigation has been the study of reaction time in brain damaged children. They found that in visual and auditory reaction time tasks, a younger group of brain damaged children (6 to 9 years old) performed less rapidly than normal children of the same age, older brain damaged children, and the older normal children (Rourke and Czunder, 1972). These results are interpreted to suggest that older brain damaged children adapt to, or recover from the deficits involved in the ability to develop and maintain a state of readiness to respond.

Kitchener-Waterloo, Ontario

An interesting method of treatment of impulsive children has been studied by Dr. Donald H. Meichenbaum of the University of Waterloo Psychology Department. He has emphasized the importance of the role of verbal control of motor behavior in children, especially internal verbal control, in which a child talks to himself and therefore helps to direct his own behavior. On the assumption that impulsive children do not normally talk to themselves and therefore have difficulty in controlling their behavior, he has devised a method of training what he terms self-instruction. In several studies of a variety of motor and problem-solving tests, the children who were trained in cognitive self-guidance, that is, to talk to themselves, showed a significant improvement in performance (Meichenbaum and Goodman, 1971).

London and Ottawa, Ontario

In conjunction with the establishment of a neuropsychological laboratory, first in London at the University of Western Ontario and then in Ottawa at Carleton University, Dr. Robert Knights and Dr. George Hinton and their graduate students have conducted a series of studies concerning children with minimal brain dysfunction. The emphasis of this work has been on the use of psychometric tests in assessment. The initial papers published normative data on a battery of tests including the Reitan (1964) modifications for children of the Halstead adult tests for the assessment of the effects of cerebral lesions (Knights, 1966). Subsequent studies investigated the variables affecting children's performance on several of the tests, including the Tactual Formboard Test, and the simplified versions of the Category Test of abstract reasoning. These studies suggest that the children's versions of these tests do not necessarily provide the reliable discrimination between normal and brain damaged individuals that occur in studies of adults. Three studies related the neuropsychological test findings to learning problems as well as various seizure conditions, and found the IQ and achievement tests more sensitive to academic success than the motor, sensory, and visuo-motor tests, but differentially sensitive to different types of seizure classifications (Hinton and Knights, 1967). Two studies related global electroencephalograph (EEG) ratings to the results of the neuropsychological test battery with unexpected findings. Children with psychiatric problems who showed any type of abnormal

EEG patterns scored higher in over-all levels of performance than similar children with normal EEG patterns, and the abnormal slow-wave EEG pattern was associated with lower test performance on measures of academic achievement.

Two studies of drug efficacy, one conducted in London and one in Ottawa, found the stimulants methylphenidate and pemoline to significantly improve the behavior of hyperactive boys. These changes were most clearly demonstrated on the parent and teacher ratings, and a review paper of 18 drug studies drew similar conclusions (Knights, 1974).

A unique approach of the research program has been the use of the computer as a means of plotting a neuropsychological test profile. The child's raw scores on each subtest variable were compared with the normative data for his age group and were plotted in standard score form. This test profile was then compared with all other profiles in the data bank in an attempt to determine whether similar profiles would be produced when the cause of a child's neurological impairment was similar. Results of these studies showed high correlation when the disorder was acute and/or localized; however, the similarity of profiles decreased when the cerebral dysfunction was diffuse and/or long standing (Knights, 1973).

Montreal, Quebec

During the past 10 years, several research programs have been conducted in Montreal. An outstanding interdisciplinary team associated with the Montreal Children's Hospital and McGill University Psychology Department has emphasized studies of the hyperactive child. It has studied the effectiveness of drug treatment, the psychometric abilities of hyperactive children, and their long-term progress. An excellent summary of this work is contained in Douglas (1972).

The work on drug use has examined the effects of both tranquilizers and stimulants. Chlorpromazine, a tranquilizer, was found to produce no change in cognitive abilities, while methylphenidate was effective in assisting the hyperactive child to sustain attention and control his impulsivity.

The psychometric test data collected by Douglas and her associates have shown that hyperactive children score lower on drawing and motor ability tests. In a concept attainment task, hyperactive children demonstrated equal abilities to normal children, although their performance was more erratic. Furthermore, in the same task under partial rather than continuous reinforcement conditions, the hyperactive children's performance was more severely impaired than that of the normal children. In a vigilance task, hyperactives performed at a lower level than normals, in that they made more responses to incorrect stimuli and more misses of correct stimuli. In another attention task, autonomic measures were taken;

although hyperactive children did not differ from normals when sitting, listening to tones, they showed a completely different pattern of orienting responses in a delayed reaction-time task, indicating a relative unresponsiveness and again erratic behavior.

Another study concerning attention demonstrated that hyperactive children made more impulsive responses and, therefore, more errors in matching similar figures and in isolating imbedded figures from background fields.

These and similar studies have led this group of investigators to conclude that hyperactive children reveal no differences from normal children in language, comprehension, or conceptual abilities, or in short-term memory. Their primary problem is one of inadequate control of sustained attention and impulsivity. A review paper includes a survey of the literature on the pattern of abilities and deficits in these children and methods of treatment and training (Douglas, 1974).

The neurologically oriented studies have discovered a tendency for pre- and paranatal abnormality in the developmental histories of hyperactive children, as well as visuomotor, minor neurological, and early infantile adjustment abnormalities, although they also noted the unreliability of parent reports. EEG abnormalities also occurred, but there was a difference in the type of abnormality (slow dysrhythmia) rather than an excessive amount. A later study confirmed the excess of neurological abnormalities in hyperactive children and noted that the distinction was in soft neurological signs as revealed in sensorimotor incoordination (Werry et al., 1972).

The group of hyperactive children who were involved in the early Montreal series of studies are now being followed by Dr. Weiss and reassessed as they progress through the school system. The first report of this work is a 5-year follow-up which reveals that the activity level diminishes with age but disorders of attention and concentration persist. Furthermore, underachievement and emotional problems, both a function of the earlier hyperactivity, remained as debilitating problems to these children.

Also associated with the McGill University Psychology Department is Dr. Sam Rabinovitch. He and his students have investigated the auditory abilities of children with learning problems and these studies include comparisons of acuity and perception of sounds, tones, and nonsense sentences in good and poor readers. It was found that many children with learning problems do not differ from normal children on various auditory tasks, but they do show deficits in the areas of discrimination of pitch, simultaneous tones, successive tones, and speech sounds (Doehring and Rabinovitch, 1969) and in the ability to make use of syntactic and structural cues. Other research has investigated the lack of observed differences between normal and learning disability children in serial-ordering ability on visual, auditory, and tactual tasks. Learning disabled and normal children have also been compared on a measure of hemispheric speech lateralization, as inferred from performance on a dichotic listening task. It was noted that the learning disabled children showed a greater tendency for right hemisphere lateralization of speech rather than the usual left hemisphere specialization for speech (Witelson and Rabinovitch, 1972).

Dr. Donald Doehring, also at McGill University in the School of Human Communication Disorders, published a comprehensive study (1968) of the patterns of impairment in specific reading disability as revealed on a large neuropsychological test battery. This study of 78 normal readers and 39 poor readers, 2 years behind their expected reading level, examined their performance on 109 subtest variables which assessed motor, sensory, language, and cognitive skills. Two major findings were that the impairment in abilities shown by the poor readers included not only their reading difficulty but other more general deficits, especially in the sequential processing of visual and verbal material (Doehring, 1968).

CONCLUSION

It has always been a fact that some children learn more easily than others, but only during the last century have differences in learning skill come under scientific study. This review of the Canadian approach to the problem of learning disabilities indicates that there has been a recent national commitment to the learning disordered child—in the amount of research concerning these disabilities, in the legislation providing for educational opportunities, in parent and volunteer organizations, and in the comprehensive CELDIC and SEECC reports which have served to emphasize the urgency of the problem and to establish objectives and priorities for the implementation of treatment and educational programs.

REFERENCES

A more complete list of references for all of the studies referred to in this chapter is available from the senior author.

Canadian Association for Children with Learning Disabilities, Head Office, 4746 The Boulevard, Montreal, Quebec.
CELDIC. 1970. One Million Children. Crainford, Toronto.
Crichton, J., J. Catterson, D. Kendall, and H. Dunn. 1972. Learning Disabilities: A Practical Office Manual. Canadian Paediatric Society, Victoria.

Doehring, D. G. 1968. Patterns of Impairment in Specific Reading Disabilities. Indiana University Press, Bloomington.

Doehring, D. G., and M. S. Rabinovitch. 1969. Auditory abilities of children with learning problems. J. Learning Disabil. 2:467.

Douglas, V. I. 1972. Stop, look and listen: the problem of sustained attention and impulse control in hyperactive and normal children. Can. J. Behav. Sci. 4:259.

Douglas, V. I. 1974. Sustained attention and impulse control: implications for the handicapped child. In J. A. Swets and L. L. Elliott (eds.), Psychology and the Handicapped Child. United States Government Publications Office, Washington, D.C.

Gaddes, W. H. 1969. Can educational psychology be neurologized? Can. J. Behav. Sci. 1:38.

Halstead, W. C. 1947. Brain and Intelligence. The University of Chicago Press, Chicago.

Hardy, M. I., J. McLeod, H. Minto, S. Perkins, and W. R. Quance. 1971. Standards for Educators of Exceptional Children in Canada. Crainford, Toronto.

Hinton, G. G., and R. M. Knights. 1967. Neurological and psychological test characteristics of 100 children with seizures. In B. W. Richards (ed.), First Congress of the International Association of the Scientific Study of Mental Deficiency. Michael Jackson Company, Surrey, Eng.

Klonoff, H. 1971a. Factor analysis of a neuropsychological battery for children aged 9 to 15. Percept. Mot. Skills 32:603.

Klonoff, H. 1971b. Head injuries in children: predisposing factors, accident conditions, accident proneness and sequelae. Amer. J. of Pub. Health 61:2405.

Knights, R. M. 1966. Normative data on tests for evaluating brain damage in children 5 to 14 years. Res. Bull. No. 20, University of Western Ontario. (Mimeo)

Knights, R. M. 1973. A problem of criteria in diagnosis; A profile similarity approach. Ann. N. Y. Acad. Sci. 205:124.

Knights, R. M. 1974. Psychometric assessment of drug-induced behavior change. In Proceedings of Abbott Laboratories Symposium on The Clinical Use of Stimulant Drugs in Children. Abbott Laboratories, Chicago.

Kronick, D. Ed. 1969a. Learning Disabilities: Its Implications to a Responsible Society. Developmental Learning Materials, Chicago.

Kronick, D. Ed. 1969b. They Too Can Succeed: A Practical Guide for Parents. Academic Therapy Publications, San Rafael, Ca.

Kronick, D. 1970. Directory of learning disabilities help across Canada. Chatelaine Mag. 43(10):100.

Kronick, D. 1973. A Word or Two About Learning Disabilities. Academic Therapy Publications, San Rafael, Ca.

Meichenbaum, D. H., and J. Goodman. 1971. Training impulsive children to talk to themselves: a means of developing self-control. J. Abnorm. Psychol. 77:115.

Reitan, R. M. 1964. Relationships between neurological and psychological variables and their implications for reading instruction. In H. A. Robinson (ed.), Meeting Individual Differences in Reading. University of Chicago Press, Chicago.

Rourke, B. P., and G. Czunder. 1972. Age differences in auditory reaction time of "brain damaged" and normal children under regular and irregular preparatory interval conditions. J. Exp. Child Psychol. 14:372.

Rourke, B. P., B. M. Dietrich, and G. C. Young. 1973. Significance of WISC verbal-performance discrepancies for younger children with learning disabilities. Percept. Mot. Skills 36:275.

Spreen, O. and W. H. Gaddes. 1969. Developmental norms for 15 neuropsychological tests age 6 to 15. Cortex 5:171.

Stott, D. H. 1966. Studies of Troublesome Children. Tavistock Publications, London.

Werry, J. 1968. Studies on the hyperactive child. IV. An empirical analysis of the minimal brain dysfunction syndrome. Arch. Gen. Psychiatry 19:9.

Werry, J. S., K. Minde, A. Guzman, G. Weiss, K. Dogan, and E. Hoy. 1972. Studies on the hyperactive child. VII. Neurological status compared with neurotic and normal children. Amer. J. Orthopsychiatr. 42:441.

Witelson, S. F., and M. S. Rabinovitch. 1972. Hemispheric speech lateralization in children with auditory-linguistic deficits. Cortex 8:412.

CHAPTER 7

Reading Problems of Chinese Children

Susan Ruth Butler
With an Addendum by Wei-fan Kuo and Mei-Ho Lin Kuo

In the People's Republic of China, Mandarin, which is based on the Peiping (Peking) dialect of Northern China, is the national language. The Chinese call it *putong hua,* or common language, emphasizing its function as a *lingua franca* throughout China. All school children learn *putong hua* and most people under 30 years of age can speak it. Many of the older people, however, speak only the dialect of the place where they live. The principal dialect in Taiwan is Mandarin, while in Hong Kong the dialect is Cantonese, a dialect of Southern China.

Spoken and written Chinese were originally closely related by pictograms. The script was developed about 1700 B.C., when the Chinese were settled along the Yellow River. Oldest examples of the writing occur as inscriptions carved in "oracle bones" which were bones used to ask gods whether the omens were good for setting out on hunting expeditions. In later centuries, the Chinese people expanded into neighboring areas where they came into contact with tribal peoples and this, combined with the passage of time, led them to produce numerous dialectal groups and subgroups.

The script, standardized in the third century, B.C., is basically the same as Confucius' time, except that the forms of many pictograms have been simplified and new words have been invented by combining various pictograms. For example, originally the word *strength* was depicted by a picture of a plow, and later it was simplified (Figure 1). The idea of *male* as being someone who employs strength in the field is conveyed by combining the two pictograms, *field* and *strength,* to form a new character, *male* (Figure 1).

PLOW

STRENGTH

FIELD

男

MALE

(EMPLOYING STRENGTH

IN THE FIELD)

Figure 1. Originally *strength* was depicted by a pictogram of a plow. Later it was simplified as shown (upper right). The word *male* became *strength* plus *field* to indicate the idea of employing strength in the field.

SOCIAL AND EDUCATIONAL BACKGROUND

Hong Kong

Unlike the People's Republic of China, where formal learning begins at 7.5 years of age, the elementary stages of learning in Hong Kong commence at 3 years of age when the children begin to recognize and write individual Chinese characters in kindergarten. Some children are taught at home and enter kindergarten later. Kindergarten is of 2 years' duration, and at the age of 5 the children enter primary school for 6 years. Education is not compulsory in Hong Kong but the majority of children attend at least primary school.

At the end of primary school, the children take a fiercely competitive public examination to determine whether they will enter government-controlled schools, government-subsidized schools, or assisted places (scholarships) in private schools. There is also a private avenue of education.

The People's Republic of China

Before the Revolution education has always been the exclusive right of the wealthy in China. Since formal education was costly and laborious only the sons of landlords, officials, and merchants could afford to spend years preparing for the highly competitive, impractical examinations which led to official appointments.

When the Communists came to power in 1949, liberation turned the old Chinese educational system on its head. Approximately 80% of the people were illiterate. Literacy meant the ability to read a newspaper, which requires the knowledge of about 3,000 ideograms (Ed. note: About 7,000 ideograms are required for "adequate" reading of Hong Kong newspapers). In 1949, the general school pattern was similar to the American, with school entry at 6 years of age.

On May 25, 1966, the Cultural Revolution began at Peking University. Some departments of the University reopened in 1970 but no postgraduate work has yet commenced. The aims of education were questioned and, as a result, the length of schooling was reduced to 5 years of primary education, 2 years of junior middle school, 2 years of senior middle school, followed by 2 years of farm or factory experience, and 2 years of tertiary education. Education was set up as a means of mobilizing the masses to accomplish the goals of nation-building and to achieve a unified proletarian society, a society based on selfless endeavor rather than individual interest. Thus education is conceived as an integral stabilizing force in the social system of China. In Hong Kong, on the other hand, some parents pressure their children to try to gain entrance to specific kindergartens and primary schools which they feel are better. The element of competition starts early and predominates throughout the system.

Also, unlike Hong Kong where the hours of school are similar to the West, in the People's Republic of China, school begins at 7:30 or 8 a.m. and usually ends at 5 p.m. It is in session from Monday through Saturday, with a half-day on Saturday. Some schools operate more than one shift and the timetable is altered accordingly while others have part-time classes. Eighty percent of the children receive 5 years of primary schooling, many in the cities complete the 2 years of junior secondary school, but as yet, few finish the full 9-year course. The schools are traditional low buildings with box-like classrooms surrounded by dirt, grass, or paved recreation areas. There are few audio-visual aids. Primary school enrollments are estimated at 95% in urban areas and 80% in rural areas, but in such a vast country this estimate of a 127,000,000 enrollment is only rough. Approximately 37,000,000 attend secondary school and another 200,000 attend universities. It is estimated that there are 3,500,000 primary and secondary school teachers. There is a shortage of teachers which is partly due to closing the universities during the cultural revolution.

It is believed that no single person has all the skills required to direct a school, hence a rural school is run by a revolutionary committee which includes teachers, peasants, soldiers and students. In the city, workers replace the peasants on this committee. This committee not only administers the school but also handles the determination of courses, teaching methods, and text books. There is a central publishing house at the national level which publishes the best of the locally produced texts. Local committees have the autonomy to use these texts or to make up their own mimeographed texts using material they feel is more relevant to their school.

Some fourth-class pupils learn English as a foreign language. During primary schooling generally two months of the year are spent in physical labor, in a factory, on a farm, or in a military unit. Some children continue beyond primary school; they are selected on the basis of political views, health, and academic performance. Similar selection operates for tertiary training with emphasis on recommendations by fellow workers.

Teaching Chinese

The approach to teaching Chinese is the same in Hong Kong as in the People's Republic of China, with the exception that the children in Hong Kong begin at an earlier age. The same Chinese characters are used in Hong Kong and the People's Republic of China. However, in Hong Kong the pronunciation of the same character would be in Cantonese rather than Mandarin.

At school the children simultaneously learn to write the characters in accordance with stroke sequence, form, and orientation (Figure 2). Generally the children begin repeatedly copying the characters presented on the chalkboard by using pencils or ball point pens on square lined paper. Subsequently they learn to hold the brush pen in the appropriate manner. Each finger has its different role to play. First the index finger is wrapped around the brush stem from the outside and it is backed up by placing the thumb on the inside. The brush is held in an upright manner perpendicular to the paper. The first section of the middle finger is wrapped on the brush immediately below the index finger and balanced with the knuckle of the ring finger on the inside. Thus the brush is set in a firm position with the little finger snugly behind the ring finger for support. The wrist is held parallel to the desk as shown in Figure 3.

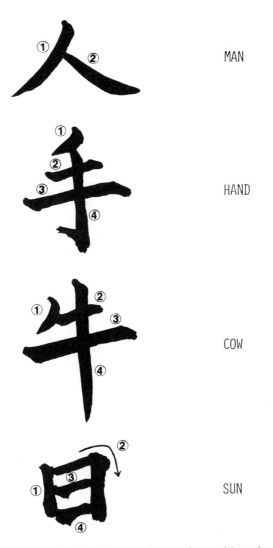

Figure 2. Children learn to write the characters in accordance with stroke sequence, form and orientation.

Like the golf grip, the brush grip is unnatural and needs practice. In the early stages of using the brush, the teacher holds the pupil's hand to guide him to achieve the correct grip. It is not unknown for the teacher to occasionally try, without any warning, to knock the brush out of the child's hand to test the child's grip. The children receive intensive practice by tracing lightly printed sets of characters.

Figure 3. Brush grip.

六

Figure 4. Lined squares used to learn writing.

風

Fl. Flexidis

Figure 5. Children learn to associate concrete objects or scenes with the pictograms. "Wind" is illustrated. Based on *General Knowledge for Kindergartens,* Book 1.

Subsequently, the children proceed to copy more stylish forms of characters by inserting a master sheet under a transparent piece of exercise paper. In a more advanced stage they begin to do free drawings of characters, imitating the master sheet. This imitation is aided by copying the characters onto lined squares to assist in the orientation of the characters (Figure 4).

The school child first learns to associate concrete objects with pictures and their relevant characters. Examples of these lessons are seen in drawings depicting "wind" and "rain" (Figures 5 and 6). The children learn to recognize and imitate characters singly and in sentences as can be seen in typical lessons depicting the morals "do not argue," and "do not litter" (Figures 7 and 8). Later the children learn to use characters to compose their own stories.

In the People's Republic of China, the method of rote teaching is similar to that of Hong Kong. The children master about 3,000 characters over a 5-year course. During the first term 340 characters are introduced,

106706

雨

Figure 6. Children learn to associate rain with the pictogram. The picture and pictogram bear a resemblance. Based on *General Knowledge for Kindergartens,* Book 1.

and by the end of the first year some 700 characters are learned. Approximately two-thirds of the primary school language course consists of learning the characters. The children learn the traditional as well as the simplified script. The emphasis, as in Hong Kong, is on the traditional mass drill. New characters are introduced, and explained, and practiced endlessly. Chinese literature is introduced as early as possible with many stories of revolutionary heroes, how the life of today is an improvement over preliberation days, and how important it is to build an industrious, selfless, strong, and happy society. The children learn to recite, speak correctly, and retell stories.

LEARNING DISABILITIES AND REMEDIAL SERVICE

Statistics concerning the incidence of learning disabilities in Hong Kong are not available. There is an awareness and interest in the problem. The special education section of the Department of Education provides

Figure 7. Chinese language lessons tend to teach morals. The picture and the characters say, "not with people argue," reading from top to bottom.

Figure 8. The text reads "litter" (on the left), "not carelessly throw" (on the right), "do not litter."

psychological, audiological, and speech assessments, and follow-up. Limited remedial services are available; there are over 30 special classes for slow-learning children, as well as special classes for blind, deaf, physically handicapped, and maladjusted children. The Department of Education provides in-service training for the teachers involved with these children.

There are also private remedial assessment and educational centers for children with learning problems, and there are private facilities to help the normal child who is not achieving at the level required by his parents or the school he is attending. The social expectation and class structure tend to affect the situation in Hong Kong.

Language Problems

Chinese children with learning difficulties encounter various types of problems. Some extreme cases of mirror reversal have been recorded by private general practitioners. Commonly, children encounter difficulty in maintaining the correct stroke sequence, distinguishing similar looking characters, pronouncing the same character in its appropriate intonation when it is used in a different context, and handling homonyms (which are frequent in the Chinese language).

Incorrect Sequence   The Chinese language requires a total visual perception of a figure at a glance. Incorrect stroke sequence of a simple figure done by a child would not cause difficulty in the recognition of the final form, since even though it may be incorrect, it would be recognizable. However, when the character has many strokes in the wrong sequence, the deformity is compounded and the orientation may be poor, leading to confusion.

Similar-looking Characters   Some characters differ from one another by the relative length of a single stroke or by the presence of an extra stroke. These situations present difficulties for certain children who have problems in distinguishing details (Figure 9).

Intonation   Some characters are pronounced differently when used in different contexts (Figure 10). Beginners with a limited vocabulary may find this confusing. In Figure 10, the two characters at the top mean "go to school" which is pronounced *sēung hau,* but the same initial character, when used in the lower pair, means "up and down" which is pronounced as *seung har.*

Homonyms   The Chinese language is very rich in homonyms. These are different characters which have the same pronunciation. For example, the Cantonese pronunciation *sum* can be written as several different characters with different meanings, including heart, forest, deep, and a proper name.

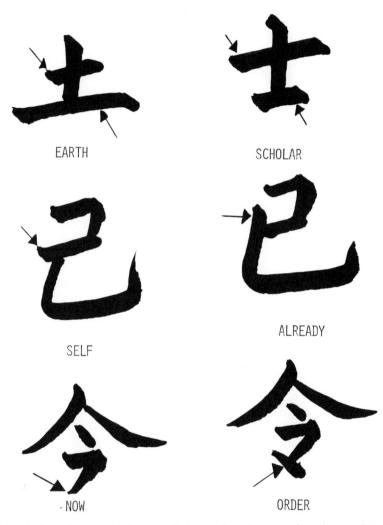

EARTH

SCHOLAR

SELF

ALREADY

· NOW

ORDER

Figure 9. Sometimes the differences between characters may be minor and thus confuse beginners.

The People's Republic of China

Early child care is generally the job of the grandmother, but the child is placed in a crèche if there is no relative to care for him. At the age of 3 he is sent to a kindergarten where he is taught many motor skills as well as the importance of community labor, such as checking the functioning of flashlight bulbs that are ready for sale in the local market.

GO TO SCHOOL

UP AND DOWN

Figure 10. Context may determine meaning.

Unlike Hong Kong where strict discipline was visible for misdemeanors, the child who misbehaves is not disciplined by adults. Instead, the other children collectively persuade him to think of his shortcomings. The approach is for each child to correct his own mistakes and guard against them.

Children who have specific problems in learning are assisted on a regular basis by the children who excel. They have extra coaching by these better pupils or by the teachers during the two periods each day set aside for self-study. Extra coaching may also be arranged at home with help from other pupils or from the retired worker whose job it is to supervise the homework of the children in his area. As in Hong Kong, special attention is focused on stroke sequence and character orientation. Much of the learning continues to be repetitive. If the extra coaching is insufficient to bring the child up to standard, he will be required to repeat his class.

There are other avenues by which a child can excel besides school work. Children's palaces provide extracurricular activity. In Shanghai the building had been the home of a British "imperialist." There is an enrollment of 2,000 children at this center, ranging from 7 to 16 years of age. The children attend once or twice a week and learn to develop different interests and hobbies. Their school teachers receive in-service training in extracurricular activities at the center, and the children return to school and teach the others. The hobbies vary from playing table tennis to making model planes, learning Morse code, learning about acupuncture, or learning how to play a musical instrument. Children are selected for activities because of talent or for their good behavior.

There are also spare-time physical culture centers for children from 7 to 16 years of age where those with special aptitudes may attend 3 times a week from 5 to 7 p.m. Exercise is an integral part of every school day as well. The only special school appears to be the Kwangchow Deaf Mute School which caters to children in Kwangchow (Canton) and the surrounding area. Much of the learning is similar to the rote learning of the other schools. The success rate is claimed to be 80%, but no controlled research has been carried out as yet. Acupuncture as well as antibiotics are used in treatment of the deaf. The only other provision for children requiring special schooling is found in a few departments in hospitals.

Teacher Training

In Hong Kong there are in-service training courses for teachers of special schools and special classes; however, in the People's Republic of China the in-service training program has been set up to teach general rather than specialized skills. In Kwangchow (Canton) for instance, due to the teacher shortage, postgraduates of general courses spend part of each week studying at a special in-service center. In some areas, senior middle school graduates begin teaching after 6 to 12 months of training, while in other areas it has been necessary to fill the teacher gap by selecting children from junior middle schools and training them for from 1 to 12 months before placing them in classrooms. In Shanghai some of the lower primary classes have teachers for the morning sessions only, and retired workers supervise in the afternoons.

Script Reform and Phonetic Alphabet

Mention must be made of the script reform which has been going on in the People's Republic of China. As stated before, the Chinese characters are semantic rather than phonetic, and some extremists advocate the use of the phonetic alphabet to replace the existing script. The advantages presumably gained by such a change would be to improve and popularize the Peking dialect as a standard language and to improve the literacy of the masses. Much planning and debate concerning the reform of the written language have been carried on since the founding of the Republic. The simplification of the existing script is intended as a transitional step towards ultimate phonetization of the written language.

Since the Chinese characters have a long history and are deeply imbedded in Chinese culture, complete eradication of these characters would be difficult. The cultural and political implications of this change would be extremely great. The common people are not used to phonetic

CLOCK

CLOCK
(SIMPLIFIED)

SCHOOL

SCHOOL
(SIMPLIFIED)

Figure 11. Many pictograms have been simplified.

EMPRESS   BEHIND

(HÓU)   (HÓU)

EMPRESS

BEHIND

(HÓU)

Figure 12. In Chinese, the word *hóu* may mean "empress," "behind," or "after." The simplest homophone "empress" is now used for all three words.

spelling, nor is the Peking dialect widespread. The abundance of homophones in the Chinese language would present a further practical problem. There is scant information on the merits and demerits of the Chinese language in terms of learning disabilities. What effect the change of written Chinese characters to a phonetic script would have on the nature and incidence of learning disabilities in Chinese children is unknown.

Since 1956, over 2,000 commonly used characters have been simplified. This has been done by reducing the number of strokes in a character. Most of the simplification has been carried out as shown in Figure 11. Another method of simplification has been to reduce the number of characters. If an existing character's use is widespread enough to cover one or more homophones, the more complex form of the homophone is eliminated. For example, in Figure 12, *hòu*, the more complex character meaning "behind" or "after," has been replaced by the simpler homophone for "empress" which now means "empress," "behind," and "after." The simplification of the ideoforms reduces the difficulty in learning the characters and makes them more convenient to write. As far as homophones are concerned, this widened use is limited to a fairly small number of cases with clearly distinguishable meanings, hence children have little difficulty deciphering the meanings from the context of the passage being read. As change comes slowly to China, especially when tradition is involved, it is unlikely that the truly phonetic script will be incorporated soon.

REFERENCES

Butler, S. R. 1974. Impressions of China Today. Paul Hamlyn, Sydney.
General Knowledge for Kindergartens. Books 1 and 4. Modern Education Research Society, Ltd., Hong Kong.

ADDENDUM[1]   *Wei-fan Kuo and Mei-Ho Lin Kuo*

Based on recent research by Dr. Wei-fan Kuo it appears doubtful that specific reading disabilities, as defined by American authors, exist among Chinese pupils. Dr. Kuo has just completed research on the academically lowest 5% of a group of eighth-grade students in Taipei, Taiwan. These 39 students were given a test battery including an intelligence scale, standardized achievement tests, study-habits inventory, self-concept test, and more than 10 diagnostic tests of attention, visual-motor coordination, visual and auditory memory, laterality, left-right awareness, visual perception, and auditory perception. The data are still being analyzed.

Only three among the 39 were suspected of having problems of visual perception, but these three did not have reading difficulties. There appear to be multivariant factors for the academic failure of these underachieving students.

On the question of the relative abilities of American and Chinese children in the area of eye-hand coordination, there seems to be no difference between these groups. Y. H. Ko, who standardized the Bender Visual Motor Gestalt Test on Chinese children, confirms that oriental and occidental children perform about the same.

---

[1] Summarized from a personal communication to the editors from Mrs. Mei-Ho Lin Kuo.

CHAPTER 8

Dyslexia in Czechoslovakian Children

Zdeněk Matějček

It is most probable that dyslexia has existed for as long as written language itself. There is no doubt that Saints Cyril and Methodius, the missionaries and linguists who in 863 brought to our land their Greek culture and their own original symbols, found not only great enthusiasm for education but also inexplicable problems in reading and writing among their pupils.

The original Glagolic (Figure 1) was soon replaced by Cyrillic (Figure 2) which was in turn replaced by Roman type and script in the early Middle Ages. At the beginning of the 15th century, Jan Hus, the church reformer and rector of Prague University, ingeniously revised Czech spelling. He introduced diacritical marks to supplement the basic Latin alphabetic characters so that each sound had a corresponding letter (Figure 3). Thus, Czech spelling became phonetically consistent. Of the European languages, Spanish is comparable in this respect. Apart from phonetic spelling, Czech is characterized by long words of three and four syllables and complicated grammar similar to Latin.

All this makes possible an analytic-synthetic method of teaching reading and writing which has varied little in recent generations. As soon as a Czech child learns the letters of the Czech alphabet and acquires the basic ability to join them, he can read any word and almost any text. Comprehension is limited only by the range of his vocabulary, which by school age should be several thousand words. Toward the end of the second grade or the beginning of the third grade, Czech children reach the "socially acceptable level" of reading, i.e., approximately 60 to 70 words a minute. This means that reading is relatively fluent and is satisfying to the child.

Parts of this manuscript have previously appeared in the *Bulletin of the Orton Society,* Volumes: XV, 1965; XVIII, 1968; XXI, 1971. Reprinted with permission.

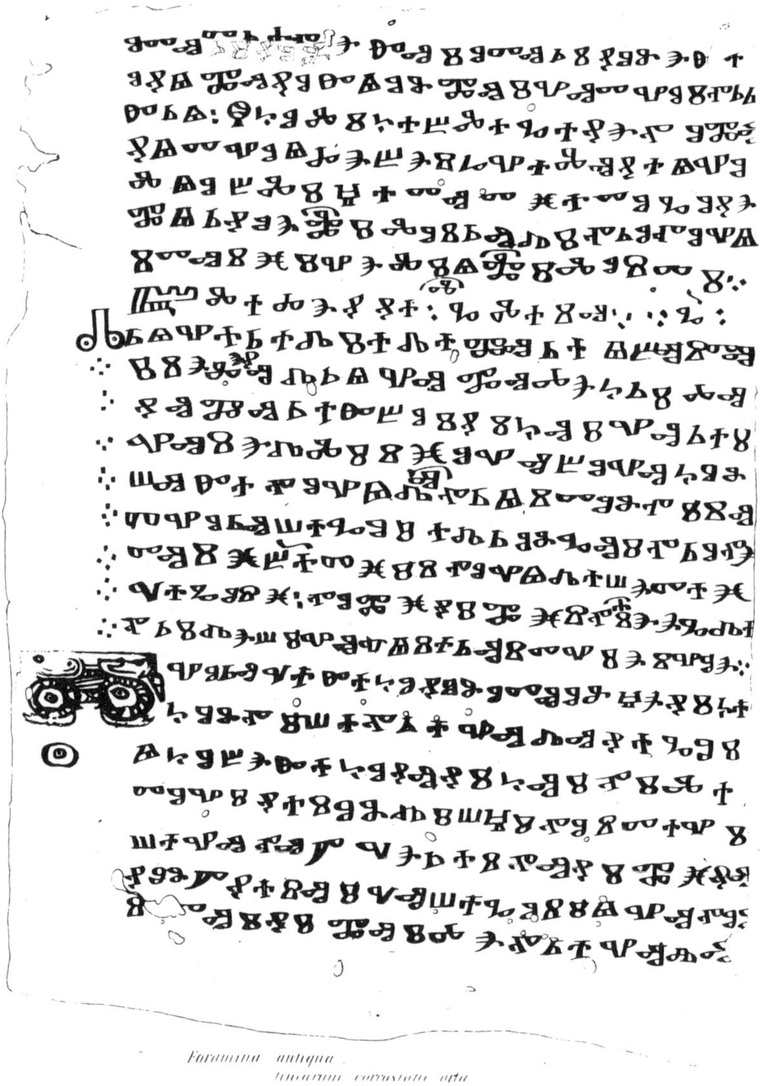

Foramina antiqua
linearum corrosione orta

Figure 1. Prague Fragments, manuscript from 11th century written in Glagolic.

He begins to enjoy books and is able to learn by reading. Reading speed, under these circumstances, is the best individual indicator of reading development. Other indicators such as accuracy and comprehension correlate highly with speed.

Reading and spelling in Czech may be considered to be easy. There are,

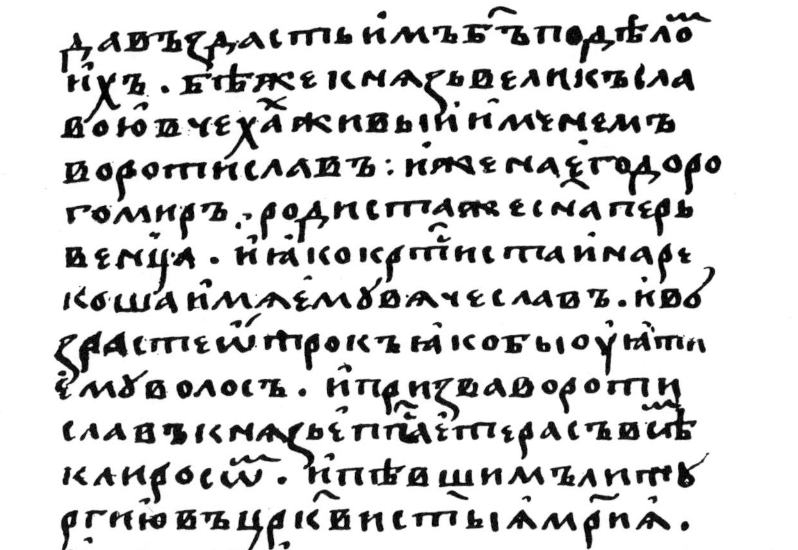

Figure 2. Legend of Saint Venceslaus, written in Cyrillic. Original manuscript from 10th century—copy from 14th century.

however, a few specific hurdles. But these, compared with English, are relatively easily overcome.

The estimate of the incidence of reading disabilities in children depends largely on how we define them, what diagnostic means are available, and to what extent the public is aware of the problem. Using the simplest measure, that is, the difference in grades between Czech language and

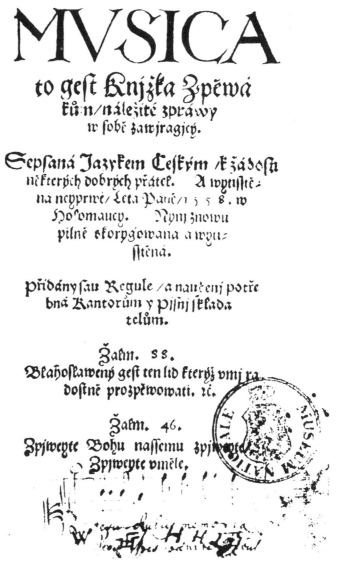

Figure 3. Title page of Jan Blahoslav's MUSICA, 1558. Gothic Latin characters with diacritical marks making the spelling phonetic.

arithmetic on a child's report we have found in schools in Prague, as well as in the country, that around 1.5% of the pupils have their achievement in Czech at least two grades lower than in arithmetic. If we also take into account children who are attending schools for the retarded because of their poor reading, and children who did not receive low grades in Czech because of their teachers' indulgence (considering their very good results in other subjects), then the number approximates 2% of our children. This corresponds to the figure indicated by H. Kirchhof in Germany, J. Roudinesco in France, de Quirós in Argentina, etc., but remains far below the estimates in English-speaking countries.

HISTORY OF DYSLEXIA IN CZECHOSLOVAKIA

Interest in specific reading disability in our land dates from the beginning of this century. The first article was published in 1904 by a professor of neurology at Prague University, A. Heveroch. The incentive for this article was the case of an 11-year-old girl who learned only the elements of reading and writing, while arithmetic and other school subjects were adequate for her age. From his detailed case history and analysis, Heveroch concluded that this was a case of "alexia," characterized not by the loss of an ability already developed, but by underdevelopment of the functional prerequisites for learning to read in her brain. He defined the disability in these words: "The same results which in some people are caused by disease, prove in others to be the result of partially unsatisfactory development. It is a learning disability for reading and writing, combined with satisfactory mental development to a degree that such a disability is unexpected or even surprising." Heveroch did not know of the previous work in English, German, and French literature of his time.

Heveroch's prediction made in this article turned out to be remarkably accurate. "In my opinion, such cases are comparatively frequent in school practice; yet it is feared that they will not come to the attention of educators as much as to neurologists." A further development in our country proved that he was correct. Systematic care for disabled readers did not develop until after World War II, at which time the initiative came from child psychiatry. The Child Psychiatric Clinic in Dolní Počernice, near Prague, became the main center concerned with the diagnosis and treatment of dyslexia. When care for the dyslexic children spread to other parts of ČSSR, the clinic took on the function of a training and methodology center. The psychiatric service in Brno established the first special classes for retarded readers in 1962. Prague followed suit in 1965 with 7 dyslexic classes—and since then there has been a steady development. Today there are 33 special classes for dyslexic children in Prague and these are quickly spreading to other centers in the country. For example, in 1971, Karlovy Vary established the first special school entirely for disabled readers. A uniform statute for special classes for dyslexic children was drawn up by the Ministry of Education in 1972.

BASIC RESEARCH

At an early period in our investigation, we found that dyslexia occurs in the Czech language substantially less frequently than reported in the English language, and also that only a small percentage of the disorders in reading occur on a mainly neurotic basis. We sought the explanation for this in the phonetic character of Czech spelling which makes reading "easier" so that it is not a suitable basis on which to fix neurotic mechanisms.

In the first stage of our work, attention was directed primarily to etiology. We investigated a group of 91 children (81 boys, 10 girls) being treated for severe dyslexia at the Children's Psychiatric Hospital Dolní Počernice, near Prague, in the years 1954 to 1960.

We soon arrived at the conclusion that our group of dyslexics was not homogenous and that it was possible to divide it according to probable etiology into three groups.

The first group, which was the most numerous (about 45%), comprised children with characteristic signs of mild encephalopathy in children (MEC); we called the group encephalopathic (E). There were mild somatic and neurological signs in conformity with the history. The psychological tests showed marked difference between the levels of verbal intelligence and nonverbal performance (Kohs and Raven tests) with low scores particularly in the drawing tests. The psychological features of MEC, hyperactivity or hypoactivity, short attention span, impulsivity, etc. were present. Dyslexia was usually more severe and its correction a difficult problem.

The second group, the hereditary (H), about 20%, did not show any specific MEC findings, but there was definite family history. The performance tests were significantly better than the verbal tests (with the exception of drawing). The defect was usually mild and successfully corrected. The fact that it was not complicated by behavior difficulties, so marked in the MEC group, was a great advantage from the therapeutic point of view.

In the third group (HE), 17% of the total group, we assumed that some cerebral lesion had developed on a group predisposed by heredity. The findings and results of the tests are approximately between the two preceding groups.

Further, we found that even in Czech, we cannot dispense with the categories of dyslexia and dysorthographia of mainly neurotic origin, even if it is usually predetermined by minor defects of encephalopathic or hereditary origin. This type of disorder rarely occurs in severe cases and comprised less than 10% of all cases. In some children of this group the central mechanism of the disturbance is anxiety; the difficulties in reading and the mistakes in orthography show a marked increase in demanding situations such as examinations, working against time, etc. Equally typical is defense against anxiety, usually elaborated in the character traits of the child in the form of lack of interest in school work, slowness, and passive resistance to school work, contrasting with alertness in other forms of activity.

It was possible to distinguish the cases of "pure" dyslexia from those in which reading disability was combined with spelling disorder. The signs which differentiated significantly between those two groups were, in the cases of children with dyslexia-dysorthographia, delayed or disturbed development of speech, specific speech disturbances (articulatory uncertainty and clumsiness, intermediate pronunciation of phonetically similar sounds, etc.), and evidence of the MEC syndrome. Tests of laterality did not differentiate between the two groups. Dyslexia-dysorthographia is thus a more complicated defect, deserving particular attention. The cases of pure dyslexia are less frequent and are predominantly linked with hereditary or neurotic etiology, while the combined dyslexia-dysorthographia occurred most frequently in cases of groups E and HE (Table 1).

This differentiation was not sufficient for practical needs such as to develop remedial teaching methods based on disturbances of functions that are connected with reading and writing. When analyzing the physiological and psychological components of these disturbances, we arrived at

Table 1. Pure dyslexia versus combined reading-spelling disorder

	Etiological groups[a]					
	H	HE	E	N	Unknown	Total
Pure dyslexia	15	5	6	5	4	35
Dyslexia-dysorthographia[b]	4	10	36	2	4	56
Totals	19	15	42	7	8	91

[a]H, hereditary; HE, heredity plus cerebral lesion; E, encephalopathic; N, neurosis.
[b]Combined reading-spelling disorder.

a system of describing various types of dyslexia which in our experience proved to be a very useful starting point for therapeutic and remedial efforts.

Investigation in Prague Schools

In the second stage of our work, we attempted to obtain a rough picture of the incidence of "mild forms" of reading disorders in the general school population, and of types of errors made by Czech children in reading. We therefore carried out an investigation in Prague schools on 380 children selected at random, 350 poorest readers in their classes, and 200 children in special schools for the mentally retarded. The children were investigated from a number of different aspects. As a basis for comparison of the frequency of different types of reading mistakes in Czech- and English-speaking children, we used the work of Bennett (1942), whose research was very similar to ours (Table 2).

Analysis of reading errors shows that some characteristics of reading which were considered as specific to dyslexia are probably only an accentuation of the given language and the methods of teaching it, and occur in the normal as well as the subnormal school population. On the

Table 2. Types of reading errors, Czech- and English-speaking children

Errors[a]	Czech children (%)		English children (%)
	2nd Grade	5th Grade	
A	36	29	31
B	12.4	13.6	16
AB/A/	18.4	24.1	6
AB/B/	11.3	13.6	4
AB	4.9	4.3	8
Median vowel	6.7	4.3	15
Reversals	4.6	1.5	12
Final "s"	+	−	5
Substitutions	2.8	8.7	3
Softening of consonants	2.8	0.9	

[a]A, unlike ending; B, unlike beginning; AB/A/, more like letters were found at the beginning of the word than at the end; AB/B/, more like letters at the end of the words than at the beginning; AB, errors in the middle part of the words; "Median vowel," stimulus word and erroneous response differ in median vowels only; "Final s," omission or addition of final "s" was sole error. Data on English-speaking children from A. Bennett (1942).

other hand, the fact that despite the different structures of the languages, we find a basic agreement in the reading errors shows that the process of relating visual impressions to sound (the understanding of the symbolic significance of visual perceptual forms) is essentially the same in both languages, since in both cases the spelling is phonetic. It is only the degree to which they are phonetic which is different, with the result that spelling is either easy or difficult. With the increasing phonetic character of spelling, the participation of auditory perception increases and disorders of auditory perception manifest themselves in spelling disorders.

DIAGNOSTIC PROCEDURES

In special centers for dyslexic children, usually a team works with the child, including psychologists, psychiatrists, pediatricians, speech therapists, and dyslexia remediation therapists. Diagnosis begins with the taking of a detailed history, especially directed to questions of heredity and early cerebral damage. This is followed by pediatric and neurological examinations, including EEG, and by ophthalmological and audiological examinations. Extensive psychological testing is focused on mental functions which may be involved in the reading disability. Great stress is placed on the examination of visual and auditory perception, the reproduction of rhythmic patterns, motor functions, handedness, and right-left orientation. As the auditory differentiation and the analysis of words into individual sounds play a primary role in Czech spelling, special tests of these functions have been developed. In other respects the diagnostic work follows the procedures generally used in other countries.

Testing a child's reading and spelling capabilities, of course, has an important role to play in the diagnosis of reading disability. Reading norms were obtained for Czech children using reading tests taken by 800 pupils in regular Prague schools and 200 pupils from schools for mentally retarded children during 1956. A revision of the norms was made in 1968, when almost 500 children from randomly selected schools in Prague and 160 mentally retarded children were tested twice during the school year.

The indicator used for reading "maturity" in Czech children is reading speed, the number of correctly read words of a standardized text per minute. Testing confirmed a highly significant correlation between speed and the accuracy of reading and understanding of the text. Cases exist where the child reads rapidly in Czech but with many mistakes and without understanding the text; however, these cases are rare.

Many teachers claim that they assess a pupil's reading not by speed, but by the quality of reading. The tests showed a high positive correlation

Table 3. Percentage of mistakes in reading easy and difficult texts (1- and 2-minute trials)

School grade (last trimester)	Easy standard text (%)		Difficult standard text (%)	
	1 min	2 min	1 min	2 min
1	3.1	5.3	12.3	9.1
2	2.1	3.3	2.9	4.6
3	1.3	2.5	3.0	2.8
4	1.6	2.2	2.7	1.9
5	1.8	1.7	1.8	1.8
6	1.3	1.6	1.4	1.3

between the speed of a child's reading and his teacher's assessment; in the second grade $r = 0.882$, in the fourth grade $r = 0.826$, in the sixth grade $r = 0.584$.

On the other hand, an insignificant correlation exists between the teacher's assessment of the pupil's reading and the number of mistakes made by the child; in the second grade $r = 0.053$, in the fourth grade $r = 0.180$, and in the sixth grade $r = 0.347$. From the second grade up, under normal conditions, our children make few reading mistakes, so that this indicator loses its differentiation value (Table 3).

Norms of reading speed for our children are expressed by converted scores calculated according to an equation proposed by Goodenough and Mauerer (Carmichael, 1954). Converted scores are comparable to intelligence quotients. When the reading-speed quotient is 25 points below the IQ, the case is considered as defective. For rapid identification of

Table 4. Number of words correctly read in 1 minute

Stage of defect	Converted scores[a]	Grade			
		2	3	4	5
Borderline	80–75	20–10	38–28	56–44	66–56
First	75–70	10	28–16	44–34	56–44
Second	69–65		16	34–22	44–34
Third	64–60			22–12	34–22
Fourth	59–55			12	22–12
Fifth	54–50				12

[a]Converted scores are standard scores that are roughly comparable to intelligence quotients. The scores were converted using a formula from Goodenough, in Carmichael (1954).

the degree of retardation in reading, a simple 5-point scale can be used (Table 4).

Besides speed and the number of mistakes made, reading achievement is also characterized by reading style; i.e., how smoothly the child reads, whether he reads individual letters or syllables, or whether he is capable of reading entire words or groups of words with correct sentence intonation (Table 5). This indicator is closely connected with reading speed; the more rapidly a child reads the more likely he is to read smoothly. It is also

Table 5. Developmental stages of reading in dyslexic children

Description of stage	Normally corresponds to grade
Reads individual letters, composes the letters into syllables, or names all letters in the word and guesses the word.	1
Reads by syllables. Pauses between individual syllables are distinct. At most, reads some short common words. Double reading, i.e., reads the word by letters silently and then pronounces the word. Pauses between individual words are thus very long. With difficult words containing groups of consonants, falls back into reading by letters.	1
Reads by syllables fluently aloud or reads syllables in the word silently and pronounces the word as a whole. Pauses between individual words are distinct. Only short familiar words are read without difficulty.	2
Reads by words, uncertainly. Stops, corrects mistakes. Pauses between words are distinct. Difficult words are read by syllables.	2
Reads by words, slowly, but without obvious difficulties—sometimes even fluently. Seldom stops to "solve" some difficult word. (In this case may fall back into reading by syllables.) Reading still lacks proper intonation.	3
Reads words and groups of words fluently, with the proper sense for content and with proper or nearly proper intonation.	4 and 5

connected with understanding the content of the text since anticipating the meaning of words and sentences makes smooth reading easier and makes it possible for the child to have correct intonation. In our tests, the connection between reading speed and the degree of acquired reading habits proved to be highly significant statistically for children in all grades and for all standardized texts. Any clear differences between speed and the manner of reading must of course serve as an inducement for analyzing the individual case.

The fifth and gravest degree of disturbance occurs when a child with good intelligence, after 5 years of school, is only able to read individual letters, to compose syllables and/or words out of them, or who must first read each letter separately and then guess the word. The mildest degree of disturbance, at the margin of normality, is reached when a child reads individual words in a more or less smooth and calm manner, without long hesitations, but his sentence intonation is not quite correct. This manner of reading is usually connected with a reading speed of approximately 60 to 70 words per minute, and under normal conditions is typical for children at the end of second or the beginning of third grade.

A qualitative analysis of the mistakes made in reading helps to find the mechanisms which participate in the reading disability. We record all incorrectly read words and evaluate the mistakes from three points of view: (1) Location of the mistake (beginning, middle, end, or the whole word); (2) quality of the mistake (which letters or syllables were read incorrectly, what was left out, what was added, etc); (3) significance of the mistake (to what extent the inaccurate word departs from the correct meaning of the word in the text is evaluated by a 4-point scale).

Understanding of a text is assessed by a 5-point scale, either according to the child's spontaneous retelling of the text or his answers to questions. Spelling is tested in a similar manner, by means of special standardized dictations.

THERAPEUTIC APPROACHES

According to the nature of the case, but also according to the personal style of the therapist and other circumstances, we usually choose one of the three methods by which the dyslexic children are introduced to remedial work.

The first technique stresses the "moment of joyful surprise." It is necessary to arrange things so that the child, as far as possible, suddenly experiences surprising success, where before he suffered only an embarrassing feeling of disappointment. In the very first exercise he must discover from his own experience that his situation is not hopeless, but that on the contrary, he already knows something and there is no doubt that he will learn more! This pleasurable experience is then linked with the method which was used and which the child now sees as "miraculous," with the person of the therapist with whom he now forms a relationship of anxiety-relieving trust, and with the surroundings in which this pleasing turning point occurred. It is natural that with the lessening suggestibility of the older child, this technique loses some of its effectiveness, but nevertheless it can be used with many children even at an older school age. The prerequisite for this is, of course, that we have recognized correctly in the diagnostic investigation just which functions in the basic prerequisites for reading are lacking and how they can be remedied and, of course, that we have a method which will lead to success. This is the case, for example, with children who could hardly manage the first elements of reading and writing with the visual-auditory procedure usual in teaching Czech and with whom the tactile and kinesthetic methods are almost certain to lead to success—at least in the initial stage. This approach shows good results where the child will remain with the therapist for a long period and where there are conditions for individual remediation. This is possible if the child is placed in a residential remedial center or in out-patient treatment with the child remaining in the care of the parents and both of them under the guidance of a specialist. It is less suitable for a special dyslexic class, where the corrective procedures are necessarily directed more at the whole group than at each child separately.

We could call the second technique "deprivational," but not in a punitive sense. It again gives best results in a remedial center, but with certain modifications it can also be used in special classes. It is based on the presupposition that the incorrect learning will tend to "fade out" if it is not reinforced and that the intensity of a need increases with short-term deprivation. Here too, a certain moment of surprise also has an effect. The child who expects that now, even more than before, he will have to learn to read, is left for a long period "without reading." Z. Zlab, who uses this method with success in the Children's Psychiatric Hospital in Dolní Počernice, recommends that for a certain period, not only should the child not be encouraged to read, but one should not even talk to him about reading. The dyslexic child has the opportunity to watch other children from a dyslexic group who are already reading with various aids, who work on special exercises, who borrow especially attractive books, and so on. It is presumed that the need to attain success in reading has not been entirely blunted in the child, but that as a result of long-term frustration of this need the child has built up defense mechanisms which are an obstacle to the direct attempt at correction. Placement in a remedial center or in a dyslexic class reduces the frustration because all of the children are similarly afflicted, and perhaps for the first time, the teacher and other members of staff treat the child's defect in an understanding way. The defense mechanisms therefore fade out and the intensity of the need to read increases. When it reaches the point where the child himself claims that he "would like to begin to read," the systematic corrective series of exercises begins. Sometimes it may be necessary to wait a month or more, but the improved motivation which is thus obtained helps to balance out this slow beginning and the result is usually very satisfactory. For the "out-patient" method of correction, this approach is not suitable, as it cannot be expected that the parents will be able to patiently "do nothing" for a sufficient length of time; and the tension which would arise in this manner could manifest itself unfavorably in other directions.

The third technique is a less extreme variation of the second and is best suited to dyslexic classes. The child is neither to be suddenly surprised nor "starved" in his yearning to read. However, he is somewhat surprised by the unexpected behavior of the teacher and somewhat strained by the postponed beginning of hard work. This approach begins from the beginning—the basic principles are quickly reviewed, whereupon the child realizes that "he does know something after all"—and then progresses systematically forward until coming to the first major difficulty. Then we begin the actual remedial exercises.

In the framework of these three initial techniques, we arrange the approach to each child according to his needs. The main idea is that the child should not have to defend himself against the corrective training, but should use his energy purposefully for cooperation with the therapist. For this, the therapist must show tact and inventiveness, for which no uniform directives can be given.

Remedial Treatment

In view of the nature of the Czech language, it was not possible to mechanically take over methods that had proved of value in English. Only in the most difficult cases and then only at the beginning of re-education, do we use Fernald's method, i.e., tracing. We soon add analysis of sound and visual units, since the inflections in Czech make it impossible to use a "word list" which is one of the essential features of the Fernald system. (Ed. note: The Fernald "word list" and Czech inflections present special problems. In a personal communication to the editors, Dr. Matějček elaborated further. "In English you say 'my dear mother,' 'to my dear mother,' 'with my dear mother,' etc. In Czech we say 'má drahá maminka,' mé drahé mamince,' 's mou drahou maminkou.' The essential part of the Fernald system is the list of words which the child has learned 'by heart' through tracing. In Czech it would be necessary to train the child to write not only the basic word but also all its forms: maminka, maminky, mamince, maminkou. That is why the tracing method has only limited value for our dyslexic children. Nevertheless, we use it with success as a departure point with severe cases of dyslexia.")

To train the child in the analysis and synthesis of syllables and words, we use colored bricks (Figure 4), each representing one letter of the alphabet. The construction and analysis of words is done tangibly and manually. In Czech every change in pronunciation means a change in the grouping of letters, which for the child entails the changing of the bricks. For greater objectivity, the children "thread" words on a wire, and with every change in the word they have to unthread one sound (one brick) and thread another in its place (Figure 5).

For training in the differentiation between soft and hard syllables (di-ti-ni, dy-ty-ny) which is rather difficult for Czech dyslexic children, metal and rubber bricks are used (Figure 6). We try to connect tactile hardness with images of hard sounds. The child also composes words and sentences, listens carefully to the pronunciation of the therapist, repeats after him "dangerous" syllables, and then looks for the corresponding soft or hard brick. In special classes for dyslexic children, each child has a "hard" wooden plate with a y written on it and a soft strip of foam rubber with an i written on it. The teacher fastens words to a magnetic black-board where the i or y is missing. The children take the object with the correct letter on it and show it to the teacher. If they make a mistake, the learning of the word is repeated many times.

The length of the sound and correct rhythm of speech are trained by using an electric buzzer on which the child "plays" what has been dictated by the therapist (Figure 7). Since the apparatus also has a small light bulb which lights up whenever the buzzer sounds, the child follows the temporal sequence of syllables by auditory, visual, tactile, and kinesthetic means, as well as by articulation. The method can also be used in competitive games in classes for dyslexics. At the same time, speech therapy is started so that the child becomes conscious of the articulatory differences among sounds in Czech.

The "window" technique is used to train prompt checking of individual syllables and words and also to divide words into syllables. The window can also serve in the training of smooth movements of the eyes along the line. This is done in two ways.

First, the text is uncovered gradually so that the child is first exposed to the beginning of the word and only later to the whole word. We thus force him to concentrate his attention during reading on the beginning of words, to read from left to right, and not to guess the word from some letters checked at random.

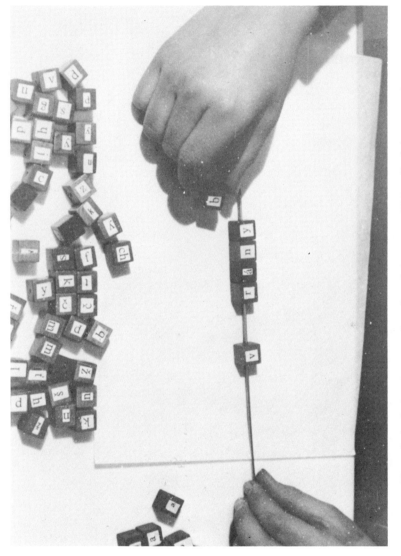

Figure 5. Analysis and construction of words by means of "threading" them on a wire.

Figure 6. Remedial exercises in differentiation between soft and hard syllables in Czech, e.g., *ty* (hard), *ti* (soft).

Figure 7. Electric buzzer used in diagnostic work and in treatment of dyslexia.

Second, the text is gradually covered. The child at first sees the whole line, then the movable window gradually covers it and "pushes" the child ahead. This tends to eliminate double reading and increases speed and smoothness.

The children also do exercises using the tachistoscope to learn words containing letters that are easily confused (*b-d, a-e, m-n,* etc.). We supplement these techniques with reading aloud with the child in a duet (usually no longer than 5 minutes). The child thus tries to adjust the pace of his speech to our speech; at the same time the child does not fully hear his own poor reading and it becomes easier to give up bad habits (Kondáš, 1965). Moreover, the child acquires correct intonation.

Great care is taken to awaken the child's desire to read. In residential centers, for example, dyslexics sleep in a special dormitory and have certain "advantages." They have their own library of selected, particularly intriguing books, and they are allowed to read in bed before going to sleep. One afternoon a week is set aside for word games and competition based on the training that the children have had.

Therapy, if carried out systematically, leads the therapist into the whole range of the problem so that he uses all types of remedial exercises, according to need. In this way therapy becomes a sort of "continuing diagnostic experiment."

CARE FOR DYSLEXIC CHILDREN IN CZECHOSLOVAKIA

Special care for disabled readers is carried out on four different levels.

Level 1

For the mildest cases of dyslexia the remedial work is part of the normal curriculum of Czech language study and is carried out in ordinary schools by classroom teachers. The child remains in his family and school, but during class he is taught somewhat differently and receives remedial exercises. The main condition for success is the teacher's acquaintance with remedial methods and his ability to put them into operation and to adapt them to the needs of each child. It is hoped that the dyslexic child in the normal class will be led in a quiet and encouraging way. Not only his achievements, but also his effort should be praised and appreciated, and the requirements made of him should correspond with his ability. This therapeutic attitude, together with some simple remedial techniques, is usually enough to help the child suffering from mild reading disability to adapt to the normal school program. Newly produced films, articles, and text books help to enlighten the public, the teachers, and also the responsible authorities.

Level 2

In the case of more pronounced reading difficulties which cannot be overcome during regular classes, special remedial exercises, out of school, are needed. In this case, also, the child remains at home and continues in his regular school, but he receives additional special individual help. The remedial exercises are carried out by specially trained workers (for example, clinical psychologists) and continue until the child is able to cope with the normal school program and to function at a level corresponding to his intelligence. This kind of remedial work is done in child psychiatric centers and in psychopedagogic centers which now exist in almost every district. The therapist sets the course and both child and parents receive detailed instructions in the first steps of remedial techniques suitable for that individual child. The therapist then checks progress regularly with parents and child and provides confidence for both that they are doing the right things in the right way. On the other hand, anxiety in the child is reduced by strictly limiting the length of lessons to 10 or, at most, 20 minutes daily. The role of "therapist" is thus passed on to the parents. This method often brings good results. One of its advantages is the deep personal concern on the part of the parents for the success of the child and their strong motivation to carry out the task. Some of the parents are quite helpful, persistent, patient and tactful—sensitive to the pedagogical aims of the situation. On the other hand, in some cases it turns out that heightened parental anxiety and lack of patience and pedagogic tact place a serious obstacle in the way of this form of remedial treatment. Under such circumstances it may be necessary to abandon this approach in favor of one in which there is less emotional involvement.

Level 3

The third level of treatment includes special classes for dyslexics, whose operation is entirely oriented to the correction of the reading difficulties of their pupils. Children accepted into these classes would otherwise hopelessly fail in the normal classes or would have to be transferred to special schools for mentally retarded children, in which category they do not belong. The special class has thus not only a remedial but also a preventive function. It prevents the child's "undeserved" school failures and all the unfavorable social outcomes that go with them.

The child is not separated from his family milieu but he is usually transferred to a different school. This very change may have a remedial influence. Our experience is that many dyslexic children are exposed in school, as well as at home, to the most deplorable misunderstanding and consequently to most inadequate treatment. In a special class for dyslexics the child at once feels in another world; the children around him suffer from defects similar to his own, and the teacher shows maxium understanding of his difficulties. The success of our special classes may be due in considerable part to this favorable "psychotherapeutic" attitude of the teachers and to the joyful atmosphere of cooperation and creativity which can be established in such a class. The child very quickly gets rid of his feeling of inferiority and makes better use of his abilities than before.

It is necessary that the number of pupils in the class be small (our classes do not exceed twelve) and that the teacher carefully masters the remedial techniques and possesses a superior sense of responsibility plus creativity and courage. *The decisive factor is the special class teacher.*

Only very experienced teachers have been chosen for this service. They attend a special course before starting their new jobs and continue to take part in regular monthly seminars, aimed at furthering their education in this field and particularly to give them an opportunity to exchange their experiences. In addition they are in constant contact with the psychiatric and pedagogic institutes for children which have responsibility for diagnosis, selection, research, and counseling. The teachers who at the beginning were full of doubts and uncertainty, now after several years of experience agree that while their job is demanding, it is also rewarding and satisfying.

Pupils attending such classes remain registered with their former schools to which they will return after their deficiencies have been sufficiently corrected. This makes it necessary for the curriculum of classes for dyslexics to include the main aspects of the general educational program used in schools for normal children. The choice and use of methods, the amounts of special exercises, and the times for different school subjects are largely left to the teacher whose main task is to meet the special language learning needs of his pupils. The principles of reading and spelling therapy permeate, of course, the entire curriculum. Four additional half-hour periods per week are dedicated primarily to special linguistic procedures and to reading and spelling exercises with each child individually. In this way, we try to cope with the individual reading disorders and to help the child find the most suitable method to meet his difficulty.

Classes for dyslexics do not have any obvious designation and so do not increase the feeling of peculiarity or of inferiority which so easily affect dyslexic children and their parents.

Spectacular changes in the attitudes of parents of the dyslexic children have been seen. Even when fully informed about the aims of the classes, they at first accepted them with deep mistrust. They were afraid, above all, that their children would be stigmatized as dull by being placed in another class and that they would miss the regular school program and become retarded, not only in reading, but in all subjects. However, the parents soon changed their opinions, and now we face two quite different dangers. 1) The parents are not willing to have the child transferred back to his former school after his difficulties have been corrected, and 2) pressure is exerted by the parents of children who have mental and behavior disorders other than reading and writing, to get their children into dyslexic classes.

The children in classes for dyslexics are not classified by means of grades, as is usual in our schools; instead the teachers evaluate their attitudes, abilities, behavior, and achievement. It is, of course, more demanding on the teacher, but very well appreciated by the parents who work in close cooperation with the schools. As for the attitudes of the children, perhaps the following episode characterizes the situation best: One boy after having received his school report with all 1's and 2's (A's and B's) instead of his usual 5 (F) for reading, and a notation that he has been "taught in a special manner," went to the teacher and exclaimed joyfully, "I congratulate you, comrade teacher! What a beautiful report—I have never received one like this in my life."

The evaluation of results at the end of the first year of special classes in Prague revealed that 30% of the pupils could be considered as very improved (i.e., they would be able to return to and continue in their former schools). Another 50% were improved but still in need of some special help, perhaps at Level 1 (in their classrooms) or Level 2 (with home help supervised by a therapist). Finally, 20% had not improved.

Level 4

Children suffering from the most severe forms of dyslexia, whose problem is whether or not they will be able to read at least a little, are subjected to concentrated therapeutic care. Such a child is placed in a special residential center and effort is directed toward correcting his basic reading difficulty and healing his secondary neurotic or behavior disorders. The tasks of those centers are a function of the child psychiatric hospitals and clinics, which are a state service, provided without cost to the parents. In these institutions all necessary equipment is available for fine diagnostic work. A thorough analysis of the child's damaged as well as undamaged mental functions serves as a starting point for remedial work. When suitable remedial methods for the individual child are found, the child can move into higher and higher levels of remedial care: into a special class; into remedial treatment by parents as directed by therapists; and finally, into his regular school. (We must admit that such spectacular progress is rare.) Children normally remain for several months to a year or more in these centers, which are really more like boarding schools than like hospitals, albeit with medically trained personnel. In addition to care for seriously disabled children, the residential centers provide treatment for children living in communities not yet equipped to minister to the needs of less severely dyslexic children.

After many years of experience, we have come to the conclusion that above all, the single most difficult task is to create a general psychotherapeutic atmosphere of understanding and acceptance for children who cannot readily cope with one of the main demands of modern society, reading and writing. It seems sometimes to be a labor of Sisyphus to prove that not punishment, enforcement, compulsion, disgrace, and rejection, but on the contrary, understanding, special help, and special care are the most essential means of solving the problems of dyslexic children. Nevertheless, the endeavor of many devoted workers in this field brings good results and progress can be seen in many ways.

REFERENCES

Bennett, A. 1942. An analysis of errors in word recognition made by retarded readers. J. Educ. Psychol. 33:25.

Fernald, G. M. 1943. Remedial Techniques in Basic School Subjects. McGraw-Hill, New York.

Carmichael, L., (Ed.) 1954. Manual of Child Psychology. John Wiley & Sons, New York.

Heveroch, A. 1904. O jednostranne' neschopnosti naučit se číst a psát při znamenité pamětl. (About specific reading and spelling difficulties in a child with excellent memory). Česká škola.

Kondáš, O. 1965. Princip interferencie v discentmej reedukacii balbuties a dyslexie. (Principles of interference in behavior therapy of stuttering and dyslexia). Psychologica 16:57.

Kučera, O. et al. 1961. Psychopatologické projevy při lehkých dětských encefalopatiích. (Psychopathological manifestations in children with mild encephalopathy). SZN, Praha.

Kučera, O., Z. Matějček, and J. Langmeier. 1963. Dyslexia in children in Czechoslovakia. Amer. J. Orthopsychiatry 33:448.

Matějček, Z. 1965. The care of children with reading disability in Czechoslovakia. Bull. Orton. Soc. 15:24.

Matějček, Z. 1968. Dyslexia, an international problem. Bull. Orton Soc. 18:13.

Matějček, Z. 1971. Dyslexia: diagnostic and treatment findings. Bull. Orton Soc. 21:53.

Matějček, Z. 1972. Vývojové poruchy čtení. (Developmental reading disability). SPN, Praha.

Vrzal, V., E. Kloboukova, and V. Reinerová. 1969. Naše pětileté zkušenosti se speciálni tridou pro dyslektiky. (Our experiences with special classes for dyslexic children). Cs. Psychiat. 65:43.

Žlab, Z. 1969. Zkušenosti s třídami pro dyslektické děti v Praze. (Experiences with classes for dyslexic children in Prague). Otázky defektol. 5:169.

CHAPTER 9

Special Education in Denmark

Mogens Jansen, Arne Søegård,
Mogens Hansen, and Bjørn Glæsel

All children of "normal" development may be admitted to elementary school. The criterion of normal development is the ability to get along socially and educationally at school. No intelligence tests are given prior to the start of school. Thus, all children in elementary school would be defined as children with normal development and normal intellectual functions.

In a few years, elementary schooling in Denmark will include part of the group of moderately mentally retarded children who are now instructed in welfare institutions for the mentally deficient under the Ministry of Social Affairs. These children will then be considered normal. The concept of normality is slowly changing as the group of children being taught in elementary school becomes more heterogeneous. In this way, an attempt is being made to change the traditional statistical concept of normality based on psychometry to one based on the child's functioning in school.

Compulsory education starts when the child is 7 years of age. Until 1972, it lasted for 7 years; then it was extended to 9 years. However, in preceding years, about 95% of the children completed 9 years of education on a voluntary basis. In 1970, the school week was changed from 6 to 5 days and at the same time a minor reduction in the number of lessons per week occurred. Teaching goes on 200 days per year, or 40 weeks.

Not all children receive their education in state elementary schools. About 5% are educated in private schools—often established on the initiative of organizations or groups of parents for religious, ideological, and/or pedagogical reasons. Private schools receive considerable governmental support in the form of very long-term loans (85% of the amount spent on children in public schools).

A small group of children (1%) is brought up and educated in 24-hour institutions. These are mainly moderately and severely mentally retarded children, children with family problems and behavior disorders, and children with severe motor and sensory handicaps.

The elementary school program for the special education of children with learning difficulties is based on the new elementary school law of 1973 which states that "children whose development requires special consideration and support, should be rendered special instruction or some other kind of special pedagogical assistance." Therefore, in principle, special instruction may be given whenever the child seems to get along poorly in class. The child is not necessarily placed in a diagnostic category or classification. (It is not required, for instance, that the school psychologist has diagnosed specific learning disability.) Even though, in principle, no emphasis is put on the classification of a child's difficulties at school, but rather on the pedagogical-diagnostic description based on the educational environment, the organization of special education is based upon a "system of boxes" derived from acknowledged groups of children with learning disabilities. The government circulars and instructions are also based upon classification.

The special education system of the elementary school has been greatly extended during the last 15 years with individual support programs, group instruction, clinical education, special classes, and special schools. Danish schools today have a nationwide system of special education at their disposal to which school psychological regional offices are attached for guidance, advice, and diagnostic service.

PERCENTAGE OF CHILDREN INVOLVED IN SPECIAL EDUCATION

In elementary school, 93% of the children between 7 and 16 years of age are admitted and educated. However, elementary education in Denmark is also available in private schools attended by 5.4% of the children (Table 1). More than 10% of elementary school pupils receive special attention.

It is estimated that a prevalence (prevalence is defined as the percentage of pupils in special education classes at a given time during the school year) of about 5% reading retarded pupils gives an incidence of about 15 to 20% (incidence is defined as the percentage of pupils who have received special education during the total school year). A 1972 study of the incidence of reading retarded pupils during the first 7 grades in a Copenhagen suburban municipality gave an incidence of 24.2%. This high inci-

Table 1. Population and education in Denmark, 1972

Total population	4,975,653
Children 7 to 16 years[a]	757,140
Children in preschool (5 to 6 years)	31,325
Children in elementary school (grades 1 to 10)	673,375
Children in private schools (grades 1 to 10)	41,222

Source: Collection of Statistical Tables, 1972:II. Danmarks Statistik, Copenhagen 1972. Elementary School, etc. Statistics 1971–1972, Ministry of Education, Copenhagen 1972.

[a]About 40% of children in first grade are 6 years old. About 20% of a class leave school before the termination of tenth grade. Within the present structure of school (school law, 1958), the pupils are divided after seventh grade into a "realafdeling" and an ordinary part, with roughly 50% in each. After 1975 the school structure will be changed, so that the pupils are undivided until after ninth grade.

dence is probably due to the fact that this population of children mainly consists of newcomers with low socioeconomic status.

Special education in the elementary school includes supplementary instruction in special classes or schools (see Table 2). Seventy-five percent of the children given special education remain in their regular classes while getting supplementary lessons for 2 to 5 hours per week in groups or in individual instruction in a clinic.

Children with behavior disorders have come into focus for special pedagogical measures within the last few years. During 1969 and 1971, two different studies were made in suburban Copenhagen municipalities with a rather high socioeconomic status, showing that the numbers of elementary school pupils with behavior disorders severe enough for special education range from 2 to 2.3%. There is a high predominance of boys with serious behavior disorders; the proportion of girls to boys is respectively 1 to 3 and 1 to 6 in the two studies.

In 1972, the Ministry of Education issued special instructions regarding the education of children with behavior disorders. As a result, there has been a considerable increase in the special education arrangements for maladjusted children. Special education in the elementary school is often offered to children between 7 and 14 years of age. There is a pronounced development towards the establishment of special pedagogical arrangements early in schooling—preferably as early as the first year of school.

Table 2. Children in special education[a]

Special education classes	Percentage of children
Special classes and schools 1971—1972	
Severely reading retarded	0.87
Deficient in intelligence (IQ about 70—90 Danish Binet, 1943; average today, IQ 110—120)	1.64
Severely maladjusted	0.10
Children with defective hearing	0.05
Speech handicapped	0.06
Sight handicapped (N = 52)	0.04
Motor handicapped (in centers for severely handicapped)	0.04
Others (ill children, individual classes)	0.04
Total	2.80
Supplementary Lessons 1968—1969 (estimated figures)	
Reading retarded	4.2
Deficient in intelligence (IQ 70—90)	0.4
Maladjusted (1971—1972)	0.5
Hearing retarded	0.5
Speech retarded	1.2
Sight retarded	0.05
Children with motor problems	0.1
Children retarded in arithmetic	0.9
Total	7.85
Special education total	10.65

[a]These figures on placement and classification of children receiving special education within elementary school are based on school population grades 1 to 10 (prevalence). About 175 children are educated in private schools for the word-blind and at the State Institute for the Speech Retarded in Copenhagen and Arhus. A number of elementary pupils are educated in centers for severely handicapped. These centers (11) are placed in various administrative areas. The pupils are transported every day from a large geographical area.

This supporting instruction is, if possible, adapted to the classroom so that the special teacher participates in the classroom as a supplementary teacher. The amount of this kind of special education with a directly preventive aim is small when viewed on a nationwide basis.

FACILITIES FOR TESTING AND DIAGNOSIS

In Denmark, the classroom teacher is nearly always the teacher of Danish, and he follows his class for an average of about 5 years. This permits the teacher to acquire a thorough knowledge of his pupils and to follow their educational development very carefully, and, to adapt his instruction to a certain degree, to the changing needs of the pupils. At the same time the teacher has the opportunity to evaluate the effect of his instruction; this may be crucial in the long run.

When the classroom teacher discovers that a child has serious learning difficulties he asks the school psychologist for assistance. Our facilities for testing and diagnosis consist of the school psychological offices. This staff works closely with the local school authorities. There are 5,000 to 6,000 children to a school psychological office. The following staff is required: three school psychologists, two clinical psychologists, a social worker, and school advisers for each of the traditional handicapped groups in elementary school.

There are about 300 school psychologists available, corresponding to one for every 2,000 children. Considering the speed with which school psychologists are educated at the universities and the Royal Danish School of Educational Studies, this ratio should show marked improvement in a few years. At some schools, the psychologist has trained a regular teacher in testing and preliminary diagnosis, to be performed under supervision, so that he can have more time for therapy.

The school psychological offices may draw assistance from experts of various kinds, and may recommend children for supplementary examinations by neurologists, child psychiatrists, and others. Furthermore, there is the State Institute for Speech Defects with two departments that take care of the diagnosis of the speech handicapped and severely dyslexic children. The institutes for the word-blind also do testing and diagnosis, and in some cases they instruct severely dyslexic children.

In some areas consultive centers have been established, which provide advisory assistance to families with handicapped children. The staff of psychologists and social workers investigates the causes of any learning difficulties and the child's situation at school.

Most of the larger schools are gradually setting up specially equipped rooms where a teacher may observe children with acute behavioral and learning problems for long periods of time to determine the causes of their difficulties. At the same time an attempt is made to find the most appropriate instruction for each child. The work in these observation clinics is done by teachers under the supervision of a school psychologist.

METHODS OF TESTING AND DIAGNOSIS

The Two Key Persons in Grades 1 to 10

Methods for testing and diagnosis involve two key persons, the classroom teacher and the school psychologist. An examination starts with the classroom teacher's description of the child's difficulties. The school psychologist observes and describes the child's symptoms from tests, observations inside and outside class, and interviews.

Tests

The tests at the disposal of the psychologist are few and of varied value. Most tests lack satisfactory Danish reliability and validity studies. There-fore, most test results require experts to interpret. Binet Simon's intelli-gence tests were standardized in Denmark in 1930 and revised in 1943. Danish norms have also been worked out for the Wechsler Intelligence Scales (WISC, WPPSI), and partly for the Illinois Test of Psycholinguistic Abilities (ITPA). Otherwise, tests translated from English tend to be used with the original norms. This situation will be little changed in the coming years because psychologists are abandoning omnibus tests.

For testing reading ability, two types of oral reading tests have been used: word-reading and paragraph-reading tests. To a limited extent, silent reading and content comprehension were measured. However, today, silent reading and understanding are always examined.

The Child's Functioning—A Vital Concern in Diagnosis

Danish society is socially, culturally, and economically relatively homo-geneous. Therefore, it is natural to evaluate the pupil's reaction to the demands on him. The school psychologist should consider whether the child has a teacher who is the right or wrong person for him, whether his schoolmates help him or have a bad effect on him, whether he has good friends or not, and so on. The child's way of functioning at school becomes a key factor in the diagnostic procedures. There is also a built-in correction due to the close cooperation between the teacher and school psychologist, since they have different points of observation.

For the reading retarded a new method called diagnostic instruction is under development. This treatment is based on a continuing analysis of pupil reaction to the instruction given him. In this method, testing, diagnosis, and treatment are functionally tied together.

FACILITIES FOR REMEDIATION

The facilities available for remediation of learning difficulties in any country probably reflect the economic status of the country, its political climate, and its point of view about its citizens. In Denmark, education has a rather high priority; this is also true of special education. Therefore, a great part of the gross national product is invested in teachers' wages, education, school buildings, and materials. Special education is made attractive to teachers through a reduction of the required number of lessons; eight lessons are paid as nine. This gives the teachers time to plan instruction for each child, to develop materials, and to hold conferences.

Teachers' Education

Denmark requires teachers to complete 3.5 to 4 years of education beyond the high school level. In the education of teachers, the pedagogical and psychological disciplines are more and more being emphasized. Therefore, the average teacher is reasonably able to cope with minor learning diffi- culties through the use of individualized instruction in class.

At the teachers' college the student chooses one of three pedagogical special topics, which he studies for 2 years, 4 hours per week. One of these special topics aims at qualifying the teacher to teach children with learning difficulties and various other handicaps.

Facilities

At most schools it is possible to house the more severely learning-handi- capped children in special classes with an average of 9 children in each class. One-fourth of the learning-handicapped children are taught in such classes. The rest of the handicapped remain in the ordinary class but receive special group instruction in separate rooms. These rooms are being equipped to offer social activities and individual work.

Special Pedagogical Arrangements

It is becoming usual to adapt special instruction to the needs of the child. For instance, some students receive special instruction in groups for 8 to 10 hours per week during a short period, whereas others receive supple- mentary lessons for several years. In some schools special instruction can be given in the regular class by specially qualified "supporting teachers." The average class size was 19.7 in 1971–1972. There is no lower limit to class size and the upper limit is approximately 32 children.

In Denmark there are differences in various parts of the country regarding special instruction. This is due to the fact that each municipality influences how much money is invested in special instruction. However, it is not possible for the municipalities to omit special instruction.

METHODS OF REMEDIATION

Danish educators do not direct their work by their own philosophy of education. On the other hand, if an attempt were made to deduce some pedagogical principles by observation of work performed in special educa- tion, at least three basic principles would appear.

1. Base the work on the pupil's strengths and compensate for weaknesses by strengthening the strong areas.

2. Try to look at the entire situation. Recreational work alone is considered ineffective. It might, however, be effective if it is purposeful and part of a whole. In special education, recreational work is often practiced, based on the hope that the children may acquire self-confidence and security, which are essential for learning.

3. Adapt the educational program to each child's or group of children's abilities rather than relying on a program prepared beforehand. The teacher listens to the pupils, but he does not let them make the decisions. Both are participants in the direction of instruction, and which of the two has the greatest influence in the long run is difficult to say. In special education, many methods are utilized by each teacher in relation to each pupil's needs. Teachers work with phonics, words in color, specific language training, programmed instruction, shapes of letters and words, and kinesthetic and other appropriate methods.

Various methods and parts of methods must be used. Three factors are emphasized—environment, maturation, and materials. The entire linguistic environment of the child is considered. This point of view leads to a global evaluation of each child. Language is considered basic to the child's entire complex of abilities and those specific areas in which he functions as linguistically retarded are considered crucial to his entire language development.

For some years, it was believed that the teacher could wait until the child matured in language and learning while attempting to overcome emotional problems which had an effect on the learning. In some cases, waiting for maturity has not led to positive results. However, it may have freed children from teachers who were overambitious about their professional success through their pupils' glowing results, and from parents who were overambitious about their children's school success. In special education these "slow learners" functioned well because special education teachers generally accept a slower rate of development.

There is a satisfactory amount of special materials available for beginning through fifth grade instruction; these materials are also used in ordinary education. In these grades even the less experienced teachers have a chance of functioning well, guided by the materials and the accompanying suggestions as well as the methodology built into the materials. For the sixth to ninth grades there are few suitable materials available. These classes demand quite a bit of the teachers and there are relatively fewer good teachers at this level.

A summary of methodology would be impossible. Perhaps the situation could be viewed from a three-fold angle.

1. The slow-learning children need a teacher who does not emphasize time. The problems of these children cannot be solved by special instruction alone, but their situation may be remediated. If ordinary education was sufficiently individualized these children might not need to be placed in special education at all.

2. The educationally deprived are those children who have had insufficient education earlier in their school years. They may be helped by qualified instruction. For these children, materials are decidedly important, and the learning environment is of great significance.

3. The specifically disabled children are traditionally a well defined group. Maturation is a factor, and often there seem to be specific hereditary and environmental influences which, in a nonspecific way, are included in the whole problem. For these children, materials and environment are essential, and the ages at which they work with the materials may also be important.

RESULTS

There have been serious attempts to evaluate the results of special education, whereas the efficiency of ordinary elementary education, as a matter of course, has been considered optimal without any kind of "proof." The reason may be that special education children have usually been thoroughly tested. This may lead spontaneously to calculations of progress or regression. The fact that special education is rather expensive has also led to demands for documentation of results. Questions about results (in the traditional psychometric meaning of the word) are rare in other school areas.

How far are we in creating acceptance of the handicapped? This is perhaps the most important field in which positive results are necessary. There is not much tolerance towards those deficient in intelligence. They are still met by environments which seem to make very little use of them and which seem to accept their difficulties to a rather limited extent. Possibly an industrial society is not the easiest one for these young people to adapt to, but society's will to help seems to be extremely modest compared with the very large resources spent on the education of the most intelligent people.

We have definitely not succeeded in creating reasonable conditions for the maladjusted. The breaking up of social mores which is seen in society as a whole seems to have contributed to the many children caught between the norms of the school and those of their homes.

During the last few years the hearing-impaired have met with more good will than previously. Because of better technology, it has been possible to absorb these children into ordinary education to a considerable extent. The same has happened to the blind, a group which has always been favored by a very positive attitude. But in spite of this, it has been difficult for these pupils to adapt to the school surroundings and later on to a normal environment.

The reading retarded as a group have had the greatest success in adjusting to the normal school environment. In general, this is not considered a specifically limiting and exactly defined handicap. The reading retarded represent a very long continuum. Both society and the educators draw the line between the retarded and nonretarded child. This has contributed to the fact that these children have been partly absorbed into ordinary education. The very strong development of special education for the reading retarded has been an economic strain. But it has yielded much to many groups of pupils, both handicapped and normal. This kind of special education has also contributed much to the ordinary teacher's knowledge of reading retardation and, consequently, to society's acceptance of this handicap.

Another result of special education is that society is able to give those children who need it special education that, in principle, is well developed. In practice, economics sets limits on how far special education will develop. The fact that ordinary education shows a tendency toward individualization may be the most important result of special education. Another result is a broader concept of normality. And so, the stage is reached whereby the results of special education may be evaluated not only by psychometry, but also via children, teachers, school, and society.

This is not exclusive to special education. Another example might be the use of school-readiness tests, which were popular in Denmark about 15 to 20 years ago. Because of the differences in children's readiness levels as shown by these tests, the point was reached where elementary education in the mother tongue had to be individualized. In the same way, reading classes have produced a series of basic materials which are now in use in the first 2 or 3 years of instruction in Danish.

What was a good result 20 years ago is not necessarily a good result today. Society has developed; schools are developing accordingly, and special education reflects the general school image. Twenty years ago, the aim was to place some of the groups of handicapped in protected institutions for the rest of their lives. The results of a pedagogy like that must necessarily be different from the aims of today, where most of the same groups of handicapped are being prepared to live an ordinary life within the general society of adults.

MEDICATION

Drugs are used as a medical treatment for epileptics or children with specific brain damage, especially in the schools for the mentally handicapped. Drugs are not used based on educational diagnosis. Probably this is connected with the fact that special education in Denmark rarely has been inspired by medicine.

JOHN—A CASE OF READING RETARDATION

John's Family Relations

John has a brother 3 years older and a sister 4 years younger than he is. His father is a skilled mechanic. He had worked as a journeyman when the children went to school and later he became a foreman. Their mother has had various jobs. Both parents are steady people, and the children have their parents' quiet temperment.

The economics of the family has been characterized by caution and common sense. When the children went to school, the family lived in an apartment. Later, the parents bought a house in the same municipality, which is considered a rather wealthy one, and where the lower social classes are clearly a minority.

Start of School

John started school at age 7 (in the 1950's). At the beginning of the second year, he was referred for a psychological examination. His classroom teacher described John as a kind, well balanced, and very sociable boy, who worked slowly and with concentration.

The psychological examination revealed no special weaknesses apart from reading and spelling. John was about 6 months behind in reading and spelling after 1 year and 3 months at school. The problem was first discussed with the classroom teacher. Because his older brother had serious reading problems, John was offered supplementary lessons in Danish. This meant that for 3 to 4 hours a week he was taken out of ordinary instruction and trained in reading in a group with two or three other pupils his age by a reading specialist.

After having received this kind of assistance for about 1 year John was re-examined. His progress appeared so modest that a transfer to a special class for the severely reading retarded was considered. The classroom teacher was happy to have John in her class, but she felt unable to give him the help and support which he needed, and the supplementary instruction seemed insufficient. John's mother was not very happy about the idea of his moving to a special class for the severely reading retarded, but she accepted the offer because her older son Tim had such great difficulties at school that she could not manage to help Tim and John at the same time.

John in Special Class

John remained in the special class for the severely reading retarded from the 4th to 8th grades. Thereafter he continued through the 8th and 9th technical classes, and finally qualified for a teachers' college after 2 more years of secondary education.

He and another boy were intellectually superior to the other children in the special class. They were well motivated for the work but they had no opportunity to utilize their abilities and develop academically. The classroom teacher was bursting with good ideas and good intentions, but his instruction was characterized by impulsive attempts at new methods. He had little understanding of what a structured, well organized curriculum means, especially to children who are weak at reading.

John's Reading Development

Analyzing John's development in reading through tests before, during, and after his stay in the special class, it is evident that his silent reading never was very bad. He gradually developed into a normal reader as far as comprehension is concerned. Oral reading was always poor and was never acceptable for speed, although it was acceptable as far as errors were concerned. His read handicap was, and still is, spelling.

The attitude at home toward John's placement in the special class was not positive. This was expressed clearly when John's mother was asked to place her daughter in a special reading class. She declined for awhile, but later accepted the transfer. However, the parents have continually supported their three reading retarded children by sending them to receive instruction in reading and spelling at an institute for the word-blind during summer vacations.

John's Estimate of His Stay in the Special Class

After leaving school, John and some of the other former pupils from the special class for the severely reading retarded were invited to participate in a discussion of the class. John and some other pupils declared that there had been no advantage in the transfer to a special reading class because academic subjects had been neglected and the basic foreign language instruction (English and German) had been inadequate.

John especially complained about the lack of community feeling in the class. It might be characteristic of John's strong personality that, as he said, he had never felt embarrassed by his slow incoherent reading, but he dropped a hint that others might have been! John probably belongs to the group of children who will not be transferred to a special class once reading clinics are incorporated into our present system of education.

RESEARCH

Denmark is, economically, a privileged nation enjoying an extremely high living standard. However, this situation is only reflected to a very moderate degree in the amount of money "invested" in humanistic research. Scientific and especially technological research have traditionally been the best funded areas. Trade has invested large sums of money in research. In the pedagogical-psychological field very few resources have been made available. This is unfortunate, considering that few areas demand a greater amount of national research than the pedagogical-psychological. The basic psychological processes may be universal, but the conditions determining children's development, growth, and profit from education are extremely dependent on national conditions.

For many years we have uncritically accepted the educational-psychological results of research, especially from the Anglo-Saxon world. However, one should question this practice since our views on rearing and educating children are decidedly different from the Anglo-Saxon views on several points.

Governmentally Performed or Supported Research

All permanently employed educators at universities and institutions of higher education are required to use part of their time (45%) on research. Practically, this is rarely done in the pedagogical-psychological area, as the teaching demands are heavy. The results of research are rarely published. However, often the students have to do individual research as part of their final examinations. This research occasionally appears later as books.

The Danish Research Council for the Humanities in its present form dates from 1968. The council gives not only support but advice on research, works out summaries on joint research, follows its development, and takes the initiative on necessary research. Appropriations are about 1,000,000 kroner (equivalent to about $150,000) per year for the entire country for educational research.

The Research Board of Primary and Lower Secondary Education is another institution (established in 1969) which functions as an advisory body to the Ministry of Education. The Research Board registers and supports research, especially pedagogical innovation within elementary and secondary schools. Appropriations are now about 500,000 to 1,000,000 kroner per year ($75,000 to $150,000) for the entire country!

The Danish Institute for Pedagogical Research was established in 1955. A staff of 15 scholars works with tests, statistical models, etc. One of its five departments, the Department of Educational Experiments, works intensively with foreign language and mother tongue education. The most widely used research technique is classroom observation.

Other Research

Sometimes municipal authorities are persuaded to support pedagogical-psychological research and development, and in a few places advisors have been appointed to manage and support local research. Furthermore, certain cultural foundations have rendered moderate economic support. Research without economic support is rather frequent within the pedagogical-psychological area. Many people have performed such research without financial support, and also without any kind of reduction in their daily work. In spite of the circumstances such work is often of high standards.

WORD-BLINDNESS

In 1955, the neurologist Knud Hermann published his book, *On Congenital Word-Blindness.* The book was written as a "showdown" with the prevailing educational-psychological view on reading retardation. Hermann found that the study of organic brain defects might explain the difficulties of the word-blind. He pointed out a close correspondence between the symptoms of patients with Gerstmann's syndrome and persons suffering from word-blindness. Gerstmann's syndrome is characterized by a failure of directionality and the forming of conceptions allied with this function, which leads to finger-agnosia, right-left confusion, writing disturbances, and deficiency in mathematical ability.

By studying the difficulties of children and adults with congenital word-blindness, Hermann reached the following conclusion. The reading and writing difficulties and other disturbances of symbols connected with congenital word-blindness depend on a defective directional function. This defect, which is inherited, is the only general feature of constitutional dyslexia. The incidence was estimated as 10 to 15% of the population.

Types of Mistakes

A persisting tendency to make reversal mistakes and to turn letters on their axis was emphasized as characteristic symptoms of congenital word-blindness. Hermann's explanation of the cause of word-blindness was received with strong reservations by many pedagogues and psychologists. The reason for this might be the importance placed on reading and spelling reversals in the diagnosis of word-blindness, especially when good readers and spellers with an inclination for reversals were spoken of as suffering from a mild degree of word-blindness.

In 1958, Tordrup published a report in which he compared reversal mistakes in oral reading, spelling, and writing from dictation from the same list of words. The participants in the experiments were 130 children from the fourth to seventh grade special classes for the severely reading retarded, and 92 children chosen at random from the second grade. In 1965, Tordrup issued a monograph comparing the types of spelling errors made by 69 children of the fifth normal class and the sixth special class for severely reading retarded children. The study was based on the results of three dictations consisting of 232 words.

Tordrup found that reading, oral spelling, and writing from dictation each created their own reversals and, consequently, it could not be concluded that a strong tendency to reversals in oral reading will reflect corresponding reversals in oral spelling or in writing. Furthermore, he documented the fact that the percentage of reading errors which could be called reversal errors rises with increasing ability in oral reading, when reading isolated words. The percentage of reversal errors compared with other errors appeared to be greater for normal readers than for the poor readers and the word-blind at the same class level.

RESULTS OF READING RETARDATION

Severely Reading Retarded

In 1951–1952, an examination of 220 severely reading retarded children's school years and later circumstances was made in Copenhagen where special classes for such children had existed for about 15 years. The IQ range for these children was 91 to 144, with an average of 111. It was found that some of the children had been transferred to ordinary classes and had gotten along well in school. Of the children who left school directly from special classes, few were able to read satisfactorily. About half of them performed on a third- or fourth-grade level, and about 19% were at a second-grade level. While the children's reading standards improved after they left school, their spelling ability decreased. These children tended to choose their father's occupational level. Many pupils felt severely embarrassed by their reading and spelling handicaps.

Effect of Supplementary Lessons for Reading Retarded

In 1955–1956 and in 1958–1959, data to illustrate the effects of supplementary lessons for reading retarded pupils were gathered. The data were obtained from two groups of retarded readers, 80 children in each group drawn from 10 schools. The children were selected from among 300 pupils who at the end of their first year of school had been recommended for special education in reading. Statistically the two groups were equivalent in intelligence and reading levels. One group of 80 had supplementary lessons (SL) for 4 hours a week, and was divided into small groups of four

(SL group). The other group had no special aid and acted as the control group (C group).

After 9 months of supplementary education, the reading level of the SL group was found to be slightly better than that of the C group; however, the difference was not significant. Nevertheless, the number of children transferred to special classes for the severely reading retarded from the C group was twice the number transferred from the SL group. Thus supplementary lessons had the effect of preventing segregation of the children. The same tendency was found in interviews with the SL group's Danish teachers, who emphasized the positive influence the special lessons had had on the emotional development of several children.

In a similar examination of children from the third grade—this time with two groups of 53 children—it was found that the SL group made obvious progress in writing, spelling, and word reading, whereas paragraph reading was equivalent in both groups (Larsen, 1960).

For some time, it seemed as if this study, published by the Danish Institute for Educational Research, would stop the allocation of supplementary lessons to pupils at the second grade level. However, Tordrup showed, by dividing the material into two groups of poor readers (severely and slightly retarded), that supplementary lessons had a marked effect on the most severely retarded pupils.

A School for Pupils with Great Reading Difficulty

From 1951 to 1964, Tordrup managed the Hyldesgaardsskolen, a special school for children with very great difficulties in reading. During this period he followed the pupils of his school closely, and in 1967 at the age of 72, he published the monograph, *Reading Development of Pupils with Great Reading Difficulties* (Tordrup, 1967).

Children are transferred to the Hyldegaardsskolen after receiving supplementary lessons for 1 year without satisfactory progress. Usually this happens at the start of the third grade. In the Hyldegaardsskolen, 2 to 3% of the poorest readers in elementary school with normal intelligence (average IQ about 110, Danish Binet, revision 1943) are educated. The pupils may remain there for their entire school life, or they may be transferred back to ordinary school whenever they are ready. Tordrup has followed the development of 16 special classes with a total of 220 pupils. He found very small differences in the reading levels of the classes, as measured by oral reading tests, and concluded that if children have great difficulty in reading, it is impossible to accelerate their development in oral reading by educational means.

Forty-eight pupils with extreme reading difficulties were followed from third to eighth grade. At the end of the eighth year of school, these extremely poor readers had oral reading levels varying between the end of second grade and the end of fourth grade. Tordrup considers it dangerous to place the main emphasis on oral reading tests. The essence of reading is the understanding of the content of a text, and experience has shown that generally the severely reading retarded manage reading with understanding far better than oral reading.

Following those weak in reading who leave the Hyldegaardsskolen and continue their schooling, terminating with an examination, Tordrup found that the reading retardeds' handicaps only inhibit their acquisition of foreign languages (English, German) and not their progress in mathematics, history, etc. Therefore, he deemed it worth while to give them aid and support.

Owing to his personal knowledge of the pupils of the Hyldegaards-skolen, Tordrup succeeded in carrying through follow-up examinations and interviews with 60 former pupils. It was found that, on the whole, the former pupils managed satisfactorily in reading, although two-thirds of the children were still poor spellers. Most of them had been happy with the Hyldegaardsskolen, and permanent psychological damage caused by their reading handicap apparently did not occur. As a whole, the reading retarded seemed to manage in the professions they had chosen. The most essential point appeared to be that the pupils possessed the ability and the maturity necessary for their chosen professions.

RESEARCH PROJECTS

There have been few properly controlled research projects. At the moment, however, there are at least three extensive studies. Two of these are longitudinal studies of children born with pregnancy and birth complications. Data are available, at present, from only one of these studies.

Prospective Study of Children of Low Birth Weight

A project group attached to the National Association of School Psychologists is doing a follow-up study of the education of a number of children with low birth weight. At the University Hospital in Copenhagen, pediatricians did a prospective study of 9,182 children born between September 1959 and December 1961. Information on pregnancy and birth had been gathered. The children were examined during the postnatal period until 1 year of age. As far as possible, the children were re-examined at 3 and 6 years of age.

The project group has continued the re-examination of over 200 children with birth weights below 2,500 grams. These children were living and going to school in Copenhagen. As a control group, 200 children were selected at random from school grades in Copenhagen corresponding to the grade levels of the experimental group.

Two articles have been published (Røne-Jeppesen et al., 1971; and Hesselholdt and Zachau-Christiansen, 1973). The 1971 study showed that the experimental group of children (prematurely born) performed more poorly, as a group, on the Binet test (Danish version) and certain WISC subtests (Similarities, Picture Arrangement, Object Assembly, and Coding). In the 1973 study some data from the deliveries of about 9,000 infants were analyzed. Sixteen percent, 3 times the normal rate, were premature and weighed below 2,500 grams. About 22% of the premature group (4 times the normal rate) showed evidence of motor retardation upon re-examination at 1 year of age. In the first week of life, a subgroup including about 35% of the premature infants showed signs of cerebral dysfunction (convulsions, spastic paralysis, mental retardation). At 1 year of age, this subgroup had decreased to about 8% or (2 to 3 times the normal rate). This drastic decrease in cerebral dysfunction during the first year led to the conclusion that signs of cerebral dysfunction early after delivery are not significant indicators of later development. Retarded development may be explained by three sets of factors: (1) retarded maturation; (2) mother anxiety or deprivation, and child deprivation caused by lack of human contact when the child was in the incubator; (3) cerebral dysfunction caused by anoxia and jaundice.

CONCLUSION

The aim of special education in Denmark has never been the integration of all pupils. On the other hand, segregation has never been viewed as advisable except for small groups of severely handicapped or disturbed pupils. Consequently, educational research seldom represents an either/or attitude.

Thus, research that is rooted in the Danish educational tradition tends to reflect the attitude in special education that integration of handicapped children is important when possible, but that segregation of some children may be required by practical considerations.

Educational and psychological diagnoses are based on both classroom observation and testing. In individual cases, both the teacher's experience and the psychologist's insight are emphasized. It is also accepted that school has a great influence on the daily lives of children and that contact with society outside of school is equally important.

ACKNOWLEDGMENTS

The authors wish to thank those who have contributed in various ways to this article, especially Mrs. Ruth Jensen for valuable contacts and Mrs. Bente Søgaard for translation.

REFERENCES

Danmarks statistik, Statistisk årbog. 1971. (Yearbook of Statistics, 1971). Danmarks statistic, Copenhagen. (With English index).

Developments Towards a Coherent System of Education for the Handicapped. 1970. Ministry of Education, International Relations Division, Denmark.

Downing, J. 1973. Comparative Reading. Cross-National Studies of Behavior and Processes in Reading and Writing. Macmillan, New York.

General Survey and Brief History of the Development of Service Systems in Denmark including the Act No. 192 of June 5, 1959. Edited by The Danish National Service for the Mentally Retarded.

Hansen, E. J. 1968. De 14—20 åriges uddannelsessituation 1965. (The educational situation for the 14—20 year age group 1965). Vol. I. Social og geografisk rekruttering. (Social and Geographical Recruitment), pp. 180—216. Social Research Institute, Copenhagen. (With English abstract and English summary).

Hesselholdt, S., and B. Zachau-Christiansen. 1973. Forklaringer på for tidligt fødte børns vanskeligheder. (Explanations of the difficulties of prematurely born infants). Skolepsykologi, 10(2):79. (With English summary).

Jansen, M. 1968. Hvor laenge vil vi blive ved med at vente på den store græskarmand? (How long will we go on waiting for the great Pumpkin?). Skand. Tidskrift Läspedag. 2:6. (Available in English).

Jansen, M. 1969. Danske læsebøger, 1.-7. skoleår. (Danish Readers and Textbooks, Grades 1—7). Vol I. Registration and analysis. Vol. II. Bibligraphy. Denmarks pædagogiski Institut (The Danish Institute for Educational Research) (with English summary).

Jansen, M. et al. 1970. New cities, educational traditions and the future. In J. A. Lauwerys, and D. Scanlon. (eds.), Education in Cities, World Year Book of Education, London.

Larsen, C. A. 1960. Om undervisning af børn med læse- og stavevanskeligheder i de første skoleår. (On the teaching of children with reading difficulties in the first years of school). Dansk pædagog. tidsskrift 8:199. (With English summary).

Røne-Jeppesen, E. et al. 1971. Psykologiske og pædagogiske undersøgelser af børn med lav fødselsvægt. Sammenligning med en repræsentativ kontrolgruppe i Københavns amt. (A psychological and educational study of infants of low birthweight. A comparison with a representative control group from suburban Copenhagen. Main results from testing with Binet-Simons intelligence tests and WISC. A preliminary report). Skolepsykologi 8(3):139.

School Systems-Guide. 1970. Ministry of Education, International Relations Division, Denmark.

Special Education for Handicapped Children in the Municipal Schools in Denmark. 1969. I. Skov Jørgensen, Superintendent for Special Education, Frederiksholms Kanal 26, 1220 Copenhagen K. Denmark.

Tordrup, S. A. 1958. Reversaler-reversaltendens. Nordisk Psykologi 10:117.

Tordrup, S. A. 1965. Stavefejl og fejltyper hos elever fra 5. normalklasse og fra 5. og 6. læseklasse. Skolepsykologi 2(1):1 (inkl. hefte med tabeller og figurer).

Tordrup, S. A. 1967. Læseudviklingen hos elever med store læsevanskeligheder (An investigation of reading progress among pupils with major reading difficulties). Skolepsykologi 4(1):3 (with English summary).

CHAPTER 10

Reading-Writing Disabilities in Finland

Raija Syvälahti

The problem of reading and writing disabilities of nonretarded children is not new in Finland but we have not yet been able to arrange the best educational help for all children who need it.

The instruction of the children who have reading and writing disabilities began in 1949. Two classes were established in Helsinki for the Finnish-speaking elementary school children. They were both changed into reading clinics in 1950 and 1951, because the reading clinic was more suitable. For a long time these two clinics were the only educational help available. There were seven reading clinic teachers in different parts of Finland in 1965. In 1968 there were 18, and by 1973 they numbered nearly 300. Some of these teachers also teach children with speech defects.

The education of the special teachers for this field began in Jyväskylä University in 1966. The education consists of a 1-year course for elementary school teachers. The elementary school teachers may also take special summer university courses and then they, in turn, are able to give this special instruction a few hours weekly to full-time special teachers in the schools.

In 1968, figures for the frequency of occurrence of reading and writing impairment (from 9 to 22%) were publicized in many different places in Finland. (Lasten erityishuolto ja-opetus Suomessa, 1970.) According to an investigation made in Finland, 14.8% of the elementary school pupils of classes II to VIII in the community of Espoo were in need of extra instruction in reading and writing (Arajärvi et al., 1971). In general, about 10% of the children in normal elementary classes are in need of this extra instruction.

175

TESTING AND DIAGNOSIS

In Finland, the testing and diagnosis of reading and writing impairment are done by a special teacher. On the basis of the test tasks it is possible to decide whether the pupil is suffering from a specific reading and writing impairment or whether his difficulties lie primarily in the auditory, visual, or visual-motor area and further, whether he has difficulties in auditory or visual memory.

Standardized tests in reading and writing have been devised for the second and third classes of elementary school. The teachers also use tasks invented by themselves, and their evaluation is based on the knowledge of how the child should be able to perform the tasks of each grade. The Institute for Education Research, University of Jyväskylä, which has published the tests, is doing research to develop more diagnostic tasks.

Auditory tests:

1. Recall the sounds corresponding to letters
2. Analyzing the sounds of words (6 different tasks)
3. Remembering the sections read aloud
4. Taking dictation
5. Reproduction

Visual tests:

1. Recognition of letters and remembering their direction and form
2. Recognition of numerals and remembering their direction and form
3. Analyzing visual words
4. Reading of text and separate words
5. Transcription

The ideal situation is one where the physician, psychologist, and special teacher each makes his own investigation for every child who has learning disabilities. This is only possible in child psychiatric hospitals and in some child guidance clinics. Usually it is only the special teacher who makes the investigation and diagnosis of reading and writing impairment. In severe cases she can ask help from the child guidance clinic or school psychologist, if there are such, or ask the parents to visit some private physician or child psychiatric hospital. We know what the situation is now and what it should be, and we are working for improvement in the future.

FACILITIES FOR REMEDIATION

The children who have reading and writing disabilities continue studying in their regular classes but they have extra instruction given by a special teacher, generally 2 hours weekly in groups of three to five pupils. Sometimes, in severe cases, there may be only one pupil at a time. A full-time special teacher takes care of about 50 to 70 pupils.

In the beginning of special instruction all children are given the diagnostic tasks by the special teacher. Because the disability varies in different children, the instruction must be individual. Though there are several children in a group, they all must have individual tasks. We do not have very much published instructional material in Finland yet. The teachers must prepare material of their own to supplement the published materials.

The starting point is the child, not the method. The basis for remediation is to know the child as well as possible and to know if the difficulties of the child are auditory, visual, or visual-motor. After determining the strongest and the weakest areas, the teacher designs the training program for each child. We have to observe and find which methods can help each child. We change the program as remediation occurs, and when necessary. In the remediation of reading and writing disabilities, we have gotten much from other Scandinavian countries, especially Denmark, and we know and use some American methods also.

RESULTS

We try to begin special instruction at the beginning of the third class of elementary school, sometimes earlier in severe cases. We think that the earlier we can help the child, the better the results. As for the duration of the special instruction, 2 to 3 years is usual. Some children will improve sooner, some will need many more years in spite of their very high intelligence. Slight cases may improve by themselves to a certain degree, but medium and severe cases need special instruction. Because the disability is very individual, improvement is also individual.

An important part of remediation is the therapeutic aspect. Many of these children are also emotionally disturbed. Some may need psychotherapy at first, or at the same time as instruction, but in most cases the understanding and therapeutic attitude of the special teacher will help the child to improve. This teacher attitude is a necessary basis for the remediation.

ORGANIZATIONS

We do not have any parent-professional organizations helping these children, but some parents have been talking about it. For special teachers in this area we have had an organization since 1968, and since 1971 this organization has been a member of the International Reading Association (IRA).

REFERENCES

Arajärvi, T., K. Louhivuori, H. Hagman, R. Syvälahti, and A. Hietanen. 1965. The role of specific reading and writing difficulties in various school problems. Ann. Paediat. Fenn. 11:138.

Arajärvi, T., R. Syvälahti, and H. Hagman. 1971. On the specific reading and writing difficulties of children. Psychiatria Fennica, pp. 185–190.

Arajärvi, T. Senior lecturer in child psychiatry, personal interview.

Erityisopetuksen Suunnittelutoimikunnan I osamietintö. Komitean-mietintö 1971:A26. Helsinki.

Erityisopetuksen Suunnittelutoimikunnan II osamietintö. Komitean-mietintö 1971:A26. Helsinki.

Lasten erityishuolto ja-opetus Suomessa. 1970. Helsinki.

Niskanen, E. Leading inspector of special education, personal interview.

Ruoppila, Isto-Röman, Kyllikki-Västi, Maire. 1969. KTL:n diagnostisia kirjoituskokeita peruskoulun II ja III luokille. Report No. 50 Institute for Educational Research, University of Jyväskylä, Finland.

Ruoppila, Isto-Röman, Kyllikki-Vasti, Maire. 1968. KTL:n diagnostisia lukukokeita peruskoulun II ja III luokille. Report No. 41. Institute for Educational Research, University of Jyväskylä, Finland.

Syvälahti, Raijo. 1970. Erityisiin lukemis- ja kirjoittamisvaikeuksiin liittyvät auditiiviset ja visuaaliset häiriöt. Fonetiikan b-linjan pro-gradututkielma kev. Helsingin Yliopisto.

CHAPTER 11

Learning Disabilities: The German Perspective

Edith Klasen

During ten years of involvement in clinical work with learning disabled children and their parents in California, I saw and evaluated more than 1,500 children, followed by at least one parent conference in each case. Research on 500 of these cases has been published (Klasen, 1972). Thus I have experienced the courageous battle of American parents and their learning disabled children. Having also taught college classes in special education, I am familiar with the teachers' quest for knowledge and their dedication to their pupils.

For the past two years I have been back in Germany working with the German Caritas Association, the largest nongovernmental welfare agency in Germany. Since it is a member of the International Caritas, as well as of the International Catholic Child Bureau, I am in the fortunate position of meeting with a variety of experts in child welfare and education.

Since my return to Germany, two things were of particular impact: Germany's size, and the degree of its Americanization. After my years in America, West Germany appeared quite small. I realized how difficult it is for Germans to have a true picture of the enormous expanse of North America—just as it must come as a surprise to Americans traveling in Europe to see how quickly one passes from one national border to another. The United States has 9,360,000 square miles, whereas East and West Germany together have an area of only 140,000 square miles. West Germany by itself approximates the size of Oregon. It has 70 million inhabitants—more than one third of the American population!

What really struck me most was the Americanization of Germany. It is not only apparent in advertising and pop music, in the large proportions of American-made movies and television series, in the multitude of American products, but mostly and probably more significantly, in the daily language and in the natural and social sciences.

In psychology the American influence is quite impressive. Behaviorism, learning theories, behavior modification, group dynamics, sensitivity training, nondirective psychotherapy, as well as research on intelligence, and cognitive and early learning are on the German psychology market. In a 1971 catalogue of newly announced psychology books 55% were of American origin.

In education the picture is much the same. The controversial American authors, Bloom and Doman, became widely known and quoted in Germany! According to Bloom, 50% of a child's intelligence is developed—or not developed—by 4 years of age. By age 7, 80% of his intelligence variation is accounted for and, after that, the environment has relatively little effect on IQ change. These theories are no longer accepted by most American psychologists. Doman claimed to accomplish miracles by teaching 3- and 4-year-olds to read. By now, both authors' claims, their methods, and their underlying theories, have been critically analyzed on both continents, but when these pronouncements first reached Germany, they had a powerful impact. Many other claims by American educators also were heard in Germany with great interest, including: (1) Intelligence was not fixed at birth by hereditary factors. (2) A boost to a child's intelligence must come long before 5 years of age. (3) Language is the most important single factor for early academic success in school. (4) Dr. Schaefer of the National Mental Health Institute had shown that youngsters, tutored in the home from age 15 months, enjoyed IQ's averaging 17 points more than those of controls. These and similar declarations were picked up in Germany and quickly found their way into political and election campaigns.

Germany is presently reforming its public school system on all levels. This is being done according to the reform plan by a Federal Education Commission of 1970. The planners had been aware of the American quest for more and better education for all, and that during the past 30 years the number of high school graduates increased from 38 to 75%; the number of college graduates rose from 6 to 16%; and that the number of students enrolled in college has doubled since 1965. As a result, 80% of all the research done in the world takes place in the U.S.

Unfortunately, many an American project, innovation, or scientific finding is published and hailed in Germany without understanding how limited and insubstantial it is, or how seriously questioned it may be in America. The relatively limited success of Head Start, for instance, should have made it clear that it does not pay to believe in panaceas, to set goals too high, or to indulge in the unrealistic hope that the schools alone can solve the problems of poverty, race relations, language and milieu barriers, etc. Children are formed primarily by their homes and their communities; it is there that reform must begin.

Comprehensive high schools and all-day public schools are now being established on an experimental basis in Germany despite voices of caution pointing to the fact that Germany has a different tradition and different needs. We are about to do away with our two-track educational system. Vocational and business schools, as well as the apprenticeship system, are to be incorporated into comprehensive high schools. This, the reformers claim, will ensure equal educational chances, academic learning for all, and social integration at an early age. Altzesberger (1973) expresses basic agreement with comprehensive schools, even for the handicapped, but he also warns against fostering utopian aims, against neglecting the gifted in our quest for equality, and against failure to take into account individual differences.

Germany still has problems of teacher shortage, obsolete school buildings, and crowded classes, yet it is talking of reform and patterning much of its thinking and planning after American models. All this at a time when, in the United States, moves in the opposite direction can already be discerned!

LEARNING DISABILITIES—A CHALLENGE TO THEORY

Where within the educational system are the learning disabled located? Since they are in need of special educational assistance, they belong to the larger group of exceptional, handicapped children. Their estimated number, however, exceeds by far any of the other exceptional subgroups. The prevalence of either learning disability or exceptional children can only be estimated very approximately. Different sources estimate the learning disability group as from 1 to 30% of the school population in the United States and from 2 to 20% in West Germany. On the other hand, estimates of the percentage of exceptional children are from 10 to 12% in the U.S. and about 6.6% in Germany. These figures indicate that different definitions of learning disability create a very wide variation in percentages.

Much agreement exists in the United States and in Europe as to terminology, classification, and definition of exceptionality. From the generally agreed upon elements it is possible to formulate the following definition: Exceptional children are those who for physical, mental, or social reasons deviate to such a degree from the norm that they encounter difficulties in daily life and need special educational help in order to develop to their full capacity and become fully integrated into society.

The U.S. and the 17 European countries which work together in the

Council of Europe classify the handicapped into the categories listed
below:
1. Sensory handicaps
2. Speech handicaps
3. Physical handicaps
4. Mental retardation
   a) slow learners (German term: learning handicapped)
   b) morons
   c) imbeciles
   d) idiots
5. Maladjustment
   a) behavioral
   b) emotional

The social science expected to deal with the exceptional group is called
"special education" in the United States, England, and Sweden. Germany
speaks of "special pedagogy," France of "medical-educational measures,"
Switzerland of "curative pedagogy" and the Netherlands of "clinical" or
"orthopedagogy."

In the United States intensive attention to children with minimal brain
damage has been given since the early 1940's. A shift away from the
medical toward a psycho-educational emphasis occurred in the mid-1960's
when the learning disability label became more widely known and accepted.

In Germany it is more difficult to trace the development. The Federal
Republic of Germany has no uniform law or system of rehabilitation for
the handicapped. This has historic reasons. During the past century aid
came primarily from church-oriented or humanitarian charity. Since World
War II government-based programs were expanded and modernized. In the
19th century, when available, the special schools took all kinds of handicapped children, even the severely mentally retarded. Today's special
school system still suffers from these historical roots. Ignorance and
prejudice cause many to think of mental retardation when they hear
special class. This is true although there are now two separate special
schools, each with a well defined curriculum of its own, one for those
diagnosed as "slow," the other for those who are "trainable within limits."

A group of German educators, after visiting special schools in other
European countries in 1966, said that the special school system in the
Federal Republic, with the exception of schools for the blind and deaf,
still requires considerable development. In Germany to date, no well
described subgroup of learning disabled children, comparable to the Amer-

ican category, exists. This does not mean, however, that nothing is known about or done for children with specific learning disabilities. There is less unity. The medical profession knows little about related writing in the educational or the psychological profession and vice versa. The public is little informed as yet. In Germany there first was an awareness of reading-writing disabled children, starting about 1950, and only now is there a growing awareness of the larger minimally brain injured category. So, there are the reading-spelling disabled and the minimally brain damaged, but of the learning disabled as a group not much is known as yet. This statement, although correct in its outline, presents an oversimplified picture. Here again we are confronted with the thorny issue of definition and classification.

In Germany much has been said and written on "school difficulties," "learning problems," "failure at school," etc., but here too, the concepts mean different things to different authors. A distinction is made in the educational literature between "learning difficulties" (Lernschwierigkeiten) and "learning disorders" (Lernstörungen). The former consist of progressively diminishing academic achievement, the latter of apparent discrepancy between expected and actual achievement. The brain damaged child is listed in both groups, learning difficulties and learning disorders. Reading-spelling weakness and legasthenia are considered learning disorders of the subcategory called "partial mental deficiency."

Turning from the educational to medical classifications we find that the minimally brain injured as well as the reading-spelling disabled child appear together under one heading, and this is strongly related to the learning disorders called partial mental deficiencies.

In connection with learning or partial performance disorders one sees here and there a paragraph on specific math disabilities, or dyscalculia. Learning disabilities of arithmetic appear to be much less explored than language disabilities, and there are fewer teaching facilities available for these children. This seems to be true in both Europe and the United States.

While literature on dyscalculia is still relatively restricted, the number of publications on dyslexia has gone beyond 20,000 in the United States and has grown to more than 1,000 important titles in German-speaking countries. With this heavy emphasis on language disabilities and conceptual restriction of learning disabilities to reading-spelling weakness in Germany, it does not come as a surprise that legislative and educational provisions for children with learning disabilities consist of reading-writing programs only. This widespread learning disorder alone presents a formidable challenge to the German school system.

LEARNING DISABILITIES—A CHALLENGE TO PRACTICE

In Germany the abbreviation LRS has become generally known and accepted—similar to MBD (minimal brain dysfunction) and LD (learning disabled) in the United States. LRS is the shortened form of Leserechtschreibschwäche (reading-writing weakness).

Depending on increasing degree one finds:

1. Lese-Rechtschreib-Schwäche (reading-spelling weakness)
2. Lese-Rechtschreib-Störung (reading-spelling disorder)
3. Legasthenia (dyslexia)

LRS is understood to encompass reading, penmanship, and orthographic difficulties, either in isolation or in various combinations. The condition was practically unknown before 1950. Beginning in 1951 the literature on the subject began to increase steadily and the pace at which new publications appear has not diminished. Especially noticeable currently is the first wave of popularized literature which serves to interest the German public and to mobilize parent initiative.

The city of Hamburg organized Germany's first experimental reading disability classes in 1953. The majority of schools did not provide special programs on a larger scale until the early and mid-1960's.

To date, at least six of the 11 State Departments of Education have legislated rules and regulations concerning special educational provisions for learning disabled students (Nordrhein-Westfalen was the first in 1964). Although not all school departments have legislation, some special educational measures are available everywhere.

Until recently much discussion centered on the question whether LRS programs belonged in the province of the regular or the special school system. This is a more important question than may appear at first sight. In Germany the two systems are much more clearly set apart than they are in the U.S. They have entirely separate locations, buildings, and administrations. Also, the prejudice, social stigma, and preconceptions mentioned earlier are still attached to the special schools. When it was decided to keep the reading disabled in the regular schools, the following reasons had been decisive: (1) Classes for the LRS children would never extend beyond the fourth grade; thus they would constitute only a rudimentary special school. (2) Curriculum and final educational goal, namely, at least a high school diploma, are identical with those of the regular, not the special schools. (3) Here would be an opportunity for teachers to seek promotion. Advancement for elementary school teachers is presently only possible in the form of studying a second major and then teaching in a special school.

Instead of having the best teachers drained from the elementary schools, it would be better to promote those who would be willing to teach reading disability groups.

That LRS may not become manifest, or may remain undiagnosed until after the fourth grade, or that it may call for special class attendance beyond the fourth grade, seems not to have been taken into consideration. The provision of special programs for reading-writing disabled pupils is now the responsibility of each elementary school. This finds all the more emphasis since much publicity has been given recently to equal educational opportunity for all, including the handicapped, especially during the early childhood years. Compensatory education is not only for the culturally deprived, so the argument goes, and the present-day educational ideal of the liberation of the child must be applied to the learning disabled as much as to the normal child.

If one considers 5% a realistic proportion of those definitely in need of special programs, there are yearly 50,000 children in Germany with medium-to-severe reading disorders for whom special provisions must be made. Teachers generally complain about insufficient financing of the programs. In 1973, Schwartz wrote, "What is all the research, what are all the teacher's personal efforts good for, if in the end the budget provides barely two German marks (a little more than a dollar) per child per year for special programs?"

The following is an overview of private and public provisions available.

Individual Help

This usually takes place in the form of private tutoring by teachers or informed parents who have been provided with teaching materials, private psychotherapy, or both. Some individual help is also available at public or private reading clinics and child guidance centers.

Special Groups

Within the Regular Classroom While the other children are being taught by the teacher, the small reading-disabled group works on material carefully prepared in advance and individually selected by the teacher. This form is used for mild cases.

Outside the Regular School Groups of 12 to 15 children from different schools meet 2 or 3 times weekly, outside regular school hours, for remedial help.

Within the Regular School If at least 12 children (upper limit for each group is 15) within one school need special help, they meet 4 to 6 times a week at their school during regular school hours.

Special Classes

These are referred to officially as LRS classes. They are offered in addition to the groups mentioned above and are designed primarily for first and second graders whose difficulties are pronounced. These children are transferred to wherever LRS classes are taught. Not more than 15 children are allowed in one class. The children receive regular second- or third-grade instruction in all subjects, but the emphasis is on a total therapeutic approach, and more time is allotted to areas or subjects of weakness. Instead of physical education and sports these children have music, rhythm, and dance classes, and in some cases even hydrotherapy. The goal is to have all of these children ready to return to their regular classes after the fourth grade at the latest.

Special Training during Beginning Reading

This is less a remedial than a preventive measure, intended to detect children early with potential or actual speech, motor, perceptual, or related difficulties. They have diagnostic training in small groups; some children are referred to speech therapists, others to ophthalmologists, etc.

All of these organizational forms have their disadvantages as well as advantages. Children do not like to be singled out, to be transferred, to have additional school hours, etc. Schedules are difficult to arrange when children come together from various grades, schools, or classes. Transportation—since few school buses exist—is often a major obstacle. The transfer to a new school and teacher, to new classmates, as much as the transition back to a regular class, is often not without problems. There is no doubt, however, that the advantages outweigh the disadvantages and that the programs will continue to grow.

Nothing can be done without parental consent, but that is not always easy to obtain. There are no general or widespread programs for parental involvement, parental counseling, or workshops for parents. Yet in many schools, parents are informed and counseled informally, often on the teachers' own time. Some schools provide interested parents with informational or teaching material.

LRS Teachers

The LRS teachers are usually not special teachers. Regular teachers acquire, either through private study or through courses and workshops, some specific knowledge. More and more such courses are beginning. In 40 to 60 class hours, these courses familiarize teachers with theory, methods, and programs. Of course, this cannot be much more than an over-all introduction. The number of children in need is growing faster than the number of teachers available. Student teachers practice on students of their own schools while taking the course; thus they have at least some supervision during their beginning diagnostic and teaching experiences with LRS children.

Teaching Materials

Teaching materials for LRS classes have been developed in such quantity that at least three alternatives for each area on each grade level from second to sixth grade are available. Some apply to all grade levels. There are games, workbooks, practice sheets, small mechanical devices such as letter clocks—everything a modern didactic market has to offer. Since the native language is essential in this context, most materials have been developed in Germany. Some are patterned after American models. To name just one, Frostig's testing and working materials, known in Germany for quite some time, are now becoming widely used.

Teaching materials for use by parents are also on the market in sufficient quality and variety. Several alternatives are on hand for each of the grades one through six, and above. Parents can choose from at least 10 different kinds of reading-spelling games for learning disabled children.

Teaching Methods

Teaching methods for LRS students have grown into a large body of techniques, each designed to train a particular aspect or function. It is impossible to name them all, but I will try to identify some of the major methodological principles:
1. In the beginning especially, slow, individually planned, skillfully taught, and well practiced steps should be taken.
2. Areas of strength are capitalized on first, then the weak areas are worked upon.
3. Learning steps are short to ensure success.
4. Many children with LRS are close to panic when asked to read aloud. To encourage verbal expression children need exciting events to talk about. These are provided through films, excursions, etc.
5. Poor posture, faulty breathing, poor body image, poor balance, etc., are common among these children, therefore many short breaks, and breathing and movement exercises are provided.
6. To improve motivation, interest, frustration tolerance, and attention span, the exercises and materials are as varied and attractive as possible. Understanding support is given by the teacher.
7. Multisensory training (Mehrwegiges Lernen) is provided where indicated.
8. Principles of learning theory are used: intermittent reinforcement, repetition, transfer, independent working, etc.

9. There are proponents of "diagnostic," of "therapeutic," of "encouragement centered" and other basic teaching approaches.

Much discussion still goes on as to whether competition in the classroom is good or bad for LRS groups. There can be no general answer to this; it depends on each child's personality, on the make-up of the group, the skill of the teacher, the momentary mood, the relationship between teacher and students, etc.

The didactic principle which appears to be most important is the individualization of special instruction. Each child has "his" reading-spelling disability.

Referral to LRS Classes

Selection for and referral to LRS classes are not handled uniformly. Often a principal will tell teachers which major symptoms to use to spot the children and how to report them so they can be placed in special groups. In one state, Schleswig-Holstein, all children are routinely screened by the end of second grade and all are given reading tests during the fourth grade. Screening is usually carried out by guidance counselors, a growing profession in this state. In Baden-Württemberg, regular teachers receive special training in testing methods; they then screen the children who have been recommended for LRS programs. In Rheinland-Pfalz most of the diagnostic work is done by school psychologists and special teachers. There are also parents, physicians, clergymen, psychologists, etc. who recognize the need for referral even if the classroom teacher does not.

There is no state without special legal provisions in regard to grading. As long as a child is attending an LRS program he is not graded in spelling, reading, report-writing, etc. In some districts the children need not participate in dictation exercises. Their grades in history, social studies, etc. are to be determined by oral participation and content of reporting, not by spelling mistakes, poor written expression, etc. When promotion to the next grade or transfer to a secondary school is at stake, the report card grades in reading and spelling are not to be considered in calculating the grade-point average.

The majority of those who work with children are now aware that the transfer of learning disabled children to special classes for slow learners cannot be the answer any more. A 1970 investigation found that one-third of 295 children in the slow learner classes studied had to be classified as LRS cases. The investigator pointed out that these children had been sent to special schools because their teachers still considered poor reading-spelling achievement as indicative of low mental endowment. Indeed, he adds, the obsolete yet widespread idea that a person who cannot spell correctly simply is "dumb" still exists (Müller, 1971).

In view of the enormous task still ahead of us I find myself in agreement with the concept that equal educational opportunity for normal as well as for handicapped children may be difficult to realize. However, what can and must be achieved is the betterment of educational chances for the handicapped.

The LRS Program in G.

G. is a city of 170,000 inhabitants in West Germany. In 1972, a program of special education for children with reading-writing disabilities was begun in G. Since this LRS program appears to be representative of many in Germany, it will be discussed in some detail.

The present head teacher of the program is a fully trained special teacher. She came to G. to teach a class of slow learners at a special school. She also tutored LRS children referred to her from regular schools, and she found work with them more visibly rewarding.

She was chosen to head the program in the fall of 1972 when the Education Department of G. first decided to make special provisions for LRS students. As soon as this plan became known there were more applications for children than could be admitted. On her own time, while still carrying a full teaching load, the teacher selected a test battery and began to test each child individually. She administered a full WISC and several academic and motor tests, took the medical, social, and school history of each applicant, and gave parent conferences in each case. When the new academic year started, and with it the first LRS program, she had 64 children tested and ready. This was possible because special teachers are trained in testing.

The 15 most severely disabled cases were scheduled for the LRS class to be taught by the head teacher. These children were transferred from their schools (with parental consent) to attend the new LRS class in which they would be taught a regular second-grade curriculum. Teaching materials, audio-visual equipment, books, games, etc., had also been made available.

The children in this first LRS class had the following characteristics: at least average general mental potential, reading-spelling scores below first-grade level, all knew only a few letters of the alphabet, none could read words with more than two letters, and none could write anything from dictation. All were too old for second grade. Six of the children had repeated first grade at least once, some as many as three times; two of the children had been in special schools for the mentally retarded.

By the end of their first year, six of the 15 children obtained average scores on reading achievement tests, seven were in the 12th to 20th percentile, and two remained below the 8th percentile. Among these latter was the most intelligent child of the group with an IQ of 123. The two most severely disabled children were allowed to repeat second grade in the LRS class. All children had improved in spelling; all still had difficulty in writing from dictation. The six students who had made substantial progress were referred back to their regular classes and were scheduled for afternoon LRS groups. The remaining eight children stayed in the LRS class but were promoted to third grade.

Of the 64 children originally admitted to the LRS program, the 49 less severely disabled were taught by another teacher in 8 afternoon LRS groups. These children came after school for two weekly one-hour sessions. They came from different schools and grades in the city and used the same room that was occupied in the mornings by the LRS class. These groups also improved so that the school authorities accepted as many children for the following year (1973).

The state in which G. is located issued its first legislation in 1973 concerning LRS programs. There are now funds available for testing, but the regulations state that group tests will suffice to determine general learning potential. Since the total IQ is crucial to being admitted, and learning disabled children perform poorly in groups, this is a weak spot in the legislation. The greatest shortcoming is the number of children who can be admitted. In a city with a population of 170,000 only 64 children can presently be accommodated for LRS assistance.

In the head teacher's opinion, the program will not be able to continue at its current level of quality unless the town's child guidance clinic is equipped to provide a diagnostic, therapeutic, and counseling team for close cooperation with the LRS program.

We seem to have a long way to go before we come near such ideals as pronounced in a 1973 Resolution of the Council of Europe: We must ". . . give handicapped persons every opportunity to be as much integrated as possible into society—they should be given all opportunities for their personal development and for maximum participation in the community."

REFERENCES

Atlzesberger, M. 1973. Gesamtschule—auch für behinderte kinder? Z. Heilpädagogik H.3.

Bloom, B. S. 1964. Stability and Change in Human Characteristics. Wiley, New York.

Doman, G. 1966. Wie Kleine Kinder Lesen Lernen. Freiburg.

Frostig, M., D. Lefever, and J. Whittlesey. 1964. The Marianne Frostig Developmental Test of Visual Perception. Consulting Psychologists Press, Palo Alto, Ca.

Klasen, E. 1972. The Syndrome of Specific Dyslexia. University Park Press, Baltimore.

Müller, P. 1971. Lese-rechtschreibschwäche und sonderschulbesuch. Z. Heilpädagogik H.1.

Schwartz, H. 1973. Legasthenie—Ein Pädagogisches Problem. Arbeitskreis Grundschule, Frankfurt.

CHAPTER 12

Specific Reading Difficulties in Great Britain

Beth Gessert

In Great Britain, there has been a growing concern for children with specific reading difficulties. As defined by the Tizard Report, this term describes "the problems of the small group of children whose reading (and perhaps writing, spelling, and number) abilities are significantly below the standards which their abilities in other spheres would lead one to expect" (Great Britain, 1972). Despite official recognition of the group, specific reading difficulties is not considered one of the 11 handicapping conditions which require special educational treatment.

There also continues to be serious disagreement over incidence, etiology, and terminology. The controversy over definitions is further confused by a lack of correspondence with terms commonly used in the United States. For example, in the United Kingdom, the term learning disabilities is often used to refer to children who are slow in learning or educationally subnormal (ESN), and it has even been used in connection with children with IQ's as low as 50. This group is roughly equivalent to the educable mentally retarded in the United States.

Much of the work on reading disabilities in Great Britain has been categorized under "dyslexia." This term and its attendant adjectives (specific, specific developmental, acute, childhood), have been used to describe all forms of backward reading.

THE BRITISH EDUCATIONAL SYSTEM

In Great Britain, children enter the infant school when they are 4 to 5 years old. The infant school is concerned with teaching pupils the basic skills of reading, writing, and numbers. By the age of 7 or 8, when they pass on to junior school, most children are expected to use effectively the skills presumed to have been learned in infant school. At the age of 11, children leave junior school and go to secondary school. Pupils stay in secondary school from 5 to 8 years depending on whether they intend to go to a university.

There are several points about this educational structure which are relevant to children with specific reading difficulties. Children enter the educational system 1 or 2 years earlier than in the United States. This means that children at risk of becoming poor readers could be diagnosed and treated earlier. However, the break in primary schooling may work to the detriment of a child with reading problems. For instance, the infant school teacher may feel that a child will grow out of his reading problem while the junior school teacher maintains that it is not her responsibility to teach basic reading skills. Since secondary education starts at age 11, approximately 3 years earlier than in the United States, there is a great deal more remedial education in some secondary schools than might be expected.

Parent Groups

In Great Britain, parents do not play as large a role in education as they do in the United States. It is felt by both teachers and parents that education is best left to those professionally qualified. Consequently, parent pressure groups do not operate as effectively as they do in the United States.

In 1966, the first local group of the British Dyslexia Association was formed (Thompson, 1972). There are now over 20 local groups in existence whose membership consists largely of parents and teachers of dyslexic children. In 1972, the local associations began operation on a national level.

However, it is the large and well established national organizations that are most effective in supporting research and the recognition of conditions such as specific reading difficulties. The Invalid Children's Aid Association (ICAA) is one such group which has promoted research on specific reading difficulties. It was through their efforts that the necessary funds and guidance for such projects as the Word Blind Centre were found. Another association, the National Society for Mentally Handicapped Children, has supported research into teaching techniques for children with reading difficulties.

THEORIES OF CAUSALITY

Genetic Factors

There are a number of studies which strongly suggest that genetic factors are involved in reading difficulties. Hallgren (1950) investigated children with reading disorders and their family histories and found that in 88% of the cases there was evidence of a reading disability in the immediate family. Hermann (1959) cited evidence from several studies on monozygotic and dizygotic twins. The findings of these studies indicated that in the monozygotic pairs studied both twins tended to have severe reading difficulties. However, findings for dizygotic twins showed that in only one-third of the cases both children were dyslexic. In clinics dealing with reading problems, the ratio of boys to girls appears to be 4 or 5 to 1. Hence, it has been suggested that the dyslexic disposition is a sex-linked genetic characteristic (Vernon, 1971).

Maturational Lag

Children with reading problems have many of the same problems as younger normal readers. For example, in children with specific reading difficulties there is a high frequency of letter reversal, difficulty in left-right discrimination, immature reproduction of the Bender designs, and an inadequate capacity to integrate events. This, combined with the further observation that many of these children show spontaneous improvement in reading and writing skills, has given rise to the suggestion that specific reading difficulty may be connected with delay in the maturation of certain functions of the brain (Critchley, 1964; Naidoo, 1972; Vernon, 1971).

On the other hand, it has been observed that reading problems can persist into adulthood. Vernon (1971) suggests that such defects as the extremely bizarre spelling, writing, and Bender reproductions are not usually found in normal young children. These appear to have a greater similarity to the productions of adult patients with brain injuries than to those of immature children.

Brain Dysfunction

Cerebral Dominance   The theory of cerebral dominance (weak, ambivalent lateralization in brain and motor functions), originally postulated by Orton as affecting children with reading problems, has been closely connected with the maturational lag theory (Critchley, 1964). Weak lateralization, which is often found in children with specific reading difficulties, has been related to ill-defined cortical differentiation. Weak lateralization is found in young children and also seems to persist in older children with reading problems. However, it has been pointed out that not all children with weak laterality have reading problems; nor do all children with reading problems have weak laterality.

Brain Damage   There have been many attempts to connect the difficulty some children find in reading with brain damage. Vernon (1971) has summarized evidence supporting this position in two broad categories: those studies which attempt to match known brain injuries (often in adults) with specific disabilities, and those which attempt to "connect cases of dyslexia in children with some impairment sustained during the antenatal period, delivery, or in early childhood."

On the whole, studies attempting to connect localized brain injury with specific disabilities have produced conflicting evidence. For example, in Gerstmann's syndrome, dysfunction in the parietal lobe is associated with disturbances in spatial orientation, directional concepts, finger agnosia, agraphia, and acalculia. However, there are also studies which question the presence of a definable syndrome of disabilities in connection with injuries to the parietal lobe.

There is stronger support for studies in the second group which attempt to connect evidence of early neurological damage to learning problems in children. In these studies, antenatal, delivery, and postnatal histories of children with reading difficulties have been carefully examined for evidence of some sustained injury. Estimates of brain damage for this group range from 16 to 58% (Kawi and Pasamanick, 1959; Shankweiler, 1964). Evidence for brain injury has also been gathered in matched studies carried out between children with specific reading difficulties and normal readers. It was found that in 16% of the cases of children with reading problems, there was evidence of brain injury, whereas only 1.5% of the control group showed any sign of having sustained some childhood brain damage (Kawi and Pasamanick, 1959).

Associated Disorders

Naidoo (1972) has criticized the "demand for unequivocal evidence of a single disorder of single identifiable etiology" and points out that such insistence would disqualify the use of cerebral palsy as a meaningful clinical term (Reid, 1972). She feels that the attempt to identify subgroups is not only helpful in remediation, but also theoretically sound.

Several attempts have been made to classify specific reading disorders. Vernon (1971) has suggested that there are four principal types of psychological processes which are involved in reading "and that defective functioning of any of these may give rise to difficulty in learning to read." The four processes which Vernon (1971) discusses are: (1) visual perception, (2) auditory-linguistic perception, (3) intellectual processes, and (4) motivational processes.

Ingram (1964) identified three subgroups on the basis of the difficulty the child may seem to have in reading. These were: (1) visuo-spatial difficulties, (2) speech sound difficulties, and (3) correlating difficulties.

INCIDENCE

Estimates of the incidence of specific reading difficulties range from less than 1% to more than 15% of the age range of children being tested. Franklin and Naidoo (1970) stated that "the majority of teachers in schools for normal children may never experience one dyslexic child." This would indicate that the condition is a very rare one indeed. On the other hand, the incidence of what Hallgren (1950) termed congenital word blindness among school children has been assessed as 10%. Kellmer et al. (1966) reported that 10% of the children leaving infant schools did not have even rudimentary reading skills. Clark (1970) reported that about 15% of the children "were, after 2 years at school, not yet beyond the earliest stages of learning to read."

Clark's Study of Reading Difficulties

Margaret Clark (1970) carried out her survey of reading difficulties in County Dunbarton, a local education authority on the west coast of Scotland. Approximately 70% of the county's population live in highly industrialized urban areas. At the first stage of testing the children were 7 years old. From the original group of 1,544 children, 230 were selected for further study. These children were selected because they had a reading quotient of 85 or less on the Schonell Graded Word Reading Test (1960) which meant that after 2 years at school they were still unable to read a simple book unaided. The 230 children comprised 14.9% of the original sample.

The children were tested on the WISC when they were 8 years old. Their mean full-scale IQ score was 89.8. Sixty-one of the 230 children did not have a single Full Scale, Verbal, or Performance IQ score over 90. This indicated that over one-fourth (26.5%) of the backward group did not fall within the average range of intelligence on any scales. Some of the difficulties in reading might therefore be attributed to low intelligence.

By 9 years of age, children who were severely backward in reading (2 or more years behind their expected performance) and were of average intelligence, represented 1.2% of the total population. This group was mainly composed of boys. There was also a larger group of moderately backward readers who were performing 1 to 2 years below their expected reading level, representing 5.1% of the total population.

Three years after the original group screening, the 230 "at risk" children were retested in reading. Over half of this group still required assistance in reading.

The Isle of Wight Study

The area chosen for a study by Rutter, Tizard, and Whitmore (1970) was the Isle of Wight, which lies about 4 miles off the south coast of England. Like County Dunbarton, the majority of the population live in urban areas. All 2,334 of the 9- and 10-year-old children on the Isle of Wight were given group IQ and reading tests, plus tests in arithmetic mechanics and form copying. Children were selected for individual testing if they had a score at least two standard deviations below the mean or if the pattern of their scores on the group tests was markedly irregular. There were 318 children (13.6%) who were selected on this basis for further testing. Altogether, 492 children were individually tested as a randomly selected control group.

Rutter et al. were interested in three identifiable groups: (1) children who were "intellectually retarded" (WISC score two standard deviations below the mean), (2) children "backward in reading" (reading attainment 28 months below their chronological age regardless of IQ), and (3) children "specifically retarded in reading" (28 months or more below their expected reading level based on mental age on the Neal Analysis of Reading Ability). Of the total 9- and 10-year-old group, 86 (3.7%) were identified as being specifically retarded in reading; 155 children (6.6%) were identified as backward readers. Of this latter group, 76% were also specifically retarded in reading.

Rutter et al. state that the 6.6% must be regarded as a minimal estimate of the reading retarded since 28 months is a severe degree of backwardness. From the control group it was found that 2% of the reading retarded children were missed by the group screening techniques. This would increase the incidence of specific reading retardation to a possible 5.7%, and backwardness to 8.6%. When the children with specific retardation in reading were retested 2 years later, all were still reading below their age levels. Only one child was less than 24 months retarded in reading and only seven children had made 2 years of progress in reading during this period.

FACILITIES FOR DIAGNOSIS AND REMEDIATION

Within the system provided by local education authorities, there are ten categories of children listed as needing special educational treatment.

Children who are educationally retarded or of limited ability can be classified as educationally subnormal (ESN) and be placed in an appropriate school. Children who "show evidence of emotional instability or psychological disturbance" can be placed in a school for the maladjusted (Great Britain, 1959). Most local education authorities also make some remedial provision for children who are having a great deal of difficulty with reading. There are also special facilities available for diagnosing and helping children with specific reading difficulties, though they tend to be scattered throughout both the education and health systems. Because each local education authority in Great Britain is highly autonomous, facilities for specific reading difficulties vary greatly.

Remedial Facilities in London

At the primary school level in London, there is general remedial provision for backward readers in many schools. Children whose reading problems are due to poor home conditions, disadvantaged environments, or who are slow learners, are taught in small groups, often by a teacher who has taken a 6-week course in remedial work. These teachers, however, cannot always provide the sophisticated techniques required by children with severe reading difficulties. If it is felt that more than remedial teaching is necessary, the head teacher will request that the school psychologist see the child.

It is also possible that the child will be examined in a clinic outside the formal educational system. In London there are centers for diagnosis which are attached to a hospital, but are supplied with teachers by the London schools. There are also centers specializing in diagnosis and remediation of reading problems which are run by voluntary organizations.

Hospital-associated Facilities There are several facilities in London associated with hospitals to which children with reading problems may be referred for diagnosis. As an example, the Newcomen Clinic was opened in 1964 and was the first comprehensive assessment center in the southern part of the United Kingdom. The clinic was not established with educational problems in mind. However, whether children are being examined because of birth disorders, slow development, or poor progress in school, a profile of the child's abilities and disabilities is made and the nature of his problem defined. The clinic has recently been provided with funds for further expansion, part of which will go toward a remedial teaching unit.

Centers Supported by Voluntary Organizations In 1963, following a conference held by the Invalid Children's Aid Association (ICAA), the Word Blind Centre for Dyslexic Children was established for research into identification, diagnosis, and treatment of specific reading disability (Naidoo, 1972). Children of average intelligence who were having difficulty learning to read were referred to the center. Referrals were accepted from a large variety of sources including parents. Children of low intelligence, those with cerebral palsy or other recognized neurological disorders, or those judged to be in need of psychotherapy were excluded.

The Word Blind Centre has since ceased operation. Many of the staff have joined the Ebury Centre for Language in Primary Education which is part of the Inner London Education Authority (ILEA) program for children with specific reading disabilities.

State Educational System Services, Primary Level

Psychological Services If a child is having difficulties in school with reading or social adjustment, or seems to be backward in development, his teacher or the head teacher may refer him to the educational psychologist for testing. Educational psychologists are assigned to a fairly large number of schools. They visit the schools at the request of the head teacher and help in testing and placing children who have problems. Alternatively, a child may be sent to a child guidance clinic staffed by educational psychologists, consultant psychiatrists, and psychiatric social workers.

The psychiatrist or psychologist collates a history from the parents, the results of a medical examination, the results of visual and auditory screening, and some measure of the child's intelligence.

The test results and recommendations are sent to the child's school. Sometimes the treatment is left in the hands of the regular teacher. If this is the case, it is strongly recommended that the psychological services should be involved in the development of programs for the children who have been tested. This might be done in several ways, including in-service training of teachers, consultation with the teachers concerned, and regular follow-up of the child. However, since an educational psychologist covers a fairly large number of schools, this can become very difficult. If the child's problem is severe, he might attend a child guidance clinic or reading center for part-time tuition. In London, clinics are provided with full- or part-time remedial teachers who work closely with the psychologists.

Special Classes For a child of normal ability with a severe reading problem, there are two kinds of special classes. These classes are housed in various schools in such a manner that each class draws its pupils from several schools. Children attend the classes on a part-time basis several times a week, usually for a whole morning or afternoon. The number of children attending at any one time is kept to a minimum. There are about 70 classes scattered throughout London.

Theoretically, there are two kinds of special classes and children are placed according to the nature of their problems. Children whose problems with reading seem to be of a cognitive order are placed in "remedial classes." These classes are restricted to a maximum of 15 children. On the other hand, children whose reading disorder is complicated by emotional problems are placed in schools for the maladjusted. Children who attend tutorial class are able to stay part-time in their regular class with the extra help they get in the special class.

Special Centers The Tizard Report (Great Britain, 1972) strongly recommended that remedial education centers be set up to help diagnose and remediate specific reading difficulties. They felt that the remedial center has a great advantage over the special class because the staff has the opportunity to pool its knowledge and experience. Remedial centers would offer part-time tuition for children who have been diagnosed as having a specific reading difficulty and would also act as a resource center for teachers of such children. Such centers are being established by some school districts.

State Education System Services, Secondary Level

Services at the secondary level are somewhat differently organized. These are arranged in two ways: (1) those services which originate within the school itself, and (2) those which rely upon a mobile teacher.

The organization and running of each school in Great Britain are the responsibility of the head teacher. Consequently, the range of remedial services is extremely broad even within the London area. Some secondary schools have remedial departments or classes which children with reading problems attend part-time. A few schools have small tutorial groups for these children who are withdrawn from the rest of the school for extra tutoring in basic language skills. Still other schools offer individualized reading programs and instruction for all children who need it. The testing of children for specific reading difficulties, however, is done by the educational psychologist or at a child guidance clinic, no matter what kind of remedial services the school may be operating.

There are several ways that specialized reading teachers are used at the secondary level. There is a system of peripatetic teachers, under the direction of the educational psychologists, who are assigned to particular schools. These teachers meet periodically with the educational psychologists for consultation about the progress the child is making. The service recently became reciprocal as specialized teachers are now often called in on an advisory basis to help the psychologists in assessment of children with reading problems.

The ILEA also provides about 150 home teachers for children suffering from emotional problems, including school phobia. The home teacher visits children in their homes for 8 to 15 hours a week, if for any reason the child cannot go to school. Alternatively, a child might be seen in the teacher's own home. This service was instituted for backward readers who needed a one-to-one relationship and has been effective with deprived and disturbed children.

There has recently been an enormous expansion of short courses in remedial techniques for teachers. Despite the expansion in the number of courses, trained teachers in this field are still at a premium. Remedial services are being reorganized in London. Remedial teachers will be asked to act as consultants to classroom teachers who have children with reading problems in their classes. It is felt that it is better for children with reading problems to remain in their own school and have part-time remedial instruction rather than to attend a special class outside the school.

MEDICAL EVALUATION AND CARE

In the United Kingdom detailed records of a child's development are kept from birth. Assessments are made by a physician at approximately the ages of 6 weeks, 6 months, 10 to 12 months, and at least yearly thereafter. "There is a general agreement that the younger the age at which children with physical, mental, or emotional disabilities are discovered and fully assessed, the more hopeful is the prognosis for recovery or habilitation. Case-findings depend upon the recognition of the earliest signs of deviation from normal development" (Sheridan, 1960).

Children who are considered "at risk" are noted and supervised most carefully. For example, if a child is slow in acquiring or developing speech, he may initially be identified at the baby clinic or by the Health Visitor. If there are special nurseries or day care centers near the child's home, it is often recommended that he attend one as soon as possible.

The majority of children with minor developmental imbalances will be brought to special attention once they enter into formal schooling at 4 to 5 years of age. At this time, their consultation record is sent to the School Medical Officer of Health who will then be responsible for the child's well being until he reaches 16 years of age.

If a child is referred by his teacher for testing because of a reading or behavior problem, the educational psychologist will usually ask for a report from the school, a history from the parents, and may request that the child's vision and hearing be tested. He might also decide that the child should have a medical examination and possibly a neurological examination, especially in the case of an overactive child.

In Great Britain, a careful distinction is made between children who are hyperkinetic and children who are overactive. Children with a true hyperkinetic syndrome are very rarely diagnosed. For children between the ages of 9 and 11 in a population of over 2,000, Rutter et al. (1970) found 5 children with the hyperkinetic syndrome. Bax (1972) examined

5-year-olds and found no cases of hyperkinesis in his sample of over 1,200 children.

The rigid criteria used for diagnosis probably account for the small percentage of children identified as having this syndrome. The child must have a "short attention span and excess motor activity, characteristics which are consistently observed by *all* adults who come into contact with him" (Bax, 1972).

Pharmacological Treatment

On the whole, drug therapy plays a very small role in the management of children with specific reading disorders in Great Britain. It has been said that one of the doctor's main tasks "may be to refute the suggestion of colleagues that a child will benefit from the administration of drugs" (Bax, 1972). One of the reasons stated for such caution in prescribing drugs is that there has been little agreement about their effect (Rosenbloom, 1972).

Psychological and Educational Tests

In Great Britain, the Wechsler Intelligence Scale for Children appears to be the preferred individual intelligence test. The Stanford-Binet Scale is also frequently used. Group intelligence tests are used for initial screening rather than diagnosis (Naidoo, 1972).

Tests used to make a differential diagnosis of a child's abilities and specific disabilities are selected from the following:

1. Bender Visual-Motor Gestalt Test (1946)
2. Benton Visual Retention Test (1955)
3. Brimer and Dunn, English Picture Vocabulary Test (1963) (British version of the Peabody-Picture Vocabulary Test)
4. Bristol Social Adjustment Guides (Stott and Sykes, 1963)
5. Crichton Vocabulary Scale (Raven, 1950)
6. Daniels and Diack, Standard Reading Tests (1958)
7. Frostig Developmental Test of Visual Perception (1963)
8. Goodenough-Harris Draw-A-Man Test (Harris, 1963)
9. Harris Tests of Lateral Dominance (1958)
10. Holborn Reading Scale (Watts, 1948)
11. Illinois Test of Psycholinguistic Abilities (McCarthy and Kirk, 1968)
12. Mill Hill Vocabulary Scale (Raven, 1958)
13. Neal Analysis of Reading Ability (1966)
14. Raven's Standard Progressive Matrices (1956)
15. Schonell Graded Word Reading Test (1960)
16. Vineland Social Maturity Scale (Doll, 1953)

The information gained by a thorough medical and educational diagnosis should help indicate a child's correct educational placement. It should also help the teacher to choose the remedial techniques best suited to each child. At present, however, the link between diagnosis and remediation is not very strong. The Inner London Education Authority is attempting to strengthen communication between teachers and psychologists by offering short courses for teachers on diagnostic techniques.

METHODS OF REMEDIATION

Until recently, remedial methods for children with reading problems were based on the assumption that reading difficulties can be overcome by counseling. This can be partially attributed to the influence of Sir Cyril Burt's investigations into backwardness in school children. Burt laid a strong emphasis on the critical role played by environmental and psychological factors in the causation of reading difficulties. Also, the category of reading difficulties is a relatively new one. It is based on educational criteria and is an administrative rather than a psychological category. This has meant that children whose problems might be attributed to widely varying causes have now been grouped together for educational treatment.

Educational Methods

On the whole, remedial treatment tends to be the responsibility of teachers and educational psychologists. There is no single method prescribed for all children with specific reading difficulties. Therefore, some of the more widely recognized techniques of remediation used in Great Britain will be described.

Fernald Technique   The Fernald method is based on the principle that a child will be more successful learning to read and write the words he selects rather than those chosen for him. Learning takes place through combined kinesthetic, auditory, and visual channels, making unnecessary the purely visual recognition of words. In this manner, the child eventually builds up a "look-say" vocabulary. There is no phonic training involved; recognition of new words comes from knowing parts of previously learned ones.

The child is asked to trace the word he has chosen with his finger, saying the word each time he traces it. He does this until he can write it without looking at the original copy. In this way he builds a large enough vocabulary to make his own book. The teacher types what the child has composed within 24 hours so that he can learn to read from printed material. All new words are filed alphabetically for easy reference (Cotterell, 1970).

Gillingham-Stillman Program   The Gillingham technique attempts to strengthen associations among the auditory, visual, and kinesthetic channels, emphasizing a multisensory approach. It is structured so that the child both encodes and decodes information in all three channels. Reading, writing, and spelling are taught simultaneously. The authors list eight steps in establishing cross-modal linkages. The manual, a very detailed book, is accompanied by teaching aids which include such items as letter and word cards.

Frostig Method   This method is designed for the child who needs developmental or remedial help in visual-motor skills. It is claimed that through proper use of the materials and techniques, a child with visual-motor perceptual difficulties can gradually be trained to more complex perceptual tasks. Work sheets for perceptual training are provided in five task areas, each of which is sequenced gradually from simple to complex (Frostig and Maslow, 1969).

Edith Norrie Letter Case   Edith Norrie founded the Word Blind Institute in Copenhagen. She developed a system in which visual cues help children learn the structure of words. Each word is broken into phonetic units which are color-coded. Consonants are grouped into three categories according to the position of the lips and tongue, and are then further divided into voiced and voiceless groups. All vowels are colored red and the child learns that every syllable must have a red letter in it.

Materials include a case in which the individual, colored, wooden letters are placed, and a mirror to aid the child in properly forming consonant sounds by viewing his mouth forming the sound. It is suggested that the child form words and sentences using these letters, then read back what he has put together, and when corrected, copy it into a composition book (Arkell, 1970).

Breakthrough to Literacy   The materials for this program were originally designed for use in the infant school and have since been successfully applied in remedial classes. The theory underlying this method is that a child will learn more easily if he is able to manipulate printed language directly, without the intervention of an adult. The teacher is not used as an intermediary between the child's expressive and written language since the child can choose his own words and make his own sentences from the materials provided. This is essentially a whole-word, look-say method of reading, but one with a highly individualized approach. It is not aimed at the child who has severe visual perception disabilities.

Materials include a magnet board, figurines, and sentence-maker. The child's version of the sentence-maker is in the form of a triptych with slots in which word cards can be placed. Two sides of the triptych usually consist of vocabulary which has been learned in a small group and the third side contains the child's own personally choosen words (Mackay et al., 1972).

English Colour-Code Programmed Reading Course This method was developed under the auspices of the National Society for Mentally Handicapped Children. Through the color-coding of the vowels, children are assisted in learning the irregularities of English spelling. This approach is essentially phonetic. A one-to-one association is established between a single color and a single sound. Children work through the stages of each program at their own pace.

The materials include 15 color-coded grapheme (vowel) tiles. It is felt that consonants are regular enough to make color-coding unnecessary. There are also drill, prompting tapes, and work sheets.

The programs are grouped into three stages. The taped drills and work sheets of the first stage concentrate on letter recognition, initial consonant sounds, and short vowel sounds. Stage two emphasizes the serial aspects of words and sentences. In stage three, the pupil concentrates on decoding words of three or four phonemes. During this stage the color code can gradually be withdrawn (Mosley, 1972).

Initial Teaching Alphabet (i.t.a.) The i.t.a. program represents an attempt to establish a direct relationship between written symbols and language sounds. There are 44 different symbols to be learned and each one has only a single correct sound response. Materials include alphabet cards, workbooks, and readers in the i.t.a. script. Symbols are introduced gradually, beginning with the most frequently used consonants and short vowels. Transition to traditional orthography (t o) is usually accomplished toward the end of the second year.

A great deal of research has been done on the use of the i.t.a. in comparison with t o. One study (Downing, 1972) suggested that i.t.a. reduces the incidence of poor reading and spelling. However, in the weakest 10% of the pupils there was no significant difference in attainment between the group using i.t.a. and the control group using t o.

CONCLUSION

There are a great many remedial techniques available for teaching children with specific reading difficulties. Some methods attempt to code written language, some use a phonetic approach, and others rely heavily upon look-say principles. These very differences reflect an important aspect of what must go into a successful remedial program for these children.

Children with specific reading difficulties need individual techniques to help them overcome their reading problems. This means that programs must be tailor-made for each child; it means that strengths must be utilized and weaknesses compensated for as fully as possible. Teaching should be carried out in fairly small groups, with at least some opportunity for one-to-one contact. Because these children do not learn incidentally, structured language programs are the most beneficial. Success also must be planned for and reinforcement must be both constant and consistent.

ACKNOWLEDGMENTS

I am extremely grateful to Dr. Mary Wilson and Mr. Maggs of the Inner London Education Authority for the help they have given me in gathering information.

REFERENCES

Arkell, H. 1970. The Edith Norrie Letter Case. *In* A. W. Franklin and S. Naidoo (eds.), Assessment and Teaching of Dyslexic Children. Invalid Children's Aid Association, London.

Bax, M. 1972. The Active and Over-Active School Child. Dev. Med. Child Neurol. 14:1.

Bender, L. 1946. Bender Visual-Motor Gestalt Test for Children. National Foundation for Educational Research, London.

Benton, A. L. 1955. Benton Visual Retention Test. (Rev. Ed.). Psychological Corporation, New York.

Brimer, M. A., and L. M. Dunn. 1963. English Picture Vocabulary Tests. Educational Evaluation Enterprises, Bristol.

Clark, M. 1970. Reading Difficulties in Schools. Penguin, Harmandsworth, Great Brit.

Cotterell, C. 1970. The Fernald Auditory-Kinesthetic Technique. *In* A. W. Franklin and S. Naidoo (eds.), Assessment and Teaching of Dyslexic Children. Invalid Children's Aid Association, London.

Critchley, M. 1964. Developmental Dyslexia. Heinemann, London.

Daniels, J. C., and H. Diack. 1958. The Standard Reading Tests. Chatto and Windus, London.

Doll, E. A. 1953. Vineland Social Maturity Scale. Educational Test Bureau.

Downing, J. 1972. i.t.a. and slow learners: a reappraisal. *In* J. F. Reid (ed.), Reading: Problems and Practices. Ward, Lock, London.

Franklin, A., and S. Naidoo. (Eds.) 1970. Assessment and Teaching of Dyslexic Children. Invalid Children's Aid Association, London.

Frostig, M. 1963. Developmental Test of Visual Perception. Consulting Psychologists Press, Palo Alto.

Frostig, M., and P. Maslow. 1969. Visual perception and early education. *In* L. Tarnopol (ed.), Learning Disabilities: Introduction to Educational and Medical Management. Charles C Thomas, Springfield, Ill.

Great Britain. 1959. The Handicapped Pupils and Special Schools Regulations. Statutory Instrument No. 365. HMSO, London.

Great Britain. 1972. Children with Specific Reading Difficulties. Department of Education and Science. HMSO, London.

Hallgren, B. 1950. Specific dyslexia. Acta Psychiatr. Neurol. No. 65.

Harris, A. J. 1958. Harris Tests of Lateral Dominance. Psychological Corporation, New York.

Harris, D. 1963. Children's Drawings as Measures of Intellectual Maturity. Harcourt, Brace & World, New York.

Hermann, K. 1959. Reading Disability. Munksgaard, Copenhagen.

Ingram, T. T. S. 1964. The dyslexic child. Word Blind Bull. 1:4.

Kawi, A. A., and B. Pasamanick. 1959. Prenatal and perinatal factors in the development of childhood reading disorders. Monogr. Soc. Res. Child. Dev. 24:4.

Kellmer, P. M., N. R. Butler, and R. Davie. 1966. 11,000 Seven-Year-Olds. Longmans, London.

Mackay, D., B. Thompson, and P. Shaub. 1972. Breakthrough to literacy in the remedial situation. In J. Reid (ed.), Reading: Problems and Practices. Ward, Lock, London.

McCarthy, J. J., and S. A. Kirk. 1968. Illinois Test of Psycholinguistic Abilities. University of Illinois Press, Urbana.

Moseley, D. V. 1972. The English Colour Code Programmed Reading Course. In J. R. Reid (ed.), Reading: Problems and Practices. Ward, Lock, London.

Naidoo, S. 1972. Specific Dyslexia. Pitman, London.

Neal, M. D. 1966. Neal Analysis of Reading Ability. Macmillan, London.

Raven, J. C. 1950. Crichton Vocabulary Scale. Lewis, London.

Raven, J. C. 1956. Standard Progressive Matrices. Lewis, London.

Raven, J. C. 1958. Mill Hill Vocabulary Scale. Lewis, London.

Reid, J. 1972 (ed.) Reading: Problems and Practices. Ward, Lock, London.

Rosenbloom, L. 1972. Learning disabilities and hyperkinesis. Dev. Med. Child Neurol. 14:3.

Rutter, M., P. Graham, and W. Yule. 1970. A Neuropsychiatric Study in Childhood. Heinemann, London.

Rutter, M., J. Tizard, and K. Whitmore. 1970. Education, Health, and Behaviour. Longman, London.

Schonell, F. F., and F. E. Schonell. 1960. Diagnostic and Attainment Testing, Oliver and Boyd, London.

Shankweiler, D. 1964. A Study of Developmental Dyslexia. Neuropsychologica Vol. 1.

Sheridan, M. D. 1960. The Developmental Progress of Infants and Young Children. Ministry of Health No. 102. HMSO, London.

Stott, D. H., and E. G. Sykes. 1963. Bristol Social Adjustment Guides. University of London Press, London.

Thompson, C. 1972. The British Dyslexia Association. Dyslexia Rev. 8: Winter.

Vernon, M. D. 1971. Reading and Its Difficulties. Cambridge University Press, Cambridge.

Watts, A. F. 1948. Holborn Reading Scale. Harrap, London.

CHAPTER 13

Learning and Reading Disabilities in Hungary

Sándor Illés and Ildikói Meixner

The Hungarian People's Republic is a socialist country which has common boundaries with the Soviet Union, Rumania, Yugoslavia, Austria, and Czechoslovakia. With an area of 93,030 square kilometers, Hungary is somewhat larger than Austria and a little smaller than the German Democratic Republic.

Hungary has a population of 10.5 million people. One-quarter of the population lives in towns of more than 100,000 and about one-half of the population lives in villages of less than 10,000 people.

The most important step in the direction of general public and compulsory primary education was taken in 1868 when the six-class primary school was begun. In 1940, the primary school was extended to eight classes, but this extension remained purely nominal until the end of World War II. In 1945, over 90% of the primary schools had only six grades.

BACKGROUND OF SPECIAL EDUCATION

Educational Policy in Normal Education

One of the greatest results of the educational policy in the Hungarian People's Republic is the establishment of the compulsory eight-class public school system (Table 1).

Public education begins in nursery school and includes ages 3 to 6 years. It is not compulsory. In 1973, 63% of all children of this age were in nursery schools. The compulsory primary school has eight classes for ages

209

Table 1. Numbers and percentage of pupils in various schools (1972–1973)

Schools	Ages	No. of pupils	Percentage of population
Nursery school	3–6	270,000	62.0
Primary school	6–14	1,043,600	98.3
Special schools	6–14	31,142	
Secondary school	14–18	346,543	31.5
University	18 up	90,857	

6 to 14 years. In the school year 1972–1973 roughly 1,000,000 pupils, that is, 98% of all children of this age, attended primary school. Secondary school, from age 14 to 18, is not compulsory. The university begins at the age of 18.

The system of special schools for different kinds of handicapped children developed parallel to the compulsory primary school for the ages of 6 to 14 years. In the school year 1972–1973 there were 31,142 pupils, or 2.9% of all primary school pupils, in special schools.

The basic principles of the educational policy of compulsory education are:

1. Compulsory education is public education, meaning that all primary schools and special schools are supported and controlled by the state
2. The primary schools and special schools are free
3. All primary schools have the same program of instruction that has been developed and prescribed by the state
4. All school books are developed by the Ministry of Education, and every school uses the same school books
5. According to the age of the pupils, instruction follows the same didactic principles in every school; in the instruction of the same subject there are no great methodical differences among the schools
6. The basic and general form of instruction is traditional: children sit in rows facing front, and all are instructed together; the primary teacher has about 30 to 35 pupils, while in the special school there are about 10 to 15 pupils in the class; group instruction does not allow very much individualization for the teacher

System of Special Education

Special education mainly ranges from age 6 to 14 years. Special nursery schools have been developed for pupils with vision and hearing impairment. Special vocational training is available for these two groups only. There are no special secondary schools.

Table 2. Special education institutions and number of pupils (1973–1974)

Institution	No. of institutions	No. of pupils	Percentage relative to normal pupils
Mentally retarded	499	30,131	2.92
Hearing impaired plus mentally retarded	1	105	0.01
Hard of hearing	1	279	0.03
Deaf	8	1,274	0.12
Partially sighted	2	185	0.02
Blind	1	252	0.02
Motor disordered	2	261	0.03
Speech defective	2	65	0.006
Total	516	32,552	3.15

Table 2 shows the number of special institutions and pupils and the percentages of the special pupils and the normal pupils in the school year 1973–1974. The largest area of special education is for the mentally retarded. The mentally retarded pupils are divided into two groups, educable mentally retarded (EMR) and trainable mentally retarded (TMR), on the basis of intelligence levels similar to other European countries. Mentally retarded pupils are either in special classes in a normal school, in special schools, or in special boarding schools. Eighty-seven percent of all mentally retarded children are classified as EMR and 13% as TMR. The above-mentioned basic principles of educational policy are valid also for special education.

STATUS OF READING AND LEARNING PROBLEMS

Education of Learning Disabled Children

Learning disabled children are in the normal schools and in the schools for the educable mentally retarded. Although the scientific notion of legasthenia was introduced by a Hungarian, Paul Ranchburg, in the first decade of the century, the educational care of learning disabled children is still relatively underdeveloped in Hungary. There are no special classes or special schools for these children. They are integrated into either normal classes of the primary school or special classes for EMR. Their need for special educational care has been only recently emphasized. To illustrate this situation, the next two tables summarize the distribution of the failed pupils according to subjects in the normal school and in the special schools for EMR (Tables 3 and 4).

Table 3. Percentage of failed primary school pupils (1968 through 1972)

Subjects	Grades		
	1	2	3
Reading	6.9	2.5	1.7
Writing	5.7	1.6	1.0
Composition	—	—	2.2
Grammar	—	4.3	4.1
Environmental studies	2.8	1.0	1.3
Mathematics	7.2	4.8	3.3
Practical skills	0.6	0.1	0.1
Drawing	—	0.1	0.1
Music	0.4	0.1	0.1
Physical education	0.1	—	—

In Hungary, we use a 5-step marking system. Number 5 signifies the best achievement and number 1 signifies the poorest achievement or failure. If a pupil is marked a number 1 grade at the end of the school year, he will not be promoted to the next grade. Tables 3 and 4 show that the most difficult subject is mathematics. The next most difficult group of subjects is reading, writing, and grammar, which are based on language skills. The common trend of low achievement among normal and EMR pupils suggests the possibility of relatively frequent occurrence of reading and writing disabilities among both normal and EMR pupils. These failures indicate that the learning disabled children do not have the necessary

Table 4. Percentage of failed pupils in EMR schools (1970–1971)

Subjects	Grades				
	1	2	3	4	5
Reading		8.3	4.5	2.7	1.9
Reading and Writing	24.2				
Writing		7.3	3.4	2.2	—
Speech	6.0	2.8	2.8	2.5	2.5
Composition	—	—	—	4.1	3.0
Grammar	—	—	6.5	6.4	4.9
Mathematics	15.8	7.3	6.4	5.4	4.1
Drawing	—	0.6	0.3	0.1	0.2
Music	1.1	0.2	0.3	0.1	0.2
Physical education	0.3	—	0.1	—	0.1
Practical skills	1.3	0.8	0.6	0.2	0.3

Table 5. Natural sciences: effectiveness of teaching methods and level of student reading skills (International Association for the Evaluation of Educational Achievement Study)

	Countries ranked by age groups of students		
Rank	10 years	14 years	18 years
1	Japan	Japan	New Zealand
2	Sweden	Hungary	West Germany
3	United States	Australia	Australia
4	Italy	New Zealand	Netherlands
5	Finland	West Germany	England
6	Hungary	Sweden	Scotland
7	Belgium	United States	Hungary
8	England	Scotland	Finland
9	Netherlands	England	Sweden
10	West Germany	Finland	France
11	Scotland	Italy	Italy
12	Thailand	Belgium	Belgium
13	Chile	Netherlands	United States
14	—	Thailand	Thailand

Source: United States Department of Health, Education, and Welfare (1969).

remedial help to overcome their impairments in reading, writing, and mathematics.

Standardized Achievement Tests

The first school achievement tests were recently standardized using valid statistical norms. The sample of children on which the test was standardized consisted of fourth, eighth, and twelfth grade pupils, that is, 10-, 14-, and 18-year-old normal pupils. The study was supported and controlled by the "International Association for the Evaluation of Educational Achievement." This association, which is under UNESCO control, consists of 21 member nations.

On the basis of this study, we can compare the effectiveness of teaching methods and the level of reading skills in different countries. The comparative study, using the multiple choice method, was carried out in three areas: reading comprehension, reading speed, and the natural sciences. Tables 5 to 7 were compiled by ranking the national averages of this study (United States Department of Health, Education, and Welfare, 1969).

Hungary has a relatively high rank in the natural sciences. However, in reading comprehension and reading speed, our ranking is much lower than

Table 6. Reading comprehension: effectiveness of teaching methods and level of student reading skills (International Association for the Evaluation of Educational Achievement Study)

Rank	Countries ranked by age groups of students		
	10 years	14 years	18 years
1	Sweden	New Zealand	New Zealand
2	Italy	Italy	Scotland
3	Finland	United States	England
4	England	Finland	Netherlands
5	Scotland	Scotland	Finland
6	Belgium	Belgium	Sweden
7	Netherlands	Sweden	Belgium
8	United States	Hungary	Israel
9	Hungary	England	Italy
10	Israel	Netherlands	Hungary
11	Chile	Israel	United States
12	India	Chile	Chile
13	Iran	Iran	Iran
14	–	India	India

Table 7. Reading speed: effectiveness of teaching methods and level of student reading skills (International Association for the Evaluation of Educational Achievement Study)

Rank	Countries ranked by age groups of students	
	10 years	14 years
1	India	India
2	Italy	Sweden
3	Chile	Italy
4	Belgium	Belgium
5	Netherlands	Scotland
6	Finland	England
7	England	United States
8	United States	Netherlands
9	Scotland	New Zealand
10	Sweden	Finland
11	Iran	Chile
12	Israel	Hungary
13	Hungary	Israel

the international standard. This comparative study disclosed several sociological factors which influenced these averages; chief among them is the standard of living. Of course, the different teaching methods of these countries may also have played a significant role in these results. The results warn us to reconsider our teaching methods and to pay more attention to writing and reading disabilities occurring in elementary school pupils.

Early Factors Influencing the Education of Learning Disabled Children

Why the education of learning disabled children is a relatively underdeveloped area of special education in Hungary may be explained by the following factors:

First, after World War II the government had to assume a great financial burden. It had to rebuild the schools demolished in the war and had to develop a new school system. As a result, the chief effort of educational policy has been to develop the primary school and to reach the level required by law. This educational policy was primarily concerned with the needs of normal children. Only in the last decade has the state been able to bring questions of quality into the foreground. The area of learning disabilities falls here.

Second, efforts were made to eliminate the effects of sociocultural differences in education. It is well known that these circumstances influence achievement in school. Therefore, normal education imposed the same requirements on every pupil. The slight biologically induced differences (among them learning disabilities) were neglected. Their manifestations as failures in academic skills were explained by mental retardation, inappropriate teaching methods, or by sociocultural deprivation.

Third, learning difficulty may be traced to either biological impairment or to unfavorable sociocultural conditions. If the manifestations of learning disabilities are considered as consequences of unfavorable sociocultural conditions, then the area of the effects of biological impairment will become narrower and the notion of handicap will include only the obviously biological defects. Our school systems are based upon the principle that only children with obvious neurological impairment are handicapped and therefore only they require and have the right to special education. On the basis of this consideration, it is very difficult to find a place in the school system for those children who have learning disabilities. In spite of the fact that in most cases of learning disabilities neurological damage can be either diagnosed or assumed, this does not give significant information concerning the child's learning capacity. The diagnosis of the underlying psychological processes may be far more important in the measurement of learning capacity.

Perspectives in the Education of Learning Disabled Children

As a result of the development of our society, the sociocultural differences among the population are considerably smaller than before World War II. The opportunity for a good educational experience is not equal even today, because of various family factors. There are differences in the attitudes, motivations, and the educational practices of families. Such differences exist between the families of uneducated workers and intellectuals, between those living in cities and those in remote rural areas, between the gypsies and nongypsies, between the families with many children and those with only one child, and so on. Therefore, the basic trends of the educational policy in connection with underachievement remain valid for the future.

The new educational policy developed on the basis of the decisions of the Central Committee of the Hungarian Workers' Party in the last 2 years includes two considerations which are important for the education of learning disabled children: (1) In theory and practice it has been recognized that there are children in our educational system who are neither entirely normal nor completely handicapped, who need special education temporarily, or only in some areas of psychological development in order to acquire the new academic skills. (2) Accordingly, the necessity to apply new teaching methods such as small group work and individualization in instruction has been emphasized.

As a result of these new demands in educational policy, the Ministry of Education has initiated a number of significant measures to prevent and to decrease the high incidence of learning difficulties. Several of these measures are remedial in character and indicate that remedial education of children with learning disabilities is beginning in the primary schools. These measures are the following:

1. Considerable extension of preschool education
2. Introduction of a compulsory educational maturity examination
3. Organization of correctional or remedial classes at the elementary level
4. Modification of the traditional marking system
5. Extra remedial lessons for the underachievers in the normal schools
6. Development of the network and efficiency of the day schools
7. Intensive courses for the underachievers after the school year
8. Development of the various forms of after-school help for the learning disabled children

Considerable Extension of Preschool Education

In the 1972–1973 school year, 58.8% of all first-graders had previously participated in preschool education. Besides the traditional form of preschool education, special "preparatory courses" are being developed. These courses include about 200 lessons for children of nursery school age who do not attend a nursery school. In the 1972–1973 school year, 22.2% of all first-graders had participated in these courses.

Compulsory School Maturity Examination

In the 1965–1966 school year, a compulsory school maturity examination was initiated for every child who reached school age. The basis of this examination was the medical diagnosis of the physical maturity of the child. In the 1972–1973 school year, 2% of the children examined were diagnosed as immature. In 1966–1967 this examination was extended to include maturity of the psychological functions.

Correctional Remedial Classes at Elementary Level

On the basis of the school maturity examination, immature children are classified into two groups. The somatically retarded children who are not mentally retarded may extend their stay in the kindergarten for a year. The children with normal intelligence but with abnormal ability profiles and developmental retardation may be enrolled in correctional remedial classes organized tentatively in the normal primary schools. These correctional classes are still experimental. In the school year 1972–1973 there were 115 correctional remedial classes in Hungary. The classes are organized only for the early grades of the primary schools. The average number of pupils in these classes is 12 to 15 while in the regular elementary school classes there are 30 to 35 pupils.

The aim of the correctional classes is to give individual assistance in the early school years to develop basic academic skills. If the school achievement of these children can be remediated in these classes, they can return to the regular elementary schools. If this remediation fails, the children will be placed in a school for EMR children.

There is a great need in these classes for adequate psychological diagnosis. It is very difficult to differentiate between a normal underachieving child, a child with learning disability, a mildly retarded child, and an underdeveloped, underprivileged child. On the basis of current diagnostic methods, the 6-year-old population of Budapest in the 1971–1972 school year has been classified as follows: 91.9%, normal; 1.6%, handicapped; 3.9%, pupils for correctional classes; and 2.6%, to remain in kindergarten for an additional year.

Modification of Traditional Marking System

A special way of helping children with learning disorders is to modify the traditional marking system and program. Since children have been taught by classical methods, failures have been 9 to 11%. This led to emotional disturbances. Poor grades serve not only as feedback for teachers and parents about the problems of these children, but also as a shock for the children themselves. Therefore, we are introducing a looser form of teaching which is connected with a new form of evaluation. Pupils get grades for the first time at the end of the second school year, instead of the first term of the first grade. Children will not be failed in the first grade. The teachers of the second grade may, if necessary, give some basic instruction to the weaker students, using small group teaching or individual instruction. The teachers may choose any methods they think effective.

Extra Remedial Lessons for Underachievers in Normal Schools

Those attending the first two grades of the normal primary school or the lower eight grades of the special schools for the EMR are given two to four extra lessons weekly. These lessons may be given individually or in small groups. In these extra lessons children participate who have difficulty in making progress in any subjects or who are in need of training a special ability, or who have been absent from school for a long time.

Development of Efficiency of Day Schools

Similar help is to be given at the day schools. Their purpose is to equalize the social and cultural differences from an instructional and educational point of view, as they are attended by children whose mothers are employed.

Intensive Courses for Underachievers after the School Year

If, in spite of all efforts, pupils do not achieve the basics necessary for the following class, their teachers pay special attention to them during the last quarter of the school year, both in the regular class time and during extra lessons. Their grades are left open at the end of the school year and they may attend an 11-day intensive course, giving them an opportunity to acquire the necessary material to pass to the next grade.

Extra Help for Learning Disabled Children

Extra help for children with learning disorders is given by child psychiatric clinics, child guidance centers, and speech therapy. The child psychiatric clinics are led by doctors. Neurotic children are given play therapy either individually or in groups. When necessary, medication is prescribed. The child psychiatric clinics are supported by the Ministry of Health, while the child guidance centers and the speech therapy groups are supported by the Ministry of Education and the local councils. In the first, the medical viewpoint is stressed, while the child guidance centers are educational. Sometimes they both deal with the same problem, in which case they cooperate.

The child guidance centers deal with all types of problems of behavior, socialization, mental health, home, and learning. If a child fails to pass the normal school readiness tests, it is the child guidance center that decides where he is to go for the appropriate form of instruction. With mental deficiency, the case is sent to another committee that has the right to send children to special schools. Neurotic children are given individual or group treatment. In some institutions learning therapy is the usual form of treatment.

In Hungary, speech therapy is given by special teachers who are experts not only in speech but also mental deficiency and often in teaching children with other sensory impairments. Our logopedic network deals with the correction of speech disorders of children from 4 to 5 years of age, and there are also special groups for adults. In cases of young children, the parents are given educational advice and they are taught educational play and home training. The development of this speech network is considered very important by us to prevent children with speech disorders from acquiring secondary symptoms. By treating delayed speech development and improving vocabulary, as well as sentence formation, we are often able to prevent the start of learning disturbances. Our speech network is an out-patient service only.

In most cases children get a 45-minute treatment twice weekly in small groups consisting of 3 to 6 children. About 4 to 5% of Hungarian children get these treatments, but the need is about double that amount. In smaller towns we have no experts available. We are striving to correct a great many of the speech disturbances before schooling. At present, we have no speech nursery schools, though one is to be established in the near future.

DIAGNOSIS OF LEARNING DISABILITIES

Learning disabilities are diagnosed by educational consultants and pediatric neurologists. In bigger towns the schools are attached to the district educational consulting stations or to the neurological dispensaries for children. The service is free and may be suggested by the school or by the parents. Frequently, the examination is suggested because of learning problems. However, cases frequently are found when the neurologist is consulted for psychosomatic complaints, and during the examination he may discover that the hidden motive for the complaint is a learning disability. In one case, for example, a child with epileptic symptoms was sent for examination. The neurological check was negative, but the diagnosis from the psychological tests was dyslexia. After temporarily administered mild sedatives and dyslexia re-education were started, the seizures did not occur again.

The children are examined by the special educator and/or the psychologist and neurologist. If necessary, other medical examinations may follow. In cases where the family background seems to be unfavorable, the district nurse calls on the family. In some cases the nurse or the psychologist also visits the school. The psychological tests vary according to the institutions where the examinations have been carried out. However, the child's intelligence level is determined in all cases. The tests are either the Hungarian version of the Binet intelligence test, or the Wechsler intelligence scales. When speech problems exist the nonverbal Snijders-Oomen test is used. To complement these tests, the Bender Visual Motor Gestalt Test, Raven's Progressive Matrices, the Ranchburg word couples, and the Draw-A-Man tests are used. If the child needs it, the Oseretsky Test of Motor Proficiency is also used.

Personality tests are used according to the practice of the examiner. The most frequently applied tests are the Rorschach, the Children's Apperception Test, and the Thematic Apperception Test. The Düss tales, the Thomas tales, the Lüscher tests, the color-pyramid, the Rosenzweig P.F.T., Wartegg's Drawing Test, Koch's Wood-Test, the family-drawing, the world-test, the Sceno-test, puppet plays, and various drawing tasks are also used. The examiners consider that the test procedures present favorable conditions to observe the child's behavior, and to produce detailed qualitative analyses from the test results as well.

In Hungary, teaching is carried out according to a uniform curriculum and the requirements are rather clearly defined. The task of the psychologist or special educator is to determine the level of knowledge and skills achieved by the child. The obtained results will be compared with the data from previous psychological examinations to determine the cause of the learning disability. Children who have certain problems at the beginning of schooling will attend remedial classes. These classes operate within the primary schools. In these classes the number of pupils is lower and the teaching methods are more meticulous than in the regular classes. We have no special schools or classes to deal with learning problems arising in the higher grades. It is the psychologist's or the special educator's task to consult the primary school teacher and the parents of the problem pupil, and to suggest the educational and occupational methods to be used with the child.

REMEDIAL METHODS IN READING DISABILITIES

The re-education of children with dyslexia is not yet generally organized in Hungary, though the investigation and research on dyslexia have a long history in this country. Since children with dyslexia generally turn up in the pediatric, neurological stations and in the speech therapy dispensaries, the re-education of children with dyslexia started in Hungary with the voluntary work of psychologists and speech therapists. The next step will be organized re-education.

Speech Correction and Reading Disability

Speech therapy has a long and respectable history in Hungary. The Institute for Speech Correction of Budapest was established 79 years ago. In the Institute, out-patients attend small-group therapy and usually a very good relationship between parents and therapists becomes established. Spontaneous tracing led to the discovery that children with speech defects who after successful therapy were discharged from the institute as recovered at the age of 6 to 8 years, would show symptoms of dyslexia at the age of 9 or 10.

Gradually we became aware of the particular types who became dyslexic. These were the slowly improving stammering (lisping) children. Those who at the beginning of therapy were unable to pronounce voiced consonants, or who had difficulties with speech sounds already developed during therapy, or who did not show spontaneous improvement in the course of speech therapy, or who had relapses, were high risk children.

If the well established but not yet automated s sound becomes lost or changed into an interdental sound; if in spite of the already rolling tip of the tongue, the child returns to the uvular r or if the child has forgotten the rolling of the tongue—these are the high risk cases for dyslexia. In one type of dyslexia group a rather high proportion of the children (about 60 to 70%) had a very poor sense of phrasing and a meager vocabulary. They also had difficulty in finding words and in forming sentences. In the course of intelligence testing it turned out that the IQ's of these children were normal or above average and their visual memory was several years beyond their age level, while their text memory was below their age group. If they were put in a group with lisping children, they would have difficulty imitating the lip and tongue exercises applied for the correction of lisping in spite of their clear pronunciation.

We do not pretend that this is the only type of dyslexia; however, the majority of our children with dyslexia belong to this group and so we consider the major part of dyslexia cases as having speech defects. They may be regarded as in the last stage of a speech weakness or as having a single visible symptom of a mild congenital aphasia.

TEACHING METHODS IN READING IN ELEMENTARY SCHOOLS

As a result of the above considerations, we attach great importance to the conscious correct pronunciation of the heard, proprioceptive analysis and differentiation of the phonemes. Hungarian orthography is almost phonetic. Its difficulty consists in its relatively numerous phonemes sometimes only slightly deviating from each other. On the other hand, the orthography follows the pronunciation, and where this is not the case, the deviation is controlled by rules. Probably this is the reason why mild cases of dyslexia are not immediately discovered in primary school.

At present there is no general re-education of children with dyslexia. In the institutions where they deal with this problem the work is carried out in small groups of 3 to 6 children, for 1 hour, twice a week. We do not consider this to be satisfactory. If dyslexia is in many cases a symptom of a speech defect, the re-education of dyslexic children must include vocabulary building, the development of sentence-constructing ability, correct articulation, and the development of reading memory. In addition, the teaching of special reading and writing exercises as well as some grammar and composition is also necessary.

In Hungary, the uniform and compulsory curriculum and textbook prescribe an essentially synthesizing (phonetic) reading and teaching method. The first part of the spelling book is printed in separate syllables and the consecutive reading of whole words is first taught in the second semester of the second grade. This is because in the Hungarian language the inflected words are rather elongated due to the suffixes. For this reason, on the first pages of the Hungarian spelling books the words are about one to two letters longer than, for example, those on the first pages of German spelling books. Because of its phonetic character, the Hungarian language is very suitable to teaching by synthetic methods. On the other hand, the suffixes make the application of a global method more difficult as the nouns get suffixes in all cases except the nominative and change the over-all picture of the word. This is why the global (whole word) system has been adopted experimentally in some schools.

REMEDIAL METHODS

The re-education system for reading disabled children is a synthetic one. However, within the synthetic teaching method the tendency is to make the children—if only indirectly—acquainted with the advantages of the whole word method. The particular system emphasizes two principal activities: (1) the differentiation of the letters (phonemes), and (2) the synthesis of letters, syllables, words, and sentences. The progress of the two different activities is parallel.

The phonics exercises include letters, syllables, reading, and writing from dictation. The principle is to place similar letters apart. We also pay attention to the visual similarities of the letters (*f-t-j*), though this would not cause serious problems to our dyslexic children. A serious problem comes from the letters which have phonetically similar sounds such as voiced and unvoiced couples (*f-v, t-d*). Other letters which the children mix up in a stage of lisping include *s-sh, r-l*. Particularly difficult are the letters representing both phonetic and visual similarities like *d-b, m-n, u-ü*, etc. In the first stage we dictate and have the children read only the letters, syllables, words, and texts which are very different from one another. If we have a lisping child, we withhold the teaching of the letter the child is unable to pronounce until he has learned the correct pronunciation in speech correction.

The method of teaching similar letters like *b* and *d* would be as follows. First teach *b* together with several unlike letters. Then teach *d* with a group of unlike letters ignoring *b*. Then return to the letter *b*, neglecting *d*. Finally, both letters are taught together as parts of letter and syllable rows, words, and sentences.

The distinction between voiced and unvoiced consonants is very important as they are rather numerous in the Hungarian language. This is why we attach great importance to speech. The sounds of these two groups are attached to two different colors. In order to facilitate the consecutive reading of letters, we use stories with smaller children. However, in the teaching of all children we also use, for a rather long period, meaningless rows of syllables. We found that children with speech defects had difficulty in consecutive reading if their lisping was apraxic. With these children we have to spend much time exercising, for example, the pronunciation of the syllable *ki*, where the pronunciation of *k* and the transition to *i* is performed by quite different muscle movements than the pronunciation of *ko* (in English, *ki*ng, *ko*la). In the beginning the rows of syllables are simple. With progress we increase the difficulty in order to develop the children's attention.

After the reading of rows of syllables the children read word-charts. The words always consist of letters which we are actually using in the differentiation of letters. When reading the letters we draw attention to the meanings of the words by explaining the words to the bigger children, or by comparing the words with pictures. One chart always includes words of equal rhythm, equal numbers of syllables, and changes of vowels and consonants. In the beginning we ask the children to read short words, and sentences composed of short words. Then slowly and systematically we increase the word length and neglect the hyphen between the syllables. Both methods permit the children to see the words as global units at an early stage.

In the problems made up to develop synthesis, the children use small cards to develop letters into words, or syllables into words, or words into sentences. At a lower speed, but according to similar principles, the teaching of writing is carried out with preparatory exercises and tracing, dictation of letters, syllables, words, and sentences. This is followed by sentences and stories from pictures, or the description from memory of a text which has been read.

The children's homework may be a problem-form to be solved or a painting-form to be filled in. On the problem-forms they will find instructions for problems to be solved by drawing, or faulty or meaningless texts to be corrected. The painting-form is stuck with its colorless side to one page of the copybook. On the opposite page the children find the instructions to do the painting. In the beginning the instructions will be short, but later we gradually introduce more and more sentences which have nothing to do with the execution of the painting but tell a story about the picture itself. This way a whole story book is constructed.

CASE HISTORY OF A READING DISABLED CHILD

We would like to present Stevie. He is one of the children to whom we taught reading and writing before school age. His mother brought Stevie to our dispensary because of a speech defect when he was 6 years and 5 months old. The child was lisping, had a tonic stuttering, was dysphonic, and had an open nasal voice. At an earlier age, he had been treated for asthma. Stevie is an only child. His father did not want a child because he thought that the child would not be sane. However, the mother could not explain his fear. The family history recalled stuttering, left-handedness, asthma, and migraines. During her pregnancy the mother had nervous complaints, and from the third month of pregnancy she developed an allergic cold. She had a normal delivery; the birth weight was 2,990 grams. The baby was lazy at first and did not suck properly. Development of motion and speech occurred in due time. He was toilet trained during the day from the age of 3 but suffered from eneuresis until the age of 5. At 9 months he had dysentery, and when he was 17 months old his diphtheria vaccination caused a high fever.

At admittance, the sounds which he could not pronounce were: *k, g, z, c, s, zs, cs,* and *r*. His Binet IQ was 100. His ability on performance problems was weak. The picture-description problems were solved at the 9 year old level, though his sense of phrasing was very weak. His Goodenough Draw-A-Man scored 4 years and 9 months.

Because of Stevie's various speech defects, we suggested postponing his schooling for one year. In addition to speech therapy we taught him reading, as we felt that he might develop dyslexia later. Our assumption was right, for he learned reading extremely slowly. He had to remain for at least a half-year at the reading of syllable-rows. The problem he faced was definitely an apraxia. He recognized the letters one by one but after pronouncing the first sound, he was unable to find the muscle movements leading to the second sound. For example, he declared in a loud voice in advance that the second letter was a "*u*"; however, when reading, he pronounced an "*o*." To explain himself, he turned and said: "I can't help it, my mouth is always turning aside and I cannot control it!"

Stevie was admitted to the first grade of a remedial class, and later to the normal primary school. As the teaching of reading was individual, and he was not obliged to compare his own score with the better scores of other children, he became fond of reading. At first, he was the best reader in his class. Later he lost this position, but even last year he was still one of the best readers in the fourth grade.

Stevie came to us at the age of 6.5 years and remained in our care for 2 years. When he was in the third grade, he returned to our dyslexia group because of some difficulties with orthography such as inversions, and confusion of voiced and unvoiced consonants, which were typical of dyslexics. He was weaker in grammar than in any other subject.

We were startled when we noticed that Stevie, whose lisping was perfectly controlled by the time he attended the first grade, started lisping again (though this was milder) during the period without speech therapy. He still stuttered slightly. However, neither the school nor the child took notice of these mild symptoms of dyslexia. The child is an enthusiastic reader. In the fourth grade he read a 600-page novel about Indians in one day when he was ill.

Unfortunately, a child's dyslexia generally strikes both parents and teachers in the third, fourth, and fifth grades, and at that stage remediation cannot be so successful. This is why prevention is one of our main goals. In addition we always ask the parents of the recovered and released nursery school children to come back to us immediately if they ever notice reading disabilities in the child.

REFERENCES

Education and Cultural Activities in Hungary, 1945–1970. 1970. Edited by The Ministry of Cultural Affairs, Budapest.

Statisztikai Tájékoztató 1971–72. 1972. Alsófoku oktatás. Müvelödésügyi Minisztérium Statisztikai Osztály, Budapest.

Közmüvelödési adatgyüjtemény. 1973. Központi Statisztikai Hivatal. Budapest, ápr. 25–11.

Báthory Zoltán. 1973. A haxai IEA vizsgálat eredményeiböl: Tanulási eredmények. Pedagógiai Szemle. XXIII. 7—8.

Báthory Zoltán. 1973. 7 standardizált tantárgyteszt. Országos Pedagógiai Intézet.

Cross-National Study of Educational Attainment: Stage of the I.E.A. Investigation in Six Subject Areas. 1969. Project No. 6-2527. U. S. Dept. of Health, Education, and Welfare, Washington.

CHAPTER 14

Learning Disabilities in Ireland

Thomas Kellaghan

A cursory glance at a history of education indicates that particular problems come into focus at different times. For example, at different periods the problems of the mentally handicapped, those of the physically handicapped, and more recently, the problems of the disadvantaged have each been the focus of attention. The fact that a problem does not receive widespread attention does not mean that it does not exist, as the case of learning disabilities well illustrates. Problems of children who have difficulty in acquiring basic scholastic skills are perennially present to teachers, whether or not they receive the attention of the specialists. In almost every class, one is likely to find at least a few children who have great difficulty in acquiring one or more of the basic skills: reading, writing, spelling, or computation. In some cases, the number may be much larger; a school in a poor neighborhood or the lowest stream in a tracked system may contain many children with a learning disability. Teachers learn to cope with such situations, one way or another, and with varying degrees of success. The problem of learning disabilities then can hardly be said to be new in any educational system. What is new is an increased awareness of the problem and an increase in attempts to supplement teachers' resources in dealing with it.

The fact that attempts (other than those of individual teachers) to deal with learning disabilities are relatively new in Ireland means that there has not yet been a great deal of thinking about the precise needs of children with such disabilities. While the existence of children of normal ability who have learning problems is clearly recognized, other problems, perceived as more pressing, have up to now taken most of the attention of educational administrators. Children with learning disabilities do, however,

227

benefit from a number of services that have been provided even though these services were not designed specifically for such children.

It is not possible at present in the Irish situation to speak of learning disabilities in terms of well-defined categories, their nature, distribution, and methods of treatment, as one might, for example, in an area in the United States with a much longer tradition in dealing with the problems of children who have difficulty in learning. An examination of the Irish case nevertheless has its own particular interest. It provides the opportunity to explore why such services were slow in developing as well as the particular factors which can foster development. The relatively new and growing service in Ireland can also provide the basis for a comparison with services that have developed at an earlier stage in other countries. The kind of service developed to deal with learning disabilities is likely to reflect certain views about the nature of such disabilities, their remediation and prevention, and these views in turn are likely to be based on current philosophical, social, medical, and psychological positions. Since such positions vary over time, so too we would expect variation in approaches to learning disabilities developed at different times.

LACK OF DEVELOPMENT OF SERVICES

Learning disabilities and their management should be viewed in the context of a total educational system, its organization, values, and priorities. Systems that are child-centered and strive to optimize the individual development of all children are more likely to develop strategies for dealing with learning difficulties than systems that are curriculum-oriented, lock-step, competitive, and selective. While there are always hazards in attempting generalizations, it is probably true to say that the Irish educational system in the past has fallen into the latter rather than into the former category.

At the elementary level, for example, education was primarily curriculum-oriented. A detailed syllabus of work was laid down for each grade and pupils were expected to attain a certain "standard" before proceeding to the next higher grade. This resulted in a high rate of retention of students for a second, and sometimes even for a third year in certain grades (*Investment in Education,* 1966). Some students never completed the full elementary school course. Those who did and who remained in formal education found themselves in a postprimary system that was also curriculum-oriented. Two types of school were available—a secondary grammar school which had an academic bias and which prepared students for third-level education and white-collar jobs, and a vocational school, which had a technically biased curriculum and whose students were generally destined for blue-collar occupations. Such an arrangement inevitably involved a selective process. Students who were accepted in secondary grammar schools were more intelligent, had better scholastic records and came from higher level socioeconomic homes than those who proceeded to vocational schools (Kellaghan and Greaney, 1970). So long as schools focused on standards and selection, one might not have expected too great attention to be paid to the learning problems of those individual students whose abilities did not match the system.

There were, no doubt, other reasons why the treatment of learning disabilities received little attention in Irish schools apart from that given by individual teachers. One was the general lack of development of the behavioral sciences. University courses in psychology, for example, have been developed only in the last 15 years. Even today, there is an almost complete absence of standardized and diagnostic tests developed for use in Irish schools. It is, of course, difficult to decide whether the absence of such basic instruments hindered the development of ancillary services to deal with problems like those of students with learning disabilities, or whether such instruments were not developed because of a lack of demand for them. However one interprets the situation, it is clear that no specialized services or materials were envisioned for problems associated with learning disabilities.

RECENT DEVELOPMENTS

Just as it may be argued that lack of provision for dealing with the problems of learning disabilities is part of the general educational system, so may it also be argued that changes in that system can bring about a new interest in such problems. Before considering such changes, it should be pointed out that when we speak about learning disabilities in the Irish situation, we have to use the term in a very general sense to indicate any case of a child who experiences difficulty with one or more of the basic school subjects. This is partly because of the practical situation outlined above; services for children with learning disabilities often deal with other categories of children. It is also because there are certain difficulties in accepting a definition such as that described, for example, by Clements (1969) who lists three criteria which some schools in the United States use for determining eligibility for a special program for children with learning disabilities. First, according to Clements, the child must have average or above intellectual capacity (IQ of 90 or above on either the Verbal or Performance Scale of the Wechsler Intelligence Scale for Children). Second, he must have a learning disability of significant proportion in reading, arithmetic, spelling, and/or writing. And third, the child should exhibit other characteristics such as hyperactivity, deficits in expressive language, or attentional difficulties. These last named characteristics are often associated with deviations of functions of the nervous system (minimal brain dysfunction), and their presence would not be regarded by many as essential to a diagnosis of learning disability. The first two of Clement's points when taken together also raise some problems. If they are taken to imply that a discrepancy between performances on an intelligence test and on an attainment test is of particular diagnostic value, then they are based on an assumption that is in need of considerable examination (Thorndike, 1963). In describing changes in the Irish educational system that have led to a greater awareness of children's learning problems, the term learning disabilities will be used without the qualifications often associated with the use of the term as described by Clements.

The development of interest in Ireland over the past 10 years in providing more extensive services for students with learning disabilities can be related to five factors: new thinking about the curriculum for elementary schools, a move to a more comprehensive type of postprimary education, the extension of the period of compulsory schooling, the expansion of the behavioral sciences, and a general awareness that some children in the school system experience difficulty in coping with the demands of the school.

The last of these factors will be considered first. As in other countries, the learning problems of the physically and mentally handicapped were the first to attract attention, no doubt, because they were the most obvious. There is a fairly long tradition in the education of the physically handicapped in Ireland. Special provision for the mentally handicapped also goes back to the beginning of the present century but such provision has expanded greatly over the past 10 years. Although performance on an intelligence test is not the only criterion for classification as mentally handicapped, in general an IQ of less than 70 is taken as indicating the dividing line between "handicap" and "normal." The needs of such children are now well served by special schools (day and residential), special classes, and specially trained teachers (O'Cuilleanain, 1968). Facilities for clinical assessment are also available. Recognition of the needs of students who, while not technically mentally handicapped, have difficulty in learning has been slower to develop and ancillary services are still poorly developed.

One of the factors that brought the needs of such students into focus in recent years centered around a rethinking of the curriculum for elementary schools. This thinking was marked by a move from classroom teaching to smaller groups and individualized instruction, the removal of a formal examination at the end of elementary schooling (at age 12), and most significantly perhaps, by the introduction of a child-centered curriculum in 1969 (Ireland: Department of Education, 1971).

Changes at the elementary level were paralleled by changes at the postprimary level. In particular, attempts have been made to merge the facilities offered by the two types of postprimary school and to offer a comprehensive curriculum for students 12 to 15 years of age. There were, at the same time, efforts to provide postprimary education for all students up to the age of 15. As well as certain organizational changes, this involved extending the period of compulsory schooling from 14 to 15 years of age. As a consequence of these changes, teachers are having to cope with weaker students who in the past would have terminated their education at the elementary level. Such students frequently present learning difficulties on a scale that secondary school teachers did not encounter in the past. This situation has given rise to pressures to improve facilities for dealing with them.

Side by side with these changes, the universities have increased the supply of behavioral scientists, particularly psychologists. Thus one group essential to the study and treatment of learning disabilities is becoming available to the school system. Many of the psychologists who have graduated in recent years are now working, directly or indirectly, in the field of learning disabilities—in the school service, in clinics, or in training programs.

The result of all these changes has been to produce a movement away from the strong curriculum-orientation that characterized Irish schools in the past, toward a more student-centered one. The movement has only begun but it has been strong enough to arouse considerable interest in the problems of students with learning disabilities and to lead to a search for solutions to those problems.

EXTENT OF LEARNING DISABILITIES

Given the state of development of services for students with learning disabilities in Ireland, it is not surprising that accurate figures for such students are not available. While definite estimates for the extent of mental handicap are available (Ireland: Commission of Inquiry on Mental Handicap, 1966), no similar estimates exist for children of normal ability with learning problems. There are, however, some data related to school attainment, which suggest that learning disabilities may be a serious problem in the Irish educational system.

In a survey carried out between 1962 and 1966, it was found that over one-third of students in elementary schools were one grade or more below the standard of attainment which teachers expected of students of their age. Teachers' expectations may of course be high, even unrealistic. Kellaghan et al. (1969) report that teachers of a representative sample of Irish elementary school children regarded the general progress of 25% of the children as "unsatisfactory." Furthermore, 25% of students were perceived as having difficulty in English (reading, writing, or oral), 48% as having difficulty in arithmetic (mechanics or problem-solving), and 50% as having difficulty in Irish (reading, writing, or oral), a compulsory second language in all schools. These figures are extremely high and even if teachers' expectations are unrealistic, they do suggest that students are working in a system where many of them are perceived as failing. In passing, it should be noted that the fact that all Irish children learn a second language in the elementary school is a further possible source of learning difficulties not present in other school systems. These difficulties may be specific to the second language or may have wider implications (Kellaghan and Macnamara, 1967; Macnamara, 1966).

Three surveys carried out in Irish schools provide data of a more objective kind on attainment in English. One nationwide survey carried out in 1961 found that the mean of fifth-grade children (most of whom were 11 and 12 years old) was 20 points below the mean obtained for the standardization sample in Britain (Macnamara, 1966). The test employed had been standardized with a mean of 100 and a standard deviation of 15. In two further surveys carried out with children aged 10 and 11 years in Dublin city in 1964 and in 1969, children scored 13 points below the British standardization mean (Kelly and McGee, 1967; McDonagh, in press); again a test with a mean of 100 and a standard deviation of 15 was used. There are problems in the interpretation of the findings of these surveys since the samples with which the tests were used were not drawn from the population for which the tests had been standardized. However, taken in collaboration with figures on retention rates and teachers' estimations of student difficulties, it seems probable that the school progress of a relatively large section of Irish students is less satisfactory than might be expected.

From the data available, it does not of course follow that such unsatisfactory progress is to be attributed to learning disabilities of the kind being discussed elsewhere in this volume, i.e., disabilities arising from neurological dysfunctioning, emotional disorders, or perceptual problems. We have no way of deciding this issue since tests of the kind recommended by Tarnopol (1969) for the diagnosis of learning disabilities have not been administered on a large scale to Irish children. The difficulties could perhaps be attributed to an inappropriate curriculum, to poor teaching, or to inadequate criterion measures. Be that as it may, the fact remains that many Irish schoolchildren experience learning difficulties which demand a kind of attention that the schools have not provided on any large scale in the past. Even when one makes whatever allowances might be necessary for the inappropriateness of using objective tests with children who have no experience with such tests and for the unrealistic nature of teachers' expectations, the figure for children with learning difficulties in Irish schools would seem to be in excess of the 10% that has been suggested in the case of the American public school population (Clements, 1969).

MEASURES TO DEAL WITH LEARNING DISABILITIES

The total population of the Republic of Ireland is about 3,000,000 people. Approximately 500,000 children are in attendance at elementary school (2 preschool years plus grades 1 to 6), and about 180,000 attend postprimary schools (5 grades, either secondary grammar or vocational). Children may commence preschool at about 4 years of age. Attendance is compulsory from ages 6 to 15.

The measures to deal with learning disabilities in this population may be categorized as being either remedial or preventive. The remedial approach is the more traditional and includes clinical and school services. The preventive approach is newer and more radical and its development was influenced by recent emphasis on the importance of early learning and school preparation.

Remedial Approaches

Clinical Services   In an unpublished survey carried out by the Psychological Society of Ireland last year, 14 clinics were listed as providing services for school children in the Dublin area. (There are three other clinics in the country, but no detailed information about their operation is available.) The Dublin clinics are served by 31 full-time and 17 part-time psychologists, five full-time and 15 part-time psychiatrists, 13 full-time and 14 part-time diagnostic and remedial teachers, 17 social workers, and seven speech therapists. Some clinics also have the service of a physician, neurologist, pediatrician, audiologist, or physiotherapist. The number of cases handled by clinics obviously varies with their size and function. For clinics for which figures are available, the number of cases seen per month varies from 10 to 130 with a mean of 65; about half are new cases.

Assessment and diagnostic procedures in the clinics are probably very similar to those in an American child guidance clinic. The Wechsler tests (Wechsler Intelligence Scale for Children and Wechsler Preschool and Primary Scale of Intelligence) and the Stanford-Binet Intelligence Scale are frequently used as measures of general intelligence. A variety of other tests of cognitive functions is also used: the Illinois Test of Psycholinguistic Abilities, the Bender Visual Motor Gestalt Test, the Goodenough-Harris Draw-a-Person Test, and the Frostig Developmental Test of Visual Perception as well as several other tests of auditory and visual functioning. It should be noted that none of these tests has been standardized on an Irish population and this fact obviously often presents difficulty in interpretation. There is also a lack of local normative data for personality assessment procedures commonly in use, such as Bellak's Children's Apperception Test, the Bene-Anthony Family Relations Test, the Rorschach technique, and the Holtzman Inkblot Technique. Locally standardized tests of attainment are also lacking; only one test developed for use in Ireland is available—the Marino Graded Word Reading Scale, which is a test of word recognition (O'Suilleabhain, 1970). In the absence of locally standardized tests of attainment, use is made of tests standardized in Britain, such as Schonell's diagnostic and attainment tests (Schonell and Schonell, 1960) and the reading tests of Daniels and Diack (1965).

A variety of therapeutic procedures is provided by the clinics: psychotherapy (group and individual), art and play therapy, speech therapy, perceptual and sensory training, and remedial teaching.

In their day-to-day-functioning, clinics in Ireland are probably very similar to clinics in other countries. They provide useful specialist services for, among others, children with severe learning disabilities. The number of clinics, however, is so small that they can provide therapeutic services for only a small number of the children in need of such services.

School Services In recent years the Department of Education of the Irish government has been engaged in developing facilities within the school system to assist students with learning disabilities. These facilities are being developed separately for the elementary and postprimary levels, but the approach at both levels involves in-service training of teachers and organizational modifications within schools.

At the elementary level, for the past 3 years, a number of in-service courses have been available for teachers who wish to specialize in dealing with learning disabilities. These courses focus on developing skills in diagnostic and remedial procedures. There are at present about 90 classes, with an average enrollment of 16 students, serving children with learning difficulties. Some of the children in these classes would be regarded as being technically mentally handicapped (IQ less than 70), but the vast majority would not. An alternative approach to the special class is the provision of a remedial teacher who withdraws children from their normal classes for specialized remedial work for a number of class periods each week. (The frequency of withdrawal can vary a good deal from student to student.) There are 210 remedial teachers working in elementary schools at present. On an average, each teacher deals with about 50 children per week. Remedial teachers then, either in special classes or using the withdrawal system, reach approximately 12,000 children, which is about 2.4% of the elementary school population. This number continues to grow.

At the postprimary level, an in-service course for remedial teachers run by the Department of Education is now in its second year of operation. The setting up of this course was in part a response to the increased number of students in postprimary schools with learning disabilities following the expansion of numbers of students in full-time education at this level. The course deals with techniques of remedial work as well as with methods of coping with students who will soon be leaving school. It recognizes that the problems of students at this level cannot be handled in the way in which one might handle learning disabilities in a 7- or 8-year-old child. The disabilities of students at the postprimary level are associated with a long history of school failure and the teacher's role must be as much therapeutic as it is simply remedial. Last year, during its first year of operation, 25 teachers took the in-service course for remedial work in the postprimary school; in the present year, 59 teachers are taking the course. In future years it is planned to have 50 to 60 teachers take the course each year. It is estimated that eventually 300 to 500 remedial teachers will be required in the postprimary sector.

Preventive Approaches

Side by side with the development of remedial approaches, the feasibility of preventive measures to deal with learning disabilities has been a topic of investigation in recent years. Their feasibility has been explored particularly in the context of disadvantaged populations, among whom one would expect a high incidence of learning disabilities, and in whom there is at present a strong interest in Ireland (Kellaghan, 1970). Studies are at present being carried out with a view to identifying effective means of helping preschool children from poor socioeconomic backgrounds develop the knowledge, skills, and attitudes which contribute to school adjustment and school learning. One study is being carried out in a preschool center, where 3- and 4-year-old children follow a structured program with scholastic objectives of the type for which some successes have been claimed elsewhere (Kellaghan, 1972; Kellaghan and OhUallachain, 1969). In the other study, 2-year-old children are visited in their homes and methods of mother-child interaction which are designed to foster cognitive and language development are demonstrated to mothers. The initial findings from these studies suggest that economical and effective ways of coping with some sources of learning disabilities may be found in such preventive measures. Action towards implementation at a national level will await final evaluation of the studies now under way.

CONCLUSION

The concept of learning disabilities is not a single well-defined category for which special services have been developed in Ireland. However, many children with learning disabilities benefit from the services which have been developed to serve a wider population. For example, child guidance clinics serve the needs of the mentally handicapped, but also provide facilities for the diagnosis and treatment of children of normal ability who are experiencing difficulty with one or more of the basic school subjects. Likewise, preschool programs designed to assist disadvantaged children adapt to school probably come in contact with many children who, in the absence of intervention procedures, would later exhibit learning disabilities.

Attempts to deal with problems of retardation and learning disability have gained momentum over the last few years. In some cases, the services which have been developed are very similar to those which traditionally have attempted to deal with these problems in other countries. Thus the remedial work of clinics with cases of severe disability closely resembles the work carried out in clinics elsewhere. However, because interest in learning disabilities has developed at a later date in Ireland than in the United States, for instance, other options have become available. In selecting these options, educationists in Ireland have been influenced by new emphases, interests, and research in other countries. The particular options we have considered—intervention in the home and in preschool centers—reflect beliefs about the importance of development in the preschool years and the possibility of influencing the course of development at this time. The value of the effectiveness of these approaches to reduce the incidence of learning disabilities in schools must await the final evaluation of experimental programs at present under way. If they are shown to be successful, we may expect in the future, a greater emphasis on preventive than on remedial measures in dealing with the problem of learning disabilities in our schools.

While services for children with learning disabilities are growing in Ireland, the need for expansion is still great. Expansion means more than just more teachers, more psychologists, and more clinics. It means the development of new ideas and new approaches for problems that are old. We have already seen signs of such development in the implementation of preventive measures for children in disadvantaged homes. An important feature of this measure was the enlisting of parental cooperation in the educational process. There have been moves initiated by parents also. Very recently, the Dyslexia Association of Ireland was formed by a group of parents whose children have reading problems. Parents are already widely involved in the education of the more obviously (physically and mentally) handicapped. There are also moves to increase the involvement of the community in schooling in general and in dealing with learning disabilities in particular. The development of such active kinds of involvement augurs well for the future development of services to cope with the problems of learning disabilities in schools.

REFERENCES

Clements, S. D. 1969. A new look at learning disabilities. *In* L. Tarnopol (ed.), Learning Disabilities. Introduction to Educational and Medical Management, pp. 31–40. Charles C Thomas, Springfield, Ill.

Daniels, J. C., and H. Diack. 1965. The Standard Reading Tests. Chatto and Windus, London.

Investment in Education. 1966. Annexes and Appendices to the Report of the Survey Team appointed by the Minister for Education in October 1962. Stationery Office, Dublin.

Ireland: Commission of Inquiry on Mental Handicap. 1966. Report. Stationery Office, Dublin.

Ireland: Department of Education. 1971. Primary School Curriculum. Teachers' Handbook Part 1. Dublin.

Kellaghan, T. 1970. Deprivation and disadvantage: Ireland. *In* A. H. Passow (ed), Deprivation and Disadvantage: Nature and Manifestations, pp. 179–186. UNESCO Institute for Education, Hamburg.

Kellaghan, T. 1972. Preschool intervention for the educationally disadvantaged. Irish J. Psychol. 1:160.

Kellaghan, T., and V. Greaney. 1970. Factors related to choice of post-primary school in Ireland. Irish J. Ed. 4:69.

Kellaghan, T., and J. Macnamara. 1967. Reading in a second language. *In* M. D. Jenkinson (ed), Reading Instruction: An International Forum, pp. 231–240. International Reading Association, Newark, Dela.

Kellaghan, T., J. Macnamara, and E. Neuman. 1969. Teachers' assessments of the scholastic progress of pupils. Irish J. Ed. 3:95.

Kellaghan, T., and S. OhUallachain. 1969. A project for disadvantaged preschool children. Oideas 3:28.

Kelly, S. G., and P. McGee. 1967. Survey of reading comprehension. A study in Dublin city national schools. New Res. Ed. 1:131.

Macnamara, J. 1966. Bilingualism and Primary Education. Edinburgh University Press, Edinburgh.

McDonagh, D. A second survey of reading comprehension in Dublin city national schools. Irish J. Ed. (In press).

O'Cuilleanain, T. A. 1968. Special education in Ireland. Oideas 1:5.

O'Suilleabhain, S. V. 1970. Marino Graded Word Reading Scale. Longmans, Browne and Nolan, Dublin.

Schonell, F. J., and F. E. Schonell. 1960. Diagnostic and Attainment Testing. 4th Ed. Oliver and Boyd, Edinburgh.

Tarnopol, L. 1969. Testing children with learning disabilities. *In* L. Tarnopol (ed), Learning Disabilities: Introduction to Educational and Medical Management, pp. 180–195. Charles C Thomas, Springfield, Ill.

Thorndike, R. L. 1963. The Concepts of Over- and Underachievement. Bureau of Publications, Teachers College, Columbia University, New York.

CHAPTER 15

Learning Disabilities in The Netherlands

Joep J. Dumont

Nearly 1,500,000 children go to regular schools in The Netherlands and more than 75,000 go to special schools. Therefore, of all the children who go to school, almost 5% are in special education.

As in most countries, care for exceptional children began with identifying and institutionalizing severely mentally retarded, blind, and deaf children. Residential care for those children has a long tradition and dates to the 18th and 19th centuries. Specialization then followed two different lines. One has been the trend to organize the education of exceptional children in special schools by special laws and administration. Thus, we built schools for epileptic children, schools for children who were suffering from prolonged illness, etc. Children who were moderately retarded were separated from children with severe mental retardation. Children who were hard of hearing and children with visual impairment were separated from deaf and blind children and went to their own schools. After World War II there was an increase and then almost an explosion of specialized schools. This rapid growth was facilitated by our educational laws which make it relatively easy to found a new school. The school can be established by the municipality or by a private organization, union, or society. In all cases, the school is entirely paid for by the government. Education is free and equal for all children. In principle all schools can be equally good, equally well equipped, and equally well staffed (Table 1).

It is striking how rapidly schools for children with learning disabilities have increased in number. These schools (in Dutch: school voor kinderen met leer-en opvoedingsmoeilijkheden; or LOM school) are now the fastest growing type of special schools and much of the professional attention of administrators, researchers and educators is fixed on them.

Table 1. Special education in The Netherlands

Type of school	1950	1960	1970	1972
Severely mentally retarded			93	94
Combined SMR and MMR[b]	206	318		
Moderately mentally retarded			304	304
Learning disabilities	4	51	162	175
Deaf	6	11	13	13
Hard of hearing	4	12	22	23
Blind			7	7
Visually impaired	6	9	6	6
Physically handicapped	4	12	33	35
Prolonged illness	12	15	9	9
Bad health (open air)	12	19	19	21
Epileptic	2	2	3	3
Emotionally disturbed			38	40
Foster home schools		18	16	15
Pedological institutes	3	3	7	8
Total[a]	273	500	797	819

[a]In the total are all special schools instituted by law, including schools for children belonging to the traveling population, and schools for children of barge crews.
[b]SMR = severely mentally retarded; MMR = moderately mentally retarded.

ADVANTAGES AND DISADVANTAGES OF A SPECIAL SCHOOL

Although Dutch school laws permitted the establishment of special classes, they were seldom found in our school system. Between 1920, the year the law was instituted, and 1970, the year a new school law was submitted to parliament, our system of special schools has flourished. What are the advantages and disadvantages of special schools? One disadvantage seems to be that stigmatization by segregating children and separating schools may produce severe problems. Specialization and separation seem to create a dilemma: "A normal child in a special school is a special child in a normal school."

The Advantages of a Special School are the Disadvantages of a Special Class

Educationally speaking, in a special school we can separate children according to age and ability. While some divergence of ages is an advantage, too much difference appears to be a problem in educating children. A special school has more opportunity to differentiate. The special school has more possibility of putting children together with the same range of capacities. Group instruction is easier in schools where the population is not too heterogeneous. Decrease in heterogeneity is facilitated by selection at entry to the school. A special committee composed of a psychiatrist, psychologist, and principal screens all the pupils who enter the school. This is a prescription of the law and it enables educators to select a more or less homogeneous population for their school. As for setting goals, choosing educational tools, and applying didactic methods, schools can specialize according to the needs of their pupils. On the other hand, special classes generally do not have a chance to specialize in their curriculum, because they have to enroll several types of children.

In special schools, the child is protected from the feeling of always being the slowest and the failure. The child is also protected from the cruelty of normal children, discriminating against and stigmatizing him. Moreover, the teachers are not isolated but work together in a team, helping and supporting each other, under the leadership of their principal.

The Disadvantages of a Special School are the Advantages of a Special Class

There are quite a few disadvantages with the special school. Originally it was thought that a few years of special school would be enough to help children re-enter the regular school, but this turned out to be the exception. In a sense, the special school appeared to maintain the problem instead of solving it. The way back to the normal school situation is easier when the child is in a special class in a regular school.

Another severe criticism is made against the special school. Teachers in regular schools acquire the habit of not feeling responsible for problem children. They see it as a problem special teachers have to solve; they do not see it as their problem. Another equally severe criticism relates to the fact that if the regular school is drained of all exceptional children, the average level of classroom work will increase and the curriculum will be accelerated. This will create a new group of "slow learners."

The special class guarantees an integration of special education into regular education, so the chance of teachers becoming influenced by special knowledge and skills is greater in an integrated school. In an integrated school, the child will feel more like a normal child, will feel less exceptional, and will have less chance to be isolated from his peers and neighborhood companions. The special school is a school where children come from various parts of the town. A child is in his school to prepare his entry to society. Every kind of isolation will have a negative influence on the development of his self-concept and create a feeling of inadequacy.

Also, to educate our children to become tolerant of children who are exceptional seems to be a worthwhile goal in education.

Last but not least are the parents, who are very sensitive to any possible stigmatization of the child. The parents prefer special classes because the decision to put the child in a special class appears not to be as definite as putting a child in a special school.

We may conclude that the special school is a strong educational help because of specialization of the curriculum and the professionalization of the teachers. The special class seems to be strong in socialization and destigmatization, while de-emphasizing specialization of curriculum.

Why did The Netherlands choose the system of special schools? Stigmatization is more a problem of society than it is of the school. To the extent that society is tolerant of exceptional behavior, exceptional achievement, and exceptional education, the child will experience no harm in being an exception.

We compared special schools and special classes in regular schools as models for solving educational problems by way of organization. There is also a continuum in the training of teachers to handle exceptional children starting with the regular classroom and ending with residential treatment schools.

Some theorists and researchers doubt the usefulness of a highly specialized organization in special education. Their strongest argument is that there is a discrepancy between the diagnostic work, the traditional emphasis on differential diagnosis, and the homogeneity usually found in all treatment programs. If we compare the curricula of our special schools, we would have trouble determining what differences there are. Actually, our programs have not yet arrived at that point of specialization necessary to fully justify the adjective "special."

We get the impression that the trend emphasizing "sameness" in the methods of special education, and de-emphasizing specialization, is inspired by behavior modification techniques. While stressing techniques to improve behavior and to stimulate motivation, they neglect the importance of the content of the curriculum. A combination of curriculum planning and reinforcement strategies appears to be necessary to get the best results. The Dutch schools of special education appear to be more progressive in relation to curriculum planning than they are in adopting behavioral techniques.

THE SCHOOL FOR CHILDREN WITH LEARNING DISABILITIES

We shall describe an average school for children with learning disabilities. The school actually is meant for children with learning disabilities and behavioral problems. The reasoning is that most children with learning disabilities will have emotional problems. Hyperactivity, impulsive behavior, anxieties, aggressiveness, lack of self-confidence, and feelings of inadequacy appear with learning disabilities. Children with severe problems in their behavioral and social conduct are not allowed in this school, but they go to schools for emotionally disturbed children. All big cities have one or several LOM schools for children with learning disabilities.

Children with Learning Disabilities

What kind of children attend the LOM schools? The most important characteristics of the learning disturbed children may be summarized:

1. A discrepancy exists between school achievement and justified expectations of parents and teachers

2. Poor achievement is not due to subnormal intelligence; IQ tests show normal intellectual potential

3. Psychological examination indicates that the child is in danger of being retarded in his school career and his personal development

4. Behavior problems may exist but the psychiatrist and psychologist determine whether the emotional problems seem secondary to the learning disabilities, or that the child is primarily emotionally disturbed

5. If the lack of achievement appears to be due to poor instruction, socioeconomic underdevelopment, or environmental neglect, the problem has to be solved where it exists and the child will not be placed in a special school

6. Parent cooperation is a strict requirement

In general these criteria of admittance to LOM schools seem to be in accordance with the definitions of children with learning disabilities in the United States. More and more it seems that they are adopted by the schools in the practice of diagnosing children. But there remain some problems, because practice is not that congruent with theoretical definitions. The IQ issue is one of them. The definition of learning disabilities speaks of a discrepancy between intellectual potential and scholastic achievement where intelligence is supposed to be normal. To assess intelligence, IQ tests such as the Stanford-Binet and the Wechsler Scales of Intelligence are used. Many schools are afraid to take in children with moderate intelligence and thus keep out children with IQ's below 90, and sometimes even below 100. This is a serious problem because neither the referring school nor the special school seems to be able to help the child. One formula is to take in the child provided his Verbal IQ or his Performance IQ reaches 90. This seems to be quite manageable, but it creates a new problem. In our school system slow learners belong in the regular school.

So from our regular schools we remove all exceptional children except those with borderline intelligence. Attempts were made to educate them in special schools but an administrative committee strongly dissented.

There is another problem built into our educational system. The borderline between normality and subnormality is an IQ of 80. Educationally, subnormal children are defined and labeled by means of an IQ measurement. Intellectual capacity is regarded as the most important and most valuable predictor for results later in life, although it certainly is not. Social competence seems to be a far more important criterion of achievement in organizing one's life.

The Curriculum of the Special School

Children who are referred to special schools for learning disabilities are diagnosed as such by a team, appointed by law, composed of the principal, a psychologist or educator, and a psychiatrist. There is a common battery of tests that most psychologists use. It is composed of a Stanford-Binet or a Wechsler Intelligence Scale, a visual motor test like the Bender or Frostig, and a projective test like the Social Intelligence Test, Thematic Apperception Test, or Columbus. The psychiatrist administers a routine examination, sometimes with the inclusion of EEG data. The principal gives some achievement tests that are standardized or derived from his daily school practice. After the child is admitted to the school, he is placed in a class of some 16 youngsters. The law provides teachers in the 1 to 15 ratio, which sometimes proves to be too high.

The remedial treatment program of the school can be divided into three strategies. The first strategy is the curriculum of the school and what is called the therapeutic climate. The curriculum includes the basic techniques of reading, writing, spelling, and arithmetic, and what is called an orientation to the world, or a synthesis of geography, history, and biology. Personal expression and the arts are taught in music, crafts, expressive language, and rhythmic movement.

The school is either built for or adapted to the instructional needs. Furniture is easily movable and can be quickly set up to form a circle for group discussion. Besides the facilities and equipment every modern school needs, there are some booths where children can sit quietly and concentrate. Audio-visual equipment completes the set-up of the school.

Time is programmed to give children the opportunity to concentrate on their work and to relax with their hobbies. It is considered of special importance to create time for the children so that they get the feeling of belonging to the community of the school. Many schools organize several extracurricular activities for their children to give them social experiences and the sense of the school as a place where one can live and be happy.

Children are given the opportunity to move, to withdraw, to concentrate in a special part of the classroom, to sit together, to speak together, to read aloud, and to ask questions.

With the topic of group work, we arrive at an essential part of school organization and curriculum. Traditionally, children sit in formation, two at a desk, facing the teacher's desk and the blackboard. The LOM school may do the same thing and we often see that formation taken over from the regular school. Classical instruction is followed by individual work in arithmetic, spelling, and reading. Individualization of the teaching process means individualization of instruction, not of production. Individualizing production means emphasizing competition among the pupils and is wrong in its antipedagogical aspects which may include cribbing, getting low marks, doing homework, and failing to be promoted. Group work, on the other hand, teaches the children to think, to reflect, to elaborate, and to integrate. In group work, emphasis is not placed on memorizing but on comprehension, discussion, and reasoning. In group work, children learn to work in the way they will work in their later life, to produce something together while the group leader explains, helps, and structures the process. Children learn in an active way; they manipulate subject matter while discussing it. Comprehension of the task can be checked by having pupils explain it to the group. A good school is one which combines classic explanation, group work, and helping individual needs.

"Therapeutic climate" has become a standard expression for the total educational treatment design that a school for exceptional children should exhibit. A tolerant atmosphere is needed, where the child believes that the teacher is really interested in what he is thinking and feeling, where he is accepted, and where the work is challenging. The teacher looks at behavior symptoms and sees the child struggling to get his environment and himself under control. Permissiveness as a "letting go" technique makes the youngsters insecure and confused. Structuring is the way to remedial education or treatment. Where it is too difficult for the child to behave, the teacher will be near him, anticipating failures, preventing misbehavior, guiding, making agreements, stimulating self-decisions. Structuring situations means giving as much help as is necessary again and again. Will we find the therapeutic climate as described here in the Dutch LOM school? Maybe in this respect teachers have been professionalized faster and easier than in the technical instructional areas.

The second strategy in remedial teaching is that the curriculum is remedial by itself. Programs are evolved, methods and special techniques are designed specifically to support the progress of the child. Generally speaking, the special teacher has to be an expert in the application of these methods, and some of our teachers are. If children need help from a specialist, this aid can be provided. Some schools have speech and physical therapists of their own. Under the influence of Bladergroen, some schools have developed a special program for the visual-motor training of children with learning disabilities.

Within the concept of the second strategy is psychotherapy. Most of the time problems are not "in" children but in peer-groups and in families. These relational problems have to be treated by group therapy or family therapy. Educator, social therapist, and social worker form a team with regard to the problem child or the problem family.

The third strategy is individual diagnosis and prescriptive treatment. All curriculum possibilities, all additional didactic and therapeutic techniques, all care and treatment of child and family are focused on the individual needs of the child. This convergence of observation and diagnosis with the first and second strategies constitutes the third strategy in the total treament design.

THE GENERIC-SPECIFIC ISSUE

In our country some 50 years ago, a choice was made to establish special schools and to discourage the formation of special classes in regular schools. We are fully aware of the many considerations involved in this decision, but we chose specialization. We still have to make clear how our schools are specialized. We have defended ourselves against the charge of stigmatization; now we have to speak to the principle of specialization.

In the report, *The Missouri Conference on the Categorical Noncategorical Issue in Special Education* (1971), it is stated that "here was general support for the position that much of the knowledge and many of the teaching skills required to effectively teach handicapped children are generic."

There surely is an important generic part in the curricula for exceptional children, but we think that there is also a specific aspect, in two ways. First, even if we teach reading and arithmetic in the same way, there is the difference between the retarded child and the learning disabled child. They learn at different rates of speed. The retarded child needs more explanation and repetition. The emotionally disturbed child needs an alternation of effort and relaxation. The learning disturbed child needs special auditory training or word games. If we place a diversity of children in one classroom, we would have too many different curricula. That is why the school with emphasis on the generic concept stresses individualization to solve this problem. We feel that individualization is needed, especially to help the child with his specific difficulties. Individualization, however, should not be pushed too far, because it is not able to solve all our problems.

Pedagogically speaking, the group situation is a far more favorable situation for a child. Together with others they can cooperate and learn from each other. Collaboration is valuable to erase competition among children and to create a relaxed atmosphere where they can enjoy learning. In short, in our schools we try to find an equilibrium between classical instruction (lecture, use of blackboard, television, circle discussions, etc.), group work (social studies, crafts, reading), and individual training (arithmetic, spelling, writing, special programs, programmed material).

What is special in a Dutch special school for children with learning disabilities? That is, what is special in the curriculum? There is or should be in every school a curriculum containing:
Auditory training
Visual-motor training
Training in spatial and temporal orientation
Training in conceptualization, reasoning, and language
Training in the concepts of arithmetic
Technical reading, speed reading, advanced reading
Special courses in writing and spelling

The first four topics are referred to as training of specific functions basic to learning the three academic subjects. Training and exercising these functions are necessary for almost all children with learning disabilities. Schools are really special schools insofar as they have that kind of basic training and succeed in teaching academics in a didactic way.

Traditionally, visual development has been stressed in the work with learning disabled children. The work of Strauss, Cruickshank, Kephart, and Frostig is well known in our country, as all our professional literature is oriented to American research. Based on their work, some teachers accented the visual aspects of training and gave it a large place in their school programs. For some years, there has also been the influence of Kirk and Myklebust, and recently Bannatyne, so that now more emphasis is placed on auditory training. Speech therapists especially understood the meaning of this work, and they wrote courses to train the children. The impact of sensorimotor development and spatiotemporal represention has been made clear by Piaget for normal development, and for exceptional children it is generally accepted that retardation may go back as far as the first stages of visual-motor and representional development.

Some Dutch teachers and workers have to be named, as they worked out training programs and curricula in this area. From the older generation are P. Calon, W. Bladergroen, M, Krabbe, F. Grewel, A. Nanninga-Boon, W. Schenk and A. Korndörffer, A. Heymans, W. Vliegenthart, L. van Gelder, H. Verhagen, and P. Mesker. Their work in the field has been of most important value and can be regarded as clinically oriented. Clinical material was the base for extended reflections on causes and symptoms of the condition. After them came more research-oriented studies of A. Wilmink, J. Berk, A. van de Wissel, D. Bakker, R. 'tHam, W. Nooteboom, and J. van Meel. Their influence has been that more and more the LOM schools tried to understand what kind of children was meant by the label learning disturbed. It had some impact on the curriculum but the influence was not systematic enough. Real curriculum-development work has been started by A. Heymans, A. Bulthuis, A. van der Gest, J. Dumont and J. Kok, S. Sieteram, G. Kohnstamm, and R. deGroot.

The special school is specializing more as attention is drawn to the curriculum. Up to now many schools have had a normal curriculum with additional remedial techniques. There are some signs that this situation is changing. More and more what is now additional will become fundamental and the core of the curriculum.

REFERENCES

Buitengewoon Onderwijs. 1966. Rapport van de commissie tot voorbereiding van een wettelijke regeling betreffende het Buitengewoon Onderwijs. 's Gravenhage. (Report on Special Education).

Chalfant, J. C., and M. A. Scheffelin. 1969. Central Processing Dysfunctions in Children: A Review of Research. N.I.N.D.S. Monograph 9. U. S. Department of Health, Education, and Welfare, Washington.

Doornbos, K. Inventarisatie-onderzoek L.O.M.-schoelen I en II. Utrecht 1965—1967. (Investigation of the organization and curriculum of Dutch schools for children with learning disabilities).

Dumont, J. J. 1971. Leerstoornissen. Oorzaken en behandelingsmethoden. Lemniscaat, Rotterdam.

Kok, J. F. W. 1972. Structopathic Children. Rotterdam University Press, Rotterdam.

The Missouri Conference on the Categorical Noncategorical Issue in Special Education: Proceedings. 1971. The University of Missouri, Columbia.

CHAPTER 16

Reading Disabilities in Norwegian Elementary Grades

Grete Hagtvedt Vik

A number of children enrolled in regular elementary school classes experience learning disabilities. Their enrollment in the Norwegian regular school grades presupposes average to above average intelligence, yet these children are plagued by reading disabilities that cause them to be educationally handicapped. Learning disability in this sense is to be differentiated from those difficulties encountered by children with a general intellectual delay or physical deficit. Rather, learning disability seems to be associated with some evident or inferred psychoneurological deficiency which interferes with the educational progress of those afflicted. Frequently some emotional or behavioral disorder further complicates the situation of the learning disabled child.

A learning disability might show serious and far-reaching manifestations. Often the functioning of cognitive processes, such as perception, symbolization, attention, or memory, is altered. A learning disability may also involve difficulties in acquiring adequate social competencies, as well as disorders of motor activities. Typically, the learning disabled child has problems with academic achievement in the areas of written and spoken language, reading, spelling, writing, and/or mathematics.

The most frequently encountered and reported educational problem among learning disabled children is specific reading disability.

ELEMENTARY EDUCATION IN NORWAY

In Norway, as in the other Scandinavian countries, children start school 1 or 2 years later than in many other countries, i.e., the United States and

249

England. School attendance is compulsory for all children beginning the calendar year in which they reach their 7th birthday. It has been the conviction of educators in these countries that sufficient psychological research is at hand to support the idea that it is to the advantage of children to start school as late as age 7.

A few children attend preschool or kindergarten before entering school, but there is no direct link between these programs and the regular school program. Some school systems enroll their immature school beginners in readiness classes the first year, to prepare them for a more successful start with formal academic work later on.

As far as school intake is concerned, a very liberal policy is pursued. Nearly all children are given a chance to find their place in the ordinary grades before any special measures are taken. The result is that Norwegian first grades contain highly heterogeneous groups of children, with mental age ranges of as much as 6 years, as measured with group tests (Gjessing, 1966).

The concept of reading readiness in Norway has been strongly influenced by Anglo-American views, especially in the form of practical testing and reading readiness programs. As a result, factors such as mental age, experiential background, language development, visual and auditory perception, and memory have assumed an increasingly dominant role. The Elementary and Secondary School Curriculum Plans stress the importance of preparation in primary grade reading. A thorough readiness program should create the basis upon which later acquisition of proficient reading skills is to be built. An increasing degree of active stimulation of reading readiness, before formal reading instruction, has become generally accepted among first-grade teachers. It is felt that time spent on the development of vocabulary and concepts, the ability to listen and concentrate, to discriminate visual as well as auditory stimuli, and to recall, is desirable for all school beginners. It is now common to use between 2 and 6 weeks to focus mainly on reading-readiness-related training. There is no sharp demarcation between the period in first grade when preparatory exercises for the stimulation of reading readiness take the greater part of the school session, and the period when the teaching of reading in its more formal sense starts. The first formal reading instruction should induce a feeling of security in an accepting environment, as expressed in the curriculum plan. Systematic reading instruction, often conducted as en masse presentation, is given in the first grade and part of the second grade. After this, major attention is on reading techniques and proficiency training. For most children this progression is acceptable; the majority of Norwegian children acquire the basic principles of reading during the first year in school.

It is quite common in Norwegian primary grades for the children to have the same teacher at least for 3, and sometimes as many as 6 consecutive years. If a child does not progress as rapidly as expected, this does not alarm his teacher. As a rule, he can look forward to a long period of togetherness with her, and chances are that when he is given more time and teacher attention he will finally succeed.

Norwegian primary children attend school for a relatively short period of time each day. Their schedules rarely exceed 15 sessions (each 45 minutes long), distributed over 6 weekdays. Beginning in the 1973–1974 school year, most Norwegian schools will be working on a 5-day schedule. Consequently, the first-graders will have to stay in school somewhat longer each day. Compared to their American counterparts, they spend about half as much time in school.

Approximately one-third of the total time in school is to be spent on reading and writing instruction. However, the children also practice their reading and writing skills when they study subjects such as local history and lore, and religion in the first grades.

Norwegian is a highly regular language. The orthographic concepts involved are few and highly generalized and the number of exceptions is limited. Thus, the demand on memory is low, and can usually be met by the majority of young readers.

The maximum number of students in Norwegian school classes is 30, by law. The actual size of the average class, however, is far smaller. This is because of many small schools (some having no more than 6 to 10 students) due to the scattered population and varied geographical conditions. Therefore, in a number of primary grade classes throughout the country, possibilities exist for meeting individual needs.

The Elementary and Secondary School Act of 1969 allowed the local school boards of education to utilize a system of splitting all first- and second-grade classes of more than 20 students into halves, for instruction in Norwegian and mathematics. Also, it is common for a school board to permit a certain number of extra school sessions for the purpose of helping primary grade children with reading and writing difficulties on an individual (or small group) basis. These arrangements further provide the classroom teacher with a fair chance of using diagnostic approaches and individualizing her instruction.

In spite of the advanced beginning age, the careful school start, adequate intelligence in the children, a good teacher ratio for instruction in Norwegian, and the relative regularity of the language itself, some youngsters still seem to experience insurmountable difficulties in reading.

THE READING DISABLED IN THE ELEMENTARY SCHOOL

It is estimated that approximately 11% of all first- and second-graders have a need for remedial reading instruction of some kind. Individual studies have reportedly revealed that 3 to 4% will be in need of remedial help in special reading classes or clinics. The remainder, 6 to 7%, will at least need extra help within the classroom setting (Gjessing, 1958). Since children enrolled in the first grade were taken as they came and grouping was heterogeneous, it should not be a surprise that approximately 11% of the youngsters scored low on reading tests. An appreciable portion of the poor readers appear to have intellectual abilities commensurate with their reading achievement levels. The percentage of intelligent children who encounter great reading problems during the first years in school is much lower. The percentage, of course, would depend on the criterion employed for reading disability. Probably about 5% of the elementary school population would be hindered in their academic progress due to some degree of reading disability, unless help is offered.

Diagnosis

To the American educator, it might appear striking that Norway lacks the extensive and systematic testing and evaluation tools so familiar in his home country. No IQ test score is mentioned in any Norwegian school act as a requirement for inclusion or exclusion in any educational program. Children are recommended for a different program when they have demonstrated an inability to benefit from the program they are in, as expressed in reports from the teacher, reading specialist, or the school psychologist.

Standardized reading readiness tests and reading tests for the primary grades are available, and are becoming widely used. Traditionally, poorly systematized instruction has been offered by classroom teachers. Without doubt, harm and injustice have been done to children because on-going evaluation has been ignored, and diagnostic information has been lacking.

Today most primary students undergo screening procedures to detect reading and writing disabilities during the spring semester. The tests used are developed and standardized by Norwegian school psychologists and speech therapists, and are easy to administer and score by the classroom teacher. Children who score generally low or show some remarkable discrepancies on different test items, are selected for differential diagnosis by specialists.

The Royal Ministry of Education has developed a code for special education services offered by the elementary school. This code suggests that the in-depth analysis of a child's particular difficulties should comprise the following:

1. An evaluation of the child's total situation, his personality, emotional and social status, and home milieu
2. An educational evaluation, describing the child's strengths and weak-

nesses in different school and related activities including information obtained through observation and standardized and informal reading tests 3. A thorough examination by a school psychologist, social worker, and physician. The psychological examination should include individual tests, i.e., the Revised Stanford-Binet Intelligence Scale, the Wechsler Intelligence Scale for Children (Performance section), the Columbia Mental Maturity Scale, and Raven Children's Colored Progressive Matrices. Other tests of specific abilities and aptitudes include the Bender Visual Motor Gestalt Test, the Marianne Frostig Developmental Test of Visual Perception, and the Goodenough-Harris Draw-A-Man Test.

A committee has been engaged since 1970 on the adaptation and standardization of the Norwegian edition of the Illinois Test of Psycholinguistic Abilities. This test will be ready for use in 1975.

The necessity of diagnosing reading disabled children is fully acknowledged in Norway as a prerequisite for sound remediation. Inherent in such an inclusive system of assessment lies the assumption that the diagnosis must be a team effort.

From the 1950's, school psychology offices were started in several local districts, providing services to the regular and special schools in their areas. In 1969 the initiation of such service centers was made the responsibility of each local school board. By 1980, the expansion of these services is expected to have reached all areas of the country. The ratio between school psychologists and children served has been estimated to be 1 in 3,000. The offices have been staffed by a clinical and/or school psychologist and a social worker. More recently, special teachers have been added to the team, primarily speech therapists, to take care of the increasing number of cases referred with reading disabilities. The development toward broader professional coverage has continued, and several of the earlier school psychology offices have expanded into Special Education School Psychology District Centers. Experience has revealed that the teamwork between the medical, psychological, and special education professions has been fruitful and rewarding. One of the main functions of the district centers is to register and diagnose children of preschool and school age with language disabilities. Part of the service offered is also to visit the schools to help diagnose the children and to develop remedial reading and other programs for treatment; to provide in-service training to parents, teachers, and administrators; and to serve as resource centers within special education in the district.

The speech and reading centers represent the latest addition to the service system within the regular school system. The scope of the program of these centers is to offer speech therapy and remedial reading services to the schools in the municipalities. This, in part, is achieved by scheduling children for diagnosis and treatment in the center, and in part by visits of professionals from the center to the schools for similar services. The importance of early detection and intervention is stressed, and the center offers services to the preschool as well as the school-age population. It is one of the functions of the center to screen the school population for major speech and reading disabilities. Differential diagnosis then follows the screening tests. The most severe disabilities are treated in the center, and in other cases reports with comprehensive recommendations for treatment are submitted to the children's classroom teachers, or to the home school reading specialist. Close and frequent communication between the center and the child's home and home school is considered to be of great importance. The speech and reading center staff consists of a number of speech therapists and remedial reading specialists. A school psychologist joins the staff whenever his expertise is needed.

There are two such centers in Norway today, both established and run as cooperative undertakings of a number of school districts. More centers are at the drawing-board stage, and the final goal is a decentralized service apparatus, fully staffed and equipped to give appropriate help to everyone who needs it, regardless of age.

In many schools today, especially in the urban areas, there are reading clinics. These are well equipped and staffed by a speech therapist or a reading specialist. This person is trained to utilize group tests and diagnostic reading tests and often works in a team with other professionals. Her job usually involves the screening and diagnosing of all children enrolled in her school, and sometimes in a few neighboring schools as well. She also offers her supervision and guidance to classroom teachers in their efforts to develop diagnostic reading programs.

However, in most cases the diagnosis and decision-making are not adequate. Due to insufficient availability of professional people in many small and often isolated districts in Norway, the school psychologist, the speech therapist, the reading specialist, or the classroom teacher alone constitutes the "team." Each one of these workers is proficient in his own field of specialization, but certainly is not competent in all areas required for adequate evaluation. As a consequence, many reading disabled students may not receive adequate help.

Remediation

It is a characteristic of Norwegian school organization that, generally speaking, each type of school is covered by special legislation. Special services offered to handicapped children of all the traditional categories are regulated by the Special School Act of 1951 (with additions of 1970).

According to this act, any student experiencing a severe verbal communication difficulty, including major reading and/or writing disability, is eligible to receive the services of one of the state schools for the alleviation of such problems. There are three state schools for this category of children providing services to an annual average of around 230 students. The schools are run in cooperation between the state and the local school authorities. Instruction is given to individual children or to small groups by qualified professionals, such as trained reading specialists and speech therapists. Whenever needed, as for diagnosis and/or treatment, the staff is supplemented by a psychologist, audiologist, odontologist, or physician (i.e., neurologist, psychiatrist, surgeon, ophthalmologist, ear-nose-throat specialist).

The demand for help of the kind offered by the state schools for verbal communication difficulties far exceeds their present capacity. An expansion of the number of such schools to five has been suggested by the Council for Special Schools of the Royal Ministry of Education. The further development of the speech and reading centers may, however, represent a better alternative in solving the problems of the severely disabled readers in the municipalities.

The auxiliary education provided for children with less severe reading problems within the regular school system existed for more than 75 years before it was made compulsory. This important school reform was incorporated in the valid school act in 1955. The Elementary and Secondary School Act of 1959 explained that this type of special education was aimed at those children who encountered difficulties in keeping up with their classmates and responsibilities in the regular grades, whatever the reason might be. These difficulties, by definition, should not be of such severe or permanent nature as to make the child eligible for placement in a special school or special class program. The regulations in the currently valid Elementary and Secondary School Act of 1969 state that the criterion to be met by the students is that they are in need of pedagogical help. The education of children with reading disabilities was defined as one type of this auxiliary education.

TEACHER TRAINING

As a result of the school reform of 1955, the elementary school administrators were confronted with a great special education task, namely, to provide services for all children with reading and writing problems. An enormous demand for qualified reading teachers was created. The first courses specifically aimed at the solution of this problem were initiated in 1958. During the 1960's, a drastic increase in the number of school sessions spent on auxiliary education in the regular schools was evident. Today it averages close to 10% of the total number of school sessions. In 1961 all courses that had been run to help educate teachers for auxiliary education were coordinated. That year the Norwegian Postgraduate Teacher Training Center of Special Education was started in Oslo.

The Teacher Training Center of Special Education offers two 1-year schemes of study, Part One and Part Two. Educators holding teacher or preschool teacher certificates can apply for admission to Part One. Here emphasis is on the psychology, diagnosis, and didactics of reading and reading disabilities. A general introduction to the psychology and education of all the traditional categories of handicapped children is also given. The training also includes observation and student teaching in remedial education classes and reading clinics. The Part One scheme is also offered by six of the regular teacher training colleges. Teachers can also obtain the same training by taking a series of courses during two consecutive summer quarters in special education subjects. These courses are offered by a number of special schools and institutions. In 1972–1973, between 700 and 800 students received their Part One diplomas, which qualify them to work as reading specialists, auxiliary education teachers in the elementary schools, or as special educators in special schools.

The Part One diploma, as a rule, makes the holder eligible for admission to the Part Two program. This second scheme is offered by the Teacher Training Center of Special Education exclusively, and is a 1-year course of specialization within one of five possible areas representing the major groups of handicapped children. One of these courses is a qualification for the teaching and therapy of speech and language disorders. Consequently, all speech therapists hold both teacher certificates and reading specialist diplomas (i.e., Part One diploma).

SPEECH AND READING THERAPISTS

The speech therapists traditionally serve the regular school system (in addition to their other responsibilities within special education and health care). They have a diagnostic as well as a treatment function, and also serve resource and consultation functions. Their area of competency includes both speech and reading-writing disabilities. A recent investigation revealed a ratio of 5 to 7 between professional time spent on the treatment of speech versus reading-writing disabilities in the country as a whole. From the central school administration no serious effort has been made to rationally utilize the speech therapy services. Because speech therapists are relatively rare (with an annual graduation class from the Teacher Training Center of Special Education of about 40), and at the same time represent a highly qualified and needed professional group, such an undertaking is of major importance. Currently, the reading specialists (those holding Part One diplomas) are in the process of taking over the responsibilities for one of the problem groups previously "belonging to" the speech therapists, namely the reading disabled.

Today, and in the foreseeable future, a large number of the jobs for remedial reading specialists will be held by teachers holding no more than regular teaching certificates (comparable to the American Bachelor of Arts degree in elementary education). Even though the teaching profession is held in high regard in Norway (it might be easier to enter a university than to gain admission to a teachers' college), the traditionally trained teachers are too poorly qualified to provide remedial instruction. Their college program does not provide sufficient coverage of the special techniques used for detection and remediation of reading disabilities. Teacher training is currently in a transitional phase. Experiments are being carried out in a number of the 17 colleges in Norway, some of which are programs geared toward primary grade education and the teaching of reading and reading readiness. There also seems to be a movement toward introducing special education subjects into all regular teacher training.

SPECIAL EDUCATION

As a result of the fact that special education provisions in Norway are regulated by two different school acts (Special School Act of 1951, and Elementary and Secondary School Act of 1969), much uncertainty and ambiguity as to the responsibilities of the state versus the local school authorities for certain vaguely defined categories of children have evolved. Special educators have expressed a strong desire for better coordination in the legislative regulations concerning special education in the regular school system and in special schools and classes. The Council for Special Schools under the Royal Ministry of Education proposed in 1970 that the best way of attaining this goal might be to integrate the necessary proposals regarding special education into the valid Elementary and Secondary School Act. This reform will mean that the majority of students presently enrolled in special school programs will be taught through special provisions within the regular schools. Consequently, the elementary school system will have to face and solve even more serious teacher recruitment problems. Estimates show that every fourth elementary school teacher will then need training in auxiliary and special education. This further indicates the necessity of strengthening regular teacher training in his field. It is still a major principle (according to the proposal from the Council for Special Schools) to incorporate into the new act the necessary guarantees for high professional standards in special education, so that nothing will be lost of the assets which have been secured through previous acts, and to come out stronger than before. This of course, would benefit the disabled reader, as well as any other learning disabled or otherwise educationally handicapped child within the Norwegian school system.

The fact that Norway is composed of many small isolated coastline localities, open farmland, and growing, busy cities, will make the services offered to the local school populations not quite uniform. Still, the ultimate goal of our school system is to provide the most appropriate educational program for all children within the milieu which is most suitable for each individual child. This is both a geographical and financial problem. The school system in Norway is almost entirely a public responsibility. It is in general supported either by the local authority (municipality), the regional authority (county), or by the state. The local authorities are responsible for the elementary schools and receive a proportion of their expenditure from the state. The contribution from the state is related to the economic ability of the individual local authority. By this system of financial support, the school programs throughout the country present a fairly consistent pattern. The financing of special programs for elementary age children, however, is still an issue of controversy between central and local authorities. One of the major objectives of the proposed new act for the integrated system of special and regular schools is to solve this problem so that all individuals can be offered equal opportunities for education.

There seems to be no lack of concern and commitment for any group of children in need of special education services from the central school administration. There seems to exist a relatively even distribution of resources: professionals, programs, and materials, throughout the country. The training of teachers for special education services is presently receiving high priority. Possibly for these reasons, no parent associations have as yet been formed to advocate the needs and rights of reading disabled children. In fact, the reading disabled have become the children representing the greatest concern within special education in elementary schools during the last two decades.

From an organizational point of view, the elementary school special education program is, as a rule, more flexible than that of the state. This in part explains its rapid growth during the recent years. The school act permits auxiliary education to be given to individual children and to small groups in self-contained classes in a regular school or in a special day school. Instruction may be given in all subjects, or it may be limited to one or two subjects, according to the potential and difficulties of the child. Thus, the school act allows a variety of organizational patterns.

In the local districts schools are often small. It is not unusual for two or more grade levels to be taught in the same room, and grouping for instruction naturally is done across grade levels. The student-teacher ratio is also favorable to individual and small group instruction. The situation in the cities and urban areas is different, with more restricted possibilities for meeting individual student needs. As a result, the demand for special help outside the classroom is more urgent in these areas.

The reading clinics represent one of the most common organizational settings for reading disabled children in elementary schools. The intake of students to the reading clinic is quite smooth; the classroom teacher and the reading specialist come to an agreement regarding a child who demonstrates a reading disability. The child receives immediate help in the clinic several times each week, and the treatment program is discontinued as soon as the child's problem is overcome. The reading clinics meet the need for help that becomes evident in primary grade classes, and the majority of clients are recruited from these grade levels. In the relatively few cases where the problems cannot sufficiently be alleviated by a few weekly sessions in the reading clinic, the child is transferred to a self-contained reading class. Such an intervention is rarely administered until the child reaches the third grade, and the decision is made in a consultation among the classroom teacher, the reading specialist, and the school psychologist. The reading class has a maximum enrollment of 12 children. After 1 or 2 years, the child, as a rule, goes back to his former class.

The speech and reading centers provide another setting for the remediation of reading disabilities in elementary grade children. Because the center staff represents a highly selected group of professional people, and due to the number of other functions to be served by the staff, only the most serious cases of reading disability are treated in the center. The staff, however, offers their diagnostic, program development, and supervisory services to the local schools.

Whether the remedial reading instruction is provided in a reading clinic, a reading class, or in a speech and reading center, it should always be based upon thorough knowledge of the child's profile as a learner. The purpose of the educational assessment is to determine what language functions have developed well and what functions are inadequate.

Dr. Hans-Jörgen Gjessing did the pioneer work on reading disabled children in Norway. Based on much observation, he developed a working hypothesis for the diagnosis and treatment of such children. He was able to identify several syndromes of errors in reading and writing. Based on an analysis of the types of errors, Gjessing grouped the disabled readers under the following headings:
1. Auditory dyslexia
2. Visual dyslexia

3. Audio-visual dyslexia
4. Emotional dyslexia
5. Educational dyslexia

The first three dyslexias are considered the most common types. Gjessing has defined dyslexia as synonymous with reading-writing difficulties, or reading disability.

Two American researchers, D. J. Johnson and H. R. Myklebust, about 10 years later (in 1967) presented quite comparable hypotheses on etiology, terminology, and symptomatology in relation to reading disability.

Gjessing also developed a differential methodology in accordance with his diagnostic system, which systematically aims at eliminating the basis of the disability, while at the same time developing compensatory abilities. The treatment plan is divided into several parts, each composed of a number of smaller steps. The first part gives an overview of some important special education principles. The second part aims at a thorough and systematic reading readiness program in order to develop speech, concepts, ability to listen (auditory discrimination and memory), visual perception (discrimination and memory), and motor abilities (hand-motor ability, rhythm, relaxation). The third part includes basic reading and writing skills arranged according to the stepwise development of reading ability: letters, sounds, blending of sounds, syllables and consonant blends, sight words, basic word attack skills. The fourth part aims at the more elaborate level of functional reading to widen the perception span, strengthen the ability to utilize what is read (answer questions about content in text), and to recall.

The methodology developed by Gjessing is widely used by teachers offering services to reading disabled children in Norwegian elementary schools today. An example of how the methodology is used is given in the following abstract from the educational psychologist's assessment and remedial instruction plan (1963).

CASE HISTORY BASED ON GJESSING'S METHODOLOGY

Student A

A's problem is that he cannot learn to recognize or recall letters or blend sounds. He has the ability to master mathematical problems, and seems to have good numerical concepts.

A, 7 years, 11 months of age, is presently enrolled in the first grade in a large city school. A is the eldest of 3 children. The father is a civil servant, the mother is not employed outside the home. The economic and housing conditions are satisfactory.

A is physically and psychologically normal. He seems to come from a harmonious and accepting home which has tried to back up the efforts of the school, but without pressing the child. Everything reportedly was normal during pregnancy, delivery, and early childhood, except for language development which was markedly delayed until 5 to 6 years of age.

During the assessment session, no articulatory disorder or reminiscenses of such could be detected. However, vocabulary and way of speaking, on close examination, seemed to be somewhat retarded in relation to chronological age and level of general intellectual functioning.

A knows a few letters well (for example, *R, L, J, S*), but to a pronounced degree he confuses voiced and unvoiced sounds (*D-T, B-P, G-K*) and the vowel sounds (*U-Y-I*). (These consonant and vowel sounds may appear similar to persons with weak auditory discrimination.) He demonstrates other problems of sound/letter-association as well. *A* is unable to master even the most elementary sound blendings; for example, two-sound words of the type *M-O*. However, he is able to write a few memory words; for example, *PER* (boy's name), *MOR* (mother), *FAR* (father). *A* apparently has only minor difficulties in recalling and reproducing word images. It seems that the phonetic process is failing, apparently due to some dysfunction in auditory perception, in ability to discriminate as well as to recall.

A has intellectual abilities within the normal range, or above. He seems generally mature, emotionally stable, and he likes school. His school progress and adjustment are normal except for reading. As an example, at the present time, he masters the first-grade curriculum in mathematics.

A ought to be able to continue as a student in his regular class. He should, however, as soon as possible receive remedial instruction 2 to 3 times each week (in sessions of approximately 20 minutes) in accordance with the recommendations for treatment enclosed.

Excerpts from the Treatment Plan

Problem: Cannot learn to recognize and recall letters or blends
Diagnosis: Serious auditory dyslexia
Plan for treatment:
   Step I: 9–16, 18–24
   Refer to second part of the methodology, reading readiness skills. The specific steps recommended are aimed at developing speech and concepts as well as the ability to listen, concentrate, and differentiate between sounds.
   Step II: 31, 32, 35
   Refer to the third part of the methodology, basic reading, and writing

exercises. The recommended steps include basic training in letters, sounds, blends, soundblending.

Step III: (if necessary) 36–37

Refer to the third part of the methodology concerning syllables and consonant blends.

Step IV: if necessary, after re-evaluation

Comments: Demands on *A*'s performance in the regular classroom must, as far as possible, be modified in accordance with this plan; assessment and plan for treatment are by Gjessing; the student is to be treated by P. H. alone, or in a small group.

REMEDIAL INSTRUCTION

Remedial instruction should start as soon as the reading problem has become evident, usually sometime during the spring semester in the first grade. According to authorities on clinical work with reading disabled children, a large proportion of children who are referred for help are actually helped to overcome the problems which previously hindered their progress. The prognosis seems to be best in those cases where: (1) the disability is treated in an early stage; and (2) the symptomatology seems to point to one major sensory modality as deficient, rather than presenting a diffuse pattern of symptoms associated with several kinds of sensory channel weaknesses.

The daily evidence of even seriously disabled readers learning to overcome their handicaps by the help of reading specialists and speech therapists, makes these professionals inclined to conclude that reading disability represents a real problem only in exceptional cases, providing the proper teaching has been offered. The successful endeavors of the reading specialists and speech therapists have also given a positive impulse to the regular teaching of reading in the first-grade programs. A number of specialists on reading have contributed books and materials essential to successful beginning reading instruction, since the late 1950's (i.e., Kari Wessel, Sigrun Vormeland, Elsa Aga, Calli Thaugland, and Sigvald Asheim). While the discussion several years ago concentrated on what specific method was to be recommended for beginning reading instruction, there seems to be a shift today toward utilizing assets gained from a variety of methods. This is because of the wide range of developmental ages found in the first-grade classes; and to provide for the needs of all learning types whether the auditory, visual, kinesthetic, and/or tactile sensory modality is the main avenue of learning.

Remedial teaching of reading in Norway, individually or in small groups, in reading clinics or in reading classes, does not differ markedly from the kind of teaching provided by an experienced and efficient primary teacher in the regular class. There are no basic differences as to principles and methods used within the different organizational forms of reading instruction. When differences are found, these are in degree, rather than kind. In regular education the group is usually taught as a whole, but in a varied fashion in order to meet individual needs. In special education, the teaching is diagnostic in approach, meeting individual needs. Also, the teaching of reading in the modified setting is administered by a specialist who has only a few students at a time, often only one.

The difference between materials and equipment used in the teaching of reading in the regular grades versus the kind used in a remedial reading setting, is a matter of degree rather than of kind. In general, special education programs operate on a far less restricted budget than the regular school programs. Language and reading machines, listening stations, and other audiovisual equipment, programmed instructional material, various material for reading readiness training, etc., are becoming standard equipment in reading classes, clinics, and centers. It is still common, however, for the reading specialist herself to develop a great deal of her own instructional material in order to meet individual student needs. Special readers and material for remedial projects are still quite rare in Norway. In a country with so few inhabitants, the manufacture of instructional materials for the small number of children who will need or use them is very expensive. However, new materials, books, booklets, playing cards, puzzles, program kits, etc., are constantly being introduced and published.

To secure quality as well as quantity, guidelines have been developed by the Royal Ministry of Education, describing in detail what materials and equipment should always be at hand in an auxiliary education program. These guidelines supposedly are minimum standards which should be followed by each local board of education.

It should be kept in mind, however, that special education is something more and different from placing a child in a special school, class, or clinic and providing him with programmed instructional materials, splitting a regular class in halves, introducing a teacher assistant, or utilizing a team-teaching approach. All of these organizational patterns and instructional solutions are found in the elementary school, special and regular programs. Special education occurs when the instruction is based on a differential diagnosis of the child's specific abilities and disabilities. A special teacher is not satisfactorily defined as a teacher who holds the Part One or Two diploma from the Teacher Training Center of Special Education. What is more relevant and important is, that he or she is one who masters the techniques and insight involved in utilizing and developing the child's strengths as well as strengthening his weak areas.

It is acknowledged within Norwegian elementary education that auxiliary or remedial instruction is required in order to help all children succeed in reading and writing. Provided this educational "first aid" is given at the right time by the best people and in the most fitting way, the chances are that those few who encounter the greatest problems will acquire the bare minimum of reading skills necessary to earn a living and find a way in our complex and often inhuman present-day society.

ACKNOWLEDGMENT

The author wishes to extend her deep appreciation to Dr. Hans-Jörgen Gjessing, Professor of Educational Psychology at Bergen University, who kindly offered to act as a consultant in the preparation of this manuscript.

REFERENCES

Gjessing, H. 1958. En Studie av Lesemodenhet ved Skolegangens begynnelse. Cappelens, Oslo.
Gjessing, H. 1963. Metodiske Anvisninger til Forebyggelse og Behandling av Lese/skrivevansker. Universitetsforlaget, Oslo.
Gjessing, H. 1966. The concept of reading readiness in Norway. In M. D. Jenkinson (ed.), Reading Instruction: An International Forum. *Proceedings of the First World Congress on Reading of the International Reading Association.*
Hagtvedt, G. A. 1972. A Comparison of Approaches to Reading Disability in the Elementary Grades in Norway and Ohio. Master's thesis, The Ohio State University, Columbus.
Johnson, D. J. and Myklebust, H. R. 1967. Learning Disabilities: Educational Principles and Practices. Grune & Stratton, New York.
Kirke- og Undervisnings departementet. (The Royal Ministry of Church and Education). Lov av 23. November, 1951 om Spesial-Skoler. (Special School Act, November 1951). Gröndahl & Sön, Oslo.
Kirke- og Undervisnings departementet. (The Royal Ministry of Church and Education). Lov av 13. Juni 1969 om Grunnskolen. (Elementary and Secondary School Act, June 13, 1969). Gröndahl & Sön, Oslo.

CHAPTER 17

Remedial Education
in Rhodesia

Harry H. Hall

Rhodesia is a very young country. It has been only 83 years since the British Pioneer Column arrived to develop the country which was named after Mr. Cecil Rhodes, whose ambition it was to set up British Colonies stretching from Cape Town to Cairo. Furthermore, Rhodesia has only been an independent nation since 1965.

As the Europeans settled in Rhodesia, they set up schools for their own children and subsequently for the indigenous African children. Many of these schools were established by religious bodies.

Today government schools are administered by the Ministries of African Education and of European, Colored, and Asian Education respectively. In addition numbers of private schools exist—at both primary and secondary levels—predominantly run by religious denominations. In recent years, post-school private colleges have been set up for those pupils who leave school before completing their full school program.

Beyond school level, technical and teacher-training centers are available and a single University of Rhodesia was established in 1953. Many Rhodesians of all races proceed to overseas universities at the undergraduate level and a considerable proportion proceed to postgraduate work beyond the borders.

The European population of Rhodesia is approximately 250,000 and the African population is approximately 5,500,000. All Rhodesian children are taught in English, including immigrants from Europe and Asia. African and European teachers are trained in Rhodesian teacher-training colleges and at graduate level, at the multiracial University of Rhodesia.

In both African and European schools there are 13 grades prior to university entrance. Primary education, grades one through seven, is now almost universal in both schools. Thereafter, 50% of the African students

265

are selected to proceed to high school. Of these, one-fourth will be selected for academic education while three-fourths receive more practically oriented education.

Remedial services were nonexistent when the author arrived in Rhodesia 15 years ago as educational psychologist to the Ministry of European, Colored and Asian Education. It was assumed by teachers and senior administrators alike that poor reading was synonymous with limited intellect. In the absence of a full diagnostic service many poor readers were housed in special classes for subnormal children, some of whom had been assessed as being mentally subnormal while many others were educationally retarded.

Initially, a small group of teachers volunteered to set up a part-time clinic conducted in the afternoons. In-service training was offered and mildly retarded children of at least average intelligence were carefully selected. As a consequence, considerable progress was recorded in a very short time, and on occasions, dramatic accelerated progress produced startlingly gratifying results at school—to the satisfaction of parents and the astonishment of teachers who became persuaded that perhaps there was some merit in paying specific attention to reading development.

One full-time remedial tutor was appointed to visit selected junior schools in Salisbury, the capital city. Gradually the service grew to the present six full-time tutors in Salisbury, four in Bulawayo, and one in Umtali. These tutors visit the 30 larger schools in Salisbury, and each has a caseload of approximately 100 pupils, each of whom is seen for two sessions per week. In addition, the growing awareness among the public led to the establishment of private remedial centers in Salisbury city and of private tutors in the other larger centers.

There remained the problem of the child who attended the small country schools; Rhodesia has a small population spread over a very large area. The author introduced a system whereby part-time ex-teachers were employed on a sessional basis.

It will be readily appreciated that the cases referred to were, in the main, relatively mild cases of reading retardation. The children are at least of average general intelligence. The children are selected for remediation in government schools by means of group test batteries and individually administered reading tests, whereas one private clinic conducts full-scale analyses before treatment is begun. In this latter case the children are all of average-plus ability but retarded in relation to their mental capacity. The more specific cases of spelling and writing difficulties, along with true dyslexics, are referred to private clinics where more sophisticated diagnostic and remedial services are available. However, as these are limited and in their infancy, numbers of cases are referred for treatment to the more established South African centers in Johannesburg and Durban.

The problem in the Ministry of African Education is very much more complex. African children are taught predominantly by African teachers trained in Rhodesia, although many proceed overseas for special purposes. The advances in tropical medicine have produced a very great population explosion as diseases such as malaria have been brought under control. The Ministry is therefore hard put to satisfy the massive demands for schooling, and sophisticated services are not yet available in this area. Recently, however, a psychologist has been appointed and this is the beginning of the evolution of such services.

No general organizations have yet been established which interest themselves in these specific problems, but as is happening in other countries, Rhodesia is experiencing a naming problem. "Minimal brain dysfunction" and "dyslexia" are very frequently used in conversation and in the "diagnosis" of those not well acquainted with the problem. But in the process, verbal confusion does appear to lead to increasing curiosity, which in turn leads to a growing awareness of what can be done to help these children.

CHAPTER 18

Learning Disabilities in The Republic of South Africa

George D. Logue

The Republic of South Africa is at the foot of the continent. It is washed by two great oceans, the Atlantic on the west and the Indian on the east. The total area is some 1,250,000 square kilometers, larger than France, Italy, Portugal, and West Germany combined. On the other hand, the density of population is a little over 15 to the square kilometer, as compared with the 220 of the United Kingdom. In 1970, the total population was 21,000,000. The largest group, the Africans, made up 69% of this total and the whites, 18%. The balance comprises the Asians (3%) and the coloreds or people of mixed origin, 10%.

The Republic is one of the most mineral-rich countries in the world. It is also a major industrial power in Africa, producing more steel and electricity than the rest of the continent put together. Although South Africa is a country of considerable size in relation to its population, much of the land is arid, stony, or mountainous. Furthermore, irregularity of rainfall and periodic droughts cause farming to be a hazardous and arduous business in many areas. Two factors which siphon off large amounts of money are defense and aid to all the rapidly emerging sections of the community, particularly for vocational training and education.

There are four provinces in the Republic and the councils which look after their affairs are also responsible for primary, secondary, and vocational education, as well as much of the training of teachers. In addition, there is the Department of National Education under the control of a cabinet minister. This department not only lays down the principles and framework within which education must develop, but also controls all the special schools apart from those for slow learning children.

269

THE EDUCATIONAL SYSTEM

Because of this great diversity of peoples, cultures, languages and politico-religious outlooks, it has not yet been possible to postulate common educational aims (Logue, 1960). For the rapidly emerging African population the need has been to provide university and high school education for some and primary schooling for all. At the present time, four-fifths of the African children, and wherever practicable, all Asian and colored children are at school. A network of special classes for the slow learners is also being developed. For many years, white children have had compulsory education as well as special classes. They also have access to a number of schools for the epileptic, the cerebral palsied, and the physically handicapped. Whatever the reason for the differential development of the several large population groups, the determination of aim and development is most needed at the present time. The psychological services of any country are the catalyst which transforms the needs and problems of the handicapped child into methods by which he can be helped. All the finances of African education have been channeled into the development of the normal child and, over the past 20 years, a system of universities has been provided to cater for those who matriculate. There are no psychological services in the true sense of the word. The middle group, made up of Asian and coloreds, is certainly fully alive to the value of special classes, and the psychological services which can select the pupils for such treatment are developing rapidly.

There is also a growing awareness of the need for remedial classes for pupils of normal potential who cannot read, and the University of Durban-Westville has established a clinic which is training teachers for this purpose. Among the white group, scattered remedial reading classes, both official and privately organized, have provided some sort of service for the past 20 years. However, both teachers and psychologists have come to realize that many pupils have problems which cannot be solved merely by receiving part-time help from a remedial teacher. It is, thus, only in the last decade that the stage has been set for the more detailed study of pupils whose problems are immune to attack by conventional remedial techniques.

THE CONCEPT OF LEARNING DISABILITY

Many educational developments can be traced back to a single source, but it would appear that the concept of learning disability is the end-product of a process which developed spontaneously in a number of countries at about the same time. For much of the way progress has been in the dark as physicians, psychologists, and teachers fumbled and groped along different paths which had the same destination. The physicians felt that the problem was "psychological"—a most convenient way of disposing of a difficulty which did not appear to be medical. The psychologists tried to look at it from the neurological point of view, probably and partially as a reaction to the attitude of the physician. The teachers relied mainly on the "he can, but he is too lazy to try" theory. In the background were those anxious parents, in ever-increasing number, whose children were clever and adequately motivated, but who could not learn despite home backgrounds which were physically and emotionally normal.

South African thinking on this subject was considerably assisted by a number of overseas publications (Bax and MacKeith, 1963; Getman, 1962; Johnson and Myklebust, 1967; Kephart, 1960). The first South African publication was the quarterly Phoenix Journal which has appeared regularly since 1968 (Logue, 1968). There have also been a number of books (Joubert, 1970; Logue et al., 1969; Logue et al., 1970; Logue, 1970; Logue, 1971; Logue, 1972). At the extremes, two schools of thought began to emerge. The first concentrated its attention almost exclusively on symptomatology and, by employing the methods of workers like Kephart and Getman, achieved considerable success with many children. The second followed the view that long-term progress depends on a better understanding of causation. The old wine of the conflict between environmentalists and geneticists came to be poured into many new bottles; among them are organicity, cultural deprivation, emotional distress, and developmental lag. The search for a working definition continued and it was only recently that an American writer produced one which may provide temporary relief: "I would like to suggest, however, that, irrespective of the presence or absence of diagnosed neurological dysfunction, learning disabilities are essentially and almost always the result of perceptual problems based on the neurological system" (Cruickshank, 1972).

THE MURRAY REPORT

In 1968 the Minister of National Education appointed a committee of inquiry into the education of children with minimal brain dysfunction. Their report was tabled a year later (Murray, 1969). The committee began its work by adopting the following definition: "The term 'minimal brain dysfunction syndrome' refers in this paper to children of near-average, average, or above-average general intelligence with certain learning or behavioral disabilities ranging from mild to severe, which are associated with deviations of function of the central nervous system. These deviations may manifest themselves by various combinations of impairment of perception, conceptualization, language, memory, and control of attention, impulse or motor function" (Clements, 1966).

The committee had at its disposal no research data dealing specifically with the incidence of minimal brain dysfunction among children in South Africa. Thus, leaning heavily on the valued opinions of Denhoff, Frostig, and Myklebust, with regard to such surveys already carried out in the United States, the committee decided that it might be expected that 15% of pupils with IQ's of at least 90 would have learning disabilities which would retard their progress at school. They further estimated that the incidence of minimal brain dysfunction could be expected to lie between 5 and 7% of all pupils with IQ's of at least 90. They also assumed that the smaller group would constitute an integral part of the larger one.

Although moving considerably outside their terms of reference, the committee made recommendations which covered all pupils in white South African schools with IQ's of at least 90 with learning disabilities. These children were divided into three groups. Group A would comprise those pupils who, with adequate part-time remedial help, could remain at normal schools. The estimated number was 94,435. Group B would comprise those pupils who would profit only from attendance at full-time schools established specifically for this purpose. The estimated number in this group was 28,000. Group C would comprise those pupils whose learning problems were so severe that they would not be able to profit from even the intensive instruction planned for Group B. It was felt that much was still to be learned about this group, some 3,000 to 4,000 pupils in all, before any definite proposals could be made.

Although a considerable part of the Murray Report is certainly of a controversial nature, it is an enlightened blueprint which the state could follow in this matter. There is little doubt that two factors will hamper its full and immediate implementation. The first is finance and the second is trained professional staff. The difficulty can perhaps best be seen with regard to the carrying out of the proposals for Group B pupils. Two hundred eighty new clinic schools would have to be erected, each at a cost of perhaps 1,000,000 rand. Furthermore, 3,500 specially trained remedial teachers would be required to staff these schools. It is clear that only time and honest intention will allow this vast project to develop to fruition. During this period there will be great advances in the theory and treatment of learning disability. Furthermore, as the other groups in the Republic become ready for it, such facilities must be extended to them as well.

The recommendation of the Murray Committee was that the provincial education departments should be responsible for children in Groups A and B. It was anticipated that Group C children would fall under the Department of Higher Education. So far as Group A children were concerned, the committee was simply reporting on what was already happening—the establishment and growth of remedial reading classes and clinics throughout the country. No official statement has yet been made by the Minister of National Education with regard to the other two groups. Until such a ruling is forthcoming, these pupils must remain in an educational limbo; no official funds may be channeled into this area until it has been decided whether the money should flow from provincial or central government sources. Thus, whatever help pupils in categories B and C have received was due to the initiative and dedication of private workers or committees.

It is perhaps not unnatural that the Minister of National Education should be reluctant to rush into an area where even the initiated fear to tread, because the financial implications of whatever decision he makes are vast. The present tendency is for pupil-teacher ratios to increase in the face of both economics and staff shortages. Thus, any large-scale trend which is counter to this process must be regarded with care and, perhaps even suspicion. Then there is the matter of criteria for the admission of pupils to whatever classes and schools are established. Despite the Murray Committee Report, there must still be considerable doubt in the official mind about the distinction between brain damage, brain dysfunction, and learning disability. This confusion is evidenced by the fact that not a few pupils, otherwise normal, have found their way into the schools for the cerebral palsied where they receive expert remediation among physically handicapped children. Furthermore, before any private clinic schools were established in the Republic of South Africa, the choice before the child with learning disability was either a transfer to a school for the cerebral palsied or educational stagnation.

Another difficulty which may be retarding official action in this area is the shortage of trained and experienced remedial staff, both professional and administrative. Although all the major South African universities have, for many years, offered courses for remedial reading teachers, it is only recently that one or two of them have looked beyond the actual reading problem and embraced the whole concept of learning disability. Progress here must depend on finance and facilities, staff and methods. South Africa would appear to be at a crossroad. The state can either postpone official progress in this area and, in due course, finance a scheme based on developments overseas or recognize the few private clinic schools which do exist in the country and finance them adequately along the lines of pilot schemes.

PRIVATE CLINIC SCHOOLS

It is safe to say that most of the thinking and all the developments in the field of learning disability in South Africa have taken place in the last 10 years. Three national associations have been established, as well as three full-time schools and at least one remedial clinic for children with learning disabilities. The organizations are the South African Association for Remedial Education in Johannesburg, the National Association for Children with Reading and Learning Disabilities in Stellenbosch, and the Phoenix Educational Association in Durban. The first two bodies are primarily professional in character, but the Phoenix Association, probably the largest, is far more general in its approach. It founded and runs the Phoenix School for Group B pupils, it is in the process of establishing a school for Group C children, it is responsible for a 2-year in-service teachers' course, and it produces a quarterly journal on learning disability.

One of the miracles of modern times is how the three private clinic schools ever came into existence, let alone survive in the face of ever-increasing inflation and complete lack of official financial support. It has been probably the thought that state subsidy was always just around the corner that inspired the teachers to work for ridiculously low salaries and the parents to continue paying very high school fees—all in order that the children concerned could have individual attention and the best treatment possible. It is to the credit of the authorities that the schools have been allowed to exist in the rather restricted circumstances of converted dwelling houses. This official attitude has been consistently the same—reluctant to commit itself at the present time but both sympathetic and prepared to help within its powers.

The Norwood School

This school was founded in 1966 by an occupational therapist who is also the present director. It is in Johannesburg. There are 70 full-time pupils, ranging from first to sixth grade. The aim is to help a child with his specific problems as far as possible for upwards of 2 years and then transfer him back to a regular school. In addition to certified teachers, the staff is made up of clinical psychologists and occupational and speech therapists. Norwood also provides part-time remedial help on a sessional basis for children who attend full-time regular schools.

The Crossroads School

This school is also in Johannesburg and it was founded by the present director, a speech therapist, in the same year as the Norwood School. It is staffed by certified professional personnel in the same way as the Norwood School. Both schools work closely with their medical advisory panels which are made up of neurologists, psychiatrists, and ophthalmologists. Crossroads comprises three units: therapy, preschool to grade 4, and grades 5 to 9.

The Phoenix School

This school is in Durban and was founded by the present director, an educational psychologist, in 1968. It draws its 100 pupils from all parts of Southern Africa, the United States, and Great Britain. One-quarter of the pupils are boarders. The orientation of the school is basically educational and there are no therapists on the staff. Two types of teachers are employed: certified and aides. All are encouraged to undertake the 2-year in-service course for the Phoenix Remedial Certificate. The school is divided into 3 departments: readiness, remedial, and adjustment, which is from grade 4 through grade 7. Because the Phoenix School differs considerably in basic philosophy and approach from both Norwood and Crossroads, which are very close to what is being done in the United States, it will be discussed in more detail later in this chapter.

Other Centers

Mention must also be made of some other centers which have helped many pupils in Johannesburg over the past 5 years. The first is Bellavista, which began as a school offering small classes for underachievers. A remedial department was gradually developed as the need for such a step became pressingly obvious. Another center is the Japari Remedial Clinic which was founded by the present director, a physician. It offers an entire range of psycho-educational services, among which are both full- and part-time remedial tutoring for children. A full range of remedial and therapeutic staff is used as well as 2 full-time social workers. To Japari Clinic goes the credit of having produced the only published set of remedial readers in the country (Machanick, 1969).

Finally there is a clinic which was founded by another physician 2 years ago. It is run entirely on the principles of Kephart and, although small, it is most efficiently organized.

THE PHOENIX SCHOOL

Function and Control

The aim of the Phoenix School is to educationally rehabilitate children with severe learning disability who are both physically and intellectually normal. The school is owned by the Phoenix Educational Association, a nonprofit-making body, with 500 members throughout the world. For the past 5 years, the school has been housed in a redundant regular school building; but the erection of its own new premises is about to begin on a bigger campus in Durban. When the new site is fully developed, it will comprise the Phoenix School for Group B and the Penfield Center for Group C pupils. There will also be a small prevocational training unit for any pupils who are not able to return to the regular school system. Also on the property will be an assessment center, a teacher-training unit, and a small research unit (Logue, 1971b).

There are two deputy directors who are responsible for remedial work and class work, respectively. In effect, this means that the first deputy controls the work of all pupils in the readiness and remedial departments and the second deputy controls that of the pupils in the adjustment section where the aim is to bring them up as speedily as possible to their age levels in the basic subjects prior to their return to regular schools.

An additional function of the school is the provision of facilities for the longitudinal study of pupils where it has not been possible to make a reliable diagnosis because of their manifold problems. Once the Penfield Centre (named after Wilder Penfield) has been established, it will be possible to study such pupils right through the intelligence range over extended periods of time. It is also envisioned that, as the result of both maturation and therapy, numbers of children will move from the Penfield Centre to the Phoenix School.

Diagnosis and Admission of Pupils

The enthusiasm of testers in this area for all the glittering new apparatus which is appearing and which, it is often extravagently claimed, can test specific functions, simply because their originators have said so, should be tempered by two important considerations—the time of the professional staff and any unnecessary expense to the parents. It should also be remembered that the assessment of a child is something that grows and is modified as therapy proceeds. Thus the initial testing and assessment of pupils are limited to a maximum of 2 hours at the Phoenix School; but assessment will continue for the whole of the child's stay.

Case conferences for initial assessment purposes have been found to produce more heat than light at the school. There are regular weekly case conferences but their value is to develop inter-teacher contacts and for the training of new staff. The aim at the school is the fashioning of the many-sided worker who can look at all aspects of the child instead of trying to fractionalize him in terms of a particular type of professional training. It is rare to find a child who requires specific speech, occupational, or physiotherapy here, as is the case in a school for the cerebral palsied, where the value of such personnel is so great.

The aim of the initial assessment is to produce a pen-picture of each

PUPIL M.C.

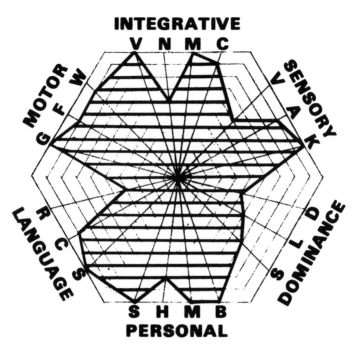

Figure 1. Hexagonal graph-profile of a child's development.

The hexagonal graph reflects the development of a student in profile. Each developmental area is scored from zero at the center to normal at the periphery.

The abbreviations are: Integrative: V, verbal IQ; N, performance IQ; M, memory; C, concentration. Sensory: V, visual perception; A, auditory perception; K, kinesthetic-tactile perception. Dominance: D, direction; L, laterality; S, sidedness. Personal: B, behavior; M, maturation; H, health; S, social adjustment. Language: R, reading level; S, speed; C, comprehension. Motor: G, gross motor; F, fine motor; W, pencil work.

child in all his many aspects. For this purpose, the Hexagonal Graph is used (Logue, 1963). The graph is made up of 10 concentric hexagons which reflect development from zero level at the center to normality at the periphery. The level of the pupil is plotted in the following six parameters: sensorimotor, integrative, language, orientational, and personality development. Thereafter the graph is drawn by joining together all of the 20 plotted points. An example of a hexagonal graph is given in Figure 1.

The illustrative graph is of a pupil, M.C., age 9 years. He has great difficulty in reading words despite the fact that comprehension is quite good. Memory, attention, and concentration are also good. The Verbal IQ is 139 and the Performance IQ is 104. There are serious figure-ground difficulties in visual perception. Sidedness has not yet been fully established, awareness of laterality is poor, and there is a serious directional problem. The pupil is motivated and well-behaved. He mixes easily with his peers but home adjustment is poor due to paternal rejection.

Medication of Pupils

Initially there was a tendency at the Phoenix School to regard the problems of the children as primarily of a medical nature. Electroencephalograms were taken as an admission requirement for every new pupil to the school, as well as neurological examinations (Joubert and Logue, 1969). Many of the entrants presented concentration problems and it was believed that the answer to this difficulty lay in medication.

The present position is that routine EEG and neurological examinations for all pupils are no longer necessary. It has been discovered over the years that the concentration problems of many of the pupils tend to diminish, or even to disappear, once they settle down in the secure and highly structured school environment. Furthermore, detailed neurological assessments are not helpful for most of the pupils because the techniques of the neurologist are still not sufficiently refined for the so-called "soft signs" of the child with learning disability. In the same way, there is a serious lack of specialists who have a profound knowledge of the neurology underlying the subtle disturbances of both speech and language (Luria, 1966, 1970).

It is therefore safe to say that at the present time the great value of the medical examination at the Phoenix School is to screen pupils who might be better placed at other types of institutions for the handicapped, and to exclude the possibility of any physical cause for the lack of further progress at school. For this purpose, a pediatrician or even a general practitioner may be adequate.

Once the pupil has been carefully observed over his first month at the school, a decision can be made on whether specialized neurological examination is desirable. The two tests most likely to be undertaken are those for glucose tolerance with a view to possible megavitamin therapy or electroencephalograms. EEG's have been found particularly valuable in respect to three types of problems where their results can provide pointers to possible medication. They are hyperkinetics, subclinical epileptics, and children with temporal lobe dysfunctions. The preferred drugs for hyperkinetics are dextroamphetamine sulphate, methylphenidate, and sometimes thioridazine. Since the withdrawal of dextroamphetamine sulphate in 1972, methylphenidate has become even more widely used. For pupils with subclinical epileptic conditions a wide range of anticonvulsants are available. These include phenobarbital, primidone, diphenylhydantoin, troxidome, and ethosuximide. Carbamazephine has proved a popular and invaluable drug for temporal lobe conditions, regardless of whether epilepsy is also present. Tranquilizers are rarely used because there is little need for them once the child has settled down in his new environment.

The School Environment

Perhaps one of the greatest mistakes that workers in this field sometimes make is to treat a learning disability instead of a child. It is for this reason that every effort has been made at the Phoenix School to develop the right type of environment for the pupils. Children who have become failures at school have very little to hold on to; often they have even been rejected by their parents. Every effort is made to help them identify with the realities about them—the Almighty, their country, and their school. Much is made of the daily assembly at which the nearness of God is often felt. Two flags are hoisted daily at that time, the national flag and the school flag with its motto, "fastina lente."

Stress is considerably reduced by the banning of all bullying and teasing. Any culprits in this direction must put on the boxing gloves the following day against opponents of their own caliber. The children know exactly what they may and may not do, and corporal punishment is administered to the nonconformists. The director's office is always open to pupils; before school and in every break it is usual for up to a dozen pupils to congregate there for informal chats. This last activity is regarded as the function of the director, which is second in importance only to his taking the daily assembly.

Every effort is made to develop in the children pride in their school, loyalty to their families, and respect for themselves. They must sweep their own classrooms and keep the school grounds clean. Their simple school uniforms must be spotless on arrival at school each day and shoes must be well polished. They must stand properly when speaking to adults and they must enunciate clearly. In some of the Western societies, all this may be looked upon as petty tyranny, but the beneficial results for the pupils at the school must be seen to be believed.

The contact with the homes of the pupils is a very close one. In the homework notebook are entered also whatever lapses or achievements the pupil has experienced at school. This the parent must read, comment on, and sign. Similar reporting is done by the parent to the class teacher about what happens at home. The result is both full understanding between parent and teacher, as well as uniformity of treatment of the child.

Only the basic subjects are taught at the school and, on admission, the child is placed in the grade which is the equivalent of his achievement level—no matter how low. It is amazing what a wonderful boost it is to the morale of the pupil to be in a group where he can actually do the work. Promotions are made whenever pupils are ready, and therein is the key to motivation.

Remediation of Pupils

Most of the remedial treatment is undertaken by the class teachers within their own group. All teachers are specially trained at the school to operate in this way. Only the most stubborn cases will be referred for further individual help to the therapy department. In the same way, very little psychotherapy is undertaken by the school psychologist. Far better results have been found to accrue by working on the larger canvas of the whole school environment.

The theories underlying remedial help and the actual treatment undertaken are based on the best that is available from overseas, particularly the United States. However, there is no water-tight division of functions among the various types of therapists. Rather, each child is helped by his own teacher who should be able to cater to all his difficulties.

School Staff

The pupil-teacher ratio at the Phoenix School is approximately 4 to 1. Most of the staff are qualified teachers and the balance are helpers. All are expected to attend the weekly lectures and case conferences, and to enter for the examinations at the end of the 2-year course. All teachers must naturally maintain records of completed work, but these are kept as simple as possible; far more emphasis is expected to be placed on the records of individual pupils. This is done, not only for obvious reasons, but also because much research leading to master's and doctoral dissertations is based on all the carefully maintained data.

Apparatus for Testing

All other things being equal, test apparatus should be economical in terms of both cost and time needed for its application. Several pieces of apparatus have been found useful at the Phoenix School, which have been either developed in South Africa or introduced from elsewhere and then adapted to local needs.

The Logue Nuts and Bolts Test (Logue, 1969) comprises a set of seven brass nuts and bolts of different lengths and thicknesses. The testee must put them together and stand them on end as quickly as possible. The test is fully standardized for pupils from 5.5 through 14.5 years. It takes less than 5 minutes to administer this test and it is useful for the observation

Reversible Series   Irreversible Series

Reversible Series			Irreversible Series		
b	p	d	X	I	O
q	Z	N	4	8	B
m	ɯ	Ɛ	Y	R	4
5	2	7	S	O	X
L	f	t	B	G	J
e	6	9	K	I	R
∪	∩	c	X	8	O
E	m	ɯ	4	J	B
Z	N	ƨ	R	S	I

Figure 2. The Super Test of Directionality. The pupil is asked to read aloud each series, and the amount of time taken is recorded. Letter and number reversals are noted.

of hand preference, directionality, visual judgments, motor perseveration, and fine muscle clumsiness.

In 1963 it was found that the Purdue Pegboard Test, a short sensori-motor test, was an efficient screening instrument to detect the presence and laterality of brain damage (Costa et al., 1966). This test has been extensively applied in South Africa to children with learning disability. Furthermore, it has been carefully standardized here for the age range of 6 to 14 years (Logue and Joubert, 1968). Although the Purdue Pegboard cannot be regarded as a screening instrument for learning disability, it is still valuable in this area, not only as an aid for establishing hand preference, but also in order to observe fine finger dexterities, and two-hand coordination. It also takes less than 5 minutes to apply.

The Super Test of Directionality was created by an optometrist in Johannesburg and has been found very valuable at the Phoenix School (Super, 1969). The pupil is asked to read out two series of letters and his time is taken for each. The first series is made up only of "irreversible" letters and digits while the second is precisely the opposite (Figure 2). The test provides a useful view of a child's directional difficulties.

Although there are no new tests in the Isaacs Diagnostic Box, it is of value because it consolidates a number of useful techniques in one unit (Logue, 1972b). This piece of apparatus is made up of five main sections: a test similar to the Kirshner Lights Test, a ring-counter of 354 sound combinations, a tape recorder, headphones (with each earpiece having its own intake channel), and a hand-eye coordination test. The Isaacs Diagnostic Box has not been manufactured for sale and its use is restricted to the Phoenix School for diagnostic and remedial purposes.

Problems and Investigations

It is only natural that in such a new and rapidly developing area as that of learning disability, theories and techniques should be constantly scrutinized and modified in terms of the exceptions which appear to break so many attractive rules. This is the raw material of progress. Unfortunately, these doubts are generally kept within each family circle and are seldom voiced at conferences or reported on in books. It is submitted that these are vitally important, and an effort will be made to reflect thinking on such subjects at the Phoenix School.

Failures in Therapy

It is customary for most remedial teachers to say that they help all their pupils in some way or other. It is also a fact that there are certain children who still do not read, despite all the expert help. This group is sometimes called dyslexic, but there is still no valid explanation for their failure. At the Phoenix School there have been nine such cases, over the past 5 years. All have been adequately motivated. There were two girls and seven boys. Of the group, five children had great disparities between verbal and performance IQ's. In three instances it was in favor of the performance score. The only common factor to the group was a great weakness in the repetition of a series of digits. It is suggested elsewhere that this may be due to a thalamic problem (Logue, 1971d) or to a verbalizing difficulty (Logue, 1973).

It was also noted that eight of the nine pupils were both blonde and blue eyed, a factor which was also mentioned to me in a personal communication by Dr. Kirshner of Montreal. It may be sheer coincidence. There is also the possible factor of phenylpyruvic acid and its relationship with similar characteristics in a certain type of mental retardation. It is planned to carry out further exploratory investigations in this area.

Intelligence and Learning Disability

There is a tendency to look upon learning disability as a handicap particular to the child of normal potential. Unfortunately, potential is reflected by performance on an intelligence test. Since learning disability can seriously affect the pupil's resultant IQ, it is extremely difficult to distinguish the chicken from the egg in this particular matter (Logue, 1971c). Since one of the admission requirements laid down by the state for the Phoenix School is intellectual normality (at least one of the IQ's above 90) it is hard to know just where to draw the line. This must surely be a universal stumbling block. It is submitted that the greater challenge in this area is with those children who score badly on intelligence tests because of learning disability.

Concept of Learning Disability

There are some workers who regard orientational and perceptual diffi-culties as discrete entities like a damaged eye or a clumsy hand. That many visual perceptual problems, for example, are due to dysfunctions or immaturities in some aspect of the visual analyzer goes without question. However, there is the other type which is a symptom of some dysfunction in the child himself. Thus, if a child does badly on a test of visual perception, it may mean that he requires visuoperceptual training or it may suggest that he needs help elsewhere. Examples of this are frequently seen in cases of subclinical epilepsy.

Case Study

The story below is of a child, age 7 years, who came to the Phoenix School from Miami, Florida, where she had received a year's intensive part-time training for a serious directional problem (Figure 3).

The parents brought her to Durban, in desperation, because it had been prognosticated that she would not read until she was 9 years old. Now, after a year, the child is in grade 3. There is little doubt that this rapid improvement was due to neither superior nor special remedial techniques. She needed, in addition to other help, the structuring of a school background all day and every day for an extended period.

This example is one of a number where a pupil has seemed to overcome such difficulties suspiciously rapidly in the full-time school

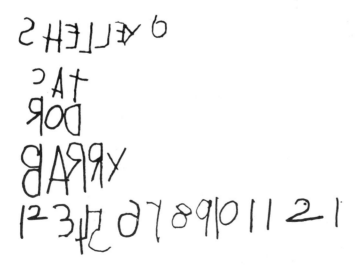

Figure 3. Shelley's directional problem.

environment. There is no doubt that, in terms of initial testing, the problems were there from the start. It is equally beyond question that the credit for their quick disappearance is not due to therapy alone.

Comprehension Problems

The most common reason for remedial help is a spectacular one; the child cannot read. The therapist and remedial teacher work around this point and far too frequently believe that their task is over when the child is reading up to his age level. It is an unfortunate fact, however, that many children who had initial reading difficulties also have serious comprehension problems. This is well brought out when they begin mathematics. It is a problem which is often as serious as the initial presenting system. Furthermore, it is not a superficial one which can be remedied simply by practice with exercises in comprehension. It may even be neurologically based (Luria, 1970).

CONCLUSION

Despite its size and also its remoteness from the main stream of world educational thinking, South Africa is vitally interested in the whole subject of learning disability. There is little doubt that all workers turn towards the United States for help in this area. However, much is being achieved here by all disciplines: psychologists, teachers, therapists, and optometrists. Despite a wholehearted acceptance of basic principles, there is a healthy lack of uniformity in many aspects of diagnosis and treatment. Much has been said about thinking and techniques at the Phoenix School, only one of the several interested centers in this country.

REFERENCES

Bax, M., and R. MacKeith. 1963. Minimal Cerebral Dysfunction. Heineman, New York.
Clements, S. 1966. Minimal Brain Dysfunction in Children: Terminology and Identification. Phase One of a Three Phase Project. U.S. Department of Health, Education and Welfare, Washington.
Cruikshank, W. M. 1972. Some issues facing the field of learning disability. J. Learning Disab. 5:7.
Getman, G. N. 1962. How to Develop Your Child's Intelligence. Announcer Press, Lucerne, Minn.
Johnson, D. J., and H. R. Myklebust. 1967. Learning Disabilities. Grune and Stratton, New York.
Joubert, M. J. 1970. Psychoneurological Dysfunction in School-going Children. Thesis for Doctor of Medicine, University of Pretoria, So. Africa.

Joubert, M. J., and G. D. Logue. 1969. The Electroencephalogram. Phoenix J. 2:1.

Kephart, N. C. 1960. The Slow Learner in the Classroom. Merrill, Columbus, Ohio.

Logue, G. D. 1963. The Hexagonal Graph. Phoenix J. 2:3.

Logue, G. D. 1968. Editorial. Phoenix J. 1:1.

Logue, G. D. 1960. Aims and Methods in Western Education. Juta.

Logue, G. D., and M. J. Joubert. 1968. The Purdue Pegboard Test. Phoenix J. 1:1.

Logue, G. D., U. Martins, and Y. Campbell. 1969. Psychoneurological Dysfunction—The Role of the Parent. Phoenix Publications, Dublin.

Logue, G. D. 1969. The Nuts and Bolts Test. Phoenix J. 2:3.

Logue, G. D., U. Martins, F. Muller, M. J. Joubert, and Y. Campbell. 1970. Psychoneurological Dysfunction—The Role of the Teacher. Phoenix Publications, Dublin.

Logue, G. D. 1970. Psychoneurological Dysfunction—The Role of the Specialist. Phoenix Publications, Dublin.

Logue, G. D. 1971a. The Late Developing Child. Phoenix Publications, Dublin.

Logue, G. D. 1971b. Specific Learning Disabilities. Phoenix J. 4:2.

Logue, G. D. 1971c. Psychoneurological Dysfunction and Learning Problems. Part I. Phoenix J. 4:3.

Logue, G. D. 1971d. Psychoneurological Dysfunction and Learning Problems. Part II. Phoenix J. 4:4.

Logue, G. D. 1972a. The Slow Learning Child. Phoenix Publications, Dublin.

Logue, G. D. 1972b. The Isaacs Diagnostic Box. Phoenix J. 5:2.

Logue, G. D. 1973. Language and Intelligence. Phoenix J. 6:1.

Luria, A. R. 1966. Higher Cortical Functions in Man. Basic Books, New York.

Luria, A. R. 1970. Traumatic Aphasia. Mouton.

Machanick, S. 1969. Sounds Travel Too. Japari.

Murray, C. H. de C. 1969. Report of the Committee of Inquiry into the Education of Children with Minimal Brain Dysfunction. Government Printer, Pretoria, So. Africa.

CHAPTER 19

Reading and Learning Disabilities in the United States (with Emphasis on California)

Lester Tarnopol and Muriel Tarnopol

Public education is controlled primarily by local boards of education in the United States. The members of each board are usually elected by the local population. Federal laws do not directly govern education in the schools. However, federal constitutional rights have been interpreted to require that, within each state, all children shall have equal opportunities and facilities for free public education.

INCIDENCE OF SPECIFIC LEARNING AND READING DISABILITIES

Silverman and Metz (1973) did a survey of a sample of 2,000 local public schools that were representative of 81,000 schools in the United States enrolling 300 or more pupils. They asked the principal of each school for an estimate of the number of pupils with specific learning disabilities (SLD) being serviced by the school, and an estimate of the number of SLD pupils who were not in special programs in each school.

From this 1970 survey, it was estimated that of 24,985,000 elementary school children (grades 1 through 6) in the United States, 465,000 (1.9%) were receiving special instruction for SLD, and a total of 779,000 (3.1%) could use such help. Of 17,839,000 pupils in secondary schools (grades 7 through 12), it was estimated that 172,000 (1.0%) were receiving special teaching and a total of 314,000 (1.8%) could use this help. The

287

total figures in both cases include those already receiving special education.

It is estimated that about 10% of the adult population of the United States are functionally illiterate. That is, their reading levels are below the fifth grade. If we assume that there are about 3% SLD children and add the 2% who are retarded and about 1.5 percent who are emotionally disturbed, the total comes to 6½%. This leaves about 4% of the functionally illiterate unaccounted for. Probably most of these come from lower socioeconomic groups, including whites, blacks, Spanish surname, and Indians.

Lower socioeconomic children are often referred to as educationally or culturally deprived. Large numbers of poor whites from such areas as Appalachia in the middle Atlantic states, and children of all ethnic groups living in city or country slums are included in this category. In the schools, it is often difficult to distinguish pure cases of cultural deprivation from those mixed with learning disabilities so that it is difficult to develop accurate SLD statistics.

An example of the effect of cultural deprivation on the reading levels of children will serve to illustrate the nature of the problem. In one California county, there are a number of elementary schools in different communities. In a primarily white, middle-class school, the average first-grade reading level was at the 62nd percentile, and climbed to the 84th by sixth grade. In a lower-class minority school, the average first-grade reading level was at the 52nd percentile, and fell to the 7th by sixth grade (Table 1). These percentiles were based on state-wide testing. Although the children in both schools started out about the same in reading, by sixth grade the middle-class children were well above average and the lower-class children were well below average.

Since the average reading levels were approximately the same in the first grade, one might assume that the children in both schools were functioning at about the same average academic level and that the percentage of children with learning disabilities in each school might be about the same. If this were true, the rapidly developing disparity between the schools would have to be explained either by a difference in teaching or a difference in the motivation of the children, or both. In the past it was claimed that schools in lower-class areas had poorer teachers with less money spent per pupil. However, in recent years, large sums of money have been spent in an attempt to overcome the effects of cultural deprivation and the amount of money spent per pupil has often become greater in schools attended by lower-class children than in those attended by middle-class children. Under these circumstances, the effects of inadequate motivation related to cultural deprivation appear to stand out. At the same

Table 1. Average reading levels in two elementary schools
in a California county

Elementary school in lower-class minority area		Elementary school in middle-class area	
Grade	Percentile[a]	Grade	Percentile[a]
1	52	1	62
2	30	2	75
3	19	3	86
6	7	6	84

[a]Percentiles are based on statewide testing.

time, there are undoubtedly a number of other complicating factors which are operating, including a probable higher rate of learning disabilities among the lower-class children than is apparent from their average first-grade reading level. Finally, we have noted that in every country with a poor ethnic minority a similar learning problem seems to exist; and in many countries, lower-class indigenous white pupils also appear to have severe learning problems (see Kellaghan's chapter on Ireland).

UNITED STATES OFFICE OF EDUCATION

The United States Office of Education is committed to assuring equal educational opportunities for all handicapped children. These efforts are coordinated through the Bureau of Education for the Handicapped. The objectives designed to implement this commitment are: to assist the states in providing appropriate educational services to the handicapped; to assure that every handicapped child receives appropriate education; to assure that every handicapped child who leaves school has had career educational training; to assure that all handicapped children in schools have trained teachers competent to aid them in reaching their full potential; and to secure the enrollment of preschool-aged handicapped children in federal, state, and local educational and day care programs.

Specific Learning Disabilities Defined

In 1970, the U.S. Office of Education defined children with *specific learning disabilities* as "those children who have a disorder in one or more of the basic psychological processes involved in understanding or in using language, spoken or written, which disorder may manifest itself in imperfect ability to listen, think, speak, read, write, spell, or do mathematical calculations. Such disorders include such conditions as perceptual handicaps, brain injury, minimal brain dysfunction, dyslexia, and developmental aphasia. Such term does not include children who have learning problems which are primarily the result of visual, hearing, or motor handicaps, of mental retardation, of emotional disturbance, or of environmental disadvantage."

The term *general learning disabilities* is similarly defined except that it refers to children who are mentally retarded. These definitions are in accordance with those proposed and accepted by the Council for Exceptional Children which is the organization of professionals in the field of exceptional children. The concept of exceptional children refers to all children outside the "normal range," and includes both the retarded and gifted as well as all forms of handicapped children.

Programs under the U.S. Office of Education

The United States Office of Education administers the Elementary and Secondary Education Act, the Higher Education Act, and the Vocational Education Act. These acts provide funds for educational and vocational projects and research, which are usually performed at the local level. The funds are given to the various state departments of education which disperse the money to approved applicants. Regional offices of the U.S. Office of Education administer scholarships, model programs, and civil rights issues.

As an example of the research funded by the Office of Education, the Bureau of Education for the Handicapped, under the Learning Disabilities Act of 1969, funded 43 Child Service Demonstration Programs involving training and research in learning disabilities. These demonstration programs were carried out in 41 states, the dependency of Puerto Rico, and through the Bureau of Indian Affairs. Brief summary descriptions (made from abstracts provided by the Bureau of Education for the Handicapped) of a few of these programs will indicate their nature.

Wisconsin Program "The Wisconsin Child Service Demonstration Program is designed to increase the competencies of the regular classroom teachers in meeting the needs of youngsters with mild to moderate learning disorders in the regular school program with the aid of the skills of qualified special education personnel. Children with moderate to severe learning disabilities are currently served by self-contained and resource programs in the state. The itinerant model currently used in this state has not been highly successful because the regular classroom teachers have not been adequately prepared to provide the necessary program and because of the inability of the itinerant teachers to spend enough time with teacher and/or student. The proposed project is designed to strengthen the itinerant teacher model while at the same time providing services to a greater number of children with learning disabilities."

Nevada Program   The Nevada Child Service Demonstration Program is an example from a state with a small population, about 580,000. "The Nevada project will establish a model center in each of the two major population centers, Reno and Las Vegas, during the first 2 years of the project, and then expand to create centers in 6 other counties, thereby servicing 95% of the state's children. The primary goal is early identification and remediation of learning disabilities. The project will create two groups of learning disability students. A group of severe learning disability children will spend part of their school day in the resource room where prescribed intervention techniques will be administered. The second group of more moderately learning disabled children will undergo prescribed intervention techniques within the regular classroom setting. It is expected that the first group of children will soon progress sufficiently to return to the regular classroom. Screening will be accomplished by adopting or modifying the behavioral assessment technique developed by the Washington State Program. This includes such tasks as saying words, saying sounds, writing letters, writing numbers, and copying geometric designs. Children found to have difficulties on the screening instrument will be studied by a psychologist who will use a variety of psychometric instruments to select children for the project. Those children selected will be provided with a program specifically designed for their needs."

Bureau of Indian Affairs Program   The Bureau of Indian Affairs Child Service Demonstration Program is an example of a special program for an ethnic minority. "As of June 1972, only 16% of the 2,748 Indian students diagnosed as learning disabled in North Carolina were receiving specialized services. The purpose of this project is to help increase these services by establishing a model resource room in an elementary school, and replicating the model in at least five administrative areas. The rationale for the proposed resource room is that by providing supportive services for the learning disabled child and his classroom teacher, the child will be able to remedy his problem with minimal isolation from his age-mates.

"The model resource room project will be staffed by a master learning specialist teacher (project coordinator), a prescriptive teacher, a relief teacher, and a teacher-aide. Services will include but not be limited to the following areas: language development, auditory perception training, basic mathematical concepts, visual perception training, social skills development, speech therapy, and psychomotor skills development. The services of specialists in mathematics and reading, a school social worker, and school psychologists will also be available. The relief teacher will substitute for classroom teachers to enable them to consult with the project staff.

"A 2-week in-service training program will be conducted for approximately 25 elementary classroom teachers and aides from the Cherokee School to introduce methods of pupil observation and acquaint teachers with the goals, objectives, and procedures of this project. Screening of all elementary school students will be conducted by the project staff and classroom teachers. It will include classroom observation by project staff, review of the child's records, and teacher referrals. If indicated, complete assessment including medical, intellectual, social-emotional, and educational evaluations will be conducted.

"Parental consent will be necessary to place a child in the program. Further parental involvement will be encouraged by providing meals, transportation, and babysitting services for visiting parents. Parents will be sent a child progress report every 6 weeks and pictures of their children in action occasionally."

Puerto Rico Program   The Puerto Rico Child Service Demonstration Project is an example from a U.S. Spanish-speaking dependency. "This project is designed as a model demonstration program for learning disabled children within the regular school program. The project has two phases: a preventative program for high-risk kindergarten and first-grade children and a resource and remedial service program for children grades 2 through 6. In addition, there is to be a great deal of in-service training for both regular and special class teachers. This program will involve restructuring the kindergarten and first-grade programs to provide for individualized instruction for children who have been identified as 'high risk.' This will be done through a readiness program for kindergarteners, emphasizing perceptual, motor, language, and behavior remediation. Part of the first-grade program would be to develop transition classes for children who are not ready for the regular first-grade curriculum.

"A diagnostic and correction program will be offered for students in grades 2 through 6. This will include the diagnosis and prescription of remedial and compensatory education for each child. When possible, children will remain in the regular classroom and service will be provided on a consultation basis. Where necessary, children will be enrolled in a resource room program.

"Another part of the project is to develop special instructional materials and evaluation instruments which can be used for screening Spanish-speaking children with potential learning disabilities."

STATE FUNCTIONS IN EDUCATION

Each of the 50 states has its own set of basic educational requirements which must be met by their local school districts. The educational process is carried out by local school districts which may comprise a town, city, county, or other unit. In general, the states provide for free public education for children from first through twelfth grades. Often free kindergartens are also available. Some states, like California, provide 2 more years of free public education through grade fourteen (the second year of college). Generally, children are required to attend school from about 6 to 18 years of age, depending on state laws.

In general, the states have special programs for children who need special education. These programs are for blind, deaf, orthopedically handicapped, cerebral palsied, mentally retarded, and emotionally disturbed children, and have existed for many years. A new group of educationally handicapped children began to be recognized about 1955. Their condition has different designations in the various states including perceptual handicap, brain damage, neurological handicap, specific learning disability, educational handicap, and so on.

PARENTS GET PROGRAMS

In America, new services for handicapped children are often obtained when parents organize and demand them. This occurs because parents are most directly faced with the problems of their children. Some parents understand their children's problems as well as, or better than many professionals (educators, psychologists, physicians, etc.). In 1965, Cruikshank wrote, "Although it is obvious that the so-called minimally brain damaged child has for many years been a part of the general child population, it has been relatively recent that sufficient information has developed within the several professions which have a concern for such children to the point where some consensus has been reached. As late as 1935, research began to develop in the United States which dealt with the psychological characteristics of these children, yet 30 years later this information is only just beginning to filter into the understanding and general practice of the professions involved. There are currently still great gaps in the knowledge about these children. . . . Parent awareness of these children has gotten ahead of professional awareness. Professional awareness is ahead of preparation of teachers, physicians, psychologists and social workers, and it is also ahead of teacher education facilities and the availability of competent college professors to teach in this complex area" (Tarnopol, 1969).

In California, local parent organizations had begun to form in the middle 1950's. In 1963, these organizations combined and formed the California Association for Neurologically Handicapped Children (CANHC). This organization was composed of parents and professionals but was controlled by the parents of these children. The legislation providing special education for educationally handicapped (EH) children was written by a parent-lawyer member of CANHC, advocated in legislative hearings by a parent-physician member of CANHC, and guided through the state legislature by a parent-salesman member of CANHC with the active backing of the organization and its members. At the same time, CANHC produced a 16mm, 42-minute, color film called *Why Billie Couldn't Learn.* This excellent film is still used in many parts of the world to demonstrate the learning problems of these children, as well as methods of remediation.

Nationwide, the Association for Children with Learning Disabilities (ACLD) was incorporated in 1964. By 1974, there were about 500 chapters in 46 states with a membership of about 30,000, including 3,500 members of CANHC which had recently affiliated. The association's major work consisted of lobbying congress for the inclusion of specific learning disabilities children as an officially designated group of handicapped children in the Elementary-Secondary Act; and holding annual international meetings on learning disabilities.

CALIFORNIA

Educationally Handicapped Children

Starting about 1958 in California, the State Department of Education funded pilot programs for children with learning disabilities in several local school districts to learn more about diagnoses and methods of remedial education. In 1963, a state law was passed making it possible for local school districts to establish special education for these children and offering extra state financial aid to the school districts based on the number of children enrolled in this program, to a maximum of 2% of each local school population. Special classes were begun in 1964 for 2,040 children in California. By 1975, there were about 80,000 pupils from kindergarten through high school (12th grade) in this program. Some school districts have already exceeded the 2% limitation of pupils in the program and others, as yet, have no program.

In California these children are designated *educationally handicapped* (EH). Educationally handicapped minors are defined as children "who by reason of marked learning or behavior disorders, or both, cannot benefit from the regular educational program, and who, as a result, require special education programs. Such learning or behavior disorders shall be associated with a neurological handicap or emotional disturbance and shall not be attributable to mental retardation" (California Administrative Code, 1967). Other programs are provided for the retarded, gifted, aphasic, blind, deaf, orthopedically handicapped, and culturally deprived. Originally, the children in the EH program usually came from middle-class homes so that the diagnosis was not confused by such factors as a poor home environment for learning, or a lower-class home where another language was spoken. However, as the program developed, it was determined that many of the children from inadequate environments also had learning disabilities. They were then placed in the program if a diagnosis fitting the description of an educationally handicapped minor could be made. As a result, a great many lower socioeconomic minority children (primarily from black and Spanish-surname families) are now served by this program. These children tend to be both "culturally deprived" and educationally handicapped.

Program for Educationally Handicapped Minors

In California there are about 600 district and county school departments which operate programs for educationally handicapped (EH) children under the state law. The growth of this program is regulated by state law to increase at the rate of 20% per year until the 2% limitation of children in the program is reached for the state. This would amount to about 88,000 out of a population of about 4.4 million children in kindergarten through twelfth grade in the California public schools.

The purpose of this program is primarily to assist pupils to overcome or compensate for their learning and/or behavior problems so that they can return to the regular classroom. Four types of help are supplied for the children. First, *learning disability groups* are provided for the children requiring least help. These children attend regular classes part time and go to their learning disability class for one or two periods each day. Here they work in small groups of not more than 8 pupils with a special teacher who may have a maximum of 32 pupils on the roll.

Second, *special day classes* are provided within the regular public schools. Each class may have a maximum of 12 pupils and a special teacher, plus a teacher's aide, in many cases. The children ordinarily attend the special class for the same number of hours as regular classes. For some children a full day is too much, in which case a child may attend for part of the school day. After catching up in their work, the children return to regular classes. Sometimes they also spend part of the day in a learning disability group for supportive help.

Third, *hospital instruction* is provided on both in-patient and out-patient services. For children confined to a hospital setting, a special teacher is provided by the local school district. Teachers may also be provided to remedial reading clinics in hospital settings where children come on an out-patient basis. These children attend regular school classes and may go to the reading clinic from 2 to 5 hours each week.

There are five such hospital-connected out-patient reading clinics in San Francisco, California. Some of these hospital reading clinics also serve special training purposes. The reading clinic at the University of California Medical Center in San Francisco trains medical students and interning pediatricians in the physician's role in learning disabilities. The reading clinic at the University of the Pacific Medical Center serves two additional roles. Special training is given to pediatric neurologists, and a Master's degree in Learning Disabilities is given for teachers.

Fourth, for those children not hospitalized, who cannot attend school because of severe behavior or other problems, *home instruction* is provided. A teacher may go to the pupil's home, or may use special telephone and computer services.

Admission to the EH Program   Pupils are admitted to the program for Educationally Handicapped Minors after a diagnostic study of the child has been reviewed by the Admission Committee. This committee is composed of a school administrator, a special education teacher, a school nurse, and a school psychologist, plus any other personnel which the committee requests such as educational specialists, optometrists, or physicians. Students (to 21 years of age) are eligible for the EH program if they have a specific learning disability (not aphasia), or a behavior disorder, or a serious emotional disturbance, or a combination of these, and their basic skills are significantly below the range expected. Moreover, they may not be mentally retarded and evidence shall be presented for a favorable prognosis for academic improvement in the EH program.

California's Master Plan for Special Education   In 1974, the California legislature passed the Master Plan for Special Education Bill. This bill requires the State Board of Education to establish a master plan whereby all children (from 3 to 21 years of age) who have exceptional educational needs shall have an educational program to meet their needs. This appears to be part of a new trend in American education whereby all children have a right to as much education as they can manage in a program suited to their special needs.

In proposing this bill, the legislature declared that previously, special education programs were developed in response to the specific needs of identifiable groups. Consequently, 28 separate programs were developed segregating pupils based on their disabilities. As a result, many children with exceptional needs were not served in any program, were inappropriately placed, or were excluded. Moreover, some programs were permissive so that not all school districts have them. "The legislature finds and declares that all individuals with exceptional needs have a right to participate in an appropriate program of publicly supported education" (Assembly Bill No. 4040, 1974).

The bill also requires that the master plan should be systematically implemented in a limited number of school districts from 1975 to 1978 after which it will be evaluated to determine if it should go into effect state-wide. Eight school districts were selected for the pilot test of the master plan. Each of these school districts devised its own method of implementing the master plan which was accepted by the State Department of Education. The legislature appropriated about $24,000,000 for the school year 1975–1976 for this purpose.

The bill creates two new educational positions, the program specialist and the resource specialist. The program specialist is to plan and coordinate programs for exceptional children, and participate in research, program development, in-service training, and the innovation of special methods. The resource specialist is to provide instruction for exceptional pupils; coordinate educational services and guidance to pupils and parents; provide consultant services to regular staff members; evaluate pupil progress; and revise individual instructional plans. The new direction of thinking seems to include retaining as many exceptional pupils as possible in regular classes with regular teachers who will receive consultation from resource teachers.

The plan appears to be somewhat grandiose in conception and a number of special education administrators and teachers doubt that it can be carried out without a great deal of modification. They point out that after 12 years of experience in developing the Program for Educationally Handicapped Children, a great many administrative personnel and most teachers are still not really qualified to do the job intended. Moreover, almost no regular teachers have been trained in special education and very few special education teachers appear sufficiently competent to undertake resource specialist positions which include acting as consultants to regular classroom teachers. The over-all concept of mandatory special education for all exceptional children is most praiseworthy. In a system with 4,400,000 children, over 10% of whom probably have exceptional educational needs, the realities of the problem appear staggering.

DIAGNOSING LEARNING DISABILITIES

The purpose of diagnosis is generally to detect: (1) medical problems which require correction (pediatric, neurological, psychiatric, hearing, or vision), (2) problems requiring speech and language therapy, and (3) the nature of the learning problems. The diagnosis of learning problems should be such that a prescription for teaching the child may be devised.

The diagnostic testing is often done by a coordinated team consisting of, at least, a physician, a psychologist, a speech, hearing, and language therapist, and a teacher of special education. The psychological evaluation usually includes intelligence testing (the Wechsler Intelligence Scale for

Children is most often used) plus other tests as required. Also customary are tests of eye-hand coordination, small and large muscle coordination, and balance. The psychologist also looks for signs of emotional disturbance. The language evaluation usually tests receptive language, integrative language processes, and expressive language. The tests may also include visual and auditory perception; speaking and writing processes; the ability to receive, understand, remember, sort, organize, and retrieve information through visual, motor, and auditory channels of communication; and automatic language processes. An educational evaluation is used to determine the child's level of reading, spelling, writing, and arithmetic. A special neuropsychiatric examination is often given which helps determine some possible underlying causes of the child's problems, and indicates if medication would be likely to help the child function better. Finally, the diagnostic team brings their reports together and works out a prescription for the medical and educational management of the child (Tarnopol, 1971).

All children do not get the benefit of the full evaluation described. In small towns, it may be impossible to find a diagnostic team capable of making a complete evaluation. Also, school districts do not usually have facilities for such a thorough testing procedure. These complete diagnostic procedures are usually done by groups connected with hospitals or learning clinics in the larger cities.

TRAINING SPECIAL TEACHERS

Of all the professional people helping children with learning disabilities, the single most important one appears to be the special education teacher. With good teaching, almost all of the EH children can learn. When they do learn, their social and psychological problems tend to become alleviated. However, getting enough trained teachers into this enormous program (the largest in special education) seems to be the most important problem, at present. The EH program grew from about 2,040 to about 80,000 children in only 11 years. The number of teachers consequently increased from about 180 to over 5,000. Teacher training simply could not keep pace with this very rapid expansion. Moreover, since no single method of teaching was found which would solve all of the children's problems, and a great many competing methods appeared, no special teacher's certificate had been developed for the EH program. A committee has prepared the requirements for this special teaching credential, which is now being given.

It has been observed that good EH teachers have certain qualities in common. For example, they tend to be hard-working, energetic people who always have enough material prepared so that the children are never without useful academic work. Observation of such a teacher's class reveals children working continuously on meaningful material with no time wasted running around the classroom, fighting, talking unnecessarily, hiding in closets, listening to a radio, or acting out in any other untoward way. In short, the teacher is able to control the children's behavior.

Teaching children with learning disabilities is extremely difficult even for a skilled teacher. By the time teachers become adequately trained, some go back to regular classes since special education demands so much of them. Because of program expansion and the high rate of turnover of the teachers in this program, there are many new teachers in the EH program each year.

Besides the in-service training provided by many school districts, there are special education courses which the teacher may take, either after school hours or during their summer vacations. These courses are given at colleges and universities. In 1965, there were very few such courses; today there are a large number available, but many are still not sufficiently practical. Professors tend to be theoretical and often teachers seem to be unable to translate this theory into practice. They usually must be shown precisely how to teach these children. There are, to be sure, some courses which are extremely practical and the number of such courses is growing as more people become trained in the required skills.

Most of the teachers in the EH program have tended to come from general education. Since it is only required to have a phonics course plus a general curriculum course for the reading part of the elementary teaching credential, many teachers enter the EH program unprepared to teach remedial reading. A reading specialist credential has recently been instituted and the schools of education have been developing curricula for this credential. In other aspects of learning disabilities, such as spelling, handwriting, arithmetic, and more advanced academic subjects, the situation is even more dismal; but courses for teachers are gradually being developed to meet these needs. However, we hasten to observe that there have always been creative self-taught teachers who have done excellent remedial work in all areas and these people have been the mainstay of the EH program.

DEFECTS IN TEACHING

Since some teachers in the EH program are relatively inexperienced, they tend to do things which create an extra burden for the already troubled children. Such teaching defects have also been observed in some regular classrooms and even among experienced teachers. Many of these problems appear to be related to the changes which have taken place in teacher training over the past 50 years. Perhaps the greatest change has been away from organization, structure and precision in teaching. Another modern innovation in teaching is one type of open classroom where four teachers and their classes may be in one large room. If any children are hyperkinetic because they are unable to suppress unwanted stimuli and must therefore react to almost all incoming stimuli, the open classroom could prove disastrous for them. Similarly, children who have auditory or visual figureground difficulties would also have severe problems attending in this situation. Another type of learning problem for some children which may be related to teacher training stems from the new educational concept that it is not necessary for teachers to use uniform pronunciation. Since teachers now pronounce words (and vowels and consonants) in many different ways, children with problems in auditory discrimination, auditory figure-ground, or auditory closure may become confused. The same holds true for writing; teachers no longer write and print in a uniform, precise manner so that children with disorders of visual perception may have difficulty recognizing letters. This also tends to occur when their texts have different type styles.

Some of the most common teaching defects observed, especially among inexperienced teachers, are the following:

1. Disorganization in the classroom
2. Lesson plans not prepared each day for each student
3. Lessons do not build continuously on previous learning
4. Lack of understanding of the linguistic forms of the English language and the application of phonics to teaching reading
5. Not enough structure in the teaching method
6. Lack of understanding of each child's individual method of learning
7. Lack of ability to diagnose what is wrong with the teaching method when a child fails to learn
8. Errors not overcome by anticipating them or immediate correction
9. Children permitted to continue to make the same mistake, thus overlearning errors
10. Teacher sits at desk when she should be moving among the children observing and correcting their work
11. Lack of understanding of individual differences in growth and development of boys and girls
12. Use of negative reinforcement (punishment) and improper use of positive reinforcement (reward)
13. Teacher unable (afraid) to tell children exactly what to do
14. Teacher unable (afraid) to control the children's behavior

Improving Instruction by Observing Pupils' Work

Children with learning disabilities have taught us more about learning and good teaching than all of the research with rats, or with college sophomores on nonsense syllables. Above average children seem to be capable of learning regardless of the methods used. On the other hand, children with learning disabilities will *not* learn as long as we continue to violate the principles of learning. Thus they represent our most valuable source of information about how children learn and so how to teach.

Make the hump letters.

Figure 1. Example of child practicing errors. This child needs more practice tracing over perfectly formed letters before going on to independent copying. The print and spacing are too small for her level of development. She requires large blackboard tracing first, then large paper tracing with continuous observation on the part of the teacher so that she does not slip into errors.

Figure 2. Weekly spelling test. This is another example of a child practicing his errors on the weekly spelling test. The words have no meaning for the student. Continuous, guaranteed failure only ensures a weekly, frustrating experience with spelling for this intermediate-aged boy. More appropriate instruction would provide spelling words from the child's spelling level.

Often teachers are not aware that certain things that they might do can confuse children with learning disabilities. However, once these matters are brought to the teacher's attention, they are usually readily understood and corrected. It has been our observation that a most common teaching defect appears to be *permitting students to practice and overlearn their errors.* Good pedagogy suggests that children learn best by practicing from a correct model followed by overlearning without the model.

Figure 1 is an example of a first-grade child's work learning to print the letters *r, n,* and *u.* Although the model is perfect, the pupil's letters are very poorly formed; she did not leave the proper space between each letter and between each word, and the word *run* soon becomes *rgn* and finally *rgnnn.* She has been practicing poor printing, essentially practicing her errors. The print is too small for this child and there are too many letters on the page. Her eye-hand coordination is inadequately developed and she needs more work tracing before she will be able to form these letters properly. The teacher should have been watching the child to prevent errors so that this would not happen.

Figure 2 is an example of an intermediate-grade child practicing his spelling errors. Every Friday, the teacher gave a test on 28 spelling words which had been given to the pupils during the week. Each week, several pupils got all the spelling words wrong. There is no point in having these pupils continue this frustrating experience each week, but no one suggested otherwise to the teacher. Either these children should be grouped according to their spelling levels, or they should be placed in individualized spellers at their own levels. Moreover, they should be taught some workable method of learning to spell so that they may achieve continuous success. The writing on this paper (and the others) indicates that these children need lined paper with the margins clearly delineated. The children will continue to learn as long as they experience success, but continuous failure can only destroy their motivation and self-esteem.

Figure 3 is an example of a pupil's work shown by an EH teacher to the supervisor. The teacher stated that she was teaching the pupil typing! It didn't occur to her that the child might not be learning anything useful by punching random keys on the typewriter. This is just one of a great many examples of unproductive "busywork" given to children.

In Figure 4, the teacher's model of the cursive letters *S s* and *T t* are incorrectly placed on the color-cued lined paper. (Color-cued lines are represented by solid and dotted lines.) Figure 5 shows how the letters should be made on this paper.

Figures 6, 7, and 8 are examples of negative reinforcement which should be avoided whenever possible when correcting the work of students. In Figure 6, the teacher has graded the child's Frostig-visual-motor exercises! They should never be graded. This would be similar to down-

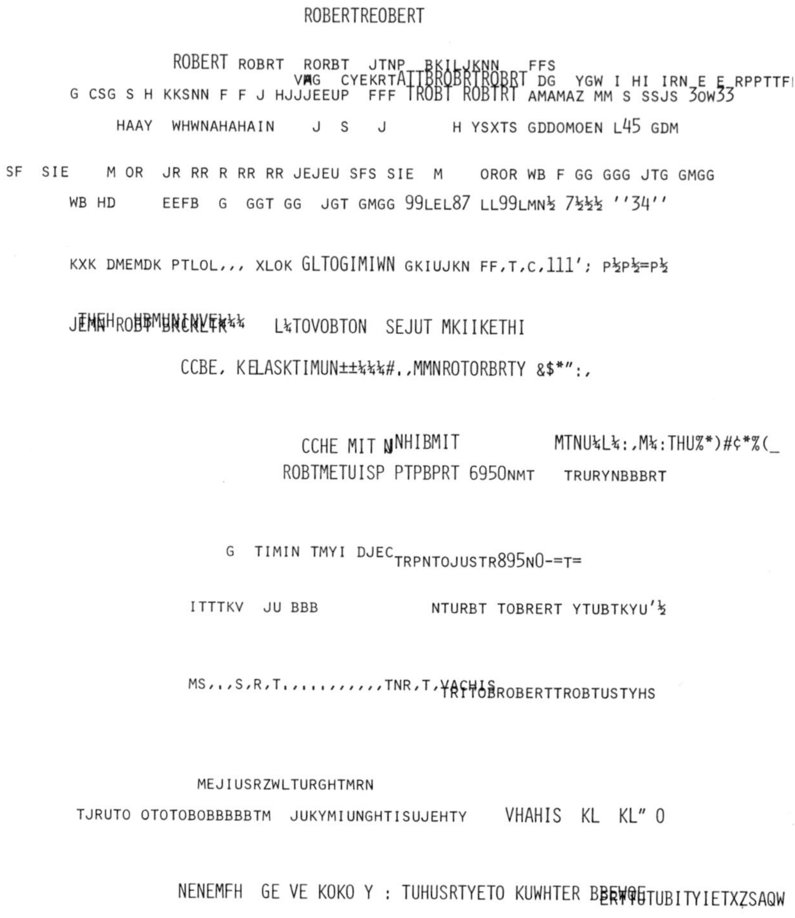

ROBERTREOBERT

ROBERT ROBRT   RORBT   JTNP   BKILJKNN   FFS
              VAG   CYEKRTAITBROBRTROBRT DG YGW I HI IRN_E E_RPPTTFI
   G CSG S H KKSNN F F J HJJJEEUP FFF TROBT ROBIRI AMAMAZ MM S SSJS 3OW33

      HAAY WHWNAHAHAIN   J S J   H YSXTS GDDOMOEN L45 GDM

SF SIE   M OR JR RR R RR RR JEJEU SFS SIE   M   OROR WB F GG GGG JTG GMGG
   WB HD   EEFB   G GGT GG JGT GMGG 99LEL87 LL99LMN½ 7½½½ ''34''

   KXK DMEMDK PTLOL,,, XLOK GLTOGIMIWN GKIUJKN FF,T,C,111'; P½P½=P½

   JFMFHRoBBMBnenVEk¼¼   L¼TOVOBTON SEJUT MKIIKETHI

      CCBE, KELASKTIMUN±±¼¼¼#,,MMNROTORBRTY &$*":,

            CCHE MIT NNHIBMIT   MTNU¼L¼:,M¼:THU%*)#¢*%(_
            ROBTMETUISP PTPBPRT 6950NMT   TRURYNBBBRT

      G   TIMIN TMYI DJEC_TRPNTOJUSTR895N0-=T=

   ITTTKV JU BBB   NTURBT TOBRERT YTUBTKYU'½

      MS,,,S,R,T,,,,,,,,,,,TNR,T,YACHIS TRTTOBROBERTTROBTUSTYHS

         MEJIUSRZWLTURGHTMRN
   TJRUTO OTOTOBOBBBBBTM JUKYMIUNGHTISUJEHTY   VHAHIS KL KL" 0

      NENEMFH GE VE KOKO Y : TUHUSRTYETO KUWHTER BBRW9GTUBITYIETXZSAQW

Figure 3. Busywork. An intermediate-aged student wanted to learn to type. No instruction was offered. His random, disorganized responses at the typing keys indicate that nothing was being learned.

grading (punishing) all of the children who have to wear corrective lenses. The fact that the child made circles indicates that the teacher was not watching and permitted him to do the exercise incorrectly. He should have been shown that lines were to be drawn between the pairs of circles similar to the stimulus figure at the top. Since the purpose of these exercises is to help the child develop his dysfunctioning visual-motor skills, he should be taught how to do the exercises and should be encouraged to develop these skills.

Figure 7 is an example of confusing, undeserved, negative reinforce-

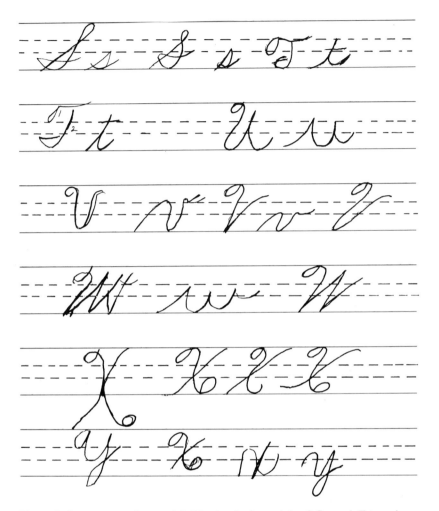

Figure 4. Incorrect teacher model. The teacher's models of *S s* and *T t* are incorrectly placed on this specially lined, color-cued paper (represented by solid and dotted lines). The student response was accordingly incorrect.

ment. This second-grade child spelled nine out of ten words correctly, missing the tenth due to a reversal, not a spelling error. The child is left-handed and such reversals are quite common for these pupils. To avoid confusion and to reinforce correct letter directions, the child should have an alphabet on his desk with the critical letters circled or color coded. He should be told to check the critical letters before printing them to be sure that they are correct. By reinforcing the correct stimulus in this manner, the pupil will avoid becoming confused by directionality problems. When

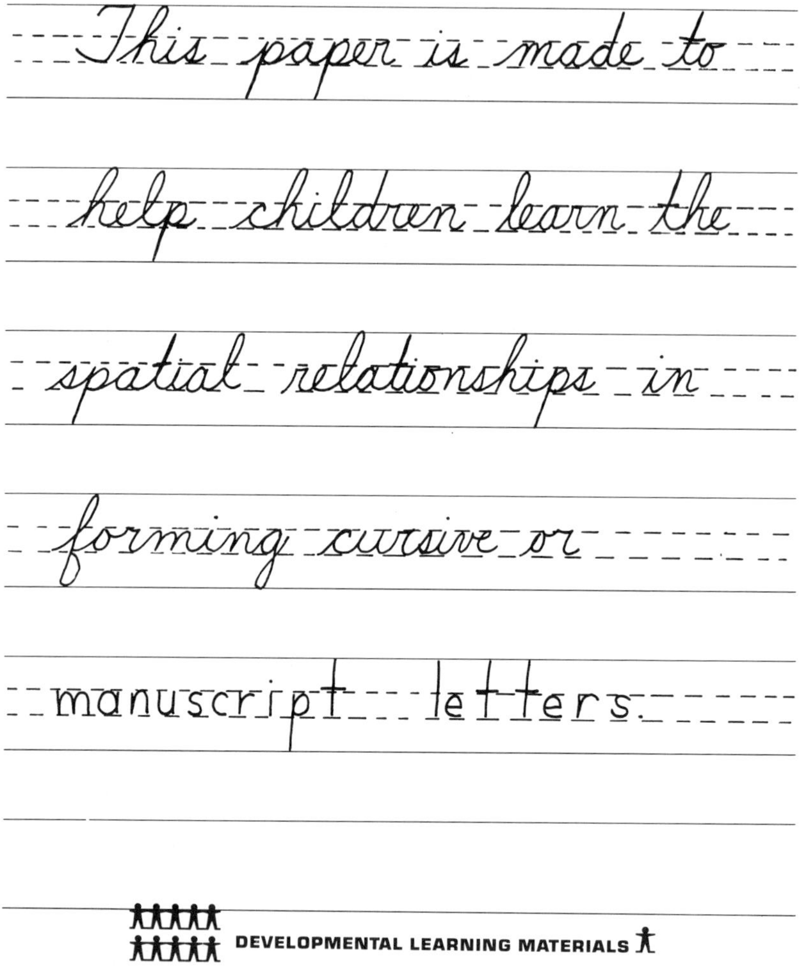

This paper is made to

help children learn the

spatial relationships in

forming cursive or

manuscript letters.

DEVELOPMENTAL LEARNING MATERIALS

Figure 5. Correct use of specially lined, color-cued paper (represented by solid and dotted lines). (Courtesy of Developmental Learning Materials, Niles, Illinois.)

the child was asked what the sad face drawn on the paper meant, he said he didn't know, but it "makes me feel bad." Discouraging little children with negative reinforcement from either sad faces or crying angels is not good pedagogy.

All children need to be taught to use margins properly and the teacher should see that this is always done. Left-handed children require special attention. They have a tendency to work too close to the left edge of the

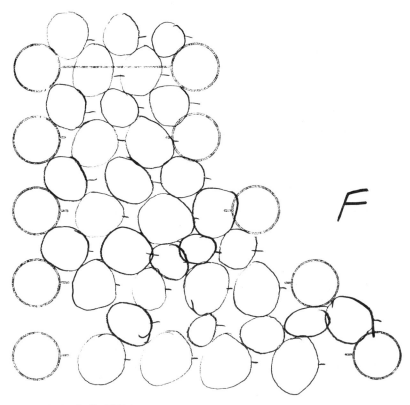

VM: Exercise 52

Figure 6. Incorrect use of Frostig exercises–negative reinforcement. These visual-motor exercises for children are to help improve motor and perceptual skills. They should certainly not be graded as is this paper which is marked F for fail. The exercise calls for the child to follow the example at the top and draw lines between the circles. The teacher should have started the child on the exercises correctly. (Exercise reproduced courtesy of Frostig Perception Program, Chicago, Illinois.)

paper. By using lined, color-coded paper with a green line for the left margin (green=left=go) and a red line for the right margin (red=right= stop), these problems will be avoided. Eventually, the habits become automatic and color-coded lines and margins are no longer needed, but they should be used as long as necessary.

Figure 8 is an example of both negative reinforcement and inconsistency on the part of the teacher. Positive reinforcement occurs when the number of right answers are scored as 15/20 (15 right out of 20) and the correct answers are checked, while there is negative reinforcment when the

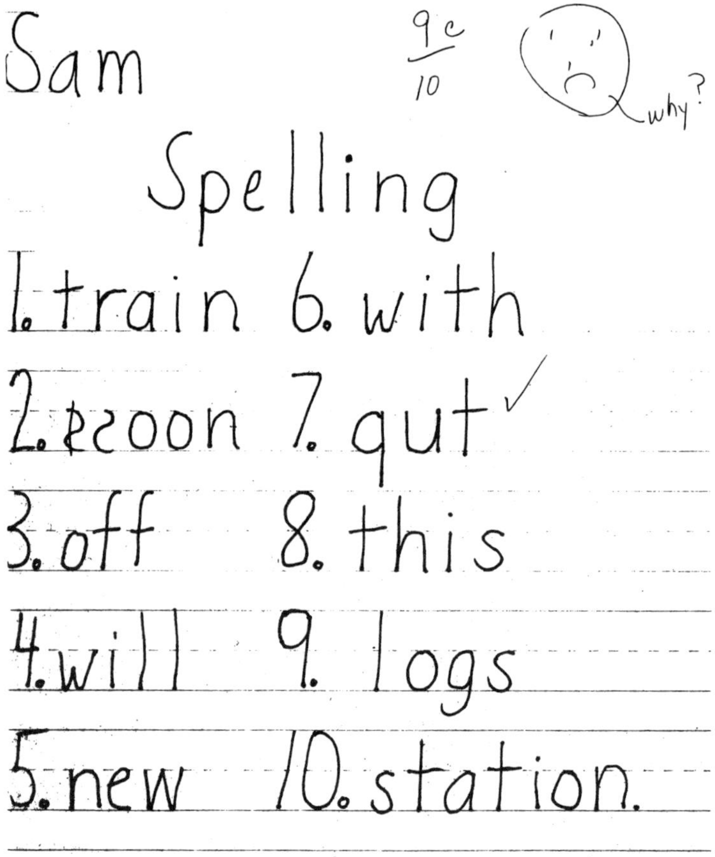

Sam $\frac{9c}{10}$ 😦 why?

Spelling

1. train   6. with

2. ?eoon   7. qut ✓

3. off   8. this

4. will   9. logs

5. new   10. station.

Figure 7. Negative reinforcement. This second-grade child achieved nine correct out of 10 spelling words, missing *put* due to a reversal, not because he couldn't spell the word. The teacher was unhappy about something so she placed a frowning face on the paper with the question, "Why?" When asked what the frowning face meant, Sam said, "I don't know but it makes me feel sad. I flunked spelling."

number wrong are marked as 5X and each word misspelled is crossed out. However, all misspelled words should be corrected. The corrections should be made beside the incorrect spelling so that both the child's work and the corrected work are clearly visible. The teacher corrected the capitalization in Atlantic and South (numbers 13 and 14) but not Atlantic and Pacific Ocean and Central America (numbers 3 and 6). Dolphin should have been dolphin and Golphin should have been dolphin (numbers 7 and 9). When these suggestions are made to teachers they usually see the value of consistency.

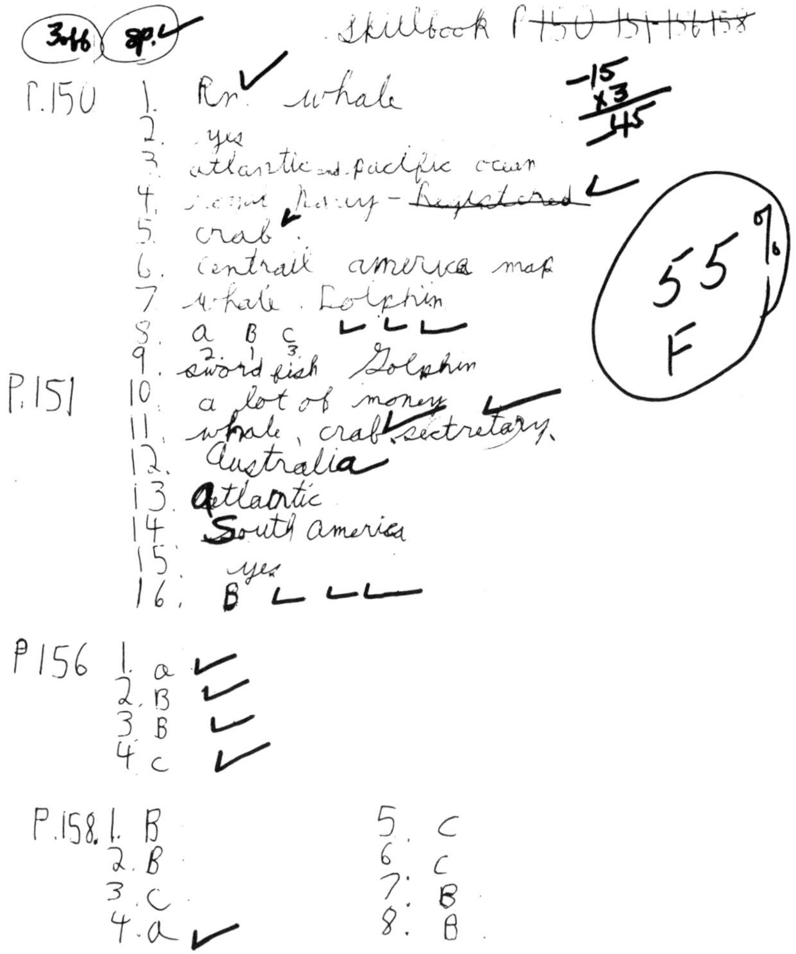

Figure 8. Negative reinforcement and improperly corrected paper. Indicating the number incorrect tends to be negative, whereas marking the number correct would be positive. It is best to write each misspelled word carefully and correctly beside the error so that the child can clearly see both his mistakes and the correct spelling. Also, all errors should be consistently corrected, not just a few.

If teachers have been properly trained in some good teaching methods (and there seem to be a great many, but none to suit all children), almost all of these problems tend to be obviated. As an example, in one suburban school district, all of the kindergarten children are screened for specific language disabilities and the "high risk" children are placed in a special program for their first 3 years. The first-grade class usually consists of 20

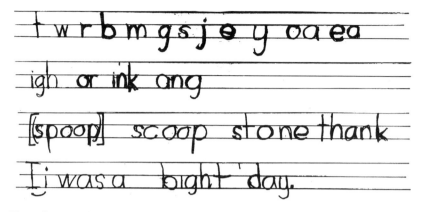

Figure 9. Special class work. This is an example of primary grade work done by a high risk child in a preventive program. The work was done from dictation. The teacher was using the Slingerland teaching method. She had 20 to 25 high risk pupils who were screened in kindergarten and who will remain in this program from 2 to 3 years. (Courtesy Menlo Park City School District, California.)

to 25 high risk children. Specially trained teachers provide a multisensory, phonics and language arts program developed by Slingerland (1971) which is said to be preventive of learning failure. Figure 9 is an example of what can be achieved with high risk children and good teaching. This is a sample of the work done by a child in a primary grade. On standardized reading tests, these children usually average above grade level throughout the 3 years. Compare this work with that of the fifth-grade, inner-city child shown in Figure 2.

Working with an EH Class

Problems such as we have discussed can usually be overcome by a combination of teacher training and experience. Once a teacher has been trained, the improvement in both the classroom appearance and the children's learning and behavior are generally readily observable and tend to be remarked upon by both the principal and other teachers, and may even be commented on by parents.

In an EH class, the teacher is expected to do diagnostic testing, plan remedial instruction for each child, prepare the materials for individualized instruction, do the record-keeping, teach the children, and manage the pupils' behavior problems. To be able to do this, both the teacher and the room must be well organized. Moreover, the teacher must do considerable preparation for each day's work. Clearly, this job requires a great deal of experience and hard work.

In a good, well-organized school district, experienced teachers can learn this job fairly quickly if they are familiar with at least one method of individualized, diagnostic teaching and are willing to continue their education. Also, teachers would not be placed in special education until they had at least a few years of general education experience, and they would be helped to learn the job by the supervisory and consulting staff of the special education section of the school district. However, in practice it does not always work out this way.

Sometimes teachers with little or no previous teaching experience are placed in special education because no experienced teacher is available and the program is expanding. Also, teachers may be hired who have had special education training which (it is later found) conflicts with the philosophy of the supervisory staff. An example will illustrate the possible resulting confusion.

Miss Jones' First Teaching Job

Miss Jones was given a full-time special day class for the educationally handicapped on her first teaching assignment, in a large school district. The class consisted of ten 9- to 11-year-old boys with moderate to severe learning and behavior problems. When the special education supervisor finally was able to visit Miss Jones' class, it was already the sixth week of school. The teacher seemed to have no idea where to begin in the curriculum, what to teach, how to teach, how to arrange the classroom, or how to determine the pupil's academic levels and learning patterns. The room was both a shambles and severely cluttered, and the children were either playing or acting out, with very little work being accomplished.

The supervisor helped the teacher clean and clear the room by removing unnecessary boxes and junk. It was then suggested that the teacher study and set up an "engineered classroom" as a way of establishing and maintaining order, a method sometimes used in California schools.

When the supervisor returned the following week, it was found that Miss Jones had established her own version of the "engineered classroom." She had created nine learning centers instead of the usual three so that the room remained cluttered and there was inadequate work space for the children. The room remained overstimulating for hyperactive youngsters, with a large paper dragon swinging from the ceiling, pop posters on the walls, and so much art work that there was no space left on the chalkboard for the teacher to write. In order to show a pupil how to print an *M* it was necessary to move posters, boxes, furniture, and the children's drawings to clear a space at the chalkboard. By that time, the child was off doing something else.

When it was suggested that the room was overstimulating for these children, Miss Jones replied, "But we were told in college to have centers for each subject and to allow children freedom to explore on their own. It goes against everything I was taught in teacher training to have structure."

To the suggestion that a behavior modification program might help children who were hyperactive, inattentive and impulsive, Miss Jones replied, "My professors said that children need to act out because this behavior indicates inner conflicts which must be allowed to surface so that the children can understand and come to grips with their feelings."

In some of these schools, there is a tendency to keep the classroom overheated in winter, about 75° F. Also, inner-city children have a tendency to wear their hats and outdoor coats all day in school. The teacher made no attempt to get them to remove any superfluous garments even though the sweat poured down their faces onto their books and papers, nor did it occur to her to open any windows.

Children were permitted to wander about the room listening to transistor radios during class. If a favorite rock song came on, a pupil might turn up the volume of his radio and the teacher would shout across the room, "Turn that noise down," which the student might or might not do.

Some teachers who started out attempting to teach in this general manner were able to accept supervision and ultimately (in about 3 years) became very good EH teachers. Others were not able to accept suggestions and in some cases were eventually transferred out of the EH program. (Another good example of a teaching defect is given in the "Case of John" which appears in the chapter by Jansen et al. "Special Education in Denmark.")

LONGITUDINAL STUDY OF AN EH STUDENT

The case of Joe represents a 16-year study of a bright child with rather severe specific learning disabilities.

Joe was born by Caesarian section and the pediatrician reported that he appeared to be a normal, healthy infant. However, he was extremely active from birth, and seemed to have difficulty learning to suck when feeding. At the age of 4, an electroencephalogram showed right-occipital intermittent paroxysmal slow waves, and the classical symptoms of hyperactivity were noted. The neurologist predicted that the child would be unable to learn in school, but the pediatrician optimistically said that the EEG did not mean anything and the child was quite normal.

Intelligence tests given at different times gave variable results. At 6 and 11 years of age, Joe was tested with the Wechsler Intelligence Scale for Children with the following results.

Age	Verbal IQ	Performance IQ	Full Scale IQ
6	120	107	115
11	103	106	104

At age 6, high verbal, low performance IQ's are evident. However, by age 11, a characteristically reduced verbal score appears due to the child's low reading level. This occurs because the verbal IQ at age 6 depends upon language that has been learned from hearing, whereas by age 11, the average child has learned a great deal from reading, which affects the IQ score. The examiner stated that Joe probably had more intelligence than the test scores indicated, and that his scores were reduced by inattentive and impulsive behavior. Further testing revealed evidence of severe visual-motor and motor dysfunction. However, his visual and auditory acuity, perception, and memory were found to be from adequate to very good.

Joe was placed in a special class for the educationally handicapped for 3 years and at the same time he received extra help twice a week, after school, at a reading clinic. This was followed by 3 years of tutoring in English and mathematics.

Joe's reading and spelling scores on standardized tests indicate that learning to read was a very difficult task for him even though he had much extra help. From the second to the sixth grade his scores were as follows:

Reading and spelling scores (grade level)

	2/66	3/67	6/68	8/69
Word discrimination	1.4	1.8	2.2	4.2
Oral reading	0	2.7	3.8	4.1
Silent reading	1.3	2.6	3.8	4.3
Spelling	1.3	2.6	3.3	4.5
Joe's actual grade	2.5	3.6	4.9	6.0

The teachers' reports during these years indicated that Joe continued to have difficulty with letters which look alike when reversed or inverted, such as *u,* and *n; l,k,* and *f; a* and *o; p,q,d,b,* and *g.* For example, he spelled *cloub* for *cloud* and *cappage* for *cabbage,* and he lacked phonics skills.

From the sixth grade, Joe attended regular classes, and gradually received less tutoring assistance each year. He remained about 1 year behind grade level on standardized reading tests until the seventh grade. However, in the ninth grade, his reading scores on the standardized group-tests given by the school were above grade level, as shown below.

Group reading-test scores (grade level)

	Grade 7	Grade 9
Vocabulary	6.2	10.5
Comprehension	6.2	11.4
Total reading	6.2	11.0

Discussion

The great difficulty that this child had learning to read was predicted from his right-occipital brain wave dysfunction, hyperkinesis, and the relatively lower performance IQ than verbal IQ. The performance tests are considered to be right hemisphere brain functions, so that they reinforce the EEG findings. There appears to be evidence that beginning reading may be primarily a right brain hemisphere function. This would account for the early problems of learning to read.

The relatively high verbal IQ of 120 at age 6 indicates a good prognosis for future learning. It is also considered to be a left hemisphere function, and there is evidence that advanced reading (beyond perhaps fourth grade) may be a left hemisphere function. This would account for the spurt in reading level by ninth grade, when he achieved an eleventh-grade reading level test score.

MATERIALS USED IN LEARNING DISABILITIES PROGRAMS

Lewis (1972) conducted a survey of techniques and materials in use among the members of the Division for Children with Learning Disabilities of the Council for Exceptional Children, which is an organization of professionals. The techniques and materials were organized into 15 categories with the following results.

Auditory Perception

These "materials attempt to train auditory discrimination, auditory memory, auditory closure, sound blending, listening comprehension, or other auditory abilities." Of 169 responses and 58 different materials used, Developmental Learning Materials was mentioned 29 times, Teaching Resources (auditory discrimination in depth) 17 times, and the SOS Program (sound, order, sense) 13 times.

Behavior Management

Twenty-three techniques were listed among 71 responses as being used to attempt to manage, modify, or control behavior. Behavior modification was mentioned 30 times with positive reinforcement (rewards) and precision teaching each mentioned 6 times.

Games

Fifty-four responses listed 24 games. Most often mentioned were card games (6), and teacher-made games (5).

General Tests

Twenty-eight responses listed 17 tests of a general nature. Most often listed were the Wechsler Intelligence Scales (8), Wide Range Achievement Test (3), and Slossen Intelligence Test (3).

General Texts, Methods, and Authors

Twenty-three responses listed 16 authors. Cruickshank methods were listed 4 times, and Fernald 3 times.

Language Development

Two hundred sixty-three responses listed 61 materials used to stimulate vocabulary development and expressive language. Most often mentioned were the Peabody Language Development Kit (76), Valett's Remediation of Learning Disabilities (35), and the Illinois Test of Psycholinguistic Abilities (27).

Miscellaneous Materials

Five hundred seventy-five responses listed 233 miscellaneous materials used. Most often used were the Language Master (57), tapes and tape recorders (55), teacher-made instructional materials (40), and chalkboards (29).

Motor Training

Three hundred twenty-eight responses listed 106 materials used that "attempt to develop tracing ability, tactile sensitivity, body image, body orientation, balance, gross and fine motor coordination, or motor expression." Most often used were the Kephart test and program (Purdue Perceptual-Motor Survey) 51 times, balance beams (48), and balls (14).

Remedial Mathematics

One hundred eighty-five responses listed 76 materials. Most often listed were Stern Structural Arithmetic (43), cuisinaire rods (24), and Sullivan Programmed Mathematics (12).

Remedial Reading

Eight hundred ninety responses listed 221 materials used "which provide drill and instruction on the alphabet, letter sounds, sound-symbol association, word recognition, word attack skills, speed and fluency in oral and silent reading, and comprehension." Most often mentioned were the Sullivan Programmed Reading (59), SRA Reading Programs (56), Fernald VAKT method (44), Distar Reading Program (38), Orton-Gillingham-Stillman reading method (35), phonetic approach to reading (34), language experience approach (25), and Merrill Linguistic Series (22).

Social Skills

Six responses listed materials to teach "courtesy, safety, vocational attitudes, or self-concept."

Spelling

Thirty-five responses listed 25 materials specifically to teach spelling. Most often mentioned was Dr. Spello, 5 times.

Thinking Skills

Forty-one responses mentioned 26 materials used to "teach concepts, associations, classification, sequencing, or problem solving." Most often mentioned was the SRA Learning to Think Series (6).

Visual Perception

Five hundred thirty-five responses mentioned 67 materials that "attempt to train visual discrimination, visual memory, visual closure, speed of perception, or other visual abilities." Most often mentioned were the Frostig Developmental Test of Visual Perception and program (118), Developmental Learning Materials (40), pegboards (36), Michigan Tracking Program (34), various puzzles (32), parquetry (29), Continental Press materials (26), Dubnoff School Program (22), Teaching Resource Visual Materials (21), and Getman programs and materials (20).

Writing

Forty-eight responses listed 33 materials to "teach letter formation and penmanship." Write and See (Skinner and Krakower) was mentioned 7 times.

MEDICATION

Medication is sometimes used in the medical management of children with learning disabilities. Most studies of the effects of medication on children appear to have been done in the United States and Canada. In these studies, the term minimal brain dysfunction (MBD) tends to be used as the medical equivalent of specific learning disability. It should be noted that MBD does not necessarily imply brain damage. Both damaged and undamaged brains may be dysfunctioning and cause learning problems. For example, genetic differences may account for variations in pitch discrimination ranging from perfect pitch to no pitch discrimination.

Bradley (1937) reported both the paradoxical effect of stimulants in controlling hyperactivity and their positive effect on learning. He noted that a number of children with learning problems improved on Benzedrine (amphetamine) and he ascribed this effect to a change in the children's emotional attitudes, observing that they appeared to be more interested in the external environment, happier, and more zestful.

Drug Research

Subsequent to this early work, both clinical studies and controlled research have proliferated on the effects of various drugs on behavior, attention, IQ, academic performance, memory, sensory perception, motor and equilibrium control, and so forth. The first reports tended to be clinical and these had the advantage that they pointed the direction in which research might profitably proceed. Their disadvantage, of course, was that the findings were subjective and could not be accepted as scientific. By 1975, a great many controlled studies had been done and it was possible to state some of the major effects of different medications on children with specific learning disabilities. At the same time, the use of drugs to improve behavior and learning in children remains controversial.

Major Therapeutic Medications

The medications that appear from the literature to be useful in aiding children with behavior and educational problems are the following (Tarnopol, 1971):

Psychotropic Drugs

1. Psychomotor stimulants (amphetamine-like):
    Amphetamine (Benzedrine)
    Deanol (Deaner)
    Dextroamphetamine (Dexedrine)
    Magnesium pemoline (Cylert)
    Methamphetamine (Methedrine)
    Methylphenidate (Ritalin)
2. Major antidepressants (imipramine-like):
    Desipramine (Petrofrane, Norpramin)
    Imipramine (Tofrānil)
    Nortriptyline (Aventyl)
3. Major tranquilizers (chlorpromazine-like):
    Chlorpromazine (Thorazine)
    Fluphenazine (Permitil)
    Thioridazine (Mellaril)
4. Minor tranquilizer:
    Chlordiazepoxide (Librium)

318   Tarnopol and Tarnopol

Anticonvulsants
1. Diphenylhydantoin (Dilantin)
2. Ethosuximide (Zarontin)
3. Phensuximide (Milontin)
4. Primidone (Mysoline)

Psychomotor Stimulants Stimulant medication appears to be most often used for both hyperkinetic children and those with learning disabilities. The symptoms of hyperkinesis include uncontrolled and almost constant overactivity, short attention span, impulsivity, fluctuating behavior, and low frustration tolerance. These conditions may be related to a low central (reticular) arousal level. In this case, the cerebral cortex is thought to be receiving insufficient tonic stimulation from the arousal mechanism in the reticular formation, leading to behavior which the child cannot control. A stimulant drug which selectively increases the function of the reticular activating system, improves the cortical tonus and thus the child's capacity to consciously regulate his own behavior. This accounts for the apparently paradoxical effect of stimulants which tend to change random hyperactivity to more normal behavior.

The behavioral changes from stimulant medication are well known to clinicians and teachers. An example of such a change is illustrated in Figures 10 and 11 which show the difference in John's arithmetic papers with medication and on the day he "forgot pill." Teachers who have pupils on stimulant medication immediately recognize these illustrations as simi-

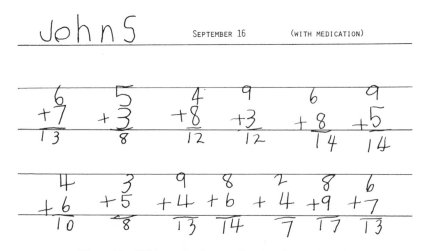

Figure 10. Child on stimulant medication, September 16.

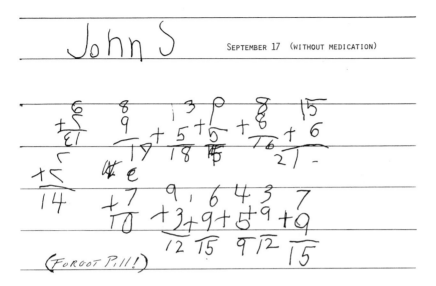

Figure 11. Child forgot to take his medication, September 17. On the day the child forgot to take his medication, disorganization set in. His visual-motor integration, spatial perception, motor coordination, and attention appear to have been disrupted.

lar to their own experience and generally claim that they can "always tell when a child has forgotten to take his medication."

Conners (1972) summarized the effects of stimulant drugs on children with learning disabilities from his studies. Two studies included 156 children (144 males) with a mean age of about 9 years, primarily white, from all socioeconomic classes. The children were randomly assigned, double-blind to dextroamphetamine, methylphenidate, or placebo in one study ($N = 75$); and dextroamphetamine, magnesium pemoline, or placebo in the second study ($N = 81$).

Significant drug improvement over placebo in the first study was reported on the WISC Full Scale IQ, WISC Verbal IQ, WISC subscales (Similarities, Digit Span, Object Assembly), Frostig Perceptual Quotient, Frostig subscales (Eye-Motor Coordination, Figure-Ground, Form Constancy), Bender Visual Motor Gestalt test, Draw-A-Man test, Porteus Mazes, verbal fluency, speech-noise test, continuous vigilance test (omissions and commissions), and teacher symptom ratings. In the second study, significant drug improvement over placebo was reported on the Porteus mazes, Frostig Perceptual Quotient, Frostig subscales (Eye-Motor Coordination, Figure-Ground), spelling, reading, teacher ratings (defiance, inattentiveness, hyperactivity), and parent ratings (conduct disturbance, impulsivity, immaturity, antisocial behavior). The major side-effects of all drugs were insomnia and some loss of appetite.

These studies provide evidence of improved behavior as well as significant drug effects on some cognitive perceptual and achievement measures. However, Conners notes some striking inconsistencies in the positive effects of medication, in both these and other studies, that he suspected were "likely to be fortuitous results of the sample composition."

Major Antidepressant Drugs The antidepressant drugs include the major psychic energizers which alleviate neurotic and psychotic depression and have an effect beyond mere stimulation. Desipramine, imipramine, and nortriptyline appear to have a favorable effect on behavior, especially when they are effective for the control of enuresis. They have also been found to have a potentiating effect with a stimulant to increase attention span. Imipramine is reported to have some possible toxic effects such as tremor and hypotension.

Major Tranquilizers Medications such as the chlorpromazine-like drugs are sedatives and create reduced attention span and motor activity. They are usually not used unless stimulants and antidepressants fail to help and relief of symptoms is highly desirable. Chlorpromazine may also be used to reduce anxiety in conjunction with a stimulant for increasing attention span.

Anticonvulsants There appears to be a close relationship between convulsive states and hyperkinetic impulse disorder. Children with seizures often exhibit hyperactive behavior and learning problems. Children who have abnormal EEG's (spike-waves, negative or diphasic spikes) generally respond to anticonvulsant medication, sometimes in conjunction with a stimulant.

Other Approaches Megavitamin therapy is being tried in a number of places, but as yet there are no definitive results from controlled studies. Another approach to behavior normalization is through the use of a stringent diet, eliminating salicylates on the assumption that some children are allergic to them and that this is the cause of their problems. Several studies of this diet are in progress as the result of preliminary work by Dr. Benjamin Feingold.

In a great many cases, it has been found that a well organized, structured school environment, in which the "hyperkinetic learning disabilities" child is able to learn, permits this child to appear normal in his behavior. When the environment becomes overstimulating for the child, hyperkinesis reappears. Therefore, as noted by several contributors to this volume, hyperactivity and secondary neurotic symptoms tend to fade when the environment is appropriate for these children.

MAJOR MBD STUDY

Gross and Wilson (1974) reported on a study of 1,056 consecutive patients at their out-patient psychiatric clinic based on data collected over 9 years. The population was primarily white, upper-lower through middle-middle class children with a mean age of 9 years, and a range of 2 to 18 years. One-half of the children were referred by schools, one-fourth by their families, and 8% by physicians. A diagnosis of minimal brain dysfunction (MBD) was made in 817 (77.4%) of the cases, 78% of whom were boys.

The chief presenting complaints for the MBD children were learning problems (75%), hyperactivity (25%), temper outbursts (20%), aggressive hostility (19%), and poor concentration (17%). The neuropsychiatric examinations of these children frequently showed some combination of fidgetiness, short attention span, clumsiness, immaturity, a tendency to rush through tasks, and lack of caution. Psychological tests frequently revealed perceptual deficits, scattering on the subscales of the WISC, distortions on the Bender Visual Motor Gestalt Test, academic problems, and impulsivity and explosiveness on projective tests. Over 50% of this population had abnormal electroencephalograms (EEG's) as compared with 3.8% of a control group composed of 160 children selected by their teachers as being "normal." The EEG's for the controls had been interspersed with those of the clinical population and were read "blind" by the physician.

Drug Therapy Results

Of the 817 MBD children, 622 were tried on medications following a placebo trial. Of 618 children tested with placebo therapy, no change was found in 92.4%, very mild improvement in 3.7%, and definite improvement in 0.7% of the cases. For those children tried on medication, 79% definitely improved, 20% showed almost no change, and 1% became worse. The medications used included methylphenidate (287 cases), dextroamphetamine (231 cases), desipramine or imipramine (74 cases), and others (30 cases). Mild side-effects were noted in about 12%, with moderate to severe side-effects, lasting a day or two, in about 6% of the cases. Loss of appetite, weight loss, and occasional slowing of growth were the only long-term side-effects observed. No cases of habituation or drug addiction were found.

Conclusions

Gross and Wilson concluded that "MBD, loosely defined as it may be, represents a real entity with a specific treatment program," and that MBD may be "the most common psychiatric disorder of children." They further conclude that observation of these children in school is often more revealing than in the physician's office, and the best observations of these children are frequently made by teachers. The EEG is too crude to be relied on for certain diagnosis but it is useful to reinforce clinical impressions. Significant improvement occurs in about 80% of the cases with stimulants, antidepressants, or anticonvulsants. Counseling parents and teachers is beneficial and an appropriate educational environment is important. Appropriate treatment may mean the difference between dropping out of school or delinquency, and completing school with socially acceptable behavior. Early detection leads to simpler treatment with better results. Psychotherapy is counterindicated for younger children. Some individual or group psychotherapy may help early adolescents or older children. However, parent counseling of a practical nature is usually more effective than psychotherapy with the child. Finally, minimal brain dysfunction (learning disabilities) may occur at all IQ levels and ages in childhood.

NEUROGENIC ETIOLOGY OF LEARNING DISABILITIES

Stimulant drug studies tend to verify the neurological basis for learning disabilities. Satterfield et al. (1973) reported on the effect of methylphenidate on children with learning disabilities. They found an approximately linear relationship between average clinical improvement and degree of neurological impairment (Table 2). A number of other studies have

Table 2. Improvement in response to methylphenidate: Four subgroups of children with minimal brain dysfunction

No.	Results of neurological and EEG tests	Average percentage of improvement
22	Both normal	25
17	Abnormal neur., normal EEG	35
6	Abnormal EEG, normal neur.	45
12	Both abnormal	55

Source: Satterfield et al. (1973).

also reported that stimulants tend to have their greatest positive effect on those learning disabilities children who have the most neurological involvement. Conversely, since 60 to 80% of these children are helped by stimulant medication, most children with learning disabilities appear to have neurological dysfunction.

Genetic Basis

Evidence of a combined genetic and neurological basis for some familial reading disabilities comes from a study by Conners (1971). In this case, there is no evidence of brain damage accompanying the neurological dysfunction.

Brain wave studies were done on the members of a family where it appeared that a familial reading disorder was present. Reading disabilities were found in all four children, their father, his brother and mother. Thus the grandmother, her two sons, and four grandchildren had tested reading disabilities. No reading disorder was found in the children's mother or her family.

The brain wave studies were performed on six family members, including the four children (two boys and two girls), and their father and

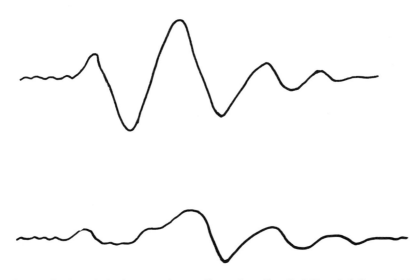

Figure 12. Genetic brain wave abnormality and reading disability. A father and his four children with reading disabilities all had the same brain wave abnormality in the visual evoked response of the left parietal lobe. Brain wave responses from the other areas were normal. Top curve is typical normal brain wave response from the left and right occipital lobes and the right parietal lobe. Bottom curve is typical abnormal left parietal response (after Conners, 1971).

mother. Visual evoked responses were used with four electrodes attached to the scalp in the left and right occipital areas, and the left and right parietal areas.

All four brain wave responses of the mother, who had no reading problems, were normal. On the other hand, each of the five family members who had a reading disability also had the same general brain wave abnormality in the left parietal response. Since the father and his four children had this same type of abnormality, this tends to give evidence of a genetic brain difference associated with a reading disorder in the absence of any traumatic brain damage (Figure 12).

CONCLUSION

Helping children of normal intelligence with learning and reading disabilities in the United States dates back to the work of Samuel Orton in about 1925. However, general recognition of these problems did not begin to develop until the 1950's when observation revealed that there were a great many apparently normal children who seemed to have the same types of learning disabilities as certain brain damaged children. This led to the conclusion that these children might be suffering from minimal (undetectable) brain damage. Further research in the 1960's established that there were probably a number of causes of minimal brain dysfunctions, including genetic differences, brain damage, allergic reactions, chemical imbalances, and so on.

In 1963, formal programs of special education for children with learning disabilities began to be established by state laws. Finally, the United States Congress passed legislation accepting specific learning disabilities as an officially designated educational handicap about 1970. By this time, most of the states had developed programs of special education for children with learning disabilities.

REFERENCES

Assembly Bill No. 4040. 1974. State of California, Sacramento.

Bradley, C. 1937. The behavior of children receiving Benzedrine. *Amer. J. Psychiatry* 94:577.

California Administrative Code. 1967. Title 5. Department of Education, Sacramento.

Conners, C. K. 1971. Cortical visual evoked response in children with learning disorders. Psychophysiology 7:3.

Conners, C. K. 1972. Psychological effects of stimulant drugs in children with minimal brain dysfunction. Pediatrics 49(5).

Gross, M. G., and C. W. Wilson. 1974. Minimal Brain Dysfunction: A

Clinical Study of Incidence, Diagnosis and Treatment in Over 1,000 Children. Brunner/Mazel, New York.

Lewis, R. 1972. Data from DCLD survey of materials. *In* D. Bryant and C. E. Kass (eds.), Leadership Training Institute in Learning Disabilities. Vol. 2. Department of Special Education, University of Arizona, Tucson.

Satterfield, J. H., L. I. Lesser, R. E. Saul, and D. P. Cantwell. 1973. EEG aspects in the diagnosis and treatment of brain dysfunction. *In* F. F. de la Cruz, B. H. Fox, and R. H. Roberts (eds.), Minimal Brain Dysfunction. New York Academy of Sciences, New York.

Silverman, L. J., and A. S. Metz. 1973. Numbers of pupils with specific learning disabilities in local public schools in the United States. *In* F. F. de la Cruz, B. H. Fox, and R. H. Roberts (eds.), Minimal Brain Dysfunction. New York Academy of Sciences, New York.

Slingerland, B. 1971. Specific Language Disability Children: A Multi-sensory Approach to Language Arts. Educators Publishing Service, Cambridge, Mass.

Special Education Memorandum. 1972. EH 72-3. Title 5 Regulations pertaining to programs for Educationally Handicapped Minors, effective March 30, 1972. Department of Education, State of California, Sacramento.

Tarnopol, L. 1969. (Ed.). Learning Disabilities: Introduction to Educational and Medical Management, p. 41. Charles C Thomas, Springfield, Ill.

Tarnopol, L. 1971. (Ed.). Learning Disorders in Children: Diagnosis, Medication, Education. Little, Brown, Boston.

CHAPTER 20

Remedial Instruction in the Virgin Islands of the United States

Rita B. Balch, Betty J. Knych, and Mary L. McGinnis

The Virgin Islands of the United States are located about 40 miles east of Puerto Rico and 1,600 miles southeast of New York City. They consist of three major islands: St. John, St. Thomas, and St. Croix. Discovered by Columbus in 1493, they had been ruled successively under French, English, Spanish, Dutch, and Danish flags. Purchased by the United States in 1917, they are a colorful conglomeration of nationalities and races.

Virgin Islanders have developed a well integrated society and a sophisticated level of human relations unparalleled in most regions of the world. Despite the sophistication of so diverse a culture, many serious problems have arisen from an educational point of view. Many people living in the Virgin Islands are from the other Caribbean Islands—British, French, Dutch, and Spanish; their children enter school coming from foreign school systems. During the past 3 years this diverse school population has jumped from approximately 16,000 to 22,000 children.

FACTORS RELATED TO MOTIVATION FOR LEARNING IN THE VIRGIN ISLANDS

Effect of Culture on Language Development

Creole is spoken by most of the current Virgin Islanders. It has been described variously as a language in its own right, a dialect of English, and simply nonstandard English. Creole is a linguistic tie—in the oral tradition—to the heritage of Virgin Islanders, as well as all other islanders in the Antilles chain. Along with the Creole language of the native children, a large number of Puerto Rican, Spanish-speaking children are entering the public schools and experiencing the problems of the bilingual child.

Creole differs from standard English in vocabulary and syntax. These differences are not necessarily consistent from island to island. Members of the community bring rich dialectical differences as they emigrate from "down-island." While ordinary communication in spoken language does not suffer because of these dialectical differences, there are important implications for the education of the children in the Virgin Islands, since standard American English is used in the classroom.

The first and most obvious implication of Creole on educational development is that the spoken language does not provide appropriate reinforcement for learning materials written and presented in the language of standard American English. While many children entering first grade have facility in Creole, they have had little experience with standard English. The materials used throughout the grades are from the mainland (continental United States), and many of the teachers in the classrooms are from the mainland as well. Thus the curriculum—whatever the content—is presented in a language only superficially similar to the Creole these youngsters are accustomed to hearing and speaking. The transitional period between acquiring a facility for both Creole and standard American English is long and occurs at the critical stage of learning basic academic material: the primary grades.

Effect of Standard versus Creole English on Motivation to Learn

Since Creole is an integral part of this culture, the use in an educational setting of American English seems to present a conflict in cultural values which leads to some educational difficulties which seem to be more related to psychological factors than ability factors.

That formal education is represented by standard English appears to become the basis for ambivalent doubts that children may develop about Creole as a source of pride. The alienation a child may feel, either imposed by education as an institution, or self-imposed, can lead to serious anxieties that accompany the rejection of one's culture. Reactions to this phenomenon are expressed as variously as the individual children involved.

For example, one notices that adults and children are more relaxed and have more facility for communication among their peers when speaking Creole. When in the school setting, children seldom interact in class discussions, possibly because they feel the poverty of content at their command in standard American English. Native Virgin Islanders, in business communication, speeches, newspaper editorials, etc., use the more archaic form of formal English—eloquently, to be sure, but without the ease and modern vocabulary they may experience from the television network or from mainland newspapers.

Recent efforts to revive a pride in native traditions have had some impact. Individual children seem to be making conscious decisions about comfortable levels of academic progress, although some administrators have not. In a recent study of high school students with low reading achievement, these students felt that their reading level was adequate for their needs. They felt comfortable with reading achievement levels averaging fifth grade, stating in interviews with counselors that they were not aware that they had a "reading problem." Administrators are alarmed that reading achievement levels of Virgin Island students are averaging 2 grade levels below mainland norms on standardized reading tests. Therefore educational demands, based on stateside levels of performance, are often conflicting and may be threatening to the youngster going through a cultural revival.

Effect of Culture on Classroom Discipline

Discipline in all of the public schools is rigorous; early school experiences, usually with native teachers, emphasize a strict socialization process. Kindergarten and first-grade children quickly learn to sit still and be quiet. Interaction is not encouraged either verbally or nonverbally. Physical reminders—a stick, ruler, etc.—are usually in evidence to support this theory. Social promotion can carry a child through high school. A quiet child with educational problems is not identified as readily as a child who is acting out and disturbing order in the classroom.

Teacher Sensitivity to the Nature of Educational Problems

While resources have existed in community agencies for the diagnosis and remediation of educational problems, teacher referrals for diagnosis of educational problems have been largely inappropriate. Inexperienced continental teachers are not aware of the nature of specific learning disabilities; thus, referrals from this group are behavior problems. Native teachers with a high cultural value on discipline also refer behavior problems.

In the past, the evaluations of these children referred to the Educational Diagnostic Center, or the mental health, public health, or social welfare agencies indicated that the majority of children had been inappropriately referred. The pathology of the problems often did not warrant the agency's specialized services. The child was then usually bounced from agency to agency, his parents became frustrated, the quest was dropped, and the child's problems continued and often multiplied in the classroom.

Identifying Children with Educational Problems

In projecting needs for educational diagnostic services, a first impression based on teacher referrals suggested a possible 30 to 50% of the public school population as potentially educationally handicapped. However, actual multidisciplinary testing of 2,500 children in grades kindergarten through twelve (1970–1973) revealed that roughly 15% of the total school population may be in need of prescriptive remediation outside of the regular classroom. Results of reading achievement testing revealed that most children were reading 2 or more years below grade level.

Problems in Specifying Learning Difficulties

A multidisciplinary screening battery, which took into account cultural differences in the standardization population (mainland norms) and the Virgin Islands population (V.I. norms), was used. Even so, three barriers to discriminating for "true" learning disability children existed, based on the complications of Creole dialect, the tenuous validity of evaluation instruments, and developmental problems in the perceptual abilities of individual children.

In a pilot project (1971–1972), the staff of the Educational Diagnostic Center screened 1,200 children in kindergarten, first, third, and sixth grades. The multidisciplinary test battery used included the following measures:

1. Learning Ability
   Verbal–Peabody Picture Vocabulary Test
   Performance–Goodenough-Harris Draw-A-Man
2. Visual Perception
   Bender Visual Motor Gestalt Test, Koppitz scoring
3. Auditory Perception
   Auditory memory
   Auditory discrimination
4. Motor Perception
   Body image
   Spatial relations
   Laterality
   Balance
5. Social maturity
6. General health
7. Vision
8. Hearing
9. Speech
10. Achievement

With the exception of the instruments noted in the areas of learning ability and visual perception, the Diagnostic Center developed 10-minute individual scales for screening the remaining areas.

This screening battery was designed to identify factors likely to interfere with learning for the individual child. Each test was administered individually by specialists in the respective disciplines who were trained to administer and interpret the test with an understanding of diagnostic implications and cultural differences. These specialists were members of the staff in each school: remedial reading teachers, speech and hearing therapists, school nurses, counselors, and physical education instructors. In smaller schools where such specialists were not available, team members filled the screening needs for that school. Normally, the school counselor served as pupil screening team coordinator for group and individual screening, acting as liaison between classroom teacher and referral agencies as well as making special arrangements for scheduling screening procedures.

Each child's performance is judged relative to his chronological age and the normal expectations for that age group. Each child is either "within normal limits," or "outside normal limits," on the basis of his age and development in each factor evaluated.

The educational screening program identifies underachieving children and coordinates this data for the Educational Diagnostic Center and other appropriate community resources which are more directly responsible for conducting an intensive study to determine the cause of underachievement and proposing solutions to effect more rewarding educational experiences for each child. The plan identifies clusters of disturbed processes that impede learning, for more meaningful programming and remediation.

Data from the pilot project strongly pointed toward the need for a preventive curriculum for children in the primary grades. Trends in the intermediate grades suggested a predictable cumulative deficit in achievement by children of average ability who may have had a learning difficulty in the early grades. It was decided to extend the project to the entire school system and to extend referrals to intra-agency resources.

In the fall of 1972, pupil-screening teams were trained in each school to deal with individual teacher referrals. After each child referred was screened, the entire team met with the classroom teacher and consultant from the Educational Diagnostic Center to make appropriate recommendations for that child based on screening data. Emphasis was placed on dealing with educational problems within the school wherever possible, as community agencies here are overwhelmed with clients and cannot realistically deal with large numbers of referrals.

METHODS OF REMEDIATION

Approximately 50% of the children enrolled in the Virgin Islands School System read below grade level. Of this group, one-half have severe enough reading problems to require enrollment in a special class or with a remedial teacher, and one-third of that group falls within the scope of learning disabilities. In this learning disabilities group, there are varied types and degrees of disabilities ranging from problems of visual perception to dysgraphia. Most of these children enter school with a background of experiences that do not prepare them for the sophisticated process of learning to read.

Among Virgin Islands children, a high percentage have auditory perceptual problems. There are also problems with spatial organization and self-concept. In view of these factors, several problems present themselves when deciding on the best techniques for remediation.

The traditional phonetic or linguistic approach often lacks the high level of interest necessary to motivate children who are so nonacademically orientated. These methods, because they are based on the sound-symbol approach, confuse these children who speak a nonstandard dialect of English. The children also appear to have an inability to identify with reading materials that are written for stateside children who, although they share the same nationality, do not share the same culture.

One typical problem encountered is the unavailability of prereading and beginning reading materials that correlate with the mental ages of the children involved. The manipulative skills that precede the verbal skills are most enjoyed by the children. Language retardation weakens the understanding of verbal stimuli, and this weakness is relatively increased with years in school and chronological age.

Kinesthetic reinforcement, as in the Fernald or Gillingham teaching methods, provides a helpful linkage for the child. The most basic contact can be made kinesthetically by the use of manipulative tools, i.e., blocks, pegs, beads, mosaics, and so forth. Primarily, the child is required to reproduce patterns of graduated difficulty. He then moves to extending patterns that are repetitive, and finally to recalling patterns flashed to him.

A problem frequently seen here is lack of transfer of learning. A perceptual skill attained in one area does not appear to be utilized in another. For this reason, some measure of success is found, for example, in the Gillingham-Orton method that incorporates the visual, auditory, and kinesthetic stimuli in learning to read, thereby ensuring multisensory reinforcement.

Much success has been found in the use of games or other gimmicks. The children are competitive and through peer pressure can achieve a certain level of motivation. Earning tokens or rewards for tasks well done provides motivation that is otherwise missing. Often, instant gratification is necessary and should probably precede any long-term goal for the children who lose sight of next week or next month.

We have found the use of gimmicks as a teaching technique most rewarding. For example, reading machines provide immediate feedback—an interesting picture and a feeling of success. Children who are inhibited or nonverbal enjoy the lack of pressure and the easy pace of a machine. Tape recorders, used to tape reading responses of the children as they read, give them the opportunity to be the performer. The Language Master appears to be highly useful as an aid in teaching vocabulary, decoding, and visual and auditory closure.

Another problem we have encountered with the children, especially those with learning disabilities, is the inability to follow directions and to organize themselves. They require individual attention and a structured environment, quite the opposite of what they find in overcrowded classrooms and the relaxed society outside the classroom. Controlled work areas and the presence of a supervising adult help these children to perform designated tasks. Well planned workbooks provide structure as well as a goal (completion) and a reward (possession of the completed book).

Many of the traditional methods of dealing with learning disabilities, although momentarily successful, often do not meet with long-term success. For instance, eye-motor control (as measured on the Bender and the Frostig) is generally well developed, while the auditory modality (measured on the ITPA) is not. The use of kinesthetic reinforcements alone is not as productive in behavior change as reinforcements that make use of the auditory modality in receptive, integrative, and expressive skills. Again, the lack of a meaningful experience plays an important role. What does all this mean to the child in his environment? How can this remedial instruction apply to his other school work?

Workshops were held to teach special teachers and regular classroom teachers diagnostic tests and remedial techniques in the perceptual areas, so that those trained became resource teachers for referrals within their schools. This program will continue next year, focusing more on remediation methods as we learn more about the effectiveness of certain approaches.

Scope of the Screening Project

While each school has been responding to individual referrals from classroom teachers, the Educational Diagnostic Center has continued with group projects—gathering data to further refine screening techniques. These projects have included screening kindergarten through high school pupils for trainable mentally retarded, educable mentally retarded, learning disabled, and emotionally disturbed children—totaling over 1,000 additional students on whom descriptive data are now available.

Since the focus of the Diagnostic Center is now on preventive remedia-

Table 1. Kindergarten screening project[a] —Virgin Islands

Screening test	Percent outside normal limits	Percent within normal limits
Auditory perception	89	11
Peabody Draw-A-Man	33	67
Bender Gestalt	29	71
Hearing acuity	27	73
Social survey	19	81
Motor	19	81
Speech	11	89
Vision acuity	6	94
Health	5	95

[a]Kindergarten children (290) screened in January and February, 1973.

tion, offsetting learning problems before they become learning disabilities for individual children, we offer here Table 1, taken from a histograph which was presented to administrators in the Department of Education, summarizing the results of our recent kindergarten project.

Referring to Table 1, we see that 89% of the kindergarten children screened were found to be outside the "normal limits" on auditory perception. This inordinately high percentage was undoubtedly related to the fact that the children often spoke Creole as their first language. This would also account for the high incidence of "hearing" problems (29% outside normal lmiits) in this population. Since the Peabody Picture Vocabulary Test was usually given in English, it was not too surprising that about one-third of the children scored below the normal limits. However, this would not account directly for the high percentages who had difficulty with both the Draw-A-Man and Bender Visual Motor Gestalt Tests (33% and 29% respectively). It is not unusual for minority children in large cities or slum conditions to evidence a high rate of visual-motor dysfunction. As yet, it is not clear what this means.

Because of the very high incidence of problems with auditory perception, it is felt that a straight phonics approach to reading would create learning problems for the children. As a result, a multisensory approach is being used to help those children who evidence reading difficulties. Also, an attempt is being made to remediate the children in the areas of their weak sensory modalities before they start to read. We are now testing the effects of kindergarten screening followed by prescriptive remediation before learning to read.

Index